Diversity and Change: Education, Policy and Selection

KT-168-160

NORTH TRAFFORD COLLEGE

00033221

WITHDRAWN

The other published volume in this series is

Contemporary Issues in Teaching and Learning
Edited by Peter Woods.

A third volume is in preparation.

This reader is one of three, and has been prepared as part of The Open University course *Exploring Educational Issues*, a broadly based multi-disciplinary course which can be studied as part of BA or BSc degrees.

It is part of an integrated teaching system; the selection is therefore related to other material available to students. Opinions expressed are not necessarily those of the course team or of the University.

If you would like to study this course or find out more about The Open University, please write to the Central Enquiry Service, PO Box 200, The Open University, Walton Hall, Milton Keynes, MK7 6YZ, or telephone 01908 653231. A copy of *Studying with the Open University* is available from the same address.

Diversity and Change

Education, Policy and Selection

Edited by John Ahier, Ben Cosin
and Margaret Hales at
The Open University

London and New York
in association with
The Open University

First published 1996
by Routledge
11 New Fetter Lane, London EC4P 4EE

Simultaneously published in the USA and Canada
by Routledge
29 West 35th Street, New York, NY 10001

Reprinted in 1999

Reprinted 2000, 2002 by RoutledgeFalmer

RoutledgeFalmer is an imprint of the Taylor & Francis Group

©1996 selection and editorial matter; The Open University; individual
chapters, the contributors

Typeset in Garamond by Datix International
Printed and bound in Great Britain by TJ International Ltd, Padstow, Cornwall

All rights reserved. No part of this book may be reprinted or reproduced or
utilized in any form or by any electronic, mechanical, or other means, now
known or hereafter invented, including photocopying and recording, or in any
information storage or retrieval system, without permission in writing from the
publishers.

British Library Cataloguing in Publication Data
A catalogue record for this book is available from the British Library

Library of Congress Cataloguing in Publication Data
A catalogue record for this book has been requested

ISBN 0-415-13720-9

Contents

Illustrations

FIGURES

TABLES

Acknowledgements

While the publishers have made every effort to contact copyright holders of material used in this volume, they would be grateful to hear from any they were unable to contact.

Chapter 1 Mueller, W. and Karle, W. (1993) 'Social selection in educational systems in Europe', *European Sociological Review*, vol. 9 (1), pp. 1–23, Oxford: Oxford University Press. Reproduced by permission of Oxford University Press and the authors.

Chapter 2 MacLean, M. (1990) 'School knowledge traditions', in *Britain and a Single Market Europe: Prospects for a Common School Curriculum*, London: Kogan Page in association with the Institute of Education, University of London, 1990. Reproduced by permission of the Institute of Education and the author.

Chapter 3 Walford, G. (1995) 'Faith-based grant-maintained schools: selective international policy borrowing from the Netherlands', *Journal of Education Policy*, vol. 10 (3), Basingstoke: Taylor and Francis.

Chapter 4 Commissioned article.

Chapter 5 Young, M. (1993) 'A curriculum for the 21st Century', *British Journal for Educational Studies*, 33 (1), pp. 203–22, Oxford: Blackwell Publishers.

Chapter 6 Phillimore, A.J. (1989) 'Flexible specialisation, work organisation and skills: approaching the "Second Industrial Divide"', *New Technology, Work and Employment*, vol.4 (2), Oxford: Blackwell Publishers.

Chapter 7 Bailey, C. (1984) 'The challenge of economic utility', in *Beyond the Present and the Particular*, London: Routledge and Kegan Paul.

Chapter 8 Roberts, K. (1993) 'Career trajectories and the mirage of increased social mobility', in Bates, I. and Riseborough, G. *Youth and Inequality*, Buckingham: Open University Press.

Chapter 9 Unwin, L. (1993) 'Training credits: the pilot doomed to succeed', in Finegold *et al.*, *The Reform of Post-16 Education and Training in England and Wales*, Harlow: Longman.

Chapter 10 Callaghan, J. (1976) Speech by the Prime Minister, the Rt Hon. James Callaghan, MP, at a foundation stone-laying ceremony at Ruskin College, Oxford, on Monday 18 October 1976. Not previously published in its entirety.

Chapter 11 Dennison, S.R. (1984) 'Public versus private provision', in *Choice in Education*, Institute of Economic Affairs.

Chapter 12 Ranson, S. (1993) 'Markets or democracy for education', *British Journal of Educational Studies*, 41 (1), pp. 333-52, Oxford: Blackwell Publishers and the SCSE.

Chapter 13 Ahier, J. (1991) 'Explaining economic decline and teaching children about industry: some unintended continuities?', in Moore, R. and Ozga, *Curriculum Policy*, Elmsford, New York: Pergamon Press.

Chapter 14 Chitty, C. (1992) 'The changing role of the state in education provision', *History of Education*, vol. 22 (1), Basingstoke: Taylor and Francis.

Chapter 15 Morris, R. (1994) 'New magistracies and commissionariats', *Local Government Studies*, vol. 20 (2), Ilford: Frank Cass Publishers.

Chapter 16 Bowe, R. and Ball, S.J. with Gold, A. (1992) 'The policy process and the processes of policy', in *Reforming Education and Changing Schools*, London: Routledge.

Chapter 17 Gewirtz, S. (1994) 'Market discipline versus comprehensive education: a case study of a London comprehensive school struggling to survive in the education market place'. This is an abridged version of a paper originally published in Kallós, D. and Lindblad, S. *New Policy Contexts for Education: Sweden and the United Kingdom*, Umea Universitet: Sweden.

Chapter 18 Jones, L. and Moore, R. (1992) 'Equal opportunities: the curriculum and the subject', *Cambridge Journal of Education*, vol. 22 (2), Carfax Publishing Company: P.O. Box 25, Abingdon, Oxfordshire, OX14 3UE.

Introduction

The four parts of this reader offer overviews into several contexts of education. Changes in those contexts and in the relation of educational systems to them, mean that such overviews are timely. The importance of the economic background of education has long been commonplace. World-wide changes in economic systems have certainly not spared the United Kingdom; and the economy of the UK has become increasingly integrated with those of continental Europe. That economic integration has been followed by increasing political links, and, since the Maastricht Treaty, educational policy has been open to EU-wide initiatives. It is reasonable, then, to begin the analyses of the contexts of education with a section on Europe. Later sections follow the first in offering means of investigating the changing nature of education and the forms of interaction between education and its social background.

We now turn to summarize the four parts of the reader and their component articles.

Part I of this reader, 'International differences and comparing traditions', begins with Müller and Karle's comparison of social selection in different European countries. Though basically quantitative in analysing different progression rates between the various transition points of education systems, it also considers some of the cultural differences which created, for example, an 'educational bourgeoisie' ('*Bildungsbürgertum*') in some Baltic countries.

This particular case is one example of their more general theme – that national traditions, arrangements and situations make a considerable difference to the rates at which boys from different social classes have progressed through the successive transitions constituted by local educational systems. Boys from the highest social class do best, but it is not the case that boys do worse the further we go down the social class structure. Rather, the complexities of each national educational system constitute educational issues for further exploration – not least as to whether and how far girls' performance is affected by the same factors. Maclean considers different traditions of knowledge more directly. The three 'traditions of knowledge' he selects – the encyclopaedic, the humanistic and the naturalistic – while being analytic abstractions, also constitute great aggregates of human and institutional experience and history. Each articulates a general world view including assumptions about reason, nature, human character, knowledge and other key concepts of education – and of human life. Each sets up a set of biases in the selection of curricular materials and valued qualities in pupils and students. Each encourages the selection of pupils or students and of curricular materials (and of assessment orientations) corresponding to those biases. He sketches out some of their salient characteristics and sets the scene for the exploration of particular national, cultural and educational systems in the light of what traditions are dominant, and what subordinate, not hesitating to allude to the history of national cultures in the light of social class cultural and political allegiances.

Walford outlines the highly segregated character of political, social, cultural and educational organization in the history of the Netherlands over the late nineteenth and most of the twentieth century. This pluralistic segregation has been proposed as an ideal model for the introduction of a 'quasi-market' in the provision of education in England and Wales. Yet the segregation of Netherlands society into separate 'pillars', each with its own political party, religious (or irreligious) denomination, trade union centre and schooling system, has been breaking down, and educational policy has been further contributing to the homogenization of educational provision (in spite of the much increased ethnic and religious diversity of Netherlands society since the 1950s). He pinpoints some of the obstacles to simple comparisons and simplistic attempts to transplant policies from one national tradition to another. In doing so he outlines some of the conflicts between efficiency, and principles of choice (preference) and equity conflicts that have driven policy developments and conflicts both within the UK and in the Netherlands. His conclusion raises in sharp relief questions about the relation between educational policy, educational provision, and the background of social and cultural life.

With Findlay's article we return to the subject-matter of education. He surveys the European dimension in UK curricular provision. Aspiration has been prominent in this area, but actual performance and provision have not been so well investigated. He sketches the overall policy development of 'European education' whether as a cross-curricular theme or as a discrete subject area. He outlines the different amount of such provision within several European countries, showing how influential the UK has been in policy development, and how teaching and learning in the UK compare with practice elsewhere in the EU.

The second part, 'Economic change and education', begins with a radical look at the 'gold standard' of English secondary education in an international light. Young criticizes the specialization of the traditional A Level, arguing that more broadly based curricular demands and provision at 18-plus are less restrictive.

Looking to the economic background, Phillimore sets out the notions of flexible specialization and its impact on the labour market and on education and training. Bailey considers the claims advanced for 'economic utility' as a criterion of educational policy and practice, and proposes an ironical approach to some of the more vaunted pieties in this contested area.

Roberts emphasizes the social impact of such policies, particularly in relation to the Youth Labour Market. He offers a detailed account of the persisting class inequalities in relation to education and career. As far as any specific effectiveness of further education and training was concerned, his finding is that the main function of this activity was not to improve job prospects, but to 'warehouse' for a while those to whom the labour market had currently nothing to offer. Roberts identifies continuing class inequalities in opportunity, noting that genuine increases in openness mean increases in downward mobility for middle-class young people. But the main impact of downward mobility, in Roberts's view, has been the increase in working-class downward mobility into unemployment.

Lorna Unwin charts the progress of the idea and reality of Training/Youth Credits. A brief survey of the variety of initiatives starts from the finding that employers seemed to be suffering from initiative fatigue, while 'the main achievement of some sixteen or so years of government-led youth training schemes has apparently been to embed a negative view of "training" in the minds of young people'. More important for Unwin, perhaps, than the complexities of funding is the fact that Training Credits are serving to expose even further the weaknesses of this country's Vocational Education and Training infrastructure. The pressure to increase staying rates in full-time education has reinforced the problems of providing for earlier leavers. Those in the minority who choose to leave full-time education to seek work may find that the credit merely buys them a re-vamped youth training place.

Part III of this reader, 'Ideologies in conflict', has as its subject-matter some of the clashes in ideologies and philosophies which have informed both the recent policy developments in education and the criticisms of those policies. It begins, however, with the full text of the Ruskin College speech, made in 1976 by the then Prime Minister, James Callaghan. This has come to be regarded by many as a significant turning point in post-war educational policy-making (see, for example, the article by Bowe *et al.* in this reader). Some have seen it as heralding a new instrumental attitude to education, while others have interpreted the content as an attack on the professional autonomy of teachers. At the very least it helped to open up many areas of education to public and political debate, while announcing that the period of simple educational expansion was over.

The following two papers give some indication of the scope of the debate that followed. The first is a direct attack on the state provision of schooling. In this paper, originally published by The Institute of Economic Affairs, S.R. Dennison attempts to show that such provision makes the teachers, administrators and bureaucrats insensitive to the demands of the consumers, and too open to coercive politicians and pressure groups. Following many developments in educational policy, which could be seen as being at least consistent with the arguments of Dennison, Stewart Ranson provides a general critique of the market coordination of education. He believes that it inevitably reinforces social divisions and undermines local democracy. In the second half of his article he makes the case for what he thinks would be a truly democratic system, based on the vision of citizens taking their full part in making decisions about their local schools and other aspects of their community. He ends with a brief indication of some of the changes in the governance and administration of schools that may help bring this about.

Ahier, in the last article of this section, looks at the way in which a broader analysis of Britain's economic and cultural history has provided both an explanation and legitimation for a distinctive programme of educational change. This example is useful because of its basis in a major *academic* debate among historians and sociologists. The so-called 'Wiener thesis' has permeated political discourses, constructing a position that has major implications for liberal–humanist cultural values in education and beyond. In his presentation and critique, Ahier explores the relationships between forms and levels of social discourse and their assumptions of value, institutional linkage and social causality.

In the final section, 'Institutions and Policies', we move from clashes of ideologies to the complexities of policy developments and processes. These articles attempt to describe some of the actual changes in educational policy over the years, and to pose questions about how we can study and understand such developments and their effects. The first, by Clyde Chitty, provides a historical overview of the role of the state in educational provision in England and Wales, making contrasts with the situation in other European countries. The key issue here is what he calls a recurring aversion to the involvement of the state in education, which he finds re-emerging in some sections of the contemporary New Right. This is not without its contradictions, however, because while some on the political Right may regret state involvement in schooling, they have been devoted, over the last twenty years, to using that state on a grand scale to change the content of the curriculum and the nature of education.

That deluge of state legislation has produced numerous new institutions for the control and governance of education, and has fundamentally affected the old. The following article by Robert Morris uses the terms magistracies and commissariats to explore the nature of two somewhat different creations of legislation. The former come between the local education authorities and the central state, whereas the latter, complete with their own staff and offices, have replaced some of the functions of those local authorities.

The last three articles raise questions about the actual effects of all these policy developments on the institutions and people within the education system. Not only is there a very indirect connection between the ideologies and philosophies expressed in Section 3, and the production of policies and legislation. There is also an equally problematic connection between policy statements and directives and the actions of teachers, children and parents. Bowe *et al.* accept that recent policy construction has been informed by a desire to minimize the power of the professionals. However, they question the extent to which even an apparently 'top-down' development, like the Technical and Vocational Education Initiative, was merely implemented by teachers on whose cooperation it depended for success. Their interest is in the ways that externally imposed policies are appropriated – how the key texts of education policy are 'translated' by those who are meant to be carrying out the aims set out within them.

Sharon Gewirtz gives us a picture of the dilemmas facing the staff and governors of a particular London comprehensive school as a result of the recent legislation. Her argument is, in part, a response to the previous article. She accepts that the way policy changes and legislation affect life in schools is, indeed, complex, but argues that there is a certain logic or set of constraints implicit in the development of market coordination of schooling which their staff cannot escape. She attempts to show how the previous comprehensive values and policies are being unavoidably compromised, and that the situation is not as open to the possibilities of reinterpretation and resistance as Bowe *et al.* suggest.

Finally, Lynn Jones and Rob Moore look at the way certain policy initiatives, aimed at correcting previous cultural and educational inequalities, depended upon a very questionable implicit theory of identity construction. This theory presumed that low attainment of certain groups can be wholly explained by negative self-images developed as a result of stereotyping and low expectations, and that this can be corrected by the promotion of positive images and high expectations. It is argued that this misunderstands the way pupils are affected by curriculum content and teaching methods in different contexts.

Part I

International differences and comparing traditions

Chapter 1

Social selection in educational systems in Europe

W. Müller and W. Karle

INTRODUCTION

The most elaborate and far-reaching theoretical attempts to explain differences across nations in educational inequalities by social origin have been made as part of a particular variant of the theory of industrial societies. Educational inequalities are understood as a crucial variable in the reproduction of social inequalities and the role education plays in this process is assumed to be systematically linked – partly through functional imperatives – to the level of industrial development. Industrialism is seen to be the driving force in changing the pattern of the dependence of educational attainment on social origin. Industrialization affects the distribution of resources, and it also affects the utility of education, particularly its utility in the labour market.

Most explicitly, the crucial hypotheses have been proposed in terms of the Blau and Duncan (1967) model of the status-attainment process in a stimulating paper by Treiman (1970). Several of these hypotheses have recently been restated: 'Industrialized societies will tend to be more open than nonindustrialized societies', and more precisely with respect to our topic here: 'The more industrialized a society, the smaller the influence of parental status on educational attainment' (Treiman and Yip 1989: 375). This tendency towards decreasing effects of social origin on educational attainment is explained by the assumption that more industrialized societies have a lower degree of status inequality. Relevant material, cultural and social resources are assumed to be distributed less unequally between the various status levels in the stratification hierarchy. In more advanced industrial societies, in consequence, decreasing differentials in educational attainment by social origin are expected. A further reason for the assumption of declining social origin differences in educational attainments is 'that free education is more readily available in industrialized societies and hence in particular is more readily available to those from low status origins' (Treiman and Yip 1989: 376). In other words, it is assumed that the costs of education decline and that, therefore, resource inequalities have a lesser impact on educational outcomes. By linking industrialization to the level of status inequality in a given society, a rather general theory for explaining differences among nations in the effects of origin status on educational attainment is pursued. Indeed, the theory should explain the decline in social-origin effects that are expected in the course of industrial development as well as differences among nations at a similar level of industrial development if the nations differ (for some additional reasons) with respect to the level of status inequality existing in them. The hypothesis that inequality of condition causes inequality of opportunity certainly has considerable power for explaining the general finding that educational attainment depends on social origin. The assumed links with industrialization, however, appear doubtful. There is so much variation in economic inequality among societies of similar industrial development that one can question the assumption that industrialization is the major factor responsible for the degree of status inequality in a given society. Furthermore, industrial societies do not continuously develop in the direction of less inequality as industrialization progresses. The developments in the United States or in Great Britain, where inequalities in the distribution of resources have clearly increased in recent years (Ryscavage and Henle 1990; Atkinson 1991), illustrate this point.

Treiman and Yip (1989) present evidence for more than 20 nations at different levels of industrial development in order to test the industrialization hypothesis. The nations included in their study range from India and the Philippines to the United States. Although the results point in the direction of the hypothesis proposed, they are not convincing. Most of the central parameters are within the margins of random error, and a sensitivity analysis shows that the results are not stable.[1] It is thus questionable whether the explanations of cross-national differences in terms of general macro-sociological changes implied by the industrialization thesis are supported by the empirical evidence that the proponents of the hypotheses present. The trend studies on the development of the inequalities in educational attainment over time that have recently become available from many countries overwhelmingly report negative evidence (see the contributions in Shavit and Blossfeld, forthcoming; Blossfeld and Shavit, forthcoming; Heath, undated). Only in a few cases do these studies find evidence of declining effects of social origin on educational attainment.

Inherent in the approaches based on general macro-structural characteristics of societies is the assumption that industrialism works the same way in all societies. The industrialization approach has scarcely paid any attention to the possibility that a different pattern of the institutionalization of education might affect the distribution of education among classes. The homogenizing pressures of modernization and industrial development may have different effects in societies where the historical development of educational institutions has differed. Education belongs to the part of the institutional infrastructure of societies that varies greatly from society to society. Societies have developed different early solutions to career preparation, and the early solutions have influenced later adaptations. If one traces the historical development of educational systems in Europe, for instance, two aspects are amazing: first, how different the educational systems are that have slowly evolved since the last century in various European countries, and second, the great extent to which the present educational systems still mirror their beginnings, although each of these systems has seen extensive reforms and adaptations (Ringer 1979; Archer 1979, 1989; König et al. 1988; Müller 1990).

As a consequence we find more or less idiosyncratic conditions present in some countries but not in others. Various properties of educational systems contribute to the fact that educational outcomes vary with the social background of children and students: the way the school system is organized into curricula; age at which the assignment to different tracks occurs; the criteria according to which selection is made at any point in the school career; the costs linked with education in private or public schools. From extensive work on school effects (Coleman et al. 1966; Jencks 1985; Sørensen and Hallinan 1986; Coleman and Hoffert 1987; Hallinan 1988; Kerckhoff 1989; Meyer 1980; Shavit 1990) we know that these and other factors are important, although the effect of each single factor tends to be small.

Recent research has also shown that there is considerable variation among different societies in the extent to which access to more or less advantageous positions in the labour market depends on qualifications obtained in the educational system (König and Müller 1986; Allmendinger 1989; König 1990). Such differences in the instrumental value of education should also differentially affect the decisions in different social classes to invest in education. The crucial factor that is addressed in this paper concerns the distribution of the various kinds of qualifications and of educational credentials that the educational institutions provide to the cohorts of students that move through the educational system. We will show that in this respect considerable differences exist among countries and that these differences also contribute to the fact that countries vary in the differential educational attainment of the offspring from different social backgrounds.

For explaining what we mean by this we can draw on Mare's (1980, 1981) suggestion of disentangling two processes in analysing class differences in educational attainment. School systems are typically organized as a series of steps which the student population moves along. At each successive step, only a fraction of the population survives. Let us call this successive shrinking of the student population the general survival

pattern. It represents the unconditional distribution of educational credentials that are made available to a cohort of students who move through
the educational system under the particular conditions of a given time in
a given nation.

This general survival pattern is not class- or colour-blind. In each of
the successive progressions, social selectivity occurs. Children of different
social origins drop out at different rates. Moreover, as has been shown
in a number of studies (Mare 1980; 1981 for the US; Smith and Cheung
1986 for the Philippines; Hout 1989 for Ireland; Cobalti 1990 for Italy;
and the contributions in Shavit and Blossfeld, forthcoming, for various
other countries), it is reasonable to assume that social selectivity varies in
a systematic way over the set of progressions. The effects of social origin
on drop-out or survival are regularly found to be stronger in the
transitions at the lower levels of education than in the transitions at
higher levels. Mare (1980, 1981, forthcoming) and Hout (1989) show
that this decline in origin effects in the sequence of transitions is partly
(but not completely) due to differences in ability among the offspring of
different social classes that survive earlier transitions. The stronger
effects of social origin in earlier progressions should also depend on the
fact that the younger a person is, the more dependent he or she will be
on the opinion of the parents and the social conditions at home. With
growing maturity, a person will be more able to decide on his or her
own and will also be less dependent on parental resources, particularly if
higher education is a more or less free good and subsidies are available
to support the economically less advantaged in acquiring it.

Educational systems differ considerably with respect to the extent to
which they allow a cohort of students to survive. One system may sort
out large proportions of students early on and let only a small minority
continue beyond a minimum level. Those selected to continue, however,
may have a high chance of surviving to the very end of the educational
course. In another system, drop-out may be organized in a more
continuous way. Considerably larger proportions of children survive
beyond the minimum educational level, but in a tournament-like process
they have to compete at each successive level, and at each level only a
limited portion of the school population survives. Eventually, only a
proportion similar to that in the first system may attain the highest
educational level. Indeed, one of the indicators Turner (1960) used in his
distinction of contest vs. sponsorship systems was precisely the point in
the life-course at which children are selected to drop out of school or to
receive further education.

If social origin affects drop-out at earlier and later transitions differently, educational systems that provide different survival opportunities
at various transition points will produce a different distribution of
educational qualifications among the social classes. In the final distribu-

tion of educational qualifications, societies may differ considerably even if at each transition they do not differ in the extent of social selectivity that occurs. Building on Mare's distinction and on research pursued in this vein, we propose to concentrate on the interplay between the institutional organization of the survival pattern and the social selectivity that occurs at various transition points in order to understand how educational credentials are distributed among social classes in different societies.

Besides this crucial mechanism producing cross-national variation in the distribution of education to different social classes, nations also may differ in more particular conditions that are responsible for the variation in the success rate of children from different social classes. Such conditions can be associated with differences in the relative location of particular classes in the class structure, with specific educational traditions followed in different classes, or with measures of educational policies intended to alter the distribution of education, for example. We will consider such peculiarities in accounting for variation across countries that remains even after controlling for differences in the general survival pattern.

Social origin is deliberately conceived in terms of social classes, and educational participation is looked at from the perspective of the intergenerational reproduction of class positions. As will become evident from the results of the analyses, this perspective is particularly suited to understand findings on educational participation that are at odds with the expectations one would hold if participation in education were to depend on the position of the family in a vertical dimension of socio-economic status or prestige.

In the following sections, we will first describe the data and methods used in the subsequent analysis. Then we will present the findings on variation in the distribution of education to different classes in the countries studied. Next we will analyse the interplay of the cross-nationally diverging organization of the general survival pattern and the cross-national similarity in social selectivity that we observed for the various educational transitions. We then report on the deviations from the basic pattern of social selectivity that we find for several nations, and finally we conclude with a short discussion of the main findings.

DATA AND METHODS

The countries in this study are the nine European nations studied in the CASMIN project: three countries of continental Western Europe (the Federal Republic of Germany, France and Sweden), four regions within the British Isles (England and Wales, Scotland, Northern Ireland and the Republic of Ireland), and two East European nations (Hungary and

Table 1.1 Class schema

I	Service class I
II	Service class II
III	Routine non-manual
IVa, IVb	Small proprietors; petty bourgeoisie
IVc	Farmers and smallholders
V/VI	Skilled manual workers
VIIa	Unskilled manual workers
VIIb	Agricultural workers

Poland). The database used in this paper is the same as the one used and described by Erikson and Goldthorpe (1992: 47–53). The total number of observations for all nations included in the analysis is 67,635.

The analysis only relates to men in the 30–65 age group. This age group has been selected in order to avoid problems of comparability linked to the fact that the different nations differ with respect to the age at which the highest educational degrees are usually acquired.

Since the data we will analyse were collected in the early 1970s, the individuals selected for study were born between 1910 and 1947. Most of the subjects studied left schools and universities before 1970. Only a very small number of them were affected in their educational careers by the educational reforms implemented in the 1960s and 1970s in the West European nations; in Eastern Europe educational reforms had been implemented earlier. Special attention will have to be given to these differences in interpreting the results.

In the analyses we will use three variables: nation, respondent's class of origin, and highest qualification obtained by the respondent up to the time of the interview. For origin class we use the class schema explained in Table 1.1, which is adopted from Erikson and Goldthorpe (1987a: 58).

For the educational classification we use a schema of qualification levels based on a detailed study of each nation's educational system that is described in detail in König *et al.* (1988). Given that the educational systems of the different nations show a considerable number of institutional differences, comparability is very difficult to establish. In the elaboration of the classification schema, we considered the establishment of functional equivalence in relation to the effects of education on processes of social mobility to be our crucial aim. The different educational categories were therefore defined so as to reflect to the greatest extent possible the typical, class-specific barriers in the educational system and grasp the differentiation in the educational courses and certificates that are relevant in the labour market.[2] In summary, our educational classification consists of the eight categories shown in Table 1.2.

Table 1.2 Educational classification

1a	Inadequately completed elementary education
1b	Completed (compulsory) elementary education
1c	(Compulsory) elementary education and basic vocational qualification
2a	Secondary, intermediate vocational qualification
2b	Secondary, intermediate general qualification
2c	Full secondary, maturity level certificate
3c	Tertiary education, lower level tertiary degree
3b	Tertiary education, higher level tertiary degree

In most of the following analyses of educational transitions, the categories 1a and 1b and the categories 2a and 2b have been collapsed. The collapsed categories represent an ordering of educational credentials in which the value of the credential on the labour market successively increases. It does not, however, exactly correspond to a strict order of educational transitions in the sense that in each case a preceding level has to be acquired before the courses leading to the next level of certificates could be entered.[3] Rather, we look at the final outcomes irrespective of the route that may have been followed to reach them. Nevertheless, using the educational classification given in Table 1.2, the set of transitions that are defined in Table 1.3 can be constructed and understood in a sociologically meaningful way if we state more precisely what is considered as success and as failure in each of the transitions.

Transition T_1 singles out as failures members of a cohort who receive only the social minimum of education or less. This level of education can be achieved by following the tracks of elementary education prescribed as minimal options by the laws on compulsory schooling. Success means continuation of education to a defined qualification level beyond the social minimum of education. Typically there are two possibilities through which the transition to a higher level of qualification (success) occurs. The first is to get access through a selective procedure to a more demanding track of secondary schooling during the period of compulsory schooling (often at ages 10–12); the second is to follow the elementary tracks of compulsory schooling but to extend education beyond the minimal legal requirement, mostly through a programme of vocationally oriented training.

Transition T_2 differentiates to a very large extent between the two success options of continuation in transition T_1. Failure at transition T_2 then means leaving the educational system with a basic level of vocationally oriented training. Success either means entrance in a course of selective secondary education (the more frequent route) or continuation on more demanding vocationally oriented courses.

Table 1.3 Definitions of educational transitions

Transition	Qualification level that is obtained at least through transition	Description of choices
T_1	1c	At most elementary education as required by compulsory schooling ('social minimum' of education) vs. continuing education beyond elementary education required by laws of compulsory schooling.
T_2	2a, 2b	*Given continuation beyond compulsory schooling* Vocationally oriented courses in addition to elementary school education vs. entrance and (at least partial) success in programmes of advanced secondary or tertiary education.
T_3	2c	*Given entrance in programmes of advanced secondary or tertiary education* Only intermediate secondary certificates vs. full secondary or tertiary education.
T_4	3a	*Given education beyond intermediate secondary certificates* Only completion of full secondary education (at maturity level) vs. educational courses leading to degrees of tertiary education.
T_5	3b	*Given tertiary education* Lower tertiary degree vs. higher tertiary degree.

At transition T_3 among those who reached secondary education or advanced occupational training, we consider as failures those who leave the educational institutions with only a certificate of intermediate qualifications. Successes are those who continue to a full secondary (maturity) certificate or to other programmes that lead to tertiary education certificates.[4]

Beyond secondary education we define two further transitions: in transition T_4 we single out as failures those members of a cohort who leave the educational system with only a certificate of full secondary education. Successes are considered to be those who enter and successfully finish any form of tertiary professional education. At transition T_5, we finally distinguish whether a person has acquired a lower or a higher degree of tertiary education. In some countries a higher degree may be achieved consecutively to a lower degree; in other countries a decision has to be taken at transition T_4 between alternative programmes of study, some of which lead to lower degrees of tertiary education and others to higher degrees.

VARIATION IN THE DISTRIBUTION OF EDUCATION AMONG DIFFERENT SOCIAL CLASSES

In the analyses of these transitions, we will pursue two lines of investigation consecutively. At the first stage we study the cross-national similarities and variations in the socially selective outcomes of the educational process. At the second stage we focus on the mechanisms through which these outcomes and their cross-national variations are achieved.

To begin, let us imagine that a cohort of children moves through the educational system defined by the transitions described above. At each transition point some children drop out in a socially selective way. As the cohort moves on, transition by transition, the social composition of the survivor group changes. Figure 1.1 illustrates one aspect of the changing social composition of the survivors in the educational course that we observe for the nations studied. It shows the changes in the proportions among the survivors who are sons of service-class fathers. In order to control for the cross-national variation in the composition of the cohorts studied according to social origin, the data are standardized to an identical origin distribution for all nations (the distribution assumed is the average size of the origin classes in all countries). Therefore all the lines in Figure 1.1 originate at the same point. This point represents the average proportion of service-class fathers in the nine countries. It corresponds to the proportion of service-class origins among the children at the stage of entrance into the school systems, that is before any social election has occurred.

As we would expect, service-class sons continually increase their share among the survivors in the educational competition. From less than 10 per cent in the student population in the first years of schooling, the service-class proportion grows to a cross-national average of about 45 per cent among those who successfully attain a higher tertiary degree. The average, however, badly represents the quite substantial variation among the nations. In the course of successive transitions, the cross-national variation clearly increases. At the end of secondary education the contrast is highest between France and all other countries, but the differentiation among the nations becomes increasingly larger

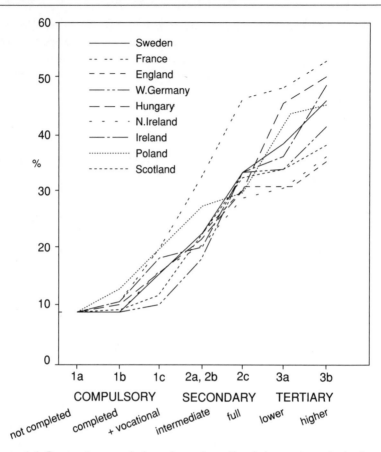

Figure 1.1 Percentages of class I or class II origin among students who attain successive qualification levels: data standardized by social origin

throughout tertiary education. Finally, at the highest educational level, we find the countries spread along a considerable range, the extremes of which are represented by France and England: in France more than 55 per cent of graduates have grown up in one of the two service classes; in England only 35 per cent do.

England does not stand alone at the lower end of social selectivity in the distribution of educational credentials. It is joined by Scotland and Northern Ireland, countries whose educational systems have much in common, at least if compared to the educational systems in other European countries. England is not just an extreme case: it shares its more egalitarian position with the other nations in Great Britain.

An interesting contrast exists between France and Germany. Already by the termination of compulsory schooling, the proportion of service-class children is highest in France, and France holds this position throughout all the transitions. In Germany, on the other hand, the proportion of service-class children is smallest until an intermediate secondary degree, but then catches up to reach an intermediate position at the end point of the educational career.

According to the indicator used here, Hungary and Poland are not among the more egalitarian countries. Hungary in particular has the second largest proportion of certificates of higher education given to the higher social classes in our list of countries.

We have illustrated this view of the socially selective participation in ever higher levels of education focusing on the proportions of service-class sons. The pattern of the lines representing the other classes is more or less the reverse of those of the service classes. Their proportions are largest at the lowest level of education considered, and they tend to become smaller as we move up the educational ladder. But what we intend to show should be sufficiently clear from Figure 1.1. Social selection in the school system is a cumulative process. At a number of transitions students drop out of the school system in a socially selective way. In this process the social composition of the student population in all countries continually changes in favour of children from service-class families, but countries clearly differ in the extent to which the most advantageous educational credentials are distributed to these classes. Even if we control for the varying class structures in the parental generation a considerable degree of cross-national variation remains.

THE SURVIVAL PATTERN AND SOCIAL SELECTIVITY IN EDUCATIONAL TRANSITIONS

In this section we examine more closely how this variation comes about. We try to disentangle the interplay between the global survival pattern and the social selectivity occurring at each of the transitions, and we try to measure the extent to which the cross-national variation in the outcomes that we have observed can be accounted for by these two constituent factors.

As we already know from earlier analyses (Müller *et al.* 1990), the nations included in this study differ greatly in the extent to which they provide opportunities for earning educational credentials to the cohorts studied here. This is reflected in the general survival pattern for the nine nations shown in Figure 1.2.

To make differences and similarities clearer, the figure is split into two parts: the upper graph documents the similarity in the survival pattern of Sweden and all nations of the British Isles. Germany, Hungary,

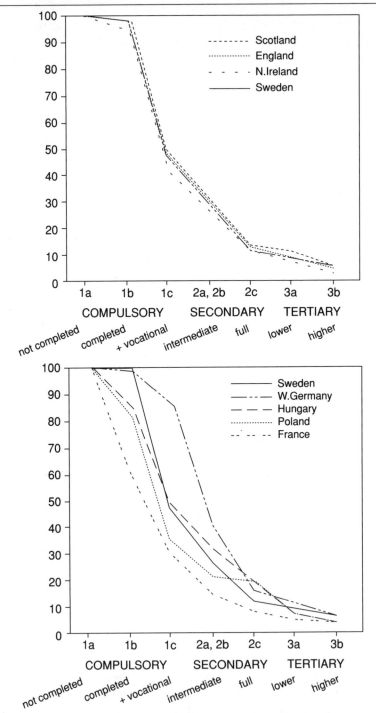

Figure 1.2 Survival rates in the educational systems of nine European

Poland and France clearly differ from this pattern and between themselves, as can be seen from the lower graph in Figure 1.2 that, in order to facilitate comparisons, also includes the pattern for Sweden. The largest contrast in Figure 1.2 is between Germany and France. In Germany 85 per cent of a cohort survives beyond completion of compulsory education and obtains at least vocational training, in France only 30 per cent. The German system also allows a higher proportion to survive until the intermediate level of secondary education, whereas France appears to be the most exclusive country throughout the educational career. In Hungary the chances of surviving through a full secondary education are better than in most of the countries. The other former socialist country, Poland, is close to France during and at the end of compulsory schooling, but only has a very low drop-out rate among those who make it into secondary schools. Indeed, together with Hungary, Poland has the highest survival rate up through a full secondary education. Given the high degree of variation among the nations in the early survival patterns, the extent of similarity at the upper end of the educational system is surprising. Indeed, at this point the differences among nations are only marginal.

In a broad sense the findings correspond to these expectations. With some exceptions, which will be discussed later, Figure 1.3 roughly reveals the expected ordering of classes. The class differences in transition rates are highest at the very first transition which leads beyond the level of compulsory schooling. At later transition the class differentials generally become smaller. In particular, the differences between the skilled and unskilled working class and between farmers and farm labourers that exist in the first two transitions disappear altogether in the three top transitions.

However, we find no point at which class of social origin becomes completely irrelevant.[5] And furthermore, the data given here do not indicate the simple linear pattern that we would expect if the class categories and educational levels represented unidimensional vertical hierarchies. The effects of origin do not continually become smaller as we move from progression to progression, nor are the classes always located in the same order. As we follow the sequence of transitions we find two inflections in the pattern of curves and we see that the agricultural classes change their position in the ordering of classes. These irregularities in the pattern are of quite substantial interest, in particular since we find the pattern to be common for all the countries studied. In attempting to understand it we propose to consider the interest that the offspring of different classes (in particular of the petty bourgeoisie and the agricultural classes) should have in different levels of education and the 'costs' of these different levels for the students.

At all transitions the petty bourgeoisie is located below the routine non-manual class. From the generally better economic conditions of the petty bourgeoisie one would rather expect the contrary. However, we have to acknowledge that for the petty bourgeoisie the intergenerational transmission of class advantages is not primarily related to education but to the direct inheritance of ownership (Yamaguchi 1983; Logan 1983; Müller *et al.* 1988). The relatively low level of educational transitions found for the offspring of the petty bourgeoisie is thus consistent with expectations to be derived from a class theory that considers the particular conditions of the reproduction of class advantages among the owning classes.

With similar considerations we can understand the peculiar pattern found for the class of farmers. It is only in the very first transition – the point in life at which it is decided whether a child receives just the social minimum of education or becomes involved in a programme of vocationally oriented training – that we find clearly higher drop-out risks for the sons of both farm classes than for the offspring of any other class. In later transitions the position of the farm classes ostensibly changes. The farmers' and farm-workers' sons who survive through full secondary education have better odds of successful transitions to one of the tertiary degrees than offspring of the working classes. At the transition to lower tertiary degrees, they have a chance of success second only to the offspring of the lower service class. This peculiar pattern for farmers' offspring can hardly be explained if we assume that origin effects chiefly result from gradual differences in the socio-economic or cultural resources of the various social classes. Under such assumptions the ordering of classes should be the same in all transitions. The peculiar reversal in the location of the farm classes, however, becomes understandable if we consider in more detail two basic options children of farmers have for their occupational future.

In status-attainment studies (Sewell and Hauser 1975; Sewell and Featherman 1975; Jencks *et al.* 1983) educational attainment is regularly found to depend on occupational plans and aspirations. In the case of farmers, however, occupational plans should lead to rather different educational choices depending on whether plans are directed to staying on the farm or to leaving agriculture. In the historical period to which our data refer, farmers' sons who intended to follow in their fathers' footsteps could scarcely gain anything from continued schooling. As long as the knowledge needed for farming is mainly transmitted from generation to generation by doing farm work, schooling and educational credentials will not be valued as a crucial resource for improving occupational prospects. This is particularly true when the institutions of vocational education mainly offer programmes for non-agricultural occupations. For farmers' and farm-labourers' children who see their occupational future in agriculture, then, it appears rational to leave the school system at the end of compulsory schooling. For becoming a farmer it is not education that counts but the opportunity to inherit a farm and to invest in these prospects through early experience and often unpaid family labour. Education will appear instrumental mainly to those who intend to leave agriculture. At more advanced levels of education, that sub-group of farmers' children will become larger and larger, and non-agricultural occupational plans will prevail more and more. In other words, the peculiar non-linear pattern in the odds of farmers' children relative to those of other classes, succeeding in the different educational transitions is interpreted as resulting from the specific 'non-educational alternative' that is available for the occupational future to at least a fraction of the farm class.

The second interesting property of the shape of the curves in Figure 1.3 concerns the inflections that we find in various lines. The first inflection results from the fact that – except for the agricultural classes – social origin effects appear to be stronger at transition T_2 than at transition T_3. The effects of origin class on surviving at least up through an intermediate degree (2a, 2b) appear to be larger than those affecting the chances of entering into basic vocational training following the end of compulsory schooling (lc). This finding is plausible, since it is a fairly general pattern in all countries that the attainment of an intermediate degree is clearly a more demanding step than continuing for vocational training after compulsory education. The attainment of an intermediate degree generally implies the transition into a selective school even before the end of compulsory schooling. Such a transition implies a compelling commitment to more demanding education. Access to vocational training can be obtained via less selective channels.[6] The inflection at transition T_2 is thus consistent with the institutionalized barriers in the educational system.

A similar inflection of the curves occurs between the last two transitions shown in Figure 1.3. A plausible account of this 'irregularity' can be found similarly in the differences in the requirements for a lower tertiary degree as opposed to a higher one. For the cohorts studied here, higher tertiary degrees could be attained almost exclusively by following the most selective academic curriculum, which implied passing the maturity examination or obtaining an equivalent certificate at the end of secondary education. Lower tertiary degrees, on the other hand, could partly be acquired from tertiary educational institutions accessible through alternative routes that did not require the maturity examination and that did not presuppose attendance at schools like the grammar school, the *gymnasium*, or the *lycée*. The institutions granting lower tertiary degrees could partly be entered by less demanding ways of upgrading intermediate secondary education, and were sometimes accessible as in the case of teacher training colleges immediately after the completion of an intermediate secondary degree. It is therefore plausible that class of origin matters more in the transition into higher tertiary degrees than in the transition to the lower, less demanding level.

In conclusion, on very general grounds, the data support the hypothesis that social selectivity is highest in the transitions at the lowest levels of the educational system and then decreases as a cohort moves up through the system. However, there are exceptions to this rule. In the European nations studied here, we do not find a neat picture according to which class effects increasingly decline as we move to higher levels of education. Furthermore, we do not find a stable order concerning the location of classes with respect to their transition probabilities. The deviations from a simple linear pattern are connected with identifiable institutional barriers in the educational system. And, particularly as the case of the farmers and of the petty bourgeoisie show, we have to take into account the differing instrumental role education plays in the intergenerational transmission of advantage in different classes.

NATIONAL VARIATION IN EDUCATIONAL TRANSITIONS

. . . [O]rigin class affects the transition pattern in very much the same way in all of the nations studied. Cross-national variation in the effects of origin class accounts for only a small proportion of the total variation in the transition pattern. But since the ever-present conditions of social selectivity lead one to expect a large degree of similarity, even small deviations from that structure are of interest, particularly if the deviations can be linked in a meaningful way to specific conditions that may explain them. In this section we will therefore discuss the findings that indicate cross-national variation.

The cross-national variations in class effects on educational transitions have been accounted for by the inclusion of three dummy variables in model II of Table 1.4. Variation with positive deviation (VPD) means that in a given nation the transition rate for a particular class is closer (or much closer, in the case of VPD+) to the transition rate of the upper service class than the transition rate for that specific class is in the average of the countries. VND indicates deviation in the negative direction: the transition rate for a particular class differs more from the upper service class in a given nation than it does in the average of all nations.

As can be seen from the top panel of Table 1.4, the estimates for VPD and VPD+ are 0.322 and 0.744. The estimate for VND is −0.327.

Table 1.4 National variation in educational transitions in nine European nations

	Strong positive deviation VPD§	Positive deviation VPD	Negative deviation VND
Estimate	0.744	0.322	−0.327
s.e.	(0.094)	(0.024)	(0.021)
Classes			
I		FRG	eng
		HUN	
		SWE	
II		HUN	
		POL	
III			
IVa, IVb	SCO		hun
IVc	ENG	FRA	frg
		IRL	hun
		NIR	pol
V/VI		HUN	eng
		POL	nir
VIIa		FRA	frg
		POL	irl
		SWE	nir
VIIb			

Thus the effects for VPD and VND are relatively small. They involve only minor shifts in the relative position of the classes involved. A change in the rank order of the position of a class for which the effect applies can occur only if two classes are relatively close to each other anyhow. In the case of VPD+ (the stronger variant of positive deviation) the effect is quite substantial. It indicates that in a given country a class may differ quite considerably from the position of that class in the average of the countries. However, this effect only occurs in two cases that do not invalidate the general conclusions drawn on the grounds of the findings in Figure 1.3.

Table 1.4 also shows in a summary way for each class the names of the countries for which dummy variable indicating deviations of the class effects from the average pattern have been included in the final model. For instance, we can see from the table that the above-mentioned two instances of strong positive deviations relate to the petty bourgeoisie in Scotland and to the class of farmers in England. As is evident from the names of countries contained in Table 1.4, the deviations are not concentrated in a small number of atypical countries. Rather most of the

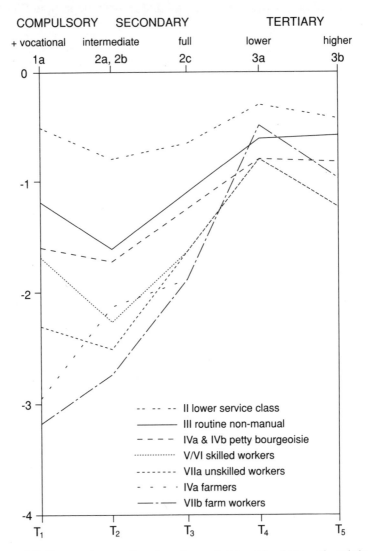

Figure 1.3 Parameter estimates for effects of class of origin on educational transitions in nine European nations according to preferred model II[a]

Note: [a]The lines indicate the differences of the transition rates of the classes shown to those of class I

nations deviate in a particular idiosyncratic instance from the cross-national average. Most of these deviations are consistent with theoretical expectations and can be linked systematically with other knowledge we have about the societies compared.

A first set of deviations that can be expected from external knowledge concerns the upper service class. For this class we find a negative deviation in England, but positive deviations in Germany, Hungary and Sweden. This finding fits with a number of historians' observations made particularly in comparative research on the *Bildungsbürgertum*. The *Bildungsbürgertum* is a status group, mainly composed of civil servants, professionals, and teachers in higher education, which forms a major fraction of the upper service class. This group shares higher education, common social values derived from it, and a high propensity to convey the goods of education to its offspring. The *Bildungsbürgertum* was probably distinguished most clearly as a status group in Germany, but it also existed in neighbouring countries that were influenced by the German traditions of higher education, such as Sweden or the Austro-Hungarian empire (Conze and Kocka 1985; Torstendahl 1985; Kocka 1989; Andorka 1988; Robert 1991). The same body of literature shows that English society was rather distinctive in not having such a broad and educational defined upper class. In England it was not primarily certified higher education that provided social recognition or that was an all-important credential in getting access to distinguished occupational positions (Fischer and Lundgreen 1975; Müller 1990). The positive deviations for Germany, Hungary and Sweden, as well as the negative deviation for England, fit well with these observations.

Another set of deviations that forms a consistent pattern concerns Hungary and Poland. In both countries the communist governments implemented a set of political measures that were intended to enhance the educational opportunities of the less-advantaged wage-earning classes and to impede the opportunities of the property-owning classes (for Hungary see Simkus and Andorka 1982; for Poland see Meyer *et al*. 1979). For Poland and Hungary one would therefore expect the wage-earning classes to show positive deviations and the self-employed classes to show negative deviations. Now, according to Table 1.4, we do indeed find positive deviations for class II, classes V/VI and class VIIa (the latter only in Poland), but negative deviations for the class of farmers and the petty bourgeoisie (the latter only in Hungary). To a large extent the data are thus consistent with expectations that can be derived from the class-linked educational policies of the communist regimes in these countries.

Outside Poland and Hungary, an egalitarian policy has been followed most consistently in Sweden (Jonsson 1987). And it is there that we find similar deviations from the cross-national average as in Hungary and Poland. Sons of families of the petty bourgeoisie have lower than average transition opportunities, and the opportunities of the sons of unskilled workers are better than the average for all the nations.

For Germany and France we find a pattern of class-specific deviation that to some extent counterbalances the effects of the general survival pattern. In Germany, as we have shown, the global survival rates in the first and second transition are by far the highest of all the countries. Large proportions of a cohort survive at those selection points for which the social selectivity (in the average of the nations) is strongest. In France, on the contrary, the school system allows only a tiny minority of the population to acquire educational credentials beyond compulsory schooling. These differences in the global survival rates between Germany and France are counterbalanced by peculiar class effects on educational transitions in the following way: in Germany the negative class factors for the educationally most disadvantaged social classes (i.e. the farmers and unskilled workers) appear to be stronger than for the average of the countries, while in France the distance in the transition rates of farmers' and unskilled workers' sons from those of the service class is smaller than for the cross-national average. The peculiarly limited opportunities of children from the unskilled working class in Germany are well documented in many studies of the German class structure and fit into a pattern that one expects from earlier research (Müller 1975; Mayer 1979; Handl 1989; Müller 1986; Erikson and Goldthorpe 1987b). For Germany, then, the beneficial effects of the global survival pattern are somewhat reduced by a stronger than average social selectivity in precisely those transitions in which selectivity is high, whereas in France the effects of the unfavourable global survival regime is mitigated by a somewhat reduced social selectivity (for corresponding findings from detailed German–French comparisons see König 1990; for France see Garnier and Hout 1981).

Other positive deviations from the average pattern are found for the class of farmers in England and both Northern Ireland and the Irish Republic. For the class of farmers in England we even have to allow a strong positive deviation (VPD +) in order to obtain an acceptable fit. The distinct social position of the class of farmers in England is well known, and it would have been surprising if we had not found a pronounced positive deviation for this class in the present analysis. The positive deviations that we also find for the class of farmers in the Republic of Ireland are consistent with the dualistic structure of farming in Ireland. The large farmers and capitalist agricultural entrepreneurs that form a specific segment of the agricultural classes in Ireland can be expected to show a similar pattern of educational participation as the farmers in England (see Jackson 1971; Peillon 1982; Erikson and Goldthorpe 1987b). However, it appears to be more difficult to find explanations from available external evidence for the better than average educational prospects of farmers' children in Northern Ireland.

A further instance for which no strong external evidence could be found concerns the position of the working classes in England, Northern Ireland and the Republic of Ireland. For England the term VND – indicating negative deviation – has to be included for the skilled working class. Since the unskilled working class does not differ in England from the cross-national average, the negative deviation for skilled workers means that the educational opportunities of sons from the skilled and unskilled working classes are less distinct from each other in England than the average across all the countries. (In spite of this fact the total range of class differentials is still smaller in England than in the cross-national average, since, as indicated above, the English upper service class is less distinct from all other classes than in the cross-national average.) In contrast to England, in Northern Ireland the educational opportunities of children of both working classes are below the cross-national average, while in the Republic of Ireland this is found only for the unskilled workers' children. Thus in Northern Ireland both the working classes and in the Republic of Ireland the unskilled fraction of it appear to be subject to a stronger class bias in educational selection than is the case for the average of the countries.

Finally, the offspring of the petty bourgeoisie have much better survival opportunities in the Scottish educational system than in any of the other countries. Indeed it is the second instance of a strong positive deviation (VPD +). We were unable to find a convincing explanation for this finding in previous work on educational attainment in Scotland. A closer analysis for the Scottish petty bourgeoisie, however, showed that in the data used for Scotland the petty bourgeoisie includes a considerably higher proportion of employers and a smaller number of self-employed/workers than the petty bourgeoisie in other nations. Thus, in the data used the Scottish petty bourgeoisie has a more advantageous composition than the petty bourgeoisie in other nations. We think that the clearly better than average educational prospects of the offspring of the Scottish petty bourgeoisie is most simply explained by this compositional difference.

Although the explanations proposed for some of the deviations are tentative – since no strong external evidence could be found – we fear that not considering these deviations that manifest themselves so clearly in the data would overstress uniformity.

SUMMARY AND CONCLUSIONS

This paper has studied similarities and differences in the educational selection processes in several European nations. The findings provide clear evidence that in these countries education is distributed in different ways and with different results to the social classes. The share of education and educational credentials that the offspring of different social classes receive varies considerably between countries.

Most of these differences in the varying distribution of education to social classes are produced through the interplay of two elements in the selection processes that occur in educational institutions. First, the general survival pattern that exists at a given time and place in the educational institutions, and second, the class-specific survival rates and their variation across transitions and nations. While the class effects on survival show a large degree of commonality in all countries, the global survival pattern varies quite extensively. It varies most among countries at precisely those transitions in which survival is most affected by the social origin of students, that is, in the early transitions. For the cohorts studied, the considerable cross-national variation in the unequal distribution of education to the various social classes thus results chiefly from cross-national variation in the global opportunities to attain the various levels of education and less from national differences in the class effects on given educational progressions. The factor that crucially induces variation among nations is the differences in the supply of education in the different national educational systems and in the channelling of the student population through the different educational institutions and transitions.

As for the similarities and differences of the class effects among nations, we should stress the large degree of commonality. No country differs fundamentally from the basic pattern of class-related advantage and disadvantage as is shown in Figure 1.3. Indeed, of all the class effects that can be accounted for in our models, 94 per cent are due to commonality among nations and only 6 per cent to variation between nations. In all countries the class effects tend to be smaller in later transitions than in earlier ones, and all nations show basically the same order in the location of the various classes in the space of higher or lower rates of transition at the various progressions. The similarity among nations also includes the 'irregularities' in the lines that were found in Figure 1.3: the inflections and the changing location of farmers. We assume that the underlying factors that are responsible for this common pattern of class effects are basically the same in all countries as well. The inflections in the pattern of class effects can be plausibly linked with the costs and institutional barriers that exist for different levels of education. In trying to understand the relative position of the various classes in the space of higher or lower transition chances at the various progressions, the adoption of a class perspective appears to be very revealing. In particular, in order to understand the location of the petty bourgeoisie and of farmers, it seems indispensable to take into account – besides the cultural and socio-economic resources available in these classes – the specific mechanisms of direct intergenerational transmission of advantage in these classes and the limited instrumental role that education plays in this process.

However, although such a common basic pattern can be discerned and meaningfully interpreted, there is also evidence that single nations deviate in specific ways from it. Commonality does not mean complete identity. The assumption that commonality exists in spite of observed deviations is supported by the fact that the variation does not result from one or a few countries that strongly deviate from another set of countries. Rather, most of the countries deviate in a specific and limited way from the cross-national average and the cross-national variation mainly entails minor differences from the basic pattern of the class-related differentials in transition rates. Most of these deviations can be interpreted sensibly in the light of existing external evidence. The findings generally indicate the relevance of factors that result from specific historical, political or institutional peculiarities existing in some of the nations but not in others. Examples are the educational orientation of the *Bildungsbürgertum* in Germany and in some other countries in which this stratum achieved a prominent position, the particular class position of farmers in England, or the class-linked educational policies in Hungary and Poland. We should also underline that the conditions that we assume to produce the cross-national variation are heterogeneous, and factors operating in different directions may overlap. In Hungary and Sweden, for instance, an above-average tendency to transmit higher education to the next generation in the highly educated upper service class is combined with effects consistent with the egalitarian policies pursued in these countries for the enhancement of the educational prospects of children of the lower classes.

Thus, concerning the more general questions that we raised at the beginning of this paper, the findings of the analysis would not seem to evoke explanations in terms of general properties such as the level of industrial or economic development. It would appear to be a difficult task to derive from such conditions the considerable differences in the supply of education and in the channelling of the student populations through the educational system as they exist, for instance, between England, France and Germany; such conditions were found to be the major factor in producing the cross-national differences in the distribution of education to the various social classes. In the same vein, the differences among nations in the class effects on education transitions hardly appear compatible with general macro-sociological differences of these nations. Rather, the findings are in line with the explanatory strategy advanced in the contributions by Erikson and Goldthorpe (1987b, 1992): that is, a strategy that elaborates on institutional, political, and other incentives and constraints that have evolved historically in specific nations and affect the behaviour of individual actors.

ACKNOWLEDGEMENTS

This paper was partly prepared while Walter Müller was a Fellow at the Center for Advanced Study in the Behavioural Sciences, Stanford. He gratefully acknowledges financial support provided by the National Science Foundation, grant BNS87-00864, the Spencer Foundation, and the Stiftung Volkswagenwerk for the grant given to the CASMIN project. An earlier version of the paper was presented by Walter Müller at the Department of Sociology, Duke University, and he wishes to thank those present for a stimulating discussion.

NOTES

1 Among the eight coefficients estimates in the crucial equations (3), (7) and (8) in the analysis by Treiman and Yip, only one coefficient is significant according to standard statistical criteria. It is the coefficient indicating that the variance explained in educational attainment in different countries depends positively on the degree of inequality in the distribution of education in the father's generation. Excluding India from the analysis, the size of this coefficient strongly decreases and it becomes statistically insignificant. Excluding India from the analysis also produces a change in sign of the coefficient estimating the effect of educational inequality in equation (8). Contrary to the assumptions of Treiman and Yip, the results without India then indicate that the coefficient relating father's occupational status to respondent's occupational status *decreases* as educational inequality in the father's generation *increases*.

2 These considerations led us to develop an educational scale with two crucial classification criteria: (1) the differentiation of a hierarchy of educational levels, based both on the length of educational experience and on the generally acknowledged value of the educational track and of the certificate obtained; (2) the differentiation between 'general' and 'vocational oriented' education (for details, see König *et al.* 1988).

3 This fact is congenial to the multi-track structure of the European school systems. Not only is there a multiplicity of parallel tracks, but alternative routes may lead to the same final outcome. It is not, therefore, the aim of this paper to model the educational decisions the students may actually have faced in their educational careers.

4 Beyond the point of intermediate secondary certificates, the school system generally provides various tracks to higher education. One typically leads through advanced secondary schools (grammar school, *gymnasium*, *lycée*) a full secondary education (with certificates like *Abitur*, A-level exam, or *Baccalauréat*). From there, a successful educational career then leads into the various programmes at the institutions of higher tertiary education. In several countries a number of opportunities exist to bypass the classical institutions of higher secondary education and to enter by alternative routes into institutions of lower tertiary degrees (such as teacher training colleges, schools for advanced technical training, schools of social work, and others).

5 As systematic statistical tests that cannot be reported here show, most of the classes differ significantly from each other even at transitions T_4 and T_5. At transition T_4 only the agricultural classes do not differ significantly from classes II and III, and only the petty bourgeoisie does not differ significantly

from classes III and V/VI. At transition T_5 class III does not differ significantly from classes II and IVa and IVb, and the agricultural classes do not differ significantly from the working classes.
6 As a rule, those who later obtain basic vocational training first follow the educational route designed for those who do not succeed in admission to advanced educational institutions or who have no intention of obtaining more education than the legal minimum. Once this is obtained one enters an institution of vocational training into which access is generally less selective than it is to the more academically oriented tracks of secondary education.

REFERENCES

Allmendinger, J. (1989) 'Career Mobility Dynamics. A Comparative Analysis of the United States, Norway, and West Germany', *Studien und Berichte*, 49. Berlin: Max-Planck-Institut für Bildungsforschung.

Andorka, A. (1988) *Comments Concerning the Results on Hungary of the CASMIN Project of International Comparison of Social Mobility*. Conference on the CASMIN Project and Comparative Sociology, Schloss Reisenburg, Germany.

Archer, M.S. (1979) *Social Origins of Educational Systems*, London: Sage.

Archer, M.S. (1989) 'Cross-National Research and the Analysis of Educational Systems', in Kohn, M.L. (ed.) *Cross-National Research in Sociology*, Newbury Park: Sage: 242–62.

Atkinson, A.B. (1991) *Poverty, Statistics, and Progress in Europe*. Discussion Paper WSP/60. London: London School of Economics.

Blau, P.M. and Duncan, O.D. (1967) *The American Occupational Structure*, New York: Wiley.

Blossfeld, H.P. and Shavit, Y. (forthcoming) 'Persisting Barriers: Changes in Educational Opportunities in Thirteen Countries', in Shavit, Y. and Blossfeld, H.P. (eds) *Persistent Inequality: Changing Educational Stratification in Thirteen Countries*, Boulder, Colo.: Westview Press.

Cobalti, A. (1990) 'Schooling Inequalities in Italy: Trends over Time', *European Sociology Review*, 6: 199–214.

Coleman, J.S. *et al.* (1966) *Equality of Educational Opportunity*, US Department of Education, Washington, DC: USGPO.

Coleman, J.S. and Hoffert, T. (1987) *Public and Private High Schools*, New York: Basic Books.

Conze, W. and Kocka, J. (1985) 'Einleitung', in Conze, W. and Kocka, J. (eds) *Bildungsbürgertum im 19. Jahrhundert. Teil I: Bildungssystem und Professionalisierung im internationalen Vergleich*, Stuttgart: Klett-Cotta: 9–28.

Erikson, R. and Goldthorpe, J.H. (1987a) 'Commonality and Variation in Social Fluidity in Industrial Nations. Part I: A Model for Evaluating the "FJH-hypothesis"', *European Sociology Review*, 3: 54–77.

Erikson, R. and Goldthorpe, J.H. (1987b) 'Commonality and Variation in Social Fluidity in Industrial Nations. Part II: The Model of Core Social Fluidity Applied', *European Sociology Review*, 3: 145–66.

Erikson, R. and Goldthorpe, J.H. (1992) *The Constant Flux. A Study of Class Mobility in Industrial Societies*, Oxford: Clarendon Press.

Fischer, W. and Lundgreen, P. (1975) 'The Recruitment and Training of Administrative and Technical Personnel', in Tilly, C. (ed.) *The Formation of National States in Western Europe*, Princeton, N.J.: Princeton University Press: 456–561.

Garnier, M.A. and Hout, M. (1981) 'Schooling Processes and Educational Outcomes in France', *Quality and Quantity*, 15: 151–77

Hallinan, M.T. (1988) 'Equality of Educational Opportunity', *Annual Review of Sociology*, 14: 249–68.

Handl, J. (1989) *Berufschancen und Heiratsmuster von Frauen*, Frankfurt: Campus.

Heath, A. (undated) *Towards Meritocracy, Recent Evidence on an Old Problem*, Oxford: Nuffield College.

Hout, M. (1989) *Following in Father's Footsteps*, Cambridge, Mass.: Harvard University Press.

Jackson, J.A. (1971) 'Ireland', in Archer, M. and Finer, S. (eds) *Contemporary Europe: Class, Status and Power*, London: Weidenfeld & Nicolson.

Jencks, C. (1985) 'How much do High School Students Learn', *Sociology of Education*, 58: 128–35.

Jencks, C., Crouse, J. and Müller, P. (1983) 'The Wisconsin Model of Status Attainment: A National Replication with Improved Measures of Ability and Aspiration', *Sociology of Education*, 56: 3–19.

Jonsson, J.O. (1987) 'Class Origin, Cultural Origin, and Educational Attainment: The Case of Sweden', *European Sociological Review*, 3: 229–42.

Kerckhoff, A.C. (1989) 'Creating Inequality in the Schools: A Structural Perspective'. Paper presented at the annual meeting of the American Sociology Association, San Francisco.

Kocka, J. (1989) 'Bildungsbürgertum – Gesellschaftliche Formation oder Historikerkonstruckt', in Kocka, J. (ed.) *Bildungsbürgertum im 19. Jahrhundert. Teil IV: Politischer Einfluss und gesellschaftliche Formation*, Stuttgart: Klett-Cotta: 9–20.

König, W. (1990) *Berufliche Mobilität in Frankreich und in der Bundersrepublik*, Frankfurt: Campus.

König, W. and Müller, W. (1986) 'Educational Systems and Labour Markets as Determinants of Worklife Mobility in France and West-Germany: A Comparison of Men's Career Mobility, 1965–1970', *European Sociological Review*, 2: 73–96.

König, W., Lüttinger, P. and Müller, W. (1988) *Comparative Analysis of the Development and Structure of Educational Systems: Methodological Foundations and the Construction of a Comparative Educational Scale*. Casmin Working Paper No. 12. Mannheim: Institut für Sozialwissenschaften.

Logan, J.A. (1983) 'A Multivariate Model for Mobility Tables', *American Journal of Sociology*, 89: 324–49.

Mare, R.D. (1980) 'Social Background and School Continuation Decisions', *Journal of the American Statistical Association*, 75: 295–305.

Mare, R.D. (1981) 'Change and Stability in Educational Stratification', *American Sociological Review*, 46: 73–87.

Mare, R.D. (forthcoming) 'Educational Stratification on Observed and Unobserved components of Family Background', in Shavit, Y. and Blossfeld, H.P. (eds) *Persistent Inequality: A Comparative Study of Educational Stratification in Fourteen Countries*, Boulder, Colo.: Westview Press.

Mayer, K.U. (1979) *Fluktuation und Umschichtung*. Habilitationsschrift. Mannheim: Universitat, Fakultat für Sozialwissenschaften.

Meyer, J.W. (1980) 'Levels of the Educational System and Schooling Effects', in Bidwell, C.W. and Douglas, M.W. (eds) *The Analysis of Educational Productivity, ii, Issues in Macroanalysis*, Cambridge, Mass.: Ballinger: 15–62.

Meyer, J.W., Tuma, N.B. and Zagorski, K. (1979) 'Education and Occupational Mobility: A Comparison of Polish and American Men', *American Journal of Sociology*, 84: 978–86.

Müller, W. (1975) *Familie, Schule, Beruf. Analysen zur sozialen Mobilitat und Statuzuweisung in der Bunderrepublik*, Opladen: Westdeutscher Verlag.

Müller, W. (1986) 'Soziale Mobilität: Die Bundersrepublik im internationalen Vergleich', in Kaase, M. (ed.) *Politische Wissenschaft und politische Ordnung*, Opladen: Westdeutscher Verlag: 339–54.

Müller, W. (1990) *Does Education Matter? Evidence from Cross-national Comparisons*, Stanford: Center for Advanced Study in the Behavioural Sciences.

Müller, W., König, W. and Luttinger, P. (1988) *Education and Class Mobility*. Casmin Working Paper No. 14. Mannheim: Institut für Sozialwissenschaften.

Müller, W. *et al.* (1990) 'Class and Education in Industrial Nations', in Haller, M. (ed.) *Class Structure in Europe*, Armonk, New York: Sharpe: 62–91.

Peillon, M. (1982) *Contemporary Irish Society*, Dublin: Gill and Macmillan.

Ringer, F.K. (1979) *Education and Society in Modern Europe*, Bloomington: Indiana University Press.

Robert, P. (1991) 'Educational Transition in Hungary from the Post-War Period to the End of the 1980s', *European Sociology Review*, 7: 213–36.

Ryscavage, P. and Henle, P. (1990) 'Earning Inequality Accelerates in the 1980s', *Monthly Labor Review*, Dec.: 3–15.

Shavit, Y. (1990) 'Segregation, Tracking and the Educational Attainment of Minorities: Arabs and Oriental Jews in Israel', *American Sociological Review*, 55: 77–88.

Shavit, Y. and Blossfeld, H.P. (eds) (forthcoming) *Persistent Inequality: Changing Educational Stratification in Thirteen Countries*, Boulder, Colo.: Westview Press.

Sewell, W.H. and Hauser, R.M. (1975) *Education, Occupation and Earnings: Achievement in Early Career*, New York: Academic Press.

Sewell, W.H. and Featherman, D.L. (eds) (1975) *Schooling and Achievement in American Society*, New York: Academic Press.

Simkus, A. and Andorka, R. (1982) 'Inequalities in Educational Attainment in Hungary, 1923–1973', *American Sociological Review*, 47: 740–51.

Smith, H.L. and Cheung, P.P.L. (1986) 'Trends in the Effects of Family Background on Educational Attainment in the Philippines', *American Journal of Sociology*, 91: 1387–1408.

Sørensen, A.B. and Hallinan, M.T. (1986) 'Effects of Ability Grouping of Growth in Academic Achievement', *American Education Research Journal*, 23: 519–42.

Treiman, D.J. (1970) 'Industrialization and Social Stratification', in Laumann, E.O. (ed.) *Social Stratification, Research and Theory of the 1970s*, Indianapolis: Bobbs-Merrill: 207–34.

Treiman, D.J. and Yip, K.B. (1989) 'Educational and Occupational Attainment in 21 Countries', in Kohn, M.L. (ed.) *Cross-National Research in Sociology*, Newbury Park: Sage: 373–94.

Torstendahl, R. (1985) 'Engineers in Sweden and Britain 1820–1914: Professionalization and Bureaucratization in a Comparative Perspective', in Conze, W. and Kocka, J. (eds) *Bildungbürgertum im 19. Jahrhundert, Teil 1: Bildungssystem und Professionalisierung im internationalen Vergleich*, Stuttgart: Klett-Cotta: 543–60.

Turner, R.H. (1960) 'Sponsored and Contest Mobility and the School System', *American Sociological Review*, 25: 855–67.

Yamaguchi, K. (1983) 'The Structure of Intergenerational Occupational Mobility: Generality and Specificity in Resources, Channels, and Barriers', *American Journal of Sociology*, 88: 718–45.

Chapter 2

School knowledge traditions

M. McLean

The divergence between national views of appropriate school knowledge is not superficially apparent from curriculum content. Primary schools throughout Europe emphasize similar computational and linguistic skills. Secondary schools have the same discrete subjects – language and literature in the national language or mother tongue of students, mathematics, sciences, one or more modern European languages, history, geography, art, music and physical education.

Even within subjects, there is much in common across the countries and not only in areas regarded as 'universal' such as mathematics and science. Literature and history are more specific to national cultures but they have similar kinds of topics – the study of select lists of important books or a chronological treatment of political, economic and social developments within the framework of a common or contingent set of European experiences.

Then commonality breaks down. There are quite different expectations of the skills and attitudes that may result from study. There are different hierarchies of status between subjects. Views diverge over what knowledge should be central and compulsory and what can be left to individual choice. Specialization occurs at different times and levels and to different degrees. Within subjects there are often differences between the kind of student cognitive and moral/emotional development that is the hoped-for outcome.

How can these differences be conceptualized in ways that are convincing, rigorous and useful? How can the perils be avoided from the opposite poles of crude and static stereotyping and of patternless complexity? On the one hand, differences should be presented with sufficient lucidity and coherence. On the other, the approach needs to build in possibilities for change within these historical patterns.

CONCEPTUALIZATION OF EUROPEAN TRADITIONS

Typification of national cultures in Europe has a long history. They became a matter for serious political theorizing in Britain with the rejection of the French revolutionary model of political change by Edmund Burke and others. The point was to make sense of the diverging political processes of Britain and France and to find a rationale for a quite different and distinctive approach in Britain. Similar analysis was encouraged in France by the central place of the revolutionary experience and in Germany and Italy by the nineteenth-century nationalist movement.

Epistemological differences were included in some of these earlier analyses. There was concern in Britain, for instance, about the impact of the 'grand tour' upon the thinking of the social élite in Britain in the early nineteenth century[1] (Collins 1868). More systematically, the revival of interest in nationality following the 1919 Versailles political settlement in Europe led to attempts to produce characterizations which included views of worthwhile knowledge. The national character types defined by Salvador de Madariaga – English 'action', French 'thought' and Spanish 'passion' – were extended to consideration of how each type related to thought (Madariaga 1970). The idea was rooted that knowledge and thought had different political and social functions in each national culture.

Comparative educationists gave attention to different epistemological traditions. Joseph Lauwerys characterized the educational knowledge philosophies of the USA, USSR, England, France and (West) Germany (Lauwerys 1965) This analysis has considerable value, especially for this study, in its typification of English moral, French rational and German metaphysical traditions. Further analyses have extended the nation-specific approach of Lauwerys by rooting the traditions in philosophical and cultural sources which have influence across countries throughout Europe (Holmes 1981). Each country has its specific and dominant knowledge tradition which is intelligible throughout Europe because it is also part of a common European culture.

There have been a number of relevant continental European studies which start from intranational conflicts about what knowledge is most worthwhile. These debates refer back to a pan-European conflict of ideas represented in the educational field by Erasmus and Comenius, the codifiers respectively of the humanist and encyclopaedist educational traditions.

Three traditions may be proposed which are specifically European and are at the same time pan-European:

1 encyclopaedism;
2 humanism;
3 naturalism.

Encyclopaedism and humanism have well-established parameters. Naturalism is shorthand for a variety of individual and community orientated views which have challenged the other two dominant traditions.[2]

Yet these views are found in different combinations in the various countries of Europe. Encyclopaedism has been powerful in France since the 1789 revolution and before. Yet it has been very weakly represented in England in the twentieth century. Naturalist views have been more strongly entrenched in England and Germany than in France. Humanism has retained a powerful place in England. Furthermore, interpretation varies from country to country and has changed over time. English and German versions of humanism diverge sharply while the French version of encyclopaedism differs from that of Germany.

How can the characteristics of each of these traditions be formulated in ways that will allow them to be used as a tool for investigation of contemporary issues of the school curriculum on a European scale? The types are cultural and sociological as much as philosophical. The need is to establish the parameters of long-established knowledge traditions. The postulations need to be made downstream from philosophy, which transcends national cultures at least in the questions posed, yet upstream from the complexity, confusion and ephemerality of everyday classroom practice.

Description might start from empirical investigation of élite schooling in the first half of the twentieth century – in the French *lycée*, German *Gymnasium*, English grammar or public school and the Italian *liceo*. The assumption is that the curriculum in these schools, on the one hand, reflected more complex configurations in higher education and in the dominant culture. On the other, this curriculum has had a major influence upon lower levels of schooling. Such patterns of curriculum are likely to have survived the democratization of secondary education in the 1960s. They represent a focal point in the whole education and cultural system over a long period of time without, at any time, totally capturing the whole and diverse spectrum of views of worthwhile knowledge prevailing at every level of education or every segment of society.

The starting point is the different dominant views of knowledge in élite secondary education before the main spurt of expanded access occurred in the 1960s. They can be constructed empirically from the statements of the aims of education and the curriculum and from the actual curriculum subjects including their specific content. They can be given greater precision by reference to philosophical, cultural and political positions which justify them.

ENCYCLOPAEDISM

A definition of encyclopaedism could start from three main principles:

- universality;
- rationality;
- utility.

Universality has two facets. First, all students should acquire as much knowledge as possible about all valid subjects. All students in countries where the universalist encyclopaedic criterion is accepted have followed the same basic core curriculum even though there may be differences in depth of study between subjects and between students. The second facet is standardization. All state schools offer the same subjects by grade, level and, when limited specialization begins, by broad orientation. Specifications include standard numbers of hours per week and the main aims and topics of each subject.

The universalist principle is now familiar in England and Wales with its adoption in the 1988 Education Reform Act for students up to the age of 16. It has been justified in other European countries on three grounds: that a standard and broad content allows students a width of capacities in later life (including higher study) which early specialization discourages; that it is a form of quality control by which all participants can judge how effectively individual schools and teachers perform against a common standard; and that it goes some way towards guaranteeing at least a limited degree of equality of opportunity through a common experience for all students of whatever backgrounds or perceived abilities (Brereton 1911).[3]

Yet universalism is the lowest common denominator of encyclopaedism. Its highest aim is rationality. In France, at least, rationalism has been historically linked with the dominant philosophy of René Descartes and with the traditional education developed by the seventeenth-century Jesuits. Since the 1789 Revolution rationality has been regarded as the means to make better people, better society, better government and better economy. At an abstract level it can make better people by imbuing each individual with the light of pure reason which is the highest good and it is the means to understanding the world by the deduction of universal principles of meaning.[4]

How is rationality used to identify central areas and approaches to knowledge? Emile Durkheim contrasted encyclopaedism in French education with humanism by arguing that the former concentrated primarily on nature and the latter on individual man (woman) (Durkheim 1977). Yet this rationality did not mean that humanity was ignored. Instead it was studied by reference to universal structures – whether of human relations or the individual psyche. So Durkheim argued that a rationalist, encyclopaedic approach would allow the child to

> understand ideas, customs, political constitutions, forms of domestic organization, ethical and logical systems other than the ones he is used to so that the child will become aware of the vital richness of human nature.
>
> (*Ibid.*: 335)

in contrast to humanism which was concerned

> with man in all the diverse ways in which he manifests himself through his moral activity as a creature of emotion and will as well as thoughts.
>
> (*Ibid.*: 279)

Durkheim was an encyclopaedist in the sense of believing that all valid knowledge should be imparted. He felt this should be approached through reason and a 'schematic knowledge of each (of the sciences) which covered those ideas most fundamental to them' (*ibid.*: 287) – repeating Comenius's demand: 'It is the principles, the causes and the uses of all the most important things in existence that we wish all men to learn' (Comenius 1907). So structure and system created and comprehended by reason were pre-eminent.

The third principle of utility was highlighted after the 1789 Revolution. Rational knowledge is not only valuable for its own sake but for its use. Social, political and economic organizations are made more efficient by the application of rational procedures. Vocational studies, at any level, should begin with rational scientific ideas. A craftsman or woman, a chef who may be an artist as well as an artisan, a technician or a professional engineer can all become more efficient by the application of rational scientific principles to practical work. The utility principle means that general academic education is organically linked to vocational studies by the same intellectual principles.[5]

Encyclopaedism is associated with a hierarchy of subjects in the school curriculum. However, it is not simply a system for assigning relative status to these subjects. It affects the selection of topics within subjects, the way they are presented, what is expected of students, their assessment and the way that teachers view themselves. Encyclopaedism can be seen as an ethos running through every aspect of the school curriculum.

Encyclopaedism and the organization of the traditional school curriculum in France

The implications of encyclopaedism for the school curriculum can be judged by confronting first the principles outlined above with the actual organization of the curriculum first in France over the last century.

Despite the claim, considered later, that there has been a movement over time from a universalist to a rationalist orientation, in certain respects universalist principles have been applied more stringently over the course of the twentieth century. In 1900, all students in secondary education followed broadly similar courses in conventional core subjects. The main cleavage was produced by the classics. Until 1902 there was a formal distinction, as in England and Germany, between the classical and modern (or mathematical/scientific) branches of secondary education. The divergence continued informally, based on a division between those taking or not taking Latin, from 1902 through to 1968, when Latin joined Greek as an optional additional subject in lower secondary education.

The provision of universal secondary education in France from 1959 was associated with a renewed application of universalism and standardization rather than with increased diversity. Universalist principles were reinforced by a commitment to achieve equality of opportunity in comprehensive schools through a common curriculum.

Universalism can imply also relative uniformity of student achievement and school quality. This has been central to French conceptions of an encyclopaedic curriculum. All students should acquire a basic knowledge appropriate to their age or grade. Class situated teacher assessment of students has been a perennial feature of French primary and secondary education throughout the twentieth century. So has grade repeating. The principle is that pupils should not move on to a higher level until they have reached a basic prescribed level of achievement for their grade.

Specialization of upper secondary schools potentially has threatened universality. Yet this process has extended the range of options without altering the relationship between a core curriculum and specialisms. In the 1980s there have been five main branches on the general, academic side and a number of others in the technical vocational section. Yet the core curriculum of French (until the penultimate grade), mathematics, physical and biological science, a modern language, history, geography and civics is still central in all full upper secondary education in France. As with streaming or setting in the lower secondary school, the only concession to differentiation is the pace and depth at which subjects are covered in different branches.

The power of the universalist principle lies in its capacity to survive continuous pressures for differentiation which have been posed by the democratization of lower secondary schooling and the diversification of upper secondary education. It is not simply system inertia but the periodic reaffirmation of commonality of educational knowledge in the face of creeping differentiation. Universalism remains central to the ethos of encyclopaedism held by participants in French education.

Rationality is the criterion by which branches of knowledge are recognized to have value in the encyclopaedic tradition. It is the justification for excluding expressive and non-intellectual elements of the curriculum, or more frequently for 'intellectualizing' them. The central place of rationality in secondary schools in nineteenth-century France was expressed in the names of the two alternative final grades of the *lycée* – the *classe de philosophie* and the *classe de mathématique* – for philosophy and mathematics were seen to be the two supremely rationalist subjects.

Curriculum subjects acquired their rational status in two ways. First, the content of the subjects themselves had to be highly logical and systematic. Second, they had to encourage the development of rational faculties among those who studied them. Some subjects acquired this status more easily than others – not only philosophy and mathematics but also the sciences (especially physical science) and languages (because of their logical structures).

The application of the rationality principle can be gauged by examining the aims, content and pedagogy of individual subjects of the curriculum. Late nineteenth- and early twentieth-century accounts may be compared with those of the last 20 years. Philosophy for the last grade of the upper secondary school had much in common at least in approach in the two periods even though the topics changed. The comment of the early twentieth century was that it emphasized the examination, analysis and classification of ideas and their arrangement into a coherent whole – something that was felt to be lacking in equivalent schools in England (Brereton 1911). A comparison might be made with the examination questions for philosophy in the *baccalauréat* in 1988. While some are contemporary – How can the journalist decide that an event is historic? For what reasons should one respect nature? The majority are relatively timeless – How can one hold to be true what has not been proved? Can taste be taught? Is it within the capacity of the state to limit its power? Can peace be made? Is there a virtue of forgetfulness? Is passion a mistake?[6]

This intellectualism featured strongly also at earlier stages of secondary schooling. Moral education for 13-year-olds in the early twentieth century was treated historically and sociologically (Hartog 1911) and encouraged children 'to look at moral issues from an intellectual rather than an emotional viewpoint (*ibid.*: 212). 'The basic texts were the fables of La

Fontaine but the exercises were firmly rationalist, including for instance questions such as: 'Distinguish modesty from humility' (*ibid.*: 216).

Though applying to an older age group (15–18), the aims of the upper secondary curriculum of 1985 differ little:

1 *To give to the student the mastery of the junction between the abstract and the concrete.*

Upper secondary students should know how to conceptualize, that is to say to move from confused global representation to clear ideas, to analyse which is to order their thinking, to model which is to construct abstract models which serve to understand reality and to act upon it. They should understand that the comprehension of the concrete is arrived at necessarily through theory and that the aim of the abstract is to allow precise understanding of the concrete.[7]

Yet some subjects, such as mathematics, are by their nature abstract and logical while others, essentially, have other goals. How can there be any rationalist mathematics when all mathematics would appear to be logical in whatever culture it is situated? How can there be a rationalist language study which has primordial goals of communication, expression and access to a literature which represents a (national) culture? How can history be rationalist when there can be 'only one safe rule for the historian: that he should recognize in the development of human destinies the play of the contingent and the unforeseen'? (Fisher 1936).

These subjects are forced into a rationalist mode in the encyclopaedic tradition of the curriculum. French mathematics teaching in secondary schools in the early twentieth century emphasized the exact presentation of theorems by students (often in front of a class ready to pounce on logical omissions) and on a rapid coverage to provide a grasp of the structure and unity of the whole subject at the expense of the endless working of examples which characterized English mathematics teaching (Hartog 1911; Brereton 1911). In the 1960s, French mathematics teaching still insisted on the communication of rules and the incorporation of 'modern' mathematics within this framework (Colomb 1985).

The logic of language, whether mother tongue or foreign (ancient or modern), would seem to be contained in its linguistic structures. This is the broader justification for language teaching (and the entry point for minority languages such as Breton or Arabic in the French curriculum in the 1970s). But rationality can be about doing as well as knowing and actual language teaching (mother tongue or foreign) concentrates on improving the capacity of students to structure and polish their French expression. Latin and Greek teaching in France in the early twentieth century gave far less attention than in English schools to translating into the classical languages and more to producing the most perfect translation into French (Brereton 1911). In French the emphasis was not on learning rules of grammar but on developing skill with expression in the language – oral and written. Most particularly there was the search for overall structure, exactitude and balance.

> The French writer is not a mere framer of happy phrases [as in England]. His chief glory consists in his skill in building up phrases into paragraphs and paragraphs into one single harmonious, symmetrical, architectural whole.
>
> (*Ibid.*)

In history, the search was for perception of overall unity and structure in the subject. There was rapid and, for English eyes, superficial coverage, but a search for meaning in the chronological patterns and attempts to find unity in the diversity of political, cultural, social, economic movements in any one period (*ibid.*: 303).

Rationality is not simply logic. It involves total comprehension through the construction of models and systems. Synthesis is important as well as analysis. It involves precision and exactitude in expression and communication. All through, the whole is more important than the parts and appreciation of structures is more important than any loss of depth.

The Enlightenment view of social, economic and political development, which was incorporated in the aims of revolutionary governments after 1789, was that rationality was the means to reconstruct society and its institutions in the most efficient, progressive and beneficial way. The means to development was central direction by a rationally trained élite. In this sense, encyclopaedism, through its emphasis on rationality, was directed at social usefulness, though the rational élite consisted of generalists rather than technical specialists (Hopper 1968).

Later twentieth-century interpretations of utility have focused on more specific technical skills. The vocational sector of upper secondary education expanded from apprenticeship centres to a wider range and higher level of vocational courses in *lycées professionnels*, which offered some courses of equal status to general academic upper secondary schooling including entry to higher education, especially technological higher education.

Technician level courses were then articulated, from the late 1960s, with general education not only in standing but also in content. That is, *baccalauréat* courses in specific branches of engineering, for instance, were based on a content (of both scientific and other general education subjects) which was common to the general *baccalauréat*. This process derived from élite education where the most prestigious higher education institutions since the early nineteenth century – the *grandes écoles* – were professional schools offering broad general education but, in most cases, giving a final qualification in engineering.

However, there is sequential progression in the three principles of universality, rationality and utility. Rationality can be developed once the framework for the transmission of a universalist curriculum is established. Utility becomes relevant once rationality has been developed. The difficulty of calling up the utility principles to justify courses at upper secondary level is that, by common understanding, rational education has hardly been completed – indeed, little more than begun – at that stage, so utility cannot be built clearly on rationality. The response of French students, their parents and employers has been to deny credibility to lower-level vocational education and to aim for higher-education-level vocational qualifications.

Debates about encyclopaedism in France

The French are encyclopaedist because they believe this is the route to liberty, equality and fraternity. Durkheim's major history of French education was a heroic story of the struggle of the forces of encyclopaedic progressiveness against humanist reaction (Durkheim 1977). Pierre Bourdieu's 'cultural capital' is humanism – acquired informally by the *mondain* who demonstrates it in 'effortless elegance'. For him encyclopaedism (or scholasticism) is egalitarian knowledge which is denied social equality by the operation of a humanist 'ethos of elective distance' (Bourdieu 1984).

Encyclopaedism is not as rigid or exclusive as it was in the nineteenth and early twentieth centuries when it took on the character of an unremitting crusade against the forces of ignorance, superstition and reaction. A distinction has been made between nineteenth-century scientism and twentieth-century formalism (Horner). Scientism emphasized the importance of learning all branches of knowledge and especially the non-literary sciences. It was associated intellectually with Auguste Comte's positivism and politically with the attack on the literary and classical humanism of the *Ancien Régime*. Its view of knowledge creation was inductive. Its structures were empirically created (*ibid.*: 67–9).

Late twentieth-century encyclopaedism on the other hand is formalist. It stresses rationality to be achieved by deduction, analysis and the creation of parsimonious structures. It is 'what remains when everything else has been forgotten' (*ibid.*: 70). In more elaborated form 'reason should not be used as a means of acquiring knowledge, but knowledge should be a means of perfecting reason' (Hignett 1958).

This abstract approach to thinking and analysis is not new. It dates back to medieval scholasticism. The criticisms made of it were those notoriously associated with angels on pinhead methodologies. As Pierre Emmanuel argued,

We baptize as 'method' a clever trick that functions no matter to what object one applies it . . . Thus intelligence by habit has come to be identified with this trick, with this infallible procedure for emptying an idea of all substance and the real of all reality.

(Zeldin *op. cit.*)

Since the 1960s there have been calls to introduce interrogative, communicative and social elements into logical analysis. Interrogative culture involves asking questions of oneself to establish 'what one does not know' (in line with the trends in Anglo-Saxon educational culture associated with the ideas of Karl Popper) and to situate thought in a social reality (Horner *op. cit.*).

However, these criticisms (which have been made across epistemological cultures since the 1960s) are made within the encyclopaedic tradition. Rationality had its limits but ultimately civilization, as known in encyclopaedic cultures, is rationalist. The alternative is not its destruction but its enrichment.

These debates have also applied in educational and pedagogical discussions in encyclopaedist cultures not only at a philosophical level but also through the dilemmas and difficulties of applying an encyclopaedism derived from élite nineteenth-century education to diverse and democratized mass education systems.

The encyclopaedic curriculum in southern Europe

How strong is encyclopaedism in the other countries of the European Community? In the projected future battle over a pan-European school curriculum, what allies can France expect to get? At some levels, encyclopaedism is part of the educational traditions of every country of continental (but not insular) Europe from the Soviet Union to Portugal and from Norway to Italy – a product not only of the historic impact of the Enlightenment and of the 1789 French Revolution.

The encyclopaedist south of Europe followed French institutional practice almost slavishly in the nineteenth century. Central control of the school curriculum until 30 years ago was almost identical, as have been the kinds of subjects and number of hours devoted to each subject in schools, the types of final school certificate, the processes of entry to higher education and the structure of courses in universities. Southern European countries have looked to France also for intellectual inspiration in the adoption of philosophies of worthwhile knowledge to underwrite the school curriculum. The forms and ideas of encyclopaedism are as much sacred idols in Italy, Belgium, Spain and Portugal as they are in France.

Like Spanish encyclopaedism, that of Italy is debased by its loss of the almost moral status that rationality has had in France. So encyclopaedism can degenerate into meaningless knowledge – into the 'rhetoric' or 'baggage' which Antonio Gramsci condemned (Gramsci 1971: 36). It faces a more powerful naturalism in Italy than in France – a demand that schooling should reflect everyday concrete experience of children which is contained not only in the critical literature (*ibid*.: 35) but in the way that teachers behave and view themselves (Newcombe 1977). There is also the idealism – the search for a higher but as yet uncomprehended unity – reflected in the influence of Benedetto Croce in Italy but which has its parallels in the tradition of the yearning for the grand and sublime in Spain.

Despite these variations, the rational principles of encyclopaedism are defended by the critics of its sterility. So, for Gramsci the school

> taught a more modern outlook based . . . on an awareness . . . that there exist objective, intractable natural laws to which man must adapt himself if he is to master them in turn – and that there exist social and state laws which are the product of human activity, which are established by men and can be altered by men in the interests of their collective developments.
>
> (Gramsci 1971)

His criticism of encyclopaedism is not about the emphasis on the abstract and formal learning of structures and connections. This is essential. What needs to be changed is only that students should carry on this teaming actively and creatively rather than passively or without comprehension (*ibid*.: 41–2). The progressive and liberating potential of encyclopaedism is affirmed even by its critics outside France.

HUMANISM

As a European intellectual movement, humanism 'meant the development of human virtue . . . not only such qualities as . . . understanding, benevolence, compassion, mercy – but also . . . fortitude, judgement, prudence, eloquence'. It had the aim of linking thought and action in ways that would encourage the grandest of human possibilities in the individual and would project the highest possibilities of the individual into the state at large (Grudin 1988). Its source for Renaissance humanists from Petrarch onwards, was the classical literature of, for instance, Plato, Cicero or Livy. It focused on the individual rather than the social group. It was moral in its emphasis on the development of human virtue but this morality was extended to include aesthetic appreciation and sensibility. In a debased form, it was associated with etiquette and polite behaviour and so was linked even more to social differentiation.

The principles of educational humanism in England and Wales

The humanist perspective on education, as entrenched in the reformed public schools and ancient universities of mid-nineteenth-century England,[8] had three major principles:

- morality;
- individualism;
- specialism.

Nineteenth-century upper-class education set out to create 'Christian gentlemen'. The qualities to be needed by this élite were moral sensibility, a commitment to duty and a capacity for decision-making based on action informed and moderated by contemplation (Wilkinson 1964). The explicit model was the philosopher-ruler class of Plato's *Republic*.

The source of élite education was not only academic study. The social organization of the public schools and universities was intended to be educative – the *esprit de corps* of the games field, and the relations between students, and between students and teachers. Literary education focused on classical texts for the moral insights and examples they might yield. The epitome of this curriculum was the classics course at Oxford – two years of Latin and Greek language and literature, leading to the pinnacle of the final two years of Literae Humaniores ('Greats') of Greek and Latin history and philosophy.

In the twentieth century, the emphasis moved to British (English) history and literature. The purpose was still the development of moral capacities. English history, following the Whig interpretation, had the motif of the heroism, the duty, but especially the moderation of the historical actors who produced what was seen to be the finest democratic polity. Literature could focus on the works of the supreme English humanist – Shakespeare. Over time history and literature were democratized. The social history of the poor became more important while literature was chosen which reflected the condition of the poor and the ordinary people. Democratization meant simply making the élite aware of the lives and struggles of the poor rather than making humanist education available to a wider section of the population.

Other subjects struggled for recognition. Mathematics and the natural sciences had notional equality in the public schools and universities, though their informal prestige was lower, whether indicated by the lower status of science teachers at the public schools or by the absence of science specialists in the political and managerial élite. Science, it seemed, gave little insight into human virtue – except that, at one remove, scientific inquiry was claimed to be a highly moral activity. Mathematics at most developed aesthetic appreciation of mathematical rules. Bereft of the rationalist panoply which was so important to the encyclopaedist justification, mathematics, sciences and, indeed, modern languages (except as a means of access to morally enhancing fine literature) were not easily admitted to the inner sanctum of humanist high status knowledge.

Technical–vocational subjects were completely outside the humanist pale. In the Platonic social system, 'training' was associated with the occupations of social groups markedly inferior to the philosopher kings for whom a humanist education was designed (Plato 1953).

The 'education vs. training' dichotomy became particularly acute in societies where the humanist tradition was pre-eminent. Training was rejected in English education because of its contemporary social-occupational associations but also because it appeared to contain no possibilities for the development of moral sensibility.

The moral criterion remained central as humanist perspectives infiltrated the state education system. The process of transfer was aided partly by a belief that democratization of the curriculum meant dissemination of elite knowledge to a mass school population. It was facilitated also by the predominantly moral orientation of late nineteenth-century mass education produced by the origin of many state schools in the religious system and by the largely moral socialization function of mass schooling which, in nineteenth-century England, unlike almost all other European countries, was established in an overwhelmingly industrial and urban society.

Individualism is central in the humanist world. Virtuous individuals create a moral world. Yet individualism is also central to the humanist conception of how humanist knowledge and humanist moral attributes are acquired. Humanism entails an individualist methodology and pedagogy.

The humanist methodology of learning, following Plato, is intuitive.[9] The learner thus reacts individually, even idiosyncratically, to the set texts which are the containers of potential moral enlightenment. Standardized, methodical, systematic learning are not reconcilable with this intuitive view of education. Even élite traditional academic knowledge was acquired at the learner's own pace, indeed, to use a religious analogy, until revelation occurred.

Pedagogy was also individualist. The moral purpose of education gave a great stress to the interaction between teacher and student. Teachers, traditionally in English education, had a pastoral as well as an intellectual function. They had to know their pupils sufficiently well to direct them individually towards total moral development. The tutorial system of Oxford and Cambridge was a model for the rest of the élite education system.

The individualism of the humanist tradition permitted connections with more naturalist, child-centred philosophies. Indeed, John Locke, whose prescriptions on the moral education of the gentleman were a major source for the revived humanist education of the nineteenth century, advocated active and child-centred approaches in the early years of schooling (Locke 1968). Individualist and humanist views coexisted and were confused in the comprehensive schools in the 1960s and 1970s.

The degree of specialization in the curriculum of schools and institutions of higher education throughout the twentieth century has separated England and Wales from all other countries of Europe (including Scotland) – and, indeed, from every other country worldwide except those directly influenced by British colonialism. The English version of the humanist curriculum is marked by an early and intense concentration on a limited range of specific subjects and even on particular topics within subjects.

Subject specialism is permitted rather than required by humanist philosophy. Yet specialization can be reconciled with humanism. The attainment of moral sensibility does not depend in any way on width of knowledge but on depth of perception and understanding. The addition of other subjects may weaken the intensity of moral enlightenment achieved by student interaction with specialist topics.

Subject specialism is also encouraged by individualism. If learning is specific to the individual then a selection of appropriate knowledge from the range of acceptable sources can be made in relation to individual needs. Hence the maxim that students should be able to concentrate on the subjects for which they have a special aptitude to the neglect of those in which they have little interest or ability.

One puzzle is that English specialism is not paralleled in the humanist traditions in other countries. Two other features of English epistemological culture then become important. First is the empirical approach to scientific inquiry which had its British roots in the epistemology of Francis Bacon and David Hume but which began to find expression in the development of research in universities in the nineteenth century. It was indicated in the expansion of single subject Honours schools at Oxford and Cambridge in the nineteenth century as the basic form of undergraduate study, which spread later to the other and newer universities. The inductive, empirical rationale for specialism is that knowledge is created cumulatively and incrementally out of small-scale inquiries from which eventually (often in hope rather than reasonable expectation) broad conclusions and patterns might emerge.

Empiricism and induction of this type could be supported in the absence of a rational tradition of logical analysis and theoretical system-building. The English version of humanism could be anti-rational. Intuition was more important than reason and intuition could be given scope in depth studies rather than in broad, schematic intellectual architecture. This empiricism also enriched the self-view of the English as having a bent for practical action.

Debates about humanism in England

The humanist tradition may have survived the democratization of education in England from the mid-twentieth century, but it has changed in the process and has been subject to criticism from the 1960s. The attacks have been made on two grounds – that the humanist view of knowledge is associated with a contempt for the material world of industry and trade and that socially it is ineluctably élitist. Perhaps most seriously, humanism is anti-rational in a world which is increasingly built on rational procedures.

The putative association of the humanist view with social élitism should be examined carefully in light of the attempts to democratize the humanist curriculum in the twentieth century. Moral appreciation of the great feats of ancient Greece and Rome – and later of English history – archetypically would encourage a muscular heroism in a District Officer in an African colony. In the course of the twentieth century, the occupational model became the sensitive aesthete – the television producer, teacher of English or advertising agency executive.

This change was linked to the emergence of English Literature as the most prestigious area of study in universities and upper secondary schooling. English Literature as defined by F.R. Leavis, the guru of the new sensibility, was supreme because

> it trains, in a way no other discipline can, intelligence and sensibility together, cultivating a sensitiveness and precision of response and a delicate integrity of intelligence
>
> (Leavis 1966)

This view was anticipated by earlier literary critics from the early nineteenth century, including Samuel Coleridge, Matthew Arnold and T.S. Eliot (*ibid.*)[10] In the twentieth century it meant a different kind of élite selection. The assumption is that delicate intelligence is not necessarily the preserve of a traditional upper class. It is still assumed to be thinly distributed in the population as a whole. The discovery of submerged artists and aesthetes became the crusade particularly of teachers of English in secondary schools from the 1950s.

This new humanism was even more susceptible to charges that it was disdainful of the world of industry and hostile to vocational education. Politicians complained that schools encouraged anti-industrial attitudes among students which were associated with the declining productivity and international competitiveness of British industry. An increasing number of studies of the persisting aristocratic values of British society and anti-industrial attitudes were influential (see Martin in Weiner 1985; Barnett 1986).

The reaction of government was to attempt to initiate curriculum change which challenged a view of worthwhile knowledge which appeared to aim at nurturing an artist 'refined out of existence, indifferent, paring his fingernails' (Joyce 1960: 215). The national curriculum of the 1988 Education Reform Act tries to ensure that all students up to the age of 16 continue to study mathematics, sciences and technology which would otherwise be neglected in the preparation of aesthetes.

Do the changes culminating in the 1988 Act really challenge the social élitism and the anti-rationalism of the humanist tradition? The propositions of the 1943 Norwood Report that three types of children – the academic, the technical and the practical – can be identified at the age of 11 (Board of Education 1943) have been rejected ostensibly with the spread of comprehensive schooling in the 1970s. It is not clear that such views, which harmonize with a humanist conception of knowledge, have been eradicated from the collective educational and national psyche.

Humanism outside England

Humanism is a European-wide – indeed global – movement since Islamic, Hindu and, especially, Confucian thought contains points of contact, particularly in a shared conception of the moral purpose of knowledge (Wilkinson 1964). Historically, humanism is among the most powerful intellectual forces in Europe and may yet be revitalized by connections with these non-European parallels.

Educational humanism has points of similarity on an international scale. The emphasis on the development of the individual rather than on understanding the world; the concern for the attainment of individual human goodness through education; a belief that understanding comes first through intuition; and a prime focus on the study of the humanities (literature, history, philosophy) are common to educational humanism throughout Europe and beyond (Maritain 1966). Indeed there is also a North American educational humanism associated with élite institutions of higher education (Hutchins 1943).

English humanism is other- rather than inner-directed. The educational humanism of the nineteenth-century public school was designed to produce men (very rarely women) of action. Thought was to inform the deed in a positive, energetic way. Moral sensibility was of value ultimately only in practice. Philosophers were to be kings and not simply philosophers (as were, for instance, the Brahmins of the Hindu system). The individual was educated through acquaintance with historical heroism, but in order to find his or her own way to be heroic in the present and future.

European humanism generally has been more inner-directed, contemplative, socially passive and politically quietist. It has concentrated upon inner contemplation and perfection divorced from action. Humanistic education has eschewed the search for social improvement. Thus it has been associated with a passive acceptance of existing patterns of social authority, especially the European Catholic version. But not only Catholic: a Greek Orthodox version of humanism is entrenched in education in Greece and is the enemy of political and social change. In these instances, humanism is socially and politically retrograde.

Humanist conservatism has been identified by both pragmatists and encyclopaedists as the main enemy of progress. John Dewey's attack on Platonic epistemology was central to his educational writing (Dewey 1961). The rejection of humanism by Durkheim and Bourdieu in France has already been described. In return humanists have reinforced their conservatism by their total rejection of pragmatism – not only Europeans such as Jacques Maritain but also Americans such as Robert Hutchins.

Inner-directed humanism, however, takes on a quite different perspective in the German metaphysical tradition. The purpose of German education is humanist in that it is 'ethical and . . . is concerned primarily with the moral personality and with the inner freedom of the individual' (Lauwerys 1965). But this humanist individualism aims to achieve individual understanding of the 'inner reality and unity in the cosmos' (*ibid.*).

The outcome is a greater individual moral awareness – even the quest for this understanding is morally enhancing. The means to the acquisition of knowledge is revelatory, intuitive, spiritual and mystical as well as rational. The subject-matter for this search for total understanding can be the humanist works of literature and history. Yet this search for *Bildung* is inner-directed or other-worldly. Indeed, German élite education has been separated from public life and a public purpose to a degree that is totally foreign to the French or the English traditions (Ardagh 1988).

Furthermore, German *Bildung* incorporates but stretches beyond a simple appreciation of humanity. It unites humanity and the world. It searches for rational understanding of the order of the natural world as well as an intuitive appreciation of human morality. It incorporates encyclopaedic rationalism as well as humanist moralism. So humanism does not exist by itself in opposition to rationalism but as part of a unity of all kinds of thinking and knowledge[11] (Plato 1953).

In practice, these great ideals remain the holy grail of ambition rather than a reasonably attainable goal – especially in the secondary education system. German philosophy from Kant and Hegel to Habermas has sought means to achieve this transcendental unity. The search is real enough to inform the way that knowledge has been transmitted in élite education. But the proof of attainment is undemonstrable.

This leads to the major weakness of humanism as a possible solution to the search for internationally common school knowledge. The individualism and morality associated with humanism have potential value in mass education in urban, industrial education which the rationalist encyclopaedist tradition has failed to offer effectively. But humanism is really only a powerful force in English education. It has this position because it has developed links with action and public morality which are missing from the relatively sterile humanist traditions of other parts of Europe. But the social élitism, the specialism and the failure to provide a meaning for rational or manual/physical expertise in English humanism ultimately deprive it of a wider international potential.

NATURALIST VIEWS

The dominant views in the public education systems of Western Europe emphasize universal ideas at such a level of abstraction that they are valid irrespective of time or place. The preceding analysis has focused on the differences between humanism and encyclopaedism. Yet they share much which also separates them from the many other views of knowledge in which immediate uses rather than universal principles and the learner rather than the subject-matter take precedence.

Naturalist views have a long history and considerable variety in Europe and beyond. Yet they have never been dominant because they have never captured the citadels of legitimate knowledge in élite education. But they have had sufficient impact on lower-level and non-élite education in various European countries for them to be considered seriously in identifying a possible European curriculum of the future, especially those elements which meet 'private' knowledge aspirations.

Naturalist views of knowledge take as a starting point concepts of how individuals develop in the 'real' world. These perceptions are then applied to programmes of formal education. They include concepts of the intellectual and moral development of children; of individualism and creativity; of interaction in social groups; and of vocational commitment.

They may start from broad views of the individual and his or her interaction with the natural world (Jean-Jacques Rousseau); they may give more emphasis to the local community (N.F.S. Grundtvig) or to work (Georg Kerschensteiner); they may focus more specifically on the nature of learning rather than on knowledge (Johann Herbart, Celestin Freinet, Maria Montessori); they may attempt to achieve a unity of psychology, sociology and pedagogy (Johann Pestalozzi, Friedrich Froebel, Ovide Decroly); or they may be designed for young children by philosophers committed to universal knowledge in the education of youth (John Locke, Immanuel Kant). They derive intellectually from psychology and sociology as well as from philosophy. Their authors developed their ideas in a wide range of European countries cited above and came from France, Germany, Denmark, Switzerland, Italy, Belgium and Britain.

In this study, the main question is what place these naturalist views have in formal and informal education in various European countries.

There are three main locations: the education of very young children as an extension of the ideal educative family; the tight-knit social grouping beyond the family; and the workplace. Their influence comes through the extension of the family upwards, the workplace downwards and the social group sideways into the school system and, with these incursions, the acceptance of epistemologies appropriate to the institutions of origin.

Naturalist views have had an influence in every European country. But they may be examined more fully in the specific cases where they were especially entrenched 'child-centred' education in England, 'work-orientation' in Germany, and community education in Denmark.

Child-centred epistemologies in England and elsewhere

Official support in England for a child-centred primary curriculum did not appear until the beginning of the twentieth century. The 1931 Hadow Report claimed that, in practice since the 1890s and especially since 1918 there had been an actual change in primary school teaching so that it

> handles the curriculum, not only as consisting of lessons to be mastered, but as providing fields of new and interesting experience to be explored; to appeal less to passive obedience and more to the sympathy, social spirit and imagination of children, relies less on mass instruction and more on the encouragement of individual and group work, and treats the school, in short, not as the antithesis of life, but as its complement and commentary.
>
> (Maclure 1968)

The last clause is crucial. The suggestion of a relationship of school learning to the actual life of children was new. Yet English child-centred education in primary schools, which reached its apotheosis of official support in the 1967 Plowden Report, remained principally a pedagogy emphasizing individual and active learning rather than a reordering of the purposes and aims of knowledge content as happened, for instance, with the adoption of a progressive pragmatic view in the USA. A major criticism at the time of the Plowden Report was that schooling was to be aligned to child psychology rather than to children as individuals or to their social environments.[12]

This emphasis on pedagogy rather than content; on process rather than final goals; on the medium rather than the message continued to be supreme, especially as child-centred approaches moved into lower secondary education. Particular comprehensive schools began to develop a reputation for organizing the whole curriculum on the basis of individual learning and creative expression at the expense of a standardized time-table (Bernbaum 1973). The debate then centred on how the active and individualist curriculum which had been well established in so many primary schools could be transferred wholesale to comprehensive lower secondary schools.

The extent of the pupil-centred pedagogic revolution in English secondary schools from the 1960s should not be exaggerated. As was argued previously, the humanist tradition has an individualist orientation and permits specialization. Prevailing intellectual currents in higher education, scholarship and research are inductive and empirical. 'Discovery methods' in lower secondary schools could derive as much from these characteristics of traditional élite knowledge as from the child-centred approaches of the primary school. In practice, the individualist curriculum of secondary schools did not usually mean the abandonment of school subject boundaries or rationales. Instead there was a development of choice and variety at school and even pupil level in the specialization in particular subjects – a rejection of standardization between schools and even between students within a school rather than a repudiation of the ultimate external and universal value of traditional subjects.

Child-centred views are less well-established in state school curricula of other European countries as a whole, though the difference is not as great as some English educationists habitually have claimed. The movement in the eighteenth and nineteenth centuries to view children as having special, individual patterns of development and needs for creative, autonomous expression was no less powerful in Germany, France, Italy and other countries than it was in England and it continues to have support among significant numbers of teachers, other educationists and parents. But the encyclopaedist insistence on the standardization of content of learning and the demand that all children should reach minimum standards of achievement restrained the total adoption of child-centred views of knowledge.

Instead an overt distinction between content and method became more important than in England where the division was blurred and content could be manipulated to suit the method or even united to form a coherence with method.

A child-centred pedagogy, in a limited interpretation that did not interfere too severely with a standardized content, was adopted to varying degrees and with differing amounts of official support in continental European countries. In Germany it had most official backing. The first all-German Reich law of 1920 on primary education was full of phrases such as 'learning through the senses', 'closeness to life', 'wholeness' and 'spontaneity' (Max Planck Institute 1983) These ideas on primary education were re-emphasized by the Federal Educational Council in 1970 with a stress upon individual initiative, cooperation and problem-solving (*ibid.*). In France, Italy and the Iberian states the movement is weaker. Reference in France is most frequently made to the approaches of, say, Freinet, who was concerned largely with method. Individual teachers may have subscribed to and pursued these methods which encourage collective activity (especially producing class newspapers) (Neiser 1979). There has also been support for this approach in Spain. Belgium has an influential child-centred movement. But these pupil-centred orientations have had little impact on the standardized primary school curriculum content.

There are doubts about whether child-centred approaches adopted in practice actually mean any alteration of the content and even the structure of knowledge to be transmitted. At most they imply methods which encourage individual self-expression and possibly a rearrangement or flexibility in the sequence of knowledge transmission. In this sense, these child-centred approaches do not necessarily comprise a distinct and different view of worthwhile knowledge. They may not be sufficient to meet future 'private' knowledge demands.

Work and community-centred approaches in Germany and elsewhere

There is a separate strand of the naturalist view which emphasizes the validity of knowledge which is connected to everyday living and the effective performance of social and work roles. They differ from dominant humanist and encyclopaedic views in that educative experiences are not necessarily intellectual. The central and shared assumption of these views is that knowledge and attitudes can be acquired by means other than literary study and intellectual exercise.

Of course, accent on activity, on cooperation in collective tasks and on the tactile as well as cognitive is found in child-centred approaches generally. The main difference in the work and community orientation is that knowledge and attitudes gained have the aim of strengthening social bonds and affinities with actual communities and with real work-roles.

The community orientation has been the weaker of the two. The school as a medium for the discovery and strengthening of local community identity and as a medium for the exploration and transmission of knowledge relevant to this aim – has been rarer in European traditions than in other continents such as Mahatma Gandhi's Basic School, or 'popular' schools in Latin–America. Examples such as the Folk High School in Denmark, inspired by Grundtvig, which tried to incorporate the activities of the community into education, were relatively rare. Indeed Grundtvig's Folk High School, like Paulo Freire's programmes in Latin America, were aimed primarily at adults.

Instead schools are organized more often as communities of children, which may have mirrored communities of the wider world – most frequently a concept of the traditional village community the admirable values of which child-centred advocates such as Pestalozzi, Froebel and, in the USA, Dewey sought to preserve in a collective and active pedagogy. But active learning, individual choice and freedom of expression and cooperative activities of students was based upon a nostalgic view of disappearing rural communities rather than the real worlds that children inhabited.

The major link between school knowledge and that of the wider community has been found in the prevocational curriculum as it emerged in a number of countries. The views of, say, Kerschensteiner in Germany on vocational education in the late nineteenth and early twentieth century did differ in a radical way from those of his mentors such as Froebel, in that Froebel, like other advocates of a child-centred view, took the psycho-physiological development of children as the starting point and wished to adapt the content of learning to this development. Kerschensteiner, in approaching the issues more crudely, did question epistemological foundations by arguing that knowledge of practical, vocational manual skills that students would later use as workers was as important as knowledge derived from books (Kerschensteiner 1966). In this, his view, though crude like that of Gandhi, was also revolutionary in the way that Gandhi was revolutionary.

The assertion that the learning of manual 'trades' could be as valid in schools as knowledge derived from books was anathema to the Platonic view of high level education. As such it was rejected, for instance, in England. Yet in Germany especially, but also to a lesser extent in a Catholic technical school tradition in Italy and other parts of southern Europe, there was a view that knowledge about a manual vocation was noble and morally enhancing. The origin in part was religious – Christ the Carpenter and the Christian acceptance of humility and resignation to the earthly human lot. It crossed the Protestant–Catholic divide in Germany and was also founded upon a particular German cultural view that every occupation required training, every occupation had dignity and the work of every occupation should be carried out with maximum commitment and thoroughness.

The particular expression of this view in the Federal Republic of Germany is the *Arbeitslehre* which was introduced in the 1960s. This involved work experience as well as formal classes in schools. It was intended to encourage work habits such as self-discipline, consistency and social responsibility, as well as learning 'generic' cognitive and motor skills. It was epistemologically radical in the sense that the intellectualism and bookishness of the encyclopaedic and humanist traditions were put aside. Yet it simply brought the 'workplace' and the epistemology of work into the school and this epistemology of work –

though perhaps more formally and institutionally expressed in Germany than in other European countries – was not uniquely German.

Naturalist views of knowledge mean, at one end, bringing the approaches of the early education of the child in the family into the school, so the reference points are the nature of growth in a child and the requirement of a pedagogy which takes account of all aspects of a child's development. Generally child-centred approaches represent a pedagogical rather than an epistemological challenge. There is little sense that these views do any more than prepare eventually for the closing of the prison house doors on the growing child and the introduction of real intellectual learning. And these approaches can be weakened by the counter-movement, with the growth of social welfare and 'compensatory' pre-school education, increasing intrusion of the formal school into the educative family.

At the other end naturalist views mean bringing work into school, that is, anticipating the epistemology and pedagogy especially of skilled trades and professions within schools. This was resisted very largely because the trades brought into schools were those conventionally associated with lower social/occupational levels and because of the aspirations that school should provide for a life wider than that of work and that it should also facilitate upward occupational mobility. But the major factor operating against this kind of vicarious transfer is the degree to which work itself is seen to require increasingly higher initial levels of school-transmitted knowledge attainments before students can be admitted into increasingly intellectualized real working occupations.

The third and marginalized element of the naturalist perspective is the view that school knowledge should inculcate private, and usually subordinated, community values. Yet school knowledge of this type does not attract support precisely because it fails to provide entry to 'public' and dominant institutions of later life (indeed private knowledge is little more than sharing of social closeness and thus the acceptance of a very limited range of small community mores). It has rarely had much impact in Europe – outside limited religious and linguistic communities – because alienation from public institutions has never been sufficient to force any orientation of major areas of schooling away from 'public' life.

The two dominant and public educational epistemologies – encyclopaedism and humanism – themselves have such obviously apparent weaknesses, that naturalist views of knowledge are very likely to be called in to shore up these flawed yet dominant epistemologies against their own contradictions, not least their foundation on traditional élite education.

NOTES

1 See, for instance, Wilkie Collins, *The Moonstone*, 1868:

These puzzling shifts and transformations in Mr. Franklin were due to the effect on him of his foreign training. At an age when we are all of us most apt to take our colouring ... he had been sent abroad and had passed from one nation to another, before there was any time for any one colouring more than another to settle itself on him firmly. As a consequence of this, he had come back with so many different sides to his character, all more or less jarring with each other, that he seemed to pass his life in a state of perpetual contradiction. He could be a busy man, and a lazy man; cloudy in the head, and clear in the head; a model of determination, and a spectacle of helplessness, all together. He had his French side and his German side, and his Italian side – the original English foundation showing through every now and again.

(Harmondsworth: Penguin, 1966, pp. 76–7)

2 The classificatory term naturalism is derived from J. J. Rousseau's distinction between man (woman) in nature and the citizen in the state (Rousseau, Jean-Jacques, *Emile*, London: Dent, 1911, p. 7). Encyclopaedism and humanism are both citizen-orientated views of knowledge as they have been applied to the school curriculum.

3 An English observer in the first decade of the twentieth century suggested that French élite secondary schools compared to their English equivalents were 'much better for training boys of average or mediocre ability'. Brereton, Cloudsley, 'A comparison between French and English secondary schools', Board of Education, *Special Reports on Educational Subjects*, Vol. 24, London: HMSO, 1911, p. 300.

4 For an excellent yet sceptical historical analysis of French rationalism in its public, cultural and educational context in the late nineteenth and early twentieth centuries, see Zeldin, Theodore, *France 1848–1945*, Vol. 2, Oxford: Clarendon Press, pp. 205–42.

5 The encyclopaedic view in the USA, adopted after 1776, and as exhibited in the work of Benjamin Franklin, came to be dominated by the utility principle so that it was transformed into pragmatism.

6 Listed in *Le Monde de L'Education*, September 1988, pp. 20–3 (my translations).

7 Contained in Centre International d'Etudes Pedagogiques, *L'enseignement en France*, mimeo, 1988, p. 61 (my translation)

8 The content of secondary and higher education in Scotland in the nineteenth and twentieth centuries has been much more encyclopaedist in character, especially in the breadth of studies and in a rationalist perspective.

9 In Plato's scheme, 'intelligence' was distinguished from and was seen to be at a higher level than 'reason'. By 'intelligence', Plato meant the innate capacity of the 'good' to perceive 'goodness' (Plato 1953: 282, 283).

10 *Ibid.* See also Mathieson, Margaret and Bernbaum, Gerald, 'The British disease: a British tradition', *British Journal of Educational Studies,* 28(2), 1988, pp. 126–74.

11 In this way it was truer to the Platonic origins of humanism as a higher *stage* of knowledge appreciation, building on earlier developed reason (Plato 1953: 282).

12 The criticism of the Plowden Report in England suggested that it started from assumptions of biological growth and that the knowledge content was then arranged according to teachers' perception of this growth. See Bern-

stein, Basil and Davies, Brian, 'Some sociological comments on Plowden', in Peters, Richard (ed.), *Perspectives on Plowden*, London: Routledge & Kegan Paul, 1969, pp. 57–8 and Wilson, P.S., 'Plowden Children', in Dale, Roger *et al.*, *Schooling and Capitalism*, London: Routledge & Kegan Paul, 1976, pp. 158–62.

REFERENCES

Ardagh, J. (1988) *Germany and the Germans*, Harmondsworth: Penguin, pp. 226, 263–4.

Bamford, T.W. (1967) *The Rise of the Public Schools*, London: Nelson, p. 118.

Barnard, H.C. (1969) *Education and the French Revolution*, Cambridge: Cambridge University Press, pp. 81–95.

Barnett, C. (1986) *Audit of War: the Illusion and Reality of Britain as a Great Nation*, London: Macmillan.

Becher, A. and Maclure, S. (1978) *The Politics of Curriculum Change*, London: Hutchinson.

Bernbaum, G. (1973) 'Countesthorpe College', in OECD/CERI, *Case Studies in Educational Innovation*, Vol. 3, Paris: OECD, pp. 7–88.

Bernstein, B. (1977) 'On the classification of education knowledge', *Class, Codes and Control*, Vol. 3, London: Routledge, pp. 85–115.

Board of Education (1943) *Curriculum and Examinations in Secondary Schools* (Norwood Report), London: HMSO, pp. 2–4.

Bourdieu, P. (1984) *Distinction*, London: Routledge & Kegan Paul, pp. 4–5, 23, 69.

Brereton, C. (1911) 'A comparison between French and English secondary Schools', Board of Education, *Special Reports on Educational Subjects*, Vol. 24, London: HMSO.

Collins, W (1868) *The Moonstone*, Harmondsworth: Penguin, reprinted 1966.

Colomb, J. (1985) 'France: development of mathematics teaching in French primary schools', Council of Europe, *Renewal of Mathematics Teaching in Primary Education*, Lille: Swets & Zeitlinger.

Comenius, John Amos (1907) *The Great Didactic*, London: Adam & Charles Black, p. 70.

Dewey, J. (1961) *Democracy and Education*, New York: Macmillan, pp. 88–91.

Durkheim, E. (1977) *The Evolution of Educational Thought*, London: Routledge & Kegan Paul, p. 334.

Fisher, H.A.L. (1936) *A History of Europe*, London: Collins, Preface.

Gramsci, A. (1971) *Prison Notebooks*, London: Lawrence & Wishart.

Grudin, R. (1988) 'Humanism', *Encyclopaedia Britannica*, Vol. 20, Chicago: Encyclopaedia Britannica Inc. (15th edn), p.723.

Hartog, P.J (1911) 'The aim of the new curricula of French secondary schools for boys', Board of Education, *Special Reports on Educational Subjects*, Vol. 24, London: HMSO.

Hignett, Marcel F. (1958) 'The primacy of the rational in French secondary education', *Yearbook of Education 1958*, London: Evans Bros., p. 235.

Holmes, B. (1981) *Comparative Education: Some Considerations in Method*, London: Allen & Unwin.

Holmes, B. and McClean, M. (1989) *The Curriculum: A Comparative Perspective*, London: Unwin Hyman.

Horner, W. (1980) 'The evolution of the notion of culture in the French pedagogical discussion', *Western European Education*, pp. 62–80.

Hopper, E. (1968) 'A typology for the classification of educational systems', *Sociology* 2, pp. 29–46.

Hutchins, R.M. (1943) *Education for Freedom*, Louisiana State University Press.

Joyce, James (1960) *Portrait of the Artist as a Young Man*, Harmondsworth: Penguin, p. 215.

Kerschensteiner, G. (1966) *The Schools and the Nation*, London: Macmillan, 1914.

Lauwerys, Joseph A. (1959) 'The Philosophical Approach to Education', *International Review of Education*, 5(3), pp. 281–98.

Lauwerys, Joseph A. (1965) *Opening Address, General Education in a Changing World*, Berlin: Max Planck Institute, pp. 7–24.

Leavis, F.R. (1966) *Uses of the Imagination: Educational Thought and the Literary Mind*, Harmondsworth: Penguin, p. 81.

Locke, J. (1968) 'Some thoughts concerning education', in Axtell, James L., *The Educational Writings of John Locke*, Cambridge: Cambridge University Press, pp. 235–9.

Maclure, J. Stuart (1968) *Educational Documents – England and Wales 1816–1968*, London: Methuen, pp. 189–90.

Madariaga, Salvador de (1970) *Englishmen, Frenchmen, Spaniards*, London: Pitman Publishing, 2nd edn.

Maritain, J. (1966) *Education at the Crossroads*, New Haven, Conn.: Yale University Press, pp. 1–2, 5, 13, 15, 56–7, 66–9.

Max Planck Institute for Human Development and Education (1983) *Between Élite and Mass Education: Education in the Federal Republic of Germany*, Albany, N.Y.: State University of New York, p. 138.

Neiser, B. (1979), 'Innovation in primary and secondary school education in France', *Western European Education*, 10(3), pp. 33–6.

Newcombe, N. (1977) *Europe at School*, London: Methuen, pp. 26–7.

Plato (1953) *The Republic*, Harmondsworth: Penguin, pp. 141–4, 156–73, 269–77, 282–3.

Sampson, A. (1982) *The Changing Anatomy of Modern Britain*, London: Hodder & Stoughton, pp. 240–59.

School of Barbiana (1970) *Letter to a Teacher*, Harmondsworth: Penguin.

Weiner, M.J. (1985) *English Culture and the Decline of the Industrial Spirit 1850–1980*, Harmondsworth: Penguin.

Wilkinson, R. (1964) *The Prefects: British Leadership and the Public School Tradition*, London: Oxford University Press.

Chapter 3

Faith-based grant-maintained schools

Selective international policy borrowing from the Netherlands

G. Walford

INTRODUCTION

Since the early 1980s educational policy borrowing has increased apace. Government ministers and civil servants have made visits to Germany, United States, Canada and elsewhere to look for transportable solutions to perceived problems in British education. This increased policy borrowing has been particularly prominent in the area of technological education and training where, for example, the Training and Enterprise Councils can be seen to have been heavily influenced by the American Private Industry Councils (Bailey 1993) and the City Technology Colleges can, at least in part, be seen as having been justified by various American magnet school programmes (Green 1993).

In practice, of course, wrenching particular policies from their historic, economic, political and social roots can result in unanticipated consequences as those in the host country react to the new implant. As Phillips (1992) argues, it is the socio-cultural setting that keeps a country's particular educational policies in place and the rather different socio-cultural setting of the borrower country that provides resistance to the implantation of ideas from other systems.

A common problem in the area of policy borrowing is that those involved in the attempt to bring about far-reaching change to the educational system are usually highly ideologically and politically committed. Partisans have incentives to use lessons from abroad to advance their policy agenda (Robertson and Waltman 1992) for those who hold particular ideological positions can advocate proposals that emulate programmes from other countries that project that ideology. Moreover, partisans are often highly selective in the elements of alternative systems that they select for promotion. They frequently identify specific elements that are in agreement with their aims, yet omit to consider closely related elements that may be in contradiction to their own views. This article examines some aspects of the process of policy borrowing that occurred preceding the 1993 Education Act's legislation for faith-based grant-maintained schools.

THE 1993 EDUCATION ACT

Since April 1994, as a result of the 1993 Education Act, it has been possible for groups of potential independent sponsors to apply to the Funding Agencies for Schools to establish their own grant-maintained schools. This important change in the way in which schools can be established is, in part, the result of a lengthy campaign by a diversity of pressure groups representing religious and other interests. The Christian Schools Campaign, in particular, was at the forefront of the political campaigning for the right to obtain state funding for faith-based schools and can be seen to have had a significant effect on the way in which the legislation has been framed (Walford 1995a, b).

The 1993 Education Act is a long and complex piece of legislation which, among other changes, gave powers to the Secretaries of State for Education and for Wales to establish new grant-maintained schools in two different ways. The first simply deals with cases where the Funding Agencies for schools see the need for a new school due to changes in population or similar circumstances, but the second allows independent sponsors to propose the establishment of new schools. Through this second procedure, if the Secretary of State approves individual proposals, the way is open for England and Wales to have state-funded schools which have the aim of fostering, for example, Muslim, Buddhist, or evangelical Christian beliefs or which wish to promote particular educational philosophies. Existing faith-based private schools are now able to apply to become re-established as grant-maintained schools. In the long term, this change may be the most significant result of the 1993 Education Act, for it further blurs the boundary between private and state provision, encourages significant private financial investment in schools, and shifts some of the responsibility for provision to local, private initiative (Walford 1990).

Technically, it was already possible for LEAs to support various religiously-based schools through voluntary aided status. Over the past few years several existing Muslim and evangelical Christian private schools have applied to their LEAs to become voluntary aided, but all such requests have so far been rejected. Usually this has happened at the LEA level, but occasionally the LEA has agreed to support a new voluntary aided school and central government has refused the request. The 1993 Act removes any barriers to the support of faith-based schools erected by local authorities, and passes the decision directly to the Department for Education. Ministers have indicated that 'denominational need' will play a significant part in the consideration of proposals for sponsored grant-maintained schools, and that over-supply of places in nearby schools (as traditionally defined within two or three mile limits) will not necessarily lead to rejection of proposals.

The campaign for the right to 'opt-in' to the state sector has involved a variety of groups including the Small Schools Movement (Meighan and Toogood 1992), several Muslim pressure groups (including the Muslim Educational Trust and, more recently, the Muslim Parliament) and the Christian Schools Campaign (CSC) which represented about 65 private evangelical Christian schools. In their desire to obtain state funding, the interests of these groups also coincided with those of the New Right who wished for further diversity in educational provision (e.g. Cox and Marks 1979), selection of pupils for particular schools (e.g. Flew 1991; Marks 1991) and the increased privatization of schooling (e.g. Sexton 1989, 1992).

This article concentrates on one specific aspect of the general Campaign – the use of international comparisons to support their case – and begins an analysis and critique of such use. The analysis presented here is based upon a larger study of the schools and the Campaign which included an interview and postal survey of the 65 schools with links to the Christian Schools Trust (Poyntz and Walford 1994), interviews with key politicians and activists involved with the Christian Schools Campaign, attendance and non-participant observation at various policy and planning meetings, and the use of documentary data.

In outline, the new Christian schools are a group of small private schools which share an ideology of Biblically-based evangelical Christianity that seeks to relate the message of the Bible to all aspects of present-day life whether personal, spiritual or educational. They are a diverse group, but most schools have been established by parents or a Church group to deal with a growing dissatisfaction with what is seen as the increased secularism of the great majority of state-maintained schools. While some schools started from nothing, others developed from the grouping together of a few parents who had withdrawn their children from school to teach them at home. The schools aim to provide a distinctive Christian approach to every part of school life and the curriculum and, in most cases, parents have a continuing role in the management and organization of the schools (Deakin 1989; O'Keeffe 1992). In general, these schools are not well provided for in terms of physical facilities and teaching staff are often on low salaries. They do not serve the 'traditional' private school market and many of the schools have progressive fee structures that are linked to the ability of parents to pay. Most of the schools wish to be open to a wide social intake and, in consequence, are often in a financially precarious position.

THE NETHERLANDS AS PARADIGM

It is inevitable that politicians and political pressure groups wish to examine what happens in other countries in order to inform British policy on faith-based schools. In the campaign to obtain state funding for a wider variety of schools, protagonists looked towards other countries to find examples where a variety of faith-based schools are supported by the state. In doing so, the two countries most commonly used as examples were the Netherlands and Denmark.

The use of the Netherlands as an example has been particularly common, for Dutch faith-based schools are supported by the state on an equal financial footing to those that the state itself provides. Moreover, this arrangement is particularly long standing, dating from 1917, and it is open for any group of parents or citizens to propose the establishment of a private school which, if certain criteria are met, will receive state funding.

Thus, Caroline Cox and John Marks (1979) argued that the example of the Netherlands shows that 'alternative methods of financing schools – which encourage diversity and choice – are both feasible and have been shown to work in practice' (1979: 33). Dennison's book, published by the Institute of Economic Affairs, gave special praise to Denmark and the Netherlands for breaking the 'state monopoly' of schooling (1984: 70). More recently Nick Seaton, Chairman of the Campaign for Real Education, argued that 'funding should . . . be available from the state for groups of parents to set up new small schools with a particular religious or philosophical ethos as is already possible in the Netherlands and Denmark' (1991: 12).

The Dutch example has been of particular importance within the Christian Schools Campaign, as it is seen as having theological as well as practical significance. For example, the original campaigning document, *The Case for Public Funding*, written by the Director of the Campaign, Ruth Deakin (1989), contains an extended discussion of how faith-based schools are established and funded in the Netherlands. She gives some of the historical background to the development of the Dutch system, outlines the way in which groups can apply to establish a new school, and indicates the most significant constraints under which state-funded Dutch private schools operate.

The Dutch case is of particular significance to several of those involved in the new Christian schools and the Christian Schools Campaign as the educational settlement that was made in 1917 was the result of the work of the Calvinist Anti-Revolutionary Party and its leader Abraham Kuyper. Kuyper was a Minister of Religion, theologian, educationalist, editor of several newspapers and politician. He was one of the leaders of the Calvinist secession from the theologically liberal State Church in 1886, when about 100,000 people formed the Reformed Churches of the Netherlands. Kuyper was one of the founding Professors of the Free University of Amsterdam in 1880 and was the Dutch Prime Minister from 1901 to 1904. He is thus seen as a model for the politically active evangelical Christian – one who is concerned and involved with politics for Christian ends.

Schooling and politics in the Netherlands

For supporters of a greater diversity of state-funded schools including faith-based schools, the Dutch system presents several features that appear to be highly desirable. The most significant of these features are that state and private schools are financed by the state on an equal basis, and that about two-thirds of all primary and secondary pupils are taught within private schools. It is open for any group of parents or others to apply to the Ministry of Education and Science to establish new schools and, if the relevant criteria are met, these new schools become state-funded. This means that, in addition to the state schools organized by the state municipalities, the Netherlands has Roman Catholic and Protestant Christian schools, Islamic, Hindu and Jewish schools. There are also several private secular schools which promote particular educational philosophies such as Montessori, Dalton, Jenaplan and Freinet schools (MOW 1994).

But aspects of the Dutch system that are so attractive to supporters of diversity cannot be understood in isolation. The nature and structure of Dutch education must be examined in the context of the wider historical, religious and political features of Dutch society. Indeed, James (1989) argues that 'the evolution of the Dutch system of primary and secondary education is unique in the Western World' in that it moved from a relatively secular state monopoly at the beginning of the nineteenth century to a highly pluralistic, largely religiously based system by the beginning of the twentieth century.

The basic cleavage between Roman Catholic and Protestant became more complex during the nineteenth century as divisions within the Dutch Reformed Church occurred and, led by such people as Abraham Kuyper, groups of orthodox Calvinist Protestants broke away from the theologically liberal Dutch Reformed Church to form their own churches. These 'little men' (de kleine luyden), who were often small shopkeepers, clerks, artisans and similar, eventually formed the Rereformed (Gereformeerde) churches. These three religious groups eventually became associated with political parties and, with the addition of a further party that developed from the socialist workers' movement and another based upon the relatively affluent Liberals (who held power until universal suffrage), still form the basis of the five current main political parties in the Netherlands.

This has meant that the Netherlands is a country of political minorities, and minorities that entertain no hope of becoming majorities (Andeweg and Irwin 1993). From 1917, when universal suffrage and proportional representation were introduced, none of the five major political parties has ever had an outright majority, or even been very near to doing so. Not only are the political parties minorities in statistical terms, they can be identified with particular minority groups that have developed histori-cally within the Netherlands. Unlike most other European countries, these political parties are divided along two dimensions. First, there is a version of the usual 'left' versus 'right' socio-economic dimension that is related to the desired degree of intervention of the state into the economy, social affairs, income distribution and so on. Second, is a religious dimension that is particularly important in social, cultural and ethical areas. This religious dimension was more important than the socio-economic dimension for most of the first half of this century.

Although Roman Catholics had never been banned, they were only given the right to establish their own schools in 1848, and the Church hierarchy was only re-established in 1853. The Catholics then joined with the growing number of Gereformeerde churches to seek state support for religious schools on an equal basis to state-provided schools. The funding of such schools became one of the two major issues in the nineteenth-century Netherlands, and was only finally resolved in the new 1917 Constitution when a Catholic–Calvinist majority coalition led to the 'Pacification' which introduced social reform, universal suffrage and the right to state funding for religious schools.

That such a change to the education system should be intertwined with issues of social justice and universal suffrage is an indication of the 'pillarization' of Dutch society that existed at the time and thrived until the late 1960s. The minority groups were not simply linked to the five political parties, but were organized social groups or subcultures which affected very many aspects of everyday life. At its strongest, for Catholics in the 1950s for example, the 'pillar' included separate hospitals, social services, television channels, newspapers, schools, universities, trades unions and employers' organizations. A Catholic 'would have lived his or her life within the confines of a homogeneous Catholic subculture and its organisational infrastructure' (Andeweg and Irwin 1993: 29).

In the first half of this century pillarization was particularly encouraged by the Roman Catholic hierarchy and the Gereformeerde churches, and less so by the Dutch Reformed Church and the other two political party groupings. It led to a situation of introversion and isolation within subcultures and distrust and hostility between the subcultures. However, Lijphart (1968) argues that, although heavily pillarized, the Dutch system is stable because there is cooperation at the élite level at the same time as segmentation at the mass level. By accepting a number of ground rules that emphasize compromise and consensus, the various groups are able to coexist fruitfully. Thus concepts such as the agreement to disagree, executive power sharing, the right of veto for minorities, and proportionality are central to the political culture and accepted by virtually all. Where compromise cannot be achieved any decisions are usually avoided altogether. Lijphart argues that this last factor is particularly important in terms of ensuring stability, but that it inhibits the society's ability to develop.

But pillarization is no longer the strength that it was. Increasing secularism and materialism, along with a greater internationalism, have meant that since the late 1960s there have been great changes in Dutch society. In particular, the importance of religion has waned. By the late 1980s some 30 per cent of Dutch people stated that they had no belief in God and only some 40 per cent claimed to attend a church service at least once a month. In Britain the comparable figures were 20 per cent and 23 per cent (Inglehart 1990: 188). Except for those in the Gereformeerde churches, religion no longer has such a strong hold. Moreover, pillarization is no longer encouraged by the Dutch élite, which has led to greater linkages between different providers of social services, education and so on. Greater social and geographical mobility has led to a diminution of social divisions based on the pillars.

This outline history shows that the principle of state support for faith-based schools where there should be 'separate but equal school systems' was the direct result of a society of minorities that was already sharply segmented along religious lines. The stability of the society as a whole is dependent upon the degree to which the various religious groups hold to a collection of fundamental shared assumptions and values about the nature of society. This situation has considerable differences from those pertaining in modern Britain, where some of the religious groups wishing to open their own schools adhere to beliefs that strongly challenge those of the mainstream. A system that, until recently, has been seen as being largely successful in the Netherlands cannot simply be wrenched from its roots and applied to Britain with its very different social, political and cultural history. Further, as is shown below, the Dutch situation is rapidly changing such that fundamental beliefs and values are being challenged, and the desirability of having such a diversity of schools is now widely questioned.

THE DUTCH SYSTEM IN PRACTICE

British advocates of a greater diversity of state-funded schools have been highly selective in the elements from the Dutch system that they emphasize, and have usually concentrated on primary level provision. The most important element discussed by most of those politically involved is the potential for groups of Dutch parents or others to apply to the government for support of a new school which will support a particular faith or philosophy. But, even with this aspect, most advocates say little about the stiff criteria that have to be met before state funding is obtained, or the conditions under which private schools operate once funded by the state. In addition, the Dutch educational system, at least at primary school level, has many features that attempt to ensure equity of provision between schools – a desire not held by most of the New Right in Britain.

Within the Netherlands there are currently about 4,000 independent school governing bodies that oversee just over 8,000 primary schools and 2,000 secondary schools. About 69 per cent of primary school pupils and 73 per cent of secondary pupils attend privately controlled schools that are funded by the state (Hirsch 1994). The vast majority of these schools are of religious foundation.

All of these schools follow a range of subjects that are specified by law. Attainment targets and the number of hours to be spent on each subject are also set. While schools are able to choose their own teaching methods, the maximum and minimum number of hours per day is prescribed. Central government even lays down the dates and length of the summer holidays which are staggered between three large national regions. Each school must produce a 'school work plan' which details (among much else) the content of teaching and assessment. This plan has to be submitted to the Education Inspectorate for approval (van Dorp and van Opdorp 1992). Although there have been some recent changes towards greater local management of schools, the normal practice is for the government to set and pay directly for all teachers, buildings and school costs. The number of teachers for each school, their salaries and conditions of work are determined by the government. A very important feature designed to ensure equity is that private schools are not allowed to charge any 'top up' fees, and may only charge (and most state and private schools do) for extra-curricular activities including visits. However, schools do have freedom to appoint their own staff and may use religion and lifestyle as appointing criteria. Further, each major faith has its own Training Colleges licensed to award teaching qualifications.

At the primary level parents and children have considerable choice in the school the child attends. The main differences between private schools and state-provided schools is that the private schools can turn away prospective pupils under certain proscribed conditions. However, state-provided schools are not allowed to reject any student that applies, and popular state schools are required to expand to accept all prospective pupils. Interestingly, this right of all pupils to attend the state school of choice can have an effect on private schools, for if a private school has spare capacity and another school nearby is popular, the private school may be forced to give up part of its buildings to the popular school (Hirsch 1994).

Many British advocates of the Dutch system seem to be unaware of changes that have recently occurred and of the reality of the system in practice. As in Britain, the Dutch government is increasingly concerned about the undue cost caused by having a great number of small schools and by attempts to respond to what might be temporary demands. Before August 1993 the state supported the establishment of new religious primary schools where a set number of pupils could be guaranteed. This number varied according to the population density of the local area but, at its highest, was 200 for a town of over 100,000, and reduced to just 80 in an area with less than 25,000 inhabitants. Since August 1993, to obtain funding for a primary school, the sponsors have to show that within five years there will be minimum number of children attending the school, but the minimum number of pupils has increased substantially and now varies from 333 in the cities to 200 in rural areas (MOW 1994). Further, the sponsors have to show that this number is likely to be maintained for a further 15 years after the first five years. These minimum numbers of pupils are now higher than pupil numbers in practically all of the existing new Christian schools in Britain (Poyntz and Walford 1994).

These changes have brought a sharp decline in the number of new schools being opened in the Netherlands. The total number of new primary schools (including municipally provided schools) was 74 in 1990, 67 in 1991 and 55 in 1992. The changes in regulations led to a mere 13 new primary schools in 1993 and just 5 in 1994 (MOW 1994). An example of the new difficulties of establishing schools is provided by a long-running controversy over a proposed Hindu school in The Hague during 1993/94. The sponsors had attracted sufficient pupil numbers for the establishment of a new school under the old regulations, but were unable to guarantee the revised figure of 333. Their application was thus rejected.

This increase in the minimum number of pupils required for state support of new schools has been accompanied by similar changes in the pupil numbers required for continued support of existing schools. The actual figures are complicated and depend upon population density, but are 143 for a 'typical' city and 69 for a sparsely populated area. While these figures appear low by British standards, there were very many Dutch schools with fewer than the required number of pupils. School closure, which usually means merger of two or more schools into one new one, has been a common feature of the recent educational environment. In 1992 there were 99 mergers (the great majority being of two schools), while in 1993 there were 270 mergers. In 1994 this figure was 264, but about twice this number is expected in 1995 as the new minimum figures will be fully enforced from 1996 (MOW 1994). Quite simply, if small schools do not merge, they close. Many of these mergers have been of schools from within the same denomination, but Hirsch (1994: 69) states that, of the schools merging in 1993, 16 per cent involved both state and private schools, 16 per cent were private schools of different denominations and 9 per cent were mergers between Christian schools and secular private schools.

The change in minimum numbers has occurred at a time of declining school rolls of about 20 per cent between 1980 and 1990 and increased secularization. The result is that many religious schools now accept children from many religious backgrounds or none. Hirsch (1994), for example, cites Catholic schools in Rotterdam and The Hague which have a majority of Muslim children. Such changes obviously pose considerable threats to the religious identities of the faith-based schools. While many of the British new Christian schools are open to pupils of other faiths, preservation of the religious identity of the schools is a particular concern of many of the promoters, and those considering opting for grant-maintained status might be well advised to ponder the effects of possible future government action on the religious identities of their schools.

It is also clear that, apart from a religious minority of parents, the religious affiliation of Dutch schools is no longer a major factor in choice. Factors such as proximity and the perceived status of the schools are generally more important and large numbers of parents now make choices that would seem to contradict their religious views. However, there is growing evidence that at secondary level private faith-based schools are beginning to produce slightly better academic results than state schools (van Laarhoven *et al.* 1990; Dronkers 1992). The effect is small and not uniform and Dronkers argues that this difference is probably due to the deliberate choice by parents and teachers towards such schools helping it to build a school community which performs better. He claims that these educational differences between private and state schools are recent and could be the start of a new form of inequality.

Another change that might concern British advocates of faith-based schools is that the Dutch Catholic or Protestant churches no longer have significant influence on the curriculum of 'their' schools, and the teaching of religious education in most religious schools has been reduced to simple factual information about different world views (Dronkers 1992). Further, there is a decline in the number of teachers in these schools who are themselves religious and in the number of teachers prepared to teach religious education.

The difficulties of establishing a primary school are nothing compared to those for a secondary school. Secondary schools are subject to the Ministry of Education and Science's annual 'Plan for Schools'. Secondary schools are expected to draw their pupils from a wider area and the Ministry only funds a new secondary school in the absence of other similar schools in the neighbourhood. Only a very few applications are funded as there are already said to be sufficient and well-distributed secondary schools (MOW 1994).

A further interesting aspect of the Dutch system is that parents are not free to educate their children at home. The Netherlands has a Compulsory Education Act, which stipulates that, from age 5 until 16, all children must attend an educational establishment that complies with statutory requirements and the standards imposed by the Ministry of Education and Science (van Dorp and van Opdorp 1992: 4). This Act protects children from parents who have idiosyncratic views on education or who wish to isolate them from interaction with peers. Further, parents have little involvement in schools once a choice of school has been made – control largely rests with the teachers (Brown 1992). Both of these elements of the Dutch system are in direct contradiction with the views of most of those concerned with the new Christian schools who believe that education is fundamentally the responsibility of parents, and that the state should only act to support parents in their task (Walford 1994a). Many of the new Christian schools developed from groups of parents who took advantage of Britain's legislation which allows parents to teach their children at home, and, without this possibility, it is unlikely that several of the schools would have formed.

EQUITY ISSUES IN DUTCH EDUCATION

At the primary school level, considerable attempts are made to try to ensure equity of treatment for all children in schools. Central government control of class size, teacher numbers, subjects of study and inspection, in particular, are designed to try to ensure that significant differences do not develop between schools provided by various sponsor groups in terms of facilities and perceived status. However, the government has not been wholly successful.

One current problem that is increasingly concerning educators and politicians is ethnic segregation in schools. The Netherlands has a growing ethnic minority population, primarily of Moroccan or Turkish origin, which is very unevenly distributed geographically. This means that in some areas, particularly the four largest cities of Amsterdam, The Hague, Rotterdam and Utrecht, the concentrations of ethnic minority children can be high. Karsten (1994) claims that at a time when the Netherlands is becoming increasingly multi-cultural, the schools are, paradoxically, becoming less integrated. Once the proportion of ethnic minority children exceeds about 50 per cent, many Dutch parents use their freedom to choose to avoid schools where non-Dutch children form a substantial proportion. This has led to some urban schools being highly ethnically divided (Louis and van Velzen 1991). White Dutch parents have been found to be much more 'mobile' in their choices than most ethnic minority groups and are prepared to take their children to schools outside their neighbourhood (Karsten 1994). In particular, as the majority of ethnic minority children are enrolled in state schools, some private religious schools are now seen as providing 'safe havens' for white pupils. They can perform this function because, although they cannot discriminate in admissions on the basis of ethnic origin, they can refuse entry to children on religious grounds.

This phenomenon of 'white flight' is seen as a problem for both academic and social grounds. There are several studies that have suggested that ethnic segregation has adverse effects on both minority and majority students (Tesser and Mulder 1990, quoted in Karsten 1994) as well as being seen as hampering social integration. While the Dutch choice of school legislation makes it difficult to try to decrease segregation, several municipalities have made significant attempts to do so (Karsten 1994).

Change in the composition of existing schools is, however, only part of what is increasingly seen as a problem of ethnic segregation in schools, for there has been a growth in the number of newly formed Muslim schools (now nearly 30) and Hindu schools. Within the Netherlands, the right to found new schools is no longer seen as having unambiguous merit, but is now viewed as having potential weaknesses as well as benefits.

However, while there is concern about possible inequities in Dutch primary schools, after they transfer to secondary school at 12, equity issues are largely ignored. Indeed, the system is highly differentiated into 'tracks' and different types of school that are hierarchically ordered from high to low. There are substantial biases in terms of class, gender and ethnicity in who attends these various schools. Secondary education is organized by both the state and the private sector, but this division is of far less significance than the form of secondary provision within the status hierarchy. Since 1968 there have been two branches of secondary education – the first consists of general secondary education and pre-university education; the second of pre-vocational and vocational education. These two branches are divided further into tracks:

VWO   pre-university education, 6 years from age 12;
HAVO   senior general secondary education, 5 years from age 12;
MAVO   junior general secondary education, 4 years from age 12;
LBO   junior secondary vocational education, 4 years from age 12;
MBO   senior secondary vocational education, 2 to 4 years between ages 16 and 18 to 20.

In the past there were firm subdivisions within each of these tracks, such that the VWO comprised three different forms of pre-university education. A reaction against such rigid streaming has recently led to slightly greater flexibility, and the first year of secondary education is now supposed to be transitional, and to offer virtually the same curriculum for all types of school. Moreover, as these different tracks of secondary schooling are not necessarily provided in five separate schools (a single school may offer several tracks), transfer between tracks is possible but not easy. Children are allocated to an 'appropriate' track of secondary schooling according to recommendations from the primary school's headteacher. The headteacher, in turn, bases this recommendation on performance throughout the past few years, examination results and his or her view of the child's particular abilities. It is very difficult for parents to go against the recommendation. The threat that a child may be 'held back' for a year if unable to complete a year's work satisfactorily acts to pressure parents into accepting the school's decision. Thus at 12 or 13 children are allocated into tracks that usually have a profound effect on their future education and subsequent careers. It is hardly surprising that there are severe class, gender and ethnic differences in who follows what track (Faasse et al. 1987).

Up-to-date data on class inequalities are difficult to obtain but James (1989: 193) argues that, apart from differences in achievement between social classes, upper-class parents are more likely to send their children to the pre-university track, despite negative advice from headteachers. In 1979, for example, over half of all high-salaried employees sent their children to VWO or VWO plus HAVO while only 16 per cent of working-class families did so. Conversely, while 43 per cent of working-class children were in vocational education, only 7 per cent of children of the most affluent were.

Gender differences are evident in the secondary track to which boys and girls are assigned. In 1988, for example, 75 per cent of girls and 63 per cent of boys entered general secondary education, while 17 per cent of girls and 23 per cent of boys entered vocational education (ten Dam and Volman 1991). Within these tracks pupils choose between subjects, and familiar gender stereotyped choices are evident. In 1989, for example, 46 per cent of girls and 76 per cent of the boys in the general secondary education chose mathematics, and 13 per cent of girls and 50 per cent of boys chose physics. Similar biases are evident in vocational education where only 4 per cent of vocational education girls chose technical courses and 2 per cent of boys followed home economics.

CONCLUSION

This paper has examined the Dutch educational system in some detail and shown that care needs to be exercised in international 'policy borrowing'. Many Christians involved with the Christian Schools Campaign looked to Abraham Kuyper as a model for Christian involvement in politics, and saw their Campaign as emulating (on a far smaller scale) the political developments of late nineteenth-century Netherlands. Yet this comparison is misleading, for Kuyper's activity was based on the pre-existence of a pillarized society and attempted to strengthen that pillarization. In contrast, few of those involved in the new Christian schools would wish to encourage religious separation or pillarization, and most of the schools are open to a proportion of pupils from other religious faiths or none. Such comparisons pay little attention to the social, economic and political realities of the time or of the present.

Those using the Netherlands as an example to be emulated have frequently been highly selective in their policy borrowing, and have failed to consider aspects which are in contradiction to their views. The lack of influence of parents in the Dutch system is a particular case in point, as is the Dutch belief that the responsibility for education lies with the state rather than with parents. Both of these are in opposition to the views of most of those involved in the new Christian schools.

Reactions to issues of equity are dependent upon the differing ideologies of the variety of people who supported faith-based grant-maintained schools. The policy was backed by an uneasy alliance between the religious supporters (many of whom have egalitarian aims) and the political New Right. Selection for a hierarchy of schools at secondary level and the linked gender, class and ethnic differences are unlikely to worry the New Right greatly. But, in contrast, some of those involved with the new Christian schools are deeply concerned with equity, as some serve areas of multiple deprivation and have fee structures based upon ability to pay. For them, comprehensive education is the ideal and selection for different schools an anathema.

In summary, a form of policy borrowing from the Netherlands was used in the British campaign to achieve state funding for a wider variety of faith-based schools. Those involved in the campaigning drew selectively from the Dutch experience rather than engage in a thorough examination of the strengths and weaknesses of the system, and were able to present many aspects that were perceived as highly desirable. The campaign achieved its objectives in obtaining legislation to allow more faith-based schools, but a closer examination of the Dutch system might have brought out some of the potential problems that are currently concerning the Dutch themselves. Indeed, the current changes to the Dutch system, where religious schools are being forced to merge with others or be closed, and where the religious identity of Christian schools is being strongly challenged, indicate that the Dutch system might be seen by British faith-based schools as more of a warning than an example to be emulated. A wider consideration of the historical, economic, social and political features of the development of the Dutch system might have raised more questions about the efficacy of such policy borrowing.

ACKNOWLEDGEMENTS

I am most grateful to those who have helped in this research and, in particular, to Ruth Deakin, Director of the Christian Schools Campaign, who provided a wealth of information and kindly gave me access to several meetings and documents. The research was funded by the Nuffield Foundation and the Strategic Innovation Research Group at Aston Business School.

REFERENCES

Andeweg, R.B. and Irwin, G.A. (1993) *Dutch Government and Politics*, London: Macmillan.

Bailey, T. (1993) 'The mission of the TECs and private involvement in training: Lessons from Private Industry Councils', *Oxford Studies in Comparative Education* 3, 1, pp. 7–26.

Brown, F. (1992) 'The Dutch experience wit' school choice: Implications for American education', in P.W. Cookson, Jr (ed.) *The Choice Controversy*, Newbury Park, California: Corwin Press.

Cox, C. and Marks, J. (1979) *Education and Freedom. The Roots of Diversity*, London: National Council for Educational Standards.

Deakin, R. (1989) *New Christian Schools: The Case for Public Funding*, Bristol: Regius.

Dennison, S.R. (1984) *Choice in Education*, London: Institute of Economic Affairs.

Dronkers, J. (1992) 'The existence of parental choice in the Netherlands', Unpublished paper.

Faasse, J.H., Bakker, B., Dronkers, J. and Schijf, H. (1987) 'The impact of educational reform: empirical evidence from two Dutch generations', *Comparative Education* 23, 3, pp. 261–77.

Flew, A. (1991) 'Educational services: Independent competition or maintained monopoly?', in D.G. Green (ed.) *Empowering the Parents: How to Break the Schools Monopoly*, London: Institute of Economic Affairs.

Green, A.G. (1993) 'Magnet schools, choice and the politics of policy borrowing', *Oxford Studies in Comparative Education*, 3, 1, pp. 83–103.

Hirsch, D. (1994) *School: A Matter of Choice*, Paris, Centre for Educational Research and Innovation: OECD.

Inglehart, R. (1990) *Culture Shift in Advanced Industrial Society*, Princeton, NJ: Princeton University Press.

James, E. (1989) 'The Netherlands: Benefits and costs of privatized public services – lessons from the Dutch educational system', in G. Walford (ed.) *Private Schools in Ten Countries: Policy and Practice*, London: Routledge.

Karsten, S. (1994) 'Policy on ethnic segregation in a system of choice: the case of The Netherlands', *Journal of Education Policy* 9, 3, pp. 211–25.

Lijphart, A. (1975) *The Politics of Accommodation: Pluralism and Democracy in the Netherlands*, 2nd edition, Berkeley: University of California Press.

Louis, K.S. and van Velzen, B.A.M. (1991) 'A look at choice in the Netherlands', *Educational Leadership* (1990/91) 48, 4, pp. 66–72.

McCarthy, R., Oppewal, D., Peterson, W. and Spykman, G. (1981) *Society, State and Schools*, Grand Rapids, Michigan: William B. Eerdmans.

Marks, J. (1991) *Standards in Schools. Assessment, Accountability and the Purposes of Education*, London: Social Market Foundation.

Meighan, R. and Toogood, P. (1992) *Anatomy of Choice in Education*, Ticknall, Derbyshire: Education Now.

Ministerie van Onderwijs en Wetenschappen (MOW) (1994) Personal communication from Public Informer, Ministerie van Onderwijs en Wetenschappen, Zoetermeer, the Netherlands.

O'Keeffe, B. (1992) 'A look at the Christian schools movement', in B. Watson (ed.) *Priorities in Religious Education*, Lewes: Falmer.

Phillips, D. (1992) 'Borrowing educational policy', *Oxford Studies in Comparative Education* 2, 2, pp. 49–55.

Poyntz, C. and Walford, G. (1994) 'The new Christian schools: a survey', *Educational Studies* 20, 1, pp. 127–43.

Praamsma, L. (1985) *Let Christ be King. Reflections on the Life and Times of Abraham Kuyper*, Ontario: Paideia Press.

Robertson, D.B. and Waltman, J.L. (1992) 'The politics of policy borrowing', *Oxford Studies in Comparative Education* 2, 2, pp. 25–48.

Rodgers, R.E.L. (1992) *The Incarnation of the Antithesis*, Durham: Pentland Press.

Seaton, N. (1991) *Higher Standards and More Choice*, London: Campaign for Real Education.

Sexton, S. (1987) *Our Schools – A Radical Policy*, Warlingham, Surrey: Institute for Economic Affairs Education Unit.

Sexton, S. (1992) *Our Schools – Future Policy*, Warlingham, Surrey: IPSET Education Unit.

ten Dam, G.T.M. and Volman, M.M.L. (1991) 'Conceptualising gender differences in educational research: the case of the Netherlands', *British Journal of Sociology of Education* 12, 3, pp. 309–21.

Tesser, P. and Mulder, L. (1990) 'Etnische scheidslijnn in het Amsterdamse basisonderwijs, een keuze?' (Ethnic dividing lines in Amsterdam primary education), *Migrantenstudies* 2, 6, pp. 31–45.

Vanden Berg, F. (1978) *Abraham Kuyper. A Biography*, Ontario: Paideia Press.

Van Brummelen, H. (1992) 'The effects of government funding on private schools: Appraising the perceptions of long-term principals and teachers in British Columbia's Christian schools', *Canadian Journal of Education*, 7, 4.

van Dorp, A. and van Opdorp, J. (1992) *The Kingdom of the Netherlands. Facts and Figures. Education and Science*, The Hague: Netherlands Ministry of Foreign Affairs.

van Laarhoven, P., Baker, B., Dronkers, J. and Schijf, H. (1990) 'Achievement in public and private secondary education in the Netherlands', in H.K. Anheier and W. Seibel (eds) *The Third Sector: Comparative Studies of Nonprofit Organizations*, Berlin: Walter de Gruyer.

Walford, G. (1990) *Privatization and Privilege in Education*, London: Routledge.

Walford, G. (1991) 'The reluctant private sector: of small schools, politics and people', in G. Walford (ed.) *Private Schooling: Tradition, Change and Diversity*, London: Paul Chapman.

Walford, G. (1994a) 'Weak choice, strong choice and the new Christian schools', in J.M. Halstead (ed.) *Parental Choice and Education*, London: Kogan Page.

Walford, G. (1994b) 'The new religious grant-maintained schools', *Educational Management and Administration*, 22, 2, pp. 123–30.

Walford, G. (1994c) *Choice and Equity in Education*, London: Cassell.

Walford, G. (1995a) 'The Northbourne Amendments: Is the House of Lords a garbage can?', *Journal of Education Policy*, 10 (4).

Walford, G. (1995b) 'The Christian Schools Campaign – a successful educational pressure group?', *British Educational Research Journal* 21 (4) (to be published).

Walford, G. and Miller, H. (1991) *City Technology College*, Buckingham: Open University Press.

Chapter 4

European dimensions in schools

I. Findlay

It is all too easy to speak confidently of the development of a 'Eurodimension' in the school curriculum at the present time, but a little more difficult to achieve a consensus on its definition. It is arguably fairly obvious why emphasis has grown on stressing its development in schools in the late 1980s and early 1990s since the growth of an educational policy has been a feature of the European Community/Union in these years, and the evolution of a single market has had several implications for the curriculum. But of course this implies that hitherto the working/conventional assumption has been that 'Europe' equals 'European Union', albeit one expanding potentially to a greater multinational membership. A good example of an attempt to discuss this issue can be seen in the following extract from the Introduction to a very substantial pack of materials produced for schools' use by EURODESK (the European section of the Scottish Community Education Council) in 1992 and subsequently adapted for use throughout the UK:

> There is still some debate as to what we mean by 'European awareness'. Currently the term is popularly used when referring to the European Community. But with more countries waiting on the threshold, pressing for admittance, from western, central and eastern Europe we recognise that the Community of twelve is likely to be an ever expanding entity. One day we may indeed see a united Europe stretching from the Atlantic to the Urals, and some believe that European awareness should encompass the whole of Europe. However the focus of this Pack is on the European Community, although its relationship with the rest of Europe and the world is addressed during different stages of the Pack.

That this element of flexibility was wise in 1992 has been proved by official developments later, e.g. in the November 1994 policy-and-practice paper of the Scottish Office Education Department (SOED, which envisages a five-year development plan taking schools through the 'Eurodimension' into international awareness. Reference will be made to this in later stages of this article. To set the scene further, the above-mentioned material provides an agenda of questions which will foreseeably underlie discussion of the educational Eurodimension for some time to come:

- Is it a study of the institutions of the EC or of the countries which make up the EC?
- Is it a study of everyday life and customs . . . of their languages . . . or is it an awareness of the impact of the development of the EC on society?
- Is it essentially much broader, even than any of these?
- Can European awareness be a discrete subject in the curriculum, or is it an essential element of existing subjects?

One question not asked in 1992, but which has been an issue since, might be expressed as 'what place does it have in the *cross-curricular* area – for example in Media Studies, Health Studies, environmental concerns and in PSE?' All of which may provide a mistaken impression that there has been no concern with such matters until the last few years. Not so. Some reference to the work of the last 50 years on the European/international dimension of national education systems by the Council of Europe, Strasbourg (still a separate and much looser entity than the European Union, though much confused in the popular mind and Press) may be useful at this point.

THE COUNCIL OF EUROPE AND EDUCATION

In general terms firstly, the Council of Europe has since its foundation in 1949 published material, produced documentation, held seminars, offered study grants for teachers (which British teachers have used very seldom in contrast to their other European colleagues) on a very wide range indeed of educational concerns and topics of potential relevance to all its member countries – who have numbered since the 1950s *c.* twice as many as had entered the European Community/Union as late as 1990. Now that the Union is expanding, it is argued in some quarters, that – in view of increasingly close co-operation between Union and Council in the 1990s – there will inevitably be a measure of closer integration in the work of the two groups in the early part of the twenty-first century, with education being an obvious area of partnership, now that it is at last taken seriously in Brussels as well as in Strasbourg. This point may serve to widen the 'horizon of discussion' within which this article deals with the 'here and now' of 'EU and education' in the 1990s context. Overarching concern with issues and problems of common interest to a number of national education systems is by no means new. Some examples of titles of publications and dates – see references at the end of this chapter – may serve to underline this observation and illustrate the intertwining strands of the Council's work in the last two to three decades.

The picture which emerges is of an organisation which has indeed combined 'Eurodimension' with international awareness, and philosophic influence with (cf. below on the growth of European thrust in UK schools '1988–now') growing emphasis on the realities facing schools in the closing years of the century.

EEC/EUROPEAN COMMUNITY/EUROPEAN UNION AND THE RELUCTANT GROWTH OF EDUCATIONAL POLICY

The Treaty of Rome of 25 March 1957 did not specifically mention education at all in its creation of the European Economic Community, one of the two original Communities to be set up (the other being that of Atomic Energy). Not until the year 1969 in fact did a belated realization develop that the EEC might – in view of the many educational changes which took place in every advanced Western European country in the intervening years – have real implications for education, and that co-operation over common issues could bear fruit. The intervening years have been described as '. . . a period when education remained a taboo subject within the corridors of the European Community . . .' (Guy Neave, 'The EEC and Education', 1984). Why so? Because, according to various views (a) the Council of Europe was acting effectively already in the field of education, culture and science, while the EEC province should be that of economics, the market and industry; (b) perhaps more tellingly, because at that period in history education systems were indissolubly linked with individual national sovereignty/culture/ identity and should therefore not be touched by policy or pressure on a supranational level (something which even today in a changed European education world is carefully hedged round by the principle of subsidiarity).

In the early 1970s, with a changed economic situation, concern about unemployment and related issues, attitudes began to change so that the importance and relevance of co-operation began to be felt – in vocational training if not in full blown concern with education as a whole. In July 1971, a meeting of the Council of Ministers adopted guidelines for this specific area, which themselves generated a climate of willingness to set up a first meeting of the Ministers of *EDUCATION* to establish the basis of co-operation among member states in education generally. Two reminders are useful here: (a) the approach was still extremely cautious and (b) the UK was still 'two years ante natal' as far as Community membership was concerned, and therefore light years away from any real consideration of its own education policy as needing any kind of 'Eurodimension'. For the first time nevertheless *GENERAL* as well as vocational further and lifelong education were envisaged as elements within the educational agenda. This can be seen as the acorn from which the oak of late 1980s and early 1990s policy has grown.

This – non-legally based – expansion of educational concern was underlined in 1973 by the Janne Report 'For a Community Policy on Education' which although not an official statement of educational policy opened the door to such familiar areas as 'the Eurodimension', mutual recognition of qualifications, foreign language teaching and lifelong learning. This was indeed the first formal denial of a taboo on wider educational matters. The Ministers of Education again met in 1974 (for the first time since UK entry, and with an incipient UK input to the discussion) and laid down ground rules for future co-operation – a big step in itself. Co-operation was to include:

- better facilities for training of guest nationals from other Community countries;
- promotion of closer relations between education systems;
- compilation of up-to-date statistics on other systems;
- increased higher education co-operation;
- improved recognition of diplomas and study periods;
- freedom of movement by teachers;
- achievement of equal opportunity of access to education.

A crucial agreement at this stage was not to accept 'harmonization' of systems, i.e. no move was to be made towards a 'European' education system. Autonomy and diversity within national systems has remained a cardinal principle ever since. All of the above thinking was embodied in funded and specific action programmes agreed upon subsequently in 1976 by the Resolution of the Ministers of Education of that year. It is still true that policy until the 1990s has developed along the lines first hammered out in 1976, at least, that is, until the Treaty of Maastricht of 1993 effected a Brussels sea change in the centrality of education within the policy and powers of the European Parliament. But in the interim the existence of an Education Committee and a Directorate for Education and Science supplied the power source needed in Brussels for non-legally based action in the field.

It is perhaps self-evident that a prime influence in the development of Community thinking in the period until 1981 was the enormous post-oil crisis economic change hitting the whole of the Western world, and that youth unemployment, preparation for working life and further education and training were high-priority concerns in policy making in this decade. The Ministers Report of 1982 added for the first time a special chapter on something which was just beginning to be called the 'European dimension in education'. This covered: knowledge about Europe, culture, history, language, civic traditions.

THE NEXT PHASE AND THE GROWTH OF UK GOVERNMENT POLICY ON THE EURODIMENSION

The event which triggered the current phase of European Community/ Union education policy (and what is even more important, UK Government committed 'policy response' to it, with subsequent policy/practice guidelines for schools by DES/DFE, DENI and SOED for England/ Wales, Northern Ireland and Scotland respectively) was the: Resolution of the ... Ministers of Education of 24 May 1988 on the European Dimension in Education.

The central objectives of this may show why it was so crucial. They were expressed in the following form:

> The purpose of this Resolution is to strengthen the European dimension in education by launching a series of concerted measures for the period 1988–1992: these measures should help to:
>
> • strengthen in young people a sense of European identity and make clear to them the value of European civilization and of the foundations on which the European peoples intend to base their development today, that is in particular the safeguarding of the principles of democracy, social justice and respect for human rights (Copenhagen Declaration, April 1978);
> • prepare young people to take part in the economic and social development of the Community and in making concrete progress towards European Union, as stipulated in the European Single Act: make them aware of the advantages which the Community represents, but also of the challenges it involves, in opening up an enlarged economic and social area to them;
> • improve their knowledge of the Community and its Member States in their historical, cultural, economic and social aspects and bring home to them the significance of the co-operation of the Member States of the European Community with other countries of Europe and the world.

Even a cursory reading of these shows the widening of the basic philosophy beyond the narrow strictures of earlier days. It also shows, of course, a certain blandness which left the various national education Departments the task of interpreting and spelling out the detailed implications for their schools and curricula! It should be pointed out, with the benefit of a few more years' hindsight on this, that such 'detailed implications' – the actual delivery of the Eurodimension in schools – have taken material form because schools and their staffs have in increasing numbers 'been provided with school focused INSET on an increasing scale', have 'taken ownership' of the Eurodimension and built it into the daily work of the school through subjects, through cross-curricular issues, and in a management sense through the school development plan. It is also crucial to highlight the variety, flexibility and 'inspired opportunism' of such development. What has become obvious in the 1990s is that there is no one way to deliver the Eurodimension and that any INSET which tries to suggest such a dogmatic, 'top-down' approach is infallibly doomed to failure. Reference at leisure to Case Studies provided below will illustrate this.

In 1990, the National Curriculum Council produced an attempt at a definitive statement for England and Wales of the Eurodimension in schools:

European dimension: NCC definition

The major purpose of the European Dimension Resolution is to strengthen pupils' sense of European identity; to prepare them to take part in the economic and social development of the Community following the European Single Act; to improve their knowledge of the European Community and of its member states; and to inform them of the significance of the cooperation between those states and the other countries of Europe and of the world.

The European dimension in education should enable pupils to live and work with a degree of competence in other European countries, to reflect critically on experiences in them so as to give an informed understanding of the predicaments and aspirations of other Europeans in order to reflect critically on or challenge existing perceptions.

(National Curriculum Council 1990)

This was spelled out in some detail by the NCC, a little repetitively, but some of the interpretations merit discussion. Firstly, the whole curriculum was seen as the context for this – an assumption which has not ceased to be debated since (e.g. 'European mathematics?'). Secondly, 'knowledge and skills acquired in various curriculum areas' are mentioned which seems vaguely to imply modern foreign language, social studies and perhaps expressive/aesthetic subjects, the vagueness being almost an invitation to do nothing about it. More usefully, the phrase 'sense of European identity' is seen as potentially to be facilitated by 'first hand experience' – presumably via exchanges, partnerships and the like. Some other aims when combined quite obviously reflect work awareness, personal enterprise within the 1990s market social/economic context and put it squarely within the European as opposed to British market – thus linking the new dimension with existing Government-promoted imperatives. On history, geography, culture, multiculturalism and 'common European ideals' the document is largely unspecific and lacking in focus.

Finally there was mention of 'Europe's interdependence with the rest of the world', an area which has gone mostly unnoticed in subsequent curricular development. Also in 1990, the General Teaching Council for Scotland (GTC) produced an extensive 12 page document incorporating the above statement from the NCC and applied it to teacher education. It went further to require that all initial courses for teachers should incorporate a European dimension with effect from the 1992/93 College year.

This in fact did happen in some centres more than others, but with initially (and perhaps unsurprisingly) no great degree of ownership by staff. Latterly its existence as a whole College dimension has been threatened by SOED guidelines reducing the number of course weeks in College, placing strong emphasis on teacher-competences and thereby recreating a perception that such an element is of low priority. European College linking may to some extent save the day. That there is a spectrum of awareness of the GTC's ruling was underlined in 1995 at a conference on 'the national level' in Eurodimension at which it became painfully clear that some College representatives had never even heard of the GTC requirement of 1990!

A more effective thrust in recent years has been through EA-based INSET for school staff by Colleges. But this in turn is victim to the financial constraints and priorities of EA staff development funding. It may be that not until the SOED reaches the stage (in 1997, cf. discussion below) of inspecting the Eurodimension in schools that a real sense of urgency is generated.

In 1991 was published 'The European Dimension in Education' – a Statement of the UK Government's Policy and Report of Activities Undertaken to Implement the EC Resolution of 24 May 1988 on the European Dimension in Education'. This came in fact from the DES, so that strictly speaking it applied only south of the Border, but the reality was that SOED and DENI contributed content and used it as a green light for official development in their own areas. It has been crucial as a platform for all that is mentioned below in fact. It began by acknowledging a clear connection with its ancestry in the 1988 Resolution, quoting it verbatim, connected the policy formulation with the rationale of the coming Single European Market in 1992 and derived a rather similar set of Objectives. But it went further to create an official framework for subsequent development placing:

1 implementation in the hands of LEAs and their Scottish and NI equivalents and
2 legislative responsibility with central government, oversight with the various Curriculum Councils in the 4 countries, and the task of embedding it in examinations and assessment with their examination boards.

Fair comment on these two areas might be that some LEAs in England and Wales now have a notable track record in 'pushing' the spread of Eurodimension in their schools; a similar situation exists in Northern Ireland, while in Scotland the level of activity is very high in the larger authorities with variability elsewhere. As far as examinations are concerned, GCSE and Standard Grade have not consciously shown so far a real change in the European direction, but in NVQ and SCOTVEC modular courses (with of course a noticeably vocational slant) there has been much evolution of short courses with language, work, cultural awareness and investigative slants. In addition to which the Scottish Examination Board has produced a clutch of 'short courses' with a similar intention.

The document also covered related areas such as support for language teaching, bilateral links and exchanges, the importance of non-governmental organisations such as UKCEE. Language teaching to age 16 has of course since then become a priority, and (as also indicated later) European Union SOCRATES/COMENIUS funding promises emphasis on school linkage. The value of UKCEE and its allies is to act as a pressure-point for the implementation of promised policy.

A further expressed aim in 1991 was that there should be no separate 'European Studies' in the curriculum – rather a 'permeation' of the whole curriculum. This has not in any sense come anywhere near reality, not least because there is much debate as to the feasibility of such permeation. Another issue is the definition of 'permeation' itself! Questions to be solved include:

- Does this mean a Eurodimension in each and every subject, but separately?
- What development is possible in the cross-curricular areas (e.g. environment media, health, communication, common study among partner schools, and the like)?
- Should there be some special areas and ages for depth treatment, e.g. in Scotland through the subject called 'Modern Studies' (an amalgam of politics, economics, current affairs, sociology), e.g. at age 14?

In March 1992, the DES issued a follow-up publication with emphasis on the managerial dimension in school and LEA/EA. This focused on guidelines for policy development and formulation at both levels. In the case of LEAs/EAs this covered such topics as guidelines for schools, the implications of the National Curriculum for the Eurodimension, INSET and resource support, guidelines for exchanges and dissemination of good practice. In the case of schools, encouragement was given for: auditing the current provision; identifying opportunities within the

National Curriculum for Eurodevelopment; appointing a school Co-ordinator; identifying staff development needs; assessing availability or lack of resources; self-evaluation of progress, etc. The main overview comment to make some years later is that what has happened in schools throughout the UK on all these issues is closely reminiscent of the proverbial patchwork quilt – with some schools at a very highly sophisticated level and with Eurodimension embedded as a priority in school development planning, while others are still asking questions such as 'how/where do we start?'. Case Studies included below will illustrate some of the former category.

Successively in 1992 and 1993, the DENI and SOED produced what have become very practical and increasingly popular guideline 'good practice' documents – both called 'Thinking European' for the schools. These contain material on:

- Strategies for Integrating a European Dimension into the Curriculum;
- the European Dimension in the Primary Curriculum;
- the European Dimension in the Postprimary (NI) Curriculum;
- the European Dimension in the Secondary (SCOT) Curriculum;
- Managing the European Dimension across the Curriculum;
- Sources and Resources to Support Teaching and Learning about Europe (or a variation on these words in the Scottish version).

A particularly useful feature of these – for the first time – was the inclusion of a range of primary and secondary Case Studies of successful (and very varied) practice. It was calculated to appeal to schools, and it has certainly done so. This may indeed be the best opportunity to provide a range of examples, from these and other sources.

Case study: a planned exchange

Buchanhaven and Dales Park Primary Schools, Peterhead

The study of France and the French is based on the development of the concepts of similarity and difference through a wide variety of skills and activities (as listed in the work plan).

Emphasis at all times is on the real France and the French people as seen through the eyes of the children's pen pals and their parents in the Normandy town of Trouville, a one time whaling station and still an important fishing town with a population equal to that of Peterhead. Such in-depth studies help each child develop a greater understanding of the people, their customs and different life-styles.

Positive attitudes are encouraged at all times in the children's work, their discussions, findings and enthusiasm.

Links were formed back in 1983 with the René Coty School in Trouville – a primary school of 250 pupils whose staff are very eager to develop educational links with a school in north–east Scotland. The headteacher was a forward-thinking person who developed the link, helping his pupils to learn more about the country of Scotland and Grampian in particular while helping our pupils to learn more about Normandy and Calvados the district, with particular emphasis on Trouville. Being a local councillor, he opened many doors and made many contacts for our visit in 1984. The present headteacher continues the original links.

Main broad aims

1 To foster co-operation between Buchanhaven and Dales Park School in joint planning of a wide range of interesting work, activities on a group, class and school basis and reciprocal visits between both staff and pupils while preparing for the trip to France and also during it, sharing and learning how to work closely together with well developed social contacts.
2 To break down artificial barriers of prejudice with Peterhead parents and children about 'foreigners' by creating a link with both parents and children of a similar primary school in Trouville, a fishing town with a population equal to the town of Peterhead.
3 To enhance friendship with the children at the school in Normandy through pen pals chosen by the children themselves according to age, hobbies and interests and, through regular correspondence with exchange of photos, videos, tapes, slides, drawings, postcards, stamps, gifts and monthly class albums, to heighten their understanding and knowledge of a different life-style.
4 To promote a greater awareness of their own immediate environment, community and town by learning how to extract and communicate information in pictorial form for their pen pals through a variety of skills including sketching, taking photographs, drawing, map making, interviewing people and involvement in the production of a video tape on their school and town.
5 To increase their understanding and enjoyment of living in another country through the actual sharing of many first hand experiences and comparative studies on visits in the town of Trouville.
6 To allow the children to mature in various ways, promoting good social and working attitudes, promoting an understanding of the difference in life-styles and cultures of another people, forming judgements and decisions while interacting with pen pals, French parents and a wide variety of people, while gaining confidence in overcoming a language and cultural barrier.

On site field work and activities planned for group visits in Trouville

1 *Visit around town*: Finding directions and map-reading assignment
   Use of street maps from tourist office and worksheets with simplified maps to find directions/street signs/traffic signs/shop signs and names/street furniture.

2 *Visit to Trouville fire station*: Comparisons assignment
   Comparing fire engines, work of a French fireman and ambulance man (combined), uniforms/equipment. Contacts: M. J Baird, Scottish fireman; Mr Perchey, fire master, Trouville station.

3 *Visit to Gendarmerie*: Comparisons assignment
   Comparing police cars/motor bikes/uniforms/use of fire arms/cells! Contacts: Community policeman, Peterhead Station; M. Maguy, Trouville station.

4 *Visit to fish market*: Comparisons assignment
   Worksheet to draw and compare shell fish. Recording/sketching shellfish/white fish/boats (with pen pals).

5 *Visit to weekly fruit/vegetable/cheeses market*: Comparisons assignment
   Worksheet assignment to compare fruits/vegetables/recognition of cheeses. Price sheet to record prices, weights (in g and kg). Recording/sketching (with pen pals to help).

6 *Visit to post office (interior)*: Recording assignment
   Compare the physical aspect of post office, its facilities, philatelic counter, postal services, etc. Contacts: The Head postmasters at both post offices.

7 *Visit to SNCF Trouville–Deauville railway station*: Recording assignment
   Assignment to compare French trains, railway station and amenities. Worksheet on train times to Paris, Rouen, Lisieux using 24 hour clock.

8 *Visit to patisserie and confiserie*
   Visit to Charlotte Corday shop to see:
   1. Demonstration on how French loaves and cakes are made.
   2. Demonstration and tasting of home made sweets (with samples).

9 *Visit to tourist office*
   Retrieval of further information on Trouville and surrounding area from brochures, posters, street maps to illustrate daily diary kept by each child and adult.

10 *Visit to boules pitch* (outside hotel)
   Learning how to play French boules (*pétanque*) with pen pals and their parents' help – much teaching and encouragement. Boules championships on last evening.

11 *Visit to aquarium*: Recording assignment
   Use of workbook on the various specimens in the aquarium (including tarantula spiders, snakes, sharks, and others).

12 *Visit to the swimming pool*
Group visits with pen pals to local pool (across the road from the hotel) for enjoyment and small competition gala.

13 *Visit to local department store*: Maths and calculations assignment
Worksheet on various prices to help children work out costs of items before deciding on presents. Visit to food hall to compare prices. Recording prices and calculations of amount of pocket money to be used.

Case Study: Local business and industry help schools into Europe

As part of a Communication Studies project, two students at Franklin Sixth Form College, L. Pickett and A. Shury, wrote this article about the Humberside 'Gateway to Europe' project.

Schools in Grimsby and Cleethorpes have been teaming up with various businesses and industrial companies in order to learn about the implications of UK membership in unified Europe. This is due to a curriculum development project supported by the Humberside Curriculum Development Initiative (TVEI), whereby school pupils and students have been encouraged to think of Grimsby as a 'Gateway for Europe'.

Entitled 'Gateway for Europe', the project asked teachers in many schools and colleges to increase European Awareness in their students as the impact of 1992 and the potential opportunities of the single community are registered. The pilot project has demonstrated how European Awareness can be delivered as a cross-curricular theme in primary, secondary and post-16 schools and colleges. The schools and colleges, including eight primary, six secondary and two post-16 colleges (including one 11–18 school), have worked with companies such as Associated British Ports, British Rail (Freight), Tioxide, Eurographics and Riverside Films and have received professional help on a wide variety of projects.

The project's aims were to establish European awareness as a theme across the whole curriculum in primary, secondary and post-16 schools and colleges and to encourage education and industry to work together in order to raise awareness of the potential for economic growth that Humberside, and in particular the Grimsby area, as a key gateway to Europe, has. It also aimed to demonstrate some of the ways in which the partnership between education and industry can enhance our young peoples' studies by giving them opportunities to undertake real commissions, work to deadlines and meet client needs, as well as to develop enterprising ideas in order to produce something of interest and value to the client company.

The primary schools projects included simple introductions to foreign languages and the application of the newly learned phrases, the requesting of information from multi-national companies and support activities such as visits to local companies and much more during the course of the projects. The secondary schools involved worked through European Awareness study units and they also were supported by trips to local companies, and work simulations involving experts from local industries as classroom consultants.

The tasks for the post-16 students, however, were a little more demanding. Five teams from the various post-16 institutions locally were set various tasks with deadlines to meet. Team One was Matthew Humberstone 6th Form working in conjunction with British Rail (Freight), Team Two was Franklin 6th Form College and Associated British Ports. Team Three was Grimsby College of Technology and Arts alongside Tioxide, and the last two teams were the Grimsby College of Technology and Arts remaining teams of BTEC students, Team Four being Business Studies students and Team Five Construction students.

After the initial contact was made with each company on behalf of the schools and colleges, preliminary visits were arranged by students, teachers and members of the company. A series of visits followed in which the students got to know more about the companies. In the case of the students working with BR and ABP this included closely super-vised (for safety reasons) visits to the ports of Immingham and Grimsby and a trip on a freight train to find out where the goods which enter and exit the country via the ports come from and go to. In the course of the visits a portfolio of information was gathered for use in the second part of the project.

The GCTA team was initially composed of students on the BTEC Business Studies course. Again, after the initial contact, the students researched with the company in Grimsby and then a visit to the Calais factory was arranged. With the help of Media Studies students the research material, which had been assembled on video tape, was turned into a promotional video which was of a highly professional standard, and this was passed on to the design team for the next stage of the project.

After discussions it was decided that the service to be offered would be the production of a trade display stand which would promote both the company and its links with Europe. As team members were all studying Art and Design, they had many of the skills required for theoretical solutions to the design problems, but not the practical and business skills. They needed to find out what was possible given that the companies were interested enough to enter into a contract for the production of the project. Further to that they needed to find out what questions to ask the companies so that they could obtain useful information about companies' requirements and they also had to find out about their materials and their suitability and availability.

To get answers to these sorts of questions the teams consulted another local company which specialises in graphics and in building trade display stands. As a result of the outcomes of those meetings, the students entered into discussions and negotiations with the companies, as a result of which contracts were entered into for the production of a modular trade display stand for ABP and BR.

The conditions of the project were that the stand had to be capable of being shown either as a unified joint stand or as two separate stands. The stand had to be of 'trade fair' standard and be easily demounted and assembled. All graphics had to comply with company policy in regard to the corporate image and the agreed price included loose graphic displays. All this had to be completed for 5 May 1992.

Once the designs were accepted by the companies, a model and rough drawings for loose graphics were produced. These were then accepted and the Franklin and Matthew Humberstone teams handed over the construction to a team of students from the Construction Department of Grimsby College of Technology and Arts (many of whom are special needs students on a Basic Skills Preparation Course). The design students then negotiated contracts for the structural graphics and began production of the finished loose graphics.

In this way the project was handed from team to team therefore utilising the specific skills that each set of students specialised in.

After being passed down and completed to that stage, the project was once more handed down this time to two Communications Studies 'A' level students at Franklin Sixth Form College. Their task was to record and evaluate the project through a video of the event, through questionnaires aimed at teachers and members of various industrial establishments, and through an article sent to various educational supplements, which you are at this time reading.

Attending the opening ceremony, held in the Banqueting Room at Grimsby Town Hall, were various people of importance, including the Mayoress of Grimsby, Councillor Kit Bell, the Mayor of Cleethorpes, Councillor J. Winn, the local MEP, Peter Crampton, the Director of Education for Humberside, Dr Garnett, and the two people who organised the project, Curriculum Development Officer David Lee and the Advisory Teacher for European Awareness, Ray Kirtley.

While in general the lessons learned from these grassroots exemplars of Eurodimension in the curriculum must be fairly self-evident, it is nevertheless useful to point out some very salient characteristics:

(a) The Eurodimension is by no means feasible only at secondary level, or with only more able students. This kind of perception is exploded by the initiatives within this group in primary schools of all kinds in rural and urban areas, in SEN situations, and at all levels from preschool onwards.

(b) Some of these schools did not wait until prodded by national or local policy was formulated, but went ahead anyway.

(c) Wherever success of this kind has been achieved, it is because a vast majority of staff with the backing of senior management have come to a motivated sense of ownership and relevance.

(d) Interpretations of the essence of the Eurodimension are almost as many as the schools themselves, precisely because they each live in a different location, climate, ethos, community, have different existing strengths and weaknesses, have used the former and attended via staff development to the latter.

(e) Parents and community have been crucial factors in many cases, perhaps especially in small rural schools, where the temptation was strongest to see the whole exercise as impossible or irrelevant.

(f) Different 'strands' of the Eurodimension come to the surface differently in such a variety of situations, e.g. language skill, exchange/partnership, PSE, the European single market, the potential for communication of new technology, etc.

(g) Finally, the sheer variety of these exemplars (which no more than exemplify a large number of similar schools in each and every subgroup represented) is currently creating a growing bank of good practice for further dissemination. The idiosyncratic nature of individual cases is also proving to be an encouragement to others to realise that it *is* possible to 'do it my way'.

SOED document

Long awaited and promised, but appearing ultimately in 1994 was the final definitive 'Policy, Strategy and Practice' document of the SOED, called 'Scottish Education and the European Community'. In the Scottish case, it was significant that this postdated the 'Thinking European' practice guide. One could speculate that in the small, tightknit, relatively innovative and fast-changing system north of the Border, the priority was felt to be 'getting the schools moving on the ground' with a modicum of historico-political rationale behind their movement and a development of assent and consensus. Then came the major thrust towards the macro-level and the 'national development plan for Scottish education'.

The document covers:

1 all that has happened (described above) since the 1991 initiative from DES;

2 the legal framework from Treaty of Rome 1957 to Single European Act 1986 to Treaty of Maastricht 1992 which amended the 1957 Act

to give the European Parliament extended powers in the education field (see below);

3 the SOED's own strategy;

4 the European dimension in practice.

Some reference to the timescale for Eurodevelopment will perhaps show how all this is meant to fit together in strategic terms. The SOED Action Plan envisages:

Phase 1 (1990–92) Clarification of Issues and setting up of operational structure

Phase 2 (1992–93) Gathering, sorting and dissemination of essential information

Phase 3 (1993–94) Focus on the development of the European dimension (cf. the Scottish example among the Case Studies supplied)

Phase 4 (1994–95) Particular effort to establish more international partnerships (obviously with SOCRATES/COMENIUS in 1995 in mind as context)

Phase 5 (1995–96) Review and consolidation of process

Phase 6 (1997–) Internationalization beyond the European Community

The above-mentioned move to 'the world beyond Europe' is targeted for c.1996–97. 'Reliable sources close to officialdom', so to speak, have indicated to the author that the SOED's intention is to 'monitor gently' the curricular development of the Eurodimension in c.1995–96, and then to hand it over to the HMIs to inspect in 1996/97. One wonders if the next few years will see a parallel development to the above in the world of the DFE (formerly DES) and schools in England and Wales, or whether the vastly greater size of the system – and the greater difficulty of embedding a Eurodimension in the still fairly prescriptive National Curriculum – will prevent equally fast progress. The 1991 DES document expressed optimism that the National Curriculum would be susceptible to European colouring. In particular the European dimension was seen as one of a number of possible cross-curricular themes. In the opinion of the UKCEE – sitting in London, now operating under the umbrella of Central Bureau, taking a view from the South East which is quite understandably 90% one of the English/Welsh system – there are very few grounds for such optimism in the mid 1990s, simply because the priorities of the National Curriculum lie elsewhere. Similar gloom is expressed about the feasibility of a real Eurodimension within teacher education south of the Border for the obvious reason that teacher education has recently changed vastly towards a school-based and therefore more fragmented process. This is in contrast to the situation in Scotland where a GTC could stipulate (or at least hope) that in five Colleges/University Institutes and one University (Stirling) a Eurodimension should exist since 1992 in all ITT. Apart from the obvious advantage of small size in the innovation business, teacher education in Scotland has not moved nearly so far away from College/Institute to schools though some such direction is discernible in SOED guidelines and terms of 'weeks-spent-in school' and resultant lack of time for areas of low priority.

MEANWHILE, BACK AT THE EU RANCH

The time has come to discuss the significance of the Treaty of Maastricht of 1992 for the process being described. The Treaty on European Union has altered the Treaty of Rome in respect of education and training, particularly the former. First of all, Article 3 of the Treaty of Rome has been amended to encompass education as well as training among its objectives. The role of the Community in respect of education and training is set out more specifically in the new Articles 126 and 127.

Article 126 states, for example:

> The Community shall contribute to the development of quality education by encouraging co-operation between Member States and, if necessary, by supporting and supplementing their action, while fully respecting the responsibility of the Member States for the content of teaching and the organisation of education systems and their cultural and linguistic diversity.

It then goes on to specify aims which Community action should pursue:

1 Developing the European dimension in education, particularly through the teaching of the languages of the Member States;
2 encouraging the mobility of students and teachers, inter alia by encouraging the academic recognition of diplomas and periods of study;
3 promoting co-operation between educational establishments;
4 developing exchanges of information and experience on issues common to the education systems of the Member States;
5 encouraging the development of youth exchanges and of exchanges of socio-educational instructors, and
6 encouraging the development of distance education.

Points to attend to as new arguably include: co-operation between educational establishments (this is now moving towards schools and further education via the SOCRATES and LEONARDO programmes mentioned below); the new emphasis on Distance education. Most of the other areas are 'enhanced quality developments' of existing priorities, but the whole message is that education is now irreversibly 'mainstream policy within Europe'.

SOCRATES and LEONARDO

What followed in May 1993 was a set of 'Guidelines for Community Action in the Field of Education and Training'. This was known as the Ruberti document after the Commissioner in charge of its production. It envisaged two action-lines of policy, with a target date of 1995 for implementation (almost certainly a schedule slippage!), i.e.

Line A: covering higher education, schools and youth activities, and incorporating elements of the old ERASMUS, LINGUA and COMETT programmes. This has later become known as 'SOCRATES'.

Line B: covering vocational education and training, e.g. with reference to youth employment, company training, the EURO market of qualifications and the like (known as 'LEONARDO').

The SOCRATES and LEONARDO programmes, together with a third to be known as 'Youth for Europe III', are in the process of appearing gradually at the time of writing. In fact SOCRATES has already 'come on stream'. These are too detailed to cover in the space available, but at least in the case of SOCRATES (which is subdivided into Chapter I (ERASMUS/LINGUA) and Chapter II (COMENIUS – on schools, etc.) one feature is worth highlighting. It is that co-operation among European schools will be promoted intensively and based on the idea of a number/group of schools focusing on a project of common concern:

> able to take on different forms, such as exchanges of correspondence or electronic mail, joint development of curriculum components or teaching modules, preparation of teaching material, development of educational innovations, exchanges of pupils and teaching staff

and

> gradual grouping of partnerships into a network for the large scale dissemination of the results of the co-operation . . . and stimulation to schools not involved in the network.

Additional comment might be that this predictably will become another step in good practice for schools such as those illustrated in the Case Studies, and that increased availability of such EU money into the twenty-first century is likely to act as a useful engine for dissemination of more widespread 'ground level' Eurodimension in schools. This was discussed in detail at the November 1994 conference of the UKCEE 'Preparing for SOCRATES' in London, and its practicalities and constraints highlighted.

THE EUROPEAN PARLIAMENT GREEN PAPER ON THE EUROPEAN DIMENSION OF EDUCATION

The picture is certainly not complete without discussion of the Green Paper mentioned above, produced by the Commission in September 1993. That it has appeared at all is a significant indication of the growing power and influence of the European Parliament after the Treaty of Maastricht (cf. above). At the time of writing in 1995, so far there is no clear indication that the widespread consultation which has ensued on its content is likely to move things towards the implied White Paper (presumably Strasbourg is following the Westminster model?). This is almost certainly because of slippage in the planned business of the Parliament. Comment in the educational press in October 1993 highlighted the Commission line that the Green Paper is 'simply continuity' of all previous initiatives since 1976. But in view of a crucial 'added value' concept in its basic philosophy, it is undoubtedly more than that. It is a departure into a different, fuller and more 'personally developmental' view of education as compared with the formerly 'economically-tied' stance of previous initiatives. An extract will illustrate this:

The general objectives of schools include contributing towards:

- equality of opportunity for everyone;
- giving all young people a sense of their responsibilities in an interdependent society;
- developing their pupils' ability to act autonomously, to make judgements, to assess matters critically and to make and adapt to innovations;
- enabling all young people to achieve their full potential in their working life and in their own personal development, especially by developing in them the taste for life-long learning;
- giving their pupils training and qualifications which will facilitate their transition to working life, in particular through being able to master technological change.

This moves the European dimension of education into PSE, citizenship, values, autonomous/effective enterprising individualism, and flexible attitudes to changing society. It would, of course, be naive to suppose that this will transform national education systems overnight, but it provides the basic philosophy and guidelines for long-term change. Since the agenda involved so obviously mirrors the British education scene of the 1980s and early 1990s, it can be concluded that this is an attempt to translate UK models on to a European plane. As indicated below in discussion of other national examples, there is no particular reason to suppose that the source is anywhere else. Atypically, the

British would appear to be leading Europe in an area of its evolution which almost never merits attention in the media.

THE UK COMMITTEE FOR EUROPEAN EDUCATION

So far this article has concerned itself with 'mainstream developments' in UK. Some brief attention is deserved, nevertheless, by the UK Committee for European education, which has been an indefatigable influence on all of this from 1979 until the present, and is now formally merged with the Central Bureau for Educational Visits and Exchanges, a move which effectively connects it also with British Council and UK Government. It will be easily seen that this has meant its working 'in early days' as pioneer within a climate of Euro-scepticism in most quarters, then through a transforming scenario in the 1980s, and now into an atmosphere of complete official acceptance of its work in the 1990s. Some colouring may be added by the following:

> The UK Centre for European Education was established in 1979. Ten years later, it merged with the Central Bureau for Educational Visits and Exchanges. The Director of the Bureau is now ex officio the Secretary of UK CEE and the Centre is fully integrated within the Bureau's management structure and works within its Schools Unit. The UK CEE has a membership of 118 institutions and associations active in the field of European education as well as a number of Local Education Authorities.
>
> UK CEE also assists schools and colleges in the organisation of conferences for older students on a European theme and maintains a register of speakers willing to take part in such events.
>
> Annual conferences have been held on a wide range of European issues since 1979, in the period from 1988 to the present. These have covered:
>
> * the European Dimension;
> * an International Perspective (to show how other systems compare to these in UK in 'delivering' the Eurodimension;
> * 'Education for Europe' (preparation for life in the Community) – Facing the Challenges of the New Europe; and
> * (in 1994) 'Preparing for SOCRATES'.
>
> In addition to this the period 1988–1991 saw a major thrust by a subcommittee of UK CEE in holding conferences all over UK to promote awareness of the Eurodimension in ITT.

It is arguable that this organisation may now have to rethink its role now that respectability has been achieved!

SOME COMMENT ON THE RELATIONSHIP OF NATIONAL CURRICULUM AND THE EURODIMENSION

The NCC of 1990 attempted a definition of the European dimension; UK CEE see it as potentially disastrous for its potential development. What is more important to observe now is that (a) the NC in its pre-Dearing form was a tight prescription within which schools were certainly most unlikely to perceive Eurodimension as a priority. In the slightly eased post-Dearing atmosphere of greater flexibility the attitude of the Schools Curriculum and Assessment Authority is that there are very many more opportunities for its insertion and the enrichment of the curriculum by it. Reference is also made to the series of cross-curricular resources produced by NCC in 1993 which included one with many ideas for its introduction at various Key Stages. In addition, certain major subjects such as Geography, History and Modern Languages contain European aspects. The writer feels that it should be added, nevertheless, that in the present climate of teacher opinion in England and Wales, perception of its importance is unlikely to change quickly for the better and commitment to its development is likely to stay low in many areas.

SIMILAR COMMENT ON THE SCOTTISH SCENE

The role of the SOED since 1990 has already been discussed. What can be added here is that (a) the Scottish Consultative Council on the Curriculum (SCCC) has been proactive in, e.g., 1989 curricular guidelines for Scottish secondary schools which set the ball rolling by 'slotting' the Eurodimension into at least one of eight curricular Modes and encouraging discussion of wider permeation; producing a Discussion Document on Values in Education which contained a section and other references to the European Dimension; devising a package of Cross-curricular Issues materials in 1993 with one of six areas devoted to the European dimension within the '5–14' programme (i.e. aimed at primary and lower secondary practice development).

The Scottish Vocational Educational Council (SCOTVEC) has over the last decade published within its modular programme several modules on Investigating Europe, Experiencing Europe, and culture/language-related courses as well. More recently it has created 'cluster courses' from these to enhance coherence, relevance and vocational motivation. The Scottish Examination Board too has a number of 'short courses' within the same general area. Since it is politically likely that SCOTVEC and SEB will merge very soon under one management, this whole area of course development is likely to become a fairly powerful resource package for schools who need 'off the shelf ideas' for their work. The

Scottish Further Education Unit also promotes thinking in the 16 + area with its regular quarterly magazine *Broadcast*.

SOME SPECULATIONS ON THE FUTURE

In the shorter term, it is reasonably likely:

- that technology will have an escalating impact on communications across European educational frontiers and between/among schools;
- that in the UK context there will be a belated marriage between European dimension and Development Education (oriented towards the Third World) with some compartments breaking down to enable the development of a concentric 'Euro/international' philosophy;
- that modern Languages will continue to have a greater relevance in UK education;
- that European work placement within a single market will increase;
- that partnerships of a multilateral nature among schools will proliferate;
- that in the longer term, attention will have to be seriously given to ITT and INSET towards the creation of a teacher able to take up the now existing entitlement to teach anywhere in the European Union. It is possible that psychological as well as linguistic barriers for British teachers may ease in view of the possibility of teaching in Sweden and Finland under certain conditions in view of a characteristic shared by these countries with the Netherlands – high-level communication skills in English particularly in the 10–19 age cohorts.

Predictably one issue which will 'never go away' is the one which this article posed at the outset – the definition and redefinition of 'Europe' in the context of the evolving education debate.

REFERENCES

General

Central Bureau (1993a) *European Dimension in Teaching* (EDIT) (March Issue) on UKCEE and other European Systems, CB, London.
Central Bureau (1993b) *The European Dimension in Education – An Inservice Training Handbook*, CB, London.
Central Bureau (1994) *Strategies and Resources for the European Dimension in Education 4–18 – A Guide for Schools and Colleges*, CB, London.
DENI (1992) *Thinking European – Ideas for Integrating a European Dimension into the Curriculum*, NU, Belfast.
Department of Education and Science (1991) *The European Dimension in Education*. A statement of the UK Government's policy and report of activities undertaken to implement the EC resolution of 24 May 1988 on the European Dimension in Education, London.

DES (1992) *Policy Models*. A guide to developing and implementing European dimension policies in LEAs, Schools and Colleges, London.

Eurodesk (1992) Scottish Community Education Council 'Understanding our European Community' – Resources/Tape/Video Pack, SCEC Edinburgh. Updated versions by Eurodesk England and Eurodesk Wales available.

European Commission (1988) *Resolution of the Council of Ministers on the European Dimension of Education*, EC, Brussels.

European Commission (1989) *Education and Training in the Community: Guidelines for the Medium Term*, EC, Brussels.

European Commission (1993) Green Paper on the European Dimension of Education, EC, Brussels.

European Commission (1993) Guidelines for Community Action in the Field of Education and Training. Commission Working Paper, EC, Brussels.

European Commission (1994) *Proposal for a decision Establishing the Community Action Programme 'SOCRATES'*, EC, Brussels.

FEU (1994) *A Curriculum for Europe*, FEU, London.

General Teaching Council for Scotland (GTC) (1990) *The European Dimension in Initial Teacher Training*, Edinburgh.

Jones M.G. (1992) *Aspects of the European Dimension in Teacher Education*, School of Education, University College of North Wales.

Kirk, G. and Glaister, R. (eds) (1992) *Scottish Education and the European Community. Professional Issues in Education*, Scottish Academic Press, Edinburgh.

NATFHE (1989) *Teacher Education and Europe*, London.

National Curriculum Council (1990) *A Definition of the European Dimension in the Curriculum*, London.

Neave, Guy (1984) *The EEC and Education*, Stoke-on-Trent, Trentham Books.

SCCC (1993) *Cross Curricular Aspects* (Pack on European Dimension, 5–14 Programme).

SCOTVEC (1993) *Cluster Packs for SCOTVEC European Studies Module*, SCOTVEC, Glasgow.

SFEU (1993) *The Ruberti Plan* (Article in *'Broadcast'* Quarterly Magazine, August 1993), SFEU, Glasgow.

Shell Education Service (1993) *Europe in the School*, Resource Pack, with 'Scottish 5–14' Supplement, Shell UK Ltd, London.

SOED (1993) *Thinking European – Ideas for Integrating a European Dimension into the Curriculum*, SCCC, Dundee.

SOED (1994) *Scottish Education and the European Community Policy, Strategy and Practice*, Scottish Office, Edinburgh.

UK Centre for European Education (1989) *Teacher Training and 1992* (15 March Conference), London, Central Bureau.

UKCEE (1991) Report on Regional Conference Series (May 1990–March 1991) on the European Dimension in Teacher Training.

Council of Europe Publications 1972–1993

(1972) *Unemployment among Young People and its Social Aspects*.

(1974) *Higher Education – Distant Study Systems*. Contemporary with an early stage of the Open University's development.

(1975)*Sociocultural Community Development*.

(1975) *Evaluation of pre-school Education*.

(1976) *Organisation, Content and Methods of Adult Education.*

(1978) *Europe in the Secondary Curriculum* (first teachers' seminar of a series over years). NB: This was at a time when the UK had been a member of the then-called 'EEC' for five years, and when embryonic attempts met in UK schools with apathy and scepticism on the part of teaching staff, hostility on the part of pupils/students.

(1978) *Permanent Education.* A rather 'French-coloured' English title for lifelong or second chance learning.

(1981) *Education for International Understanding.* Teaching about Japan (indeed the SOED is *not* first in the field with its 1997-targeted proposals on the 'world in the curriculum'!).

(1982) *Migrant Culture and Culture of Origin.*

(1982) *Europe in Secondary School Curricula* (cf. 1978 above).

(1982) *Cultural Values and Education in a Multicultural Society.* An interesting reminder that multicultural/antiracist education is itself a topic for European awareness in the curriculum.

(1983) *Migrant Culture in a Changing Society – Multicultural Europe by the year 2000.*

(1984) *Development Education in Primary Schools,* i.e. again on the world (especially Third World) and international dimension.

(1984) *Teaching about USA in Secondary Schools in Western Europe* (cf. the 'beyond Europe' emphasis with the 1981 Japanese example).

(1985) *Conference on Teaching and Learning about Each Other: the USA and Western Europe.*

(1985) *Teaching about Canada in the Secondary Schools of Western Europe* (cf. 1981 Japan and 1984 USA).

(1986) *Final Report of the Project Group on Education and Cultural Development of Migrants.*

(1989) *Guides for Intercultural Teaching Activities.* Note (a) the move towards classroom-based methodology and (b) the rethinking of values behind 'multi'-cultural education at a time when simultaneously within the European Union (and in UK schools) a demand was beginning to be felt that resources have to be provided for teaching about Europe in the classroom.

(1991) *Resolution of the Standing Conference of European Ministers of Education* (i.e. under Council of Europe auspices as opposed to similar but different meetings of those in EU) on 'The European Dimension of Education: Teaching and Curriculum Content'. NB: This coincides with the formulation of official UK government policy on the 'school Eurodimension through the (then) DES.

(1991) *Educating Society, Transmitting Values.* A reminder of the European Dimension of Values Education and School Ethos: *School Links and Exchanges a Vade Mecum* (1992). Nothing new here in a sense, but a 1990s emphasis on aims/objectives, planning, performance indicators, codes of conduct, practical organisation, and audit of existing strengths and weaknesses!

(1992) *The New Europe and Geography Teaching.* Note the significance of the phrase 'new Europe' – an obvious reference at this stage to Union as well as Council change. '*The School in the Local Community: Autonomy and Responsibility*' (1993) – an obvious coverage of the new 1990s 'external market accountability' of the school.

Part II

Economic change and education

Chapter 5

A curriculum for the twenty-first century?

Towards a new basis for overcoming academic/vocational divisions

M. Young

In the 21st century, education will be the foundation of material as well as intellectual progress. The challenge is to develop an education system adequate to the economic and social demands of the next century . . . (and) that innovative capabilities be spread throughout the whole population.

(Finegold *et al.* 1990)

INTRODUCTION

The quotation above from the beginning of the Institute for Public Policy Research (IPPR) report, *A British Baccalauréat*, captures well the aim of this paper, which is to contribute to the development of a post-compulsory curriculum 'adequate to the demands of the next century'. There are two issues here – one quantitative and concerned with levels of participation in post-compulsory education; the other qualitative, concerned with the content and quality of learning. The quantitative issue is whether a curriculum, which was established when at most 20 per cent continued in education after 15, is appropriate when at least 80 per cent are expected to continue until 18 and reach the levels of achievement that are currently reached by only 20 per cent. The qualitative issue is whether expanding participation on the basis of existing curricula, even were it to prove possible, would provide young people with the kind of skills and knowledge that are necessary in the likely circumstances of the twenty-first century. The aim of this paper is to explore those circumstances and their curriculum implications.

Taking the English and Welsh system of post-compulsory education and training has an advantage from the point of view of this analysis as it can be seen as an example of a 'worst case'. It is an extreme example of a highly industrialised country which combines low participation, deep social class divisions and a curriculum which, structurally, has changed little in half a century or more. Paradoxically, it is the backwardness of the system in England and Wales that may provide us with insights that do not arise so directly from the more developed systems on the European continent.

Let us consider, for the purposes of comparison, two cases of countries in which social class divisions are significantly less than in England and Wales. One is of a country (and I suggest that the Netherlands is a good example) which has a divided educational system, but one that is not embedded in a deeply divided social class structure. In such a situation, it is unlikely that the educational divisions will have the social consequences on levels of participation that they do in England and Wales. In other words, considerable expansion of levels of participation and achievement will be possible, even through a divided educational system.

The other case is of a country (and here I suggest Japan as an example) in which, though the academic curriculum is no less dominant than in England and Wales, social selection is deferred until the end of secondary schooling. In Japan secondary education has expanded so that now virtually all students continue until 18 or 19, despite the absence of any substantial changes in the curriculum.

Neither such possibility is open in the English and Welsh case which is characterised by a continuing cleavage between social classes, a deeply divided system of qualifications, and a narrow and elitist academic curriculum. It may be that it is the very impossibility of reforming the existing system in the UK that has led to a more radical analysis emerging and finding support (Finegold *et al.* 1990; Young and Watson 1992). Furthermore, in taking academic/vocational divisions as its focus, it may be that such an analysis will give us some insights into the curriculum that will be necessary for the twenty-first century. It is to this analysis that we now turn.

DIVIDED QUALIFICATIONS, DIVIDED CURRICULUM

The IPPR report, *A British Baccalauréat*, is probably the most comprehensive critique of the UK system (here, as in the report, UK will refer to England and Wales only) of post-compulsory education that has yet appeared. Its analysis is distinguished in two ways from the plethora of other reports on post-compulsory education that have appeared in recent years. The report begins by restating the widely agreed criticisms of the narrowness and exclusiveness of the English academic route (only 30 per cent of the cohort take it, and the vast majority take only two or three subjects), and of the poor quality and lack of availability of 'vocational' alternatives (four times as many places are available for 2-year academic courses as for full time vocational alternatives). However, it goes on to argue that the cause of these weaknesses cannot be found in the inadequacies of the separate routes, but in *the divided system itself*. In other words, they are the direct outcome of having *separate* academic and vocational *tracks* leading to separate *qualifications*. The report's prescriptions for a *unified system of qualifications* that 'will end the division between education and training' follow from this argument. Secondly, the report does not just focus on the structural issue by drawing a distinction between a divided and a unified qualifications system. It also considers the implications of a unified system of qualifications at the level of curriculum practice.

The report begins by reviewing the failure of a variety of attempts in recent years to reform the two (academic and vocational) tracks. Two such reform strategies are worth referring to as they reflect examples of 'borrowing' from other countries. Firstly, there are the attempts to diversify the academic track to give it a broader appeal and make it less exclusive – what might be called *the French solution*. Secondly, there are the efforts to enhance the status and content of vocational programmes along the lines of the German 'dual system'. The report concludes that, in the UK, these reforms have inevitably come up against the barriers of a divided system and in particular its assumption that sometime between the ages of 14 and 16 young people can be divided into two groups – the academically gifted (at least relatively), and the rest.

Attempts to diversify Advanced levels are restricted by two of the most basic features of the English academic track. Firstly, it is explicitly designed for selecting the 'top 20 per cent' and its normative referenced model of assessment is geared to this. A recent indication of this is given by some public reactions to last year's Advanced level results. The modest increase in higher pass grades was used by some not as evidence of the improved level of performance of the system but of falling standards of marking. The second feature of Advanced levels is that they are not a *curriculum framework* capable of reform and modification like the French *Baccalauréat*. They consist of individual subjects clearly separated from each other with their own rules and traditions.

The barriers confronting attempts to enhance the status and content of vocational alternatives are different but no less severe. Quite apart from the proliferation of Examining Boards and the lack of clarity of progression routes to higher levels, they face the fact, regardless of their content, that vocational qualifications are judged by employers and university admission tutors as inferior.

The IPPR Report goes on to identify *six* main weaknesses of the divided system in England and Wales:

- it is based on nineteenth-century assumptions (now being increasingly challenged) that industrial economies require the separation of mental and manual labour and which provides the justification for academic/ vocational divisions;
- it is a system dominated by selection when the problem now and in

the future is to increase both the quantity and quality of participation post-16;

- it is inflexible in that it separates students into different academic and vocational tracks and inhibits movement and transfer between them;
- it inhibits innovative combinations that can link theoretical and applied studies;
- it exaggerates differences between high and low prestige institutions and programmes, reinforces the process of educational stratification, and leads to the particular devaluation of vocational education and training that characterises the system in England and Wales;
- in combination with the unique structure of the labour market which provides incentives for early school leaving, it locks the country into a 'low skill equilibrium' (Finegold and Soskice 1988).

Finally, the main focus of the report's analysis is on the strategic role of qualifications and how a divided system of qualifications is inevitably dominated by its function of *selecting* young people for higher education or employment. A qualification system that is dominated by selection limits both levels of participation and achievement and the potential of innovative curriculum reforms. Meanwhile, the government, in its proposals for what it refers to as a *modern* system of qualifications in the 1991 White Paper, *Education and Training for the 21st Century*, has decided to stick firmly to a divided system, albeit in a reorganised and rationalised form. It is therefore not surprising that it has been the IPPR report's proposal for a *unified qualification system* that has stimulated most interest. The specific recommendations are for:

- a single national Qualifications Authority to replace the separate regulating bodies (the Schools Examinations and Assessment Council and the National Council for Vocational Qualifications) and the separate Examination Boards that currently award academic and vocational qualifications; and
- a single integrated diploma, normally to be achieved at 18, to replace the current alternatives of either a cluster of A level subjects (and in some cases AS (half A) levels) or one of the variety of vocational qualifications that are (at least in theory) available for students at 16.

This focus on the interdependence of the qualifications system and the curriculum is partly a recognition of the neglect of previous analyses of the curriculum. Qualification systems, it argues, are key factors that distinguish between systems of post-compulsory education with high and low levels of participation (Finegold *et al.* 1990: 14), and they differ according to the priority they give to *selection*, the *setting* of standards and the *empowerment* of students.

This analysis, in showing how the English qualification system is characterised by the dominance of its selective function, and its use of exclusion as the main means of maintaining standards, goes a long way to explain the persistence of low participation and achievement. The importance given to qualifications in the report also reflects the dominating role that assessment and in particular terminal examinations have had on post-compulsory education in England and Wales. In the absence of any direct role for the state, Examining Boards, which are mostly either private charities or owned by the Universities, exert considerable power. They are, in effect, the lynchpin of the qualification system and have a stranglehold over the curriculum. The *British Baccalauréat* proposals for a unifed system of qualifications and a single diploma are not, therefore, only about reforming the curriculum. They involve major institutional changes and pose a threat to major vested interests – not only the Examining Boards, but the private secondary schools, one of whose main attractions to parents as an alternative to state schools is their examination successes. In countries where the state has a more direct role in the curriculum, the *separate* significance of qualifications is likely to be much less. There are already indications of this in England and Wales in the compulsory phase of education (5–16) which is now governed by the National Curriculum as well as by the Examination Boards.

As stated at the beginning of the paper, the curriculum issue identified in the IPPR report is not only concerned with how to raise the levels of participation in post-compulsory education. It is also about the content and quality of learning. The report makes clear the inappropriateness of both the traditional academic curriculum of Advanced levels as well as one based on occupationally specific skills for the learning needs of young people who will be adult citizens seeking employment in the twenty-first century. It is therefore the social and economic basis of a new *curriculum* that is the main focus of this paper and to which I now turn.

The *British Baccalauréat* proposals for the curriculum follow from the argument for a unified qualifications system. Instead of having separate academic and vocational courses, the curriculum would consist of a range of theoretical and applied modules within a *single unified* system. Students then would choose from within a number of routes or pathways according to their interests and aspirations and taking account of their previous achievements. However, replacing a curriculum based on separate academic and vocational tracks by one consisting of a unified system of modules is not just a new way of organising the curriculum, like replacing school subjects with interdisciplinary themes. Academic/vocational divisions have their origins both in a culture which associates manual work as of low status and in an economy which was based on the separation of mental and manual labour. A unified curriculum, on the other hand, does not separate the preparation of young people for employment from the wider role of preparing them to become citizens in a democratic society. It follows that such a curriculum implies a very different form of economy to that which has been dominant in industrialised societies since the last century.

In considering the grounds for such a curriculum, and in beginning to specify the form that it might take, it is necessary to examine the economic basis of the separation of academic and vocational education and what indications there are that it may be changing. I am referring to the growing body of research in a number of countries that suggests we are at the end of an industrial era dominated by mass production of goods and services, and that there are signs of a new mode or production emerging, variously characterised as *post-Fordism* and *flexible specialisation* (Piore and Sabel 1984; Mathews 1989). All these writers recognise that the changes they describe are not inevitable and that they are political as much as economic. However, what is important from the point of view of this paper is that they all recognise the emergence of new relations between education and the economy. Whereas under mass production, the economy set severe limits on the development of the education system, flexible specialisation itself depends on prior education and political changes. We are it is argued entering an era of education (or more broadly human resource-led) economic growth, when, as Reich (1991) and others argue, it is *national systems of education and training* rather than *national economies* that will determine the fate of nations.

SPECIALISATION IN THE CURRICULUM: BEYOND THE SPECIALIST/GENERALIST DISTINCTION

Early and narrow specialisation has for long been regarded as a distinctive feature of English post-compulsory education, and is increasingly seen as a major weakness (HMSO 1988). This narrowness is expressed by the fact that the majority of those on the academic track can restrict their studies after 16 to science and mathematics or humanities/languages alone. The International Baccalaureate, Scottish Highers, as well as most post-compulsory curricula on the European continent offer a much broader curriculum with a generalist rather than a subject-specialist focus. A parallel distinction between narrow and broad curricula can be made in describing English and continental vocational qualifications. English vocational qualifications, even when they are not occupationally specific, tend to limit the horizons of students to particular occupational areas, whereas continental models adopt a Baccalaureate-type approach combining occupational and general education.

In the English context, the issue of specialisation has usually been posed in terms of the absence of any kind of framework, such as is provided by the Abitur or Baccalaureat, and trying to compensate for the unique narrowness and exclusivity of single subject Advanced levels.

Virtually every other country has some form of *baccalauréat* or matric. However, this is to concentrate only on the peculiarities of this country and neglects a second dimension of specialisation, namely the separation of knowledge from its application through academic/vocational divisions. Furthermore, concentration on subject and vocational specialisation can all too easily lead to a simplistic view that equates academic/ vocational divisions with specialisation and assumes that a unified curriculum would be generalist and less specialist.

The alternative approach that will be adopted in this paper is to recognise that the pressure to shift away from subject and vocational specialisation arises from deeper changes in the *form of specialisation*, not just as it appears in the curriculum, but in the wider division of labour and occupational structure of society. The *British Baccalauréat* proposals for a unifed curriculum are not a trend away from specialisation, but a move towards more integrative *forms of specialisation* which are not based on either insulated subject divisions or academic/vocational divisions. In curricular terms this suggests the possibility of developing new connective skills and understanding and the ability to innovate and to apply and use learning in different contexts. In *The Work of Nations* Reich refers to such knowledge as *symbolic analysis* and, from a slightly different perspective, Zuboff in *In the Age of the Smart Machine* refers to *intellective skills*. Such curricular priorities are frequently expressed by leading edge companies (e.g. British Telecom 1992). Before exploring these possibilities for a *curriculum of the future*, it is necessary to consider why specialisation is such a crucial issue in post-compulsory education at this time.

SPECIALISATION AS AN INTEGRAL ASPECT OF MODERN ECONOMIES

A high level of specialisation is an integral aspect of the state and economies of modern societies, and it is a crucial reason why such societies have been so vastly more productive than those that they replaced. The first substantial increase in specialisation occurred with the emergence of the modern state in the last decades of the nineteenth century. It developed further through the expansion of industrial economies in the twentieth century with the growth of mass production. As Piore and Sabel (1984) put it:

> the extensive division of labour in mass production (was characterised by) both the break between conception and execution of tasks and the highly specialised character of almost all production jobs.

The consequences for the newly emerging system of mass education were twofold. Curricular specialisation was fuelled by the rapid development of knowledge expressed in the growth of and divisions between new subjects and vocational areas. At the same time school-based 'education' and work based 'training' became increasingly separate as the development of mass production:

> made it possible (for the system of production) to rely on two separate institutions for training employees: the formal education system and the firm itself. The formal education system . . . providing abstract knowledge of products and production . . . the firm (providing) training for the fraction of the workforce that needs skills . . .
>
> (Piore and Sabel 1984)

Thus the main features of what will be referred to as *divisive specialisation* were established – the divisions between academic subjects and the separation of education and training.

MASS PRODUCTION AND THE DEVELOPMENT OF DIVISIVE SPECIALISATION

The correspondence between education and the economy has always been somewhat tenuous. Education is shaped by many historical mediating influences other than the economy or its leading productive processes. The parallels that can be drawn between economic organisations and the curriculum in the era of mass production, may relate less to the direct influence of the economy and more to how the economy and the education system have themselves been shaped by different cultural and political histories (Green 1991).

In England and Wales the new social divisions between managers (nearly always owners at this time) and factory workers emerged in the early nineteenth century in an environment still culturally and politically dominated by the feudal aristocracy and, in the new factories, by the traditional artisans who controlled the tools and new machines. The education of craftsmen took place almost entirely within the apprenticeship system and developed separately from the growth of mass elementary education. Thus the terms were set for the early and sharp separation between academic study and vocational education which was to become the basis for the uniquely *divisive* form of specialisation that was to emerge in England and Wales.

Relations between the expanding industry and services in the late nineteenth and early twentieth centuries and the education system were mediated by a divided qualifications system consisting of two largely separate tracks: an academic track dominated by subject-specialisation and terminal examinations and an occupationally specific vocational track, until recently consisting of work-based apprenticeships. Such a selective system also ensured that large sections of the population received only elementary education and had no access to qualifications of any kind.

It was not until the 1980s that a British government decided to rationalise vocational qualifications and attempt to extend them to the majority of the working population. The method it has adopted has been through the precise specification of job competences. This is somewhat ironic, given that it is occurring at a time when systems of production based on such a rigid specification of jobs are increasingly being questioned as the continuing basis for productivity. In the 1990s the system of qualifications and curricula for post-compulsory education in the UK can be seen as at a point of contradiction. There are (largely political) forces committed to maintaining inherited divisions with their powerful selective and restrictive functions, and there are the growing demands (largely industrial and professional) for a broader curriculum as the basis for educational expansion. Increasingly, the latter recognise that such expansion is not possible within a divided system.

These contradictions do not just express the problems of expansion and how a curriculum dominated by selection can be geared to increases in participation. They also raise the question, mentioned earlier in this paper, as to whether a divided curriculum can deliver the kind of skills and knowledge that are going to be needed if the country is to be competitive in the economic climate of the twenty-first century. In order to gain some insight into what the new combinations of skills and knowledge might be it is necessary to review briefly the arguments about current economic changes and how they are expressed in changes in the form of specialisation. It will then be possible to consider their implications for the curriculum in more detail.

NEW CONCEPTS OF SPECIALISATION IN THE ECONOMY AND EDUCATION

The idea that we are in at the beginning of a new post-Fordist era is much contested and its possible forms and destinations are far from clear. Different analyses give different emphasis to cultural and economic changes. This chapter is primarily concerned with the latter, in particular with changes in the organisation of work and the structure of occupations. The emergence in the economies of advanced capitalist countries of what has been termed 'post-Fordism' has been widely commented on. 'Post-Fordism' is a rather loose, albeit evocative, term which refers to the appearance of a collection of industrial innovations, such as flexible specialised production, new uses of information-based technologies, flatter management structures, and the new emphasis upon teamwork. Mathews *et al.* (1988) describe the changes in this way:

The industrial system that has dominated the twentieth century – a system based upon mass production, mass consumption, Taylorised fragmentation of work and deskilling – is visibly dying, and creating economic chaos as it is forced from the historical stage. A new industrial system is being born – based upon technologies of microelectronics and new materials, intelligent production, human-centred organisation, worker responsibility and multi-skilling. The *forms of specialisation* within the economy are in fact changing. They are reversing the concept of mass production and introducing the process of 'flexible specialisation'.

Flexible specialisation involves the combination of general purpose capital equipment and skilled, adaptable workers to produce a wide and changing range of semi-customised goods. Manufacturing flexibility and market responsiveness go hand in hand, allowing companies to tailor their output to sales trends and carve out new market niches by adapting products to customer needs.

The actual extent of such developments and their likely extension in particular countries is open to question, as are their social consequences. What is not in doubt is that changes from a system of mass production to one based on flexible specialisation makes quite new intellectual demands on employees at all levels. The social, intellectual and essentially *educational* basis of the new forces of production are well recognised by Castells (1989) when he states that it is the

> structurally determined *capacity of labour* to process information and *generate knowledge* that is the material basis of productivity and the (modern) source of economic growth. Yet this symbolic capacity of labour is not an individual attribute. Labour has to be formed, educated . . . etc.

> . . . In addition . . . social institutions . . . and the overall structure of society . . . will be key elements in fostering or stalling the new . . . productive forces. The more a society facilitates the exchange of information flows, the decentralised generation and distribution of information, the greater will be its collective symbolic capacity.

But the argument can be taken further. A high-participation education system linked to a high-skill system of production would require a curriculum which was congruent with it. In other words, it too must exhibit features of flexible specialisation. Hickox and Moore (1991) make the point that it may only be in the 'post-Fordist' phase, with the vastly increased pressures on industrial capitalism, that we can begin to talk with any realism about a correspondence between education and the economy. They see managers of the future having to learn that their only new sources of productivity are the potential intellectual capacities of their employees.

The new forms of work organisation associated with flexible specialisation set quite new criteria for the curriculum. Instead of the traditional screening role of academic/vocational divisions, the emphasis would be on new and innovative kinds of connectiveness between knowledge areas and different forms of specialised study interwoven with a generic core of knowledge, skills and processes. It is debatable whether such criteria, despite their origins in the demands of new occupations, should be described as a modern version of general education or a form of vocational education.

In curriculum terms there are two key issues: *flexibility* (the opportunity to make choices and combine different kinds of learning in new ways) and *coherence* (the sense of clarity that students need in order to be clear about their educational purposes and where a particular course of study (or cluster of modules) will lead to. In the *British Baccalauréat* we concluded that this combination of flexibility and coherence could be achieved through a modular curriculum, provided there were also a clear set of pathways or routes for students to identify with. This model of the curriculum has some parallels with new forms of network organisation in which teams of employees are given maximum autonomy within a clear set of overarching purposes (Morgan 1989) and in some recent educational developments (Young 1993).

It is not surprising that the educational implications of this new era have been interpreted as being 'anti-specialisation' – particularly with the recent emphasis upon generic problem-solving and the dissolution of curriculum barriers (Brown and Lauder 1991). However, as was mentioned earlier, the change is not away from specialisation, but towards new forms that can (at least in principle) free specialisation from its association with selection and insulation. *The separation of specialisation from its association with divisions and the insulation of subject areas is the key basis for distinguishing between a divided curriculum or 'curriculum of the past' and a 'curriculum of the future'.* This is the key point of this chapter, and one that I will come back to.

The issue of specialisation is central to whether changes in industrial economies can be the basis for a new curriculum. The productivity of industrial capitalism up to the middle of this century depended on what is termed here *divisive specialisation* – or increasing the division between mental and manual labour as the specialist engineers and managers designed systems of production which depended less and less on the skills and knowledge of the majority of employees (Noble 1979). This system was the most productive the world had ever known and, as knowledge grew, specialisation took the form of the principles of scientific management being applied to more and more areas of manufacturing, service and other sectors. It is this system of production and its dominant form of divisive specialisation that is under challenge from systems that depend on maximising the innovative contribution of all employees (Prospect Centre 1991/National Education Commission 1992). The origins of this change are twofold: the 'globalisation' of economies and the massive increase in the potential for competition that goes with it, and the transformative potential of information-based technologies.

A form of work organisation which seeks to maximise the intellectual potential of all employees cannot rely on a curriculum that limits itself to providing a small proportion of the population with highly specialist knowledge, while, at the same time, disregarding the level of performance of the majority. Again, Piore and Sabel (1984) make the point clearly when they state that in production based on flexible specialisation:

> designers must be so broadly qualified that they can envision product and production together (something not learnt by) book learning alone

and:

> production workers must be so broadly skilled . . . to be able to collaborate with designers to solve the problems that inevitably arise in production.

In other words, specialisation has to become part of another paradigm of what is elsewhere referred to as *connective* knowledge and skills, and the increased scope for choice, personal flexibility and high performance that enables the highest possible number of people to innovate in a constantly changing world. This 'flexible' or 'connective specialisation' contrasts sharply with the 'divisive specialisation' that underpins academic/vocational divisions. Before exploring further the idea of *flexible (or connective) specialisation* as a curricular concept, it is necessary to discuss the curricular implications of the dominance of *divisive specialisation*.

THE LANGUAGE OF DIVISIVE SPECIALISATION AND ITS CURRICULAR IMPLICATIONS

One consequence of inheriting a deeply divided system in which academic and vocational tracks are so embedded in the institutional and social structure is the absence of any embracing concepts to describe knowledge and skill development. Without such concepts it becomes difficult to extend the idea of flexible specialisation in curriculum terms. The comparison between the vocabulary and concepts available in English with the potential of the French terms 'formation' and 'qualification' and the German term 'Bildung' are very striking. In English, most of the terms and concepts which we have for discussing education and training, though never precisely defined, have limiting and often highly divisive meanings. They were established in the discourse and institutionalised in the last part of the nineteenth century but remain extremely powerful. It is possible to list some examples as follows:

knowledge – which usually refers to academic subjects;
science – which, unlike in German, refers to the natural sciences;
technical – in relation to education is invariably associated with manual work and low status occupations;
academic – meaning detached (but with high prestige);
vocational – defined as non-academic and relating to specific occupations;
skills – associated with the manual activities of craftsmen;
competences – defined in terms of observable performances.

This is the vocabulary of a deeply divided system. It is also the vocabulary of a society deeply rooted in its past, with limited intellectual resources to change or even to come to terms with the present let alone the future.

A further consequence of the power of academic/vocational divisions as a dominant form of specialisation in the United Kingdom is the extent to which rigour and standards, which are associated with the highly selective Advanced levels, have been separated from both personal and social education and preparation for future employment (which then get associated in curriculum terms with academic 'failure'). This association of rigour with academic subjects and their forms of assessment is well exemplified by the current attempts to give General National Vocational Qualifications parity of esteem with A levels through requiring externally set and marked tests. A curriculum of the future has to bring together the aims of rigour, relevance and personal development, which appear so irretrievably separate in a divided curriculum.

Although it is difficult to find examples of *flexible specialisation* in this country, this does not mean that the process of specialisation, albeit within the divisive form, is not changing. I will describe these changes in terms of the distinction between *sectional* and *corporate* forms of *divisive* specialisation. They refer to horizontal and vertical developments within and between occupational groups. I shall use these forms of divisive specialisation to contrast with the possibilities of *flexible* (or *connective*) specialisation.[1]

FORMS OF SPECIALISATION AND THEIR CURRICULUM IMPLICATIONS

The *sectional form of divisive specialisation* refers to how, in response to changing circumstances, members of professions and groups of craftsmen within an occupational area traditionally identify with their fellow professionals or craftsmen and form associations (and trade unions). In curriculum terms it describes the associations of academic or vocational subject specialists, many of which were established at the turn of the century. Exaggerated subject specialisation is characteristic of the divided curriculum and is particularly strong in England where it has been described by Bernstein (1971) in terms of the concepts 'strong classification' and 'collection code'.

The curricular priority which characterises the *sectional form of* divisive specialisation is an exclusive concentration on subject-specific content. However, this is not an inevitable feature of the behaviour of subject specialists or craft teachers. It refers only to their historically insulated forms of organisation in a divided curriculum. In the context of the much broader notion of educational purposes associated with what is elsewhere described as a 'curriculum for the future', identification with subjects and occupational areas can become the basis for developing teams of *flexible* (or *connective*) specialists (Spours and Young 1991)

Corporate specialisation is illustrated by a number of developments that can be found in both the economy and in education that are expressions of limited vertical integration. In industry it refers to how different specialists (both craft and professional) and also employees and senior managers can, in the face of external threats (e.g. global or even national competition), identify common purposes beyond their 'sectional' interests. It is much more frequently in evidence in countries other than the UK, as is indicated by the frequent reference to examples of co-determination between unions and employers in Sweden and Germany. This is partly because in the past in the UK employer/union relationships were so often adversarial. More recently, it reflects the extent to which such relationships have been actively discouraged by government.

The two main curriculum priorities of the *corporate* form of specialisation are the broad notions of integrating natural and social sciences which bring groupings of subject specialists together, and the idea of transferable (or 'core') skills which transcends and complements occupationally specific or subject-based knowledge. The former developments have, as discussed earlier, been limited by government determination to maintain the selective function of Advanced levels as single separate subjects. The idea of core skills has been widely supported by business and industrial as well as educational interests (CBI 1989, 1993) and has been a basis for collaboration across the education/industry divide. As with forms of subject integration, the implementation of core skills has been profoundly limited by the divided system of qualifications (Spours and Young 1991).

The *corporate* form of divisive specialisation can be seen to represent a transitional and even contradictory phase of divisive specialisation. It is transitional in the sense that its curricular priorities have emphasised breadth and the idea of 'core skills' in ways which go beyond the traditional forms of divisive specialisation. It is contradictory to the extent that the broad notion of skills that is being sought after in potential employees by leading edge companies (British Telecom 1992) is very different from the narrowly defined job specific concept of a vocational qualification or even the numeracy and literacy that employers are supposed to want.

In developing their concept of *flexible specialisation*, Piore and Sabel (1984) write about 'envisioning product and production together'. In relation to the curriculum. I prefer the term *connective specialisation*, as it refers explicitly to the interdependence of different specialists and contrasts with the insularity of traditional subject specialists. It refers to the importance of specialists, whether physicists, designers or guidance staff (to take only three examples) sharing an overall sense of the relationship between their specialisation and the whole curriculum. In other words, whereas divisive specialists see the curriculum from the point of view of their subjects, connective specialists see their subjects from the point of view of the curriculum.

In the sense used here, connective specialisation is concerned with the links between combinations of knowledge and skills in the curriculum and wider democratic and social goals. At the individual level it refers to the need for an understanding of the social, cultural, political and economic implications of any knowledge or skill in its context, and how, through such a concept of education, an individual can learn both specific skills and knowledge and the capacity to take initiatives, whatever their specific occupation or position.

In the context of such a deeply divided curriculum as in the UK, it is not surprising that it is difficult to find evidence of connective *specialisation* as a curriculum reality. As a curriculum concept it points to the interdependence of the content, processes and organisation (Young and Spours 1992). As a definition of educational purposes it aims to transcend the traditional dichotomy of 'the educated person' and 'the competent employee' which define the purposes of the two tracks of a divided curriculum. One example of an attempt at a more elaborate definition of connective specialisation is that it should include

> fundamental elements based upon new needs of an age of science, technology and innovation including maths, science, technological studies so that an education system produces . . .

and aims to encourage

> well-rounded, technologically literate citizens who have some insight into the processes of scientific and technological development, and the capacity and will to keep returning to the system to sharpen and broaden their skills and understanding.
>
> (Mathews *et al.* 1988)

To these themes might be added:

- economic, political and sociological understanding as part of the preparation for active and democratic citizenship;
- the development of modern languages and understanding as tools for a new internationalism;
- aesthetic and cultural understanding as a means of becoming 'competent cultural practitioners'.

How connective specialisation will be expressed concretely will vary from country to country and depend on historical circumstances. In England, where divisive specialisation remains dominant, it is likely to be expressed in a variety of local attempts to create *integrating frameworks* and networks (Spours 1992; Young 1993). They may take the form of credit frameworks to assist progression and student transfer, new forms of compact between schools and colleges of higher education, or groups of teachers writing modules or developing learning resources within shared curriculum purposes. In each case they represent attempts to express the curriculum aims of *connective specialisation* within and between institutions when such changes are limited by the constraints of a divided qualification system. There are signs that industrial interests, at least as reflected in the Confederation of British Industry (CBI 1993) are going beyond their traditional positions and arguing for overarching qualifications and credit transfer.

SUMMARY AND CONCLUSIONS – A CURRICULUM FOR THE FUTURE?

The aim of this chapter has been to examine analyses of changes in work organisation and the economy and to suggest that they point to a new basis for overcoming the academic/vocational divisions that dominate the post-compulsory curriculum in England and Wales. Starting from the narrow and exclusive form of curriculum specialisation found in England and Wales, the focus of the analysis has been on the theme of specialisation and the interdependence of changes in the *forms of specialisation* in the economy and the curriculum.

The post-compulsory curriculum in the UK is analysed in terms of the concepts *divisive* and *flexible (or connective) specialisation*. The major features of *divisive specialisation* as found in England and Wales are identified as:

- sharp academic/vocational divisions;
- insulated subjects;
- absence of any concept of the curriculum as a whole.

Two forms of divisive specialisation, the *sectional* and the *corporate*, are distinguished. These concepts are used to point to current changes in post-compulsory education in the UK.

Finally, it is argued that current economic changes could provide the basis for a very different form of *flexible (or connective) specialisation* in work organisation and in a curriculum for the future. Such a curriculum, it is suggested, would need to build on and give specificity to the principles of the IPPR's *British Baccalauréat* of:

- breadth and flexibility;
- connections between both core and specialist studies and general (academic) and applied (vocational) studies;
- opportunities for progression and credit transfer;
- a clear sense of the purpose of the curriculum as a whole.

At the end of their book, Piore and Sabel (1984) state that whether societies of the future will be based on mass production or flexible specialisation will 'depend in part on the capacity of nations and social classes to envision the future that they want'. This chapter can be seen as an extension of their argument by proposing that if this country is to have an economy based on flexible specialisation it has to develop a curriculum that is designed for that future. In the UK, at least prior to April 1992 and the fourth consecutive Conservative Party General Election victory, a unified curriculum along the lines of the IPPR's *British Baccalauréat* had begun to look more and more like the future (Young and Watson 1992). With such a future now looking very distant we need to remember, as Gramsci wrote, that 'what "ought to be" is concrete ... it alone is history in the making and philosophy in the making, it alone is politics'.

NOTE

1 This distinction between three forms of specialisation is indebted to Gramsci's idea of 'levels of consciousness'. The link between levels of consciousness and forms of specialisation owes much to Sassoon's (1988) interpretation of Gramsci's ideas.

REFERENCES

Bernstein, B. (1971) *Class, Codes and Control*, London: Routledge.
British Telecom (1992) *Matching Skills: Report of a Collaborative Project*, London: BT.
Brown, P. and Lauder, H. (1991) (eds) *Education and Economic Survival: From Fordism to Post-Fordism*, London: Routledge.
Castells, M. (1989) *The Informational City*, Oxford: Blackwell.
Confederation of British Industry (1989) *Towards a Skills Revolution*, London: CBI.
Finegold, D. and Soskice, D. (1988) The Failure of Training in Britain, in G. Esland (ed.) *Education Training and Employment*, Milton Keynes: Open University Press.

Finegold, D., Keep, E., Miliband, D., Raffe, D., Spours, K. and Young, M. (1990) *A British Baccalauréat: Ending the Divisions Between Education and Training*, London: Institute for Public Policy Research.

Gleeson, D. (ed.) (1991) *Training and Its Alternatives*, Milton Keynes: Open University Press.

Green, A. (1991) *The Reform of Post-16 Education and Training*, Post-16 Education Centre Working Paper No. 11, London: Institute of Education, University of London.

Department for Education (1991) *Education and Training for the 21st Century*, London: HMSO.

Her Majesty's Stationery Office (1988) *Advancing A Levels*, Report of the Committee chaired by Professor Higginson, London: HMSO.

Hickox, M. and Moore, R. (1991) 'Post-Fordism and education', in P. Brown and H. Lauder (1991).

Mathews, J. (1989) *Tools for Change: New Technology and the Democratisation of Work*, Sydney, Australia: Pluto Press.

Mathews, J., Hall, G. and Smith, H. (1988) 'Towards flexible skill formation and technological literacy: challenges facing the education system', *Economic and Industrial Democracy*, 9(4).

Morgan, G. (1989) *Images of Organisation*, London: Sage.

National Education Commission (1992) *Towards a Well Qualified Workforce*, London: NEC.

Noble, D. (1979) Social choice in machine design: the case of numerically controlled machine tools, in A. Zimbalist, *Case Studies on the Labour Process*, New York and London: Monthly Review Press.

Piore, D. and Sabel, C. (1984) *The Second Industrial Divide*, New York: Basic Books.

Prospect Centre (1992) *Growing an Innovative Workforce*, Kingston: Prospect Centre.

Reich, R. (1991) *The Work of Nations*, London: Simon & Schuster.

Royal Society (1991) *Beyond GCSE*, London: Royal Society.

Sassoon, A. (1988) *Gramsci's Politics*, London: Hutchinson.

Spours, K. (1992) *Recent Developments in Qualifications at 14+*, Post-16 Education Centre Working Paper, London: Institute of Education, University of London.

Spours, K. and Young, M. (1991) 'Beyond Vocationalism', in Gleeson (1991).

Young, M. and Spours, K. (1992) *A Curriculum for the Future*, Post-16 Education Centre Discussion Paper, London: Institute of Education, University of London.

Young, M. (1993) 'Modularisation and the Outcomes Approach: Towards a Strategy for a Curriculum of the Future', in J. Burke (ed.) *Outcomes and the Curriculum*, London: Falmer.

Young, M. and Watson, K. (1992) *Beyond the White Paper: The Case for a Unified System at 16+*, Post-16 Education Centre Discussion Paper, London: Institute of Education, University of London.

Zuboff, S. (1988) *In the Age of the Smart Machine*, London: Heinemann.

Chapter 6

Flexible specialization, work organization and skills

Approaching the 'second industrial divide'

A.J. Phillimore

It is becoming commonplace to argue that the advanced industrialized countries are currently living in an era of great transformation. Whether it be the onset of 'The Third Wave', the 'Farewell to the Working Class', or the 'End of Organized Capitalism', the post-1945 world of cheap energy US-dominated trade and Keynesian demand management is recognized as having ended (Toffler 1980; Gorz 1982; Lash and Urry 1987). Its symptoms are high and persistent unemployment, a rapidly changing balance of international economic power, and a political and economic convergence by governments of East and West alike towards more reliance on market forces, less government intervention and the widespread adoption of new, microelectronics-based technology.

It was into this debate that Piore and Sabel introduced their own 'era of transformation' book, *The Second Industrial Divide*. They argue that the present deterioration in economic performance results from the limits of the model of industrial development that is founded on mass production: the use of special-purpose (product-specific) machines and of semi-skilled workers to produce standardized goods (Piore and Sabel 1984). The advanced industrial economies now face a choice between building on the organization of mass production, or shifting to an era based on flexible specialization (FS). This epochal redefinition of markets, technologies and industrial hierarchies' (Sabel 1982) will have different implications for industries, regions, national economies, consumers and workers, depending upon what choices are made, when, and by whom.

Piore and Sabel's book is important for a number of reasons. First, it summarized a great deal of material that had been gathered about the renaissance of the small firm, the entrepreneur, and the growing 'industrial districts' based on these successful firms. Second, it linked changes at the level of production (which had already been noted in many European analyses under the rubric of neo-Fordism (Blackburn *et al.* 1985; Coriat 1981), with the macro-economic and global crises and shifts of power. Third, and perhaps most importantly, it sounded a distinctly optimistic tone: the future was not determined; choices did exist. Politics reassumed a central role, with the recognition that particular technologies, the organization of production and even whole technology systems, were not 'given', but *socially* determined and, in the present era, 'up for grabs'.

This optimistic tone was perhaps the primary cause of the controversy which the book aroused at all points on the political spectrum. On the positive side, the book was seen as a 'tour de force' (Webber 1985). FS was seen as a 'third wave' for the Left between monetarism and Keynesianism (Murray 1985), and as a possible avenue of advance for small and Third World countries who could build upon their craft traditions through the judicious use of new technology (Poon 1988). On the negative side, Piore and Sabel were seen as 'incurably romantic' (Williams *et al.* 1988); going from one nostalgia (the mass-production worker) to another (the craft worker) (Block 1985); FS was seen to 'spell a return to the worst excesses of industrial capitalism', and to be 'bad news for the trade unions' and the labour movement in general (Murray 1987).

The Second Industrial Divide covers a vast area, ranging from the global economic regulatory system to shop-floor industrial relations. The focus of this article will be more narrow in scope. It will concentrate on the changes occurring at the level of production, and in particular on the application and implications of FS on the organization of work and on the labour force. This concentration on production is, however, crucial to Piore and Sabel's thesis, for their basic starting point is that changes at the level of production are the primary determinants of the current economic crisis at all levels. As one set of critics caustically points out, 'seldom in the history of intellectual endeavour, can so much have been built on the foundation of one opposition' – that is, the opposition between mass production (or Fordism) and FS (neo-Fordism) (Williams *et al.* 1987).

THE CONCEPT OF FLEXIBLE SPECIALIZATION

Even confined to the level of production, FS is an elusive, if not elastic, concept, with no single defining feature. To some, the technology used in production is the key; to others, it is the smaller size of the production unit, or of the production run. Still other analysts focus on the labour requirements (both in terms of skills and of numbers), while some see innovatory management as most important. In essence, however, FS is a relative concept, defined in relation to another, different type of production system – mass production, or Fordism. Table 6.1 summarizes ten of the principal differences between Fordism and FS.

According to Piore and Sabel, the shift from mass production to FS arose from two main factors. The first was the increasing labour unrest of the late 1960s and early 1970s. This encouraged firms to decentralize

Table 6.1 Fordism and flexible specialization (FS) compared

1 Production concept	Mass production; economies through fixed capital and labour productivity within the production process	FS/flexible automation; economies through working capital productivity between production processes and in distribution
2 Technology	Machines purpose-built and dedicated; R&D functionally separate and discontinuous	General-purpose and adaptable machinery; importance of design
3 Products	Limited range of standardized products	Specialization, product variety; 'niche' markets
4 Inputs	Materials and energy-intensive	Materials and energy-saving; information-intensive
5 Work process and skills	Fragmented and standardized tasks; strict division between mental and manual labour; semi-skilled workers	Open-ended tasks/ closer integration of manual and mental tasks/core of multi-skilled workers linked to subcontract and semi-skilled labour
6 Payment system	Rate for the job; formalized pay bargaining	Payment for person; rising income for skilled core; more informal wage settlement
7 Organization and management	Managerial hierarchies; centralization; multi-divisional corporation	Flatter hierarchies; centralized information and planning systems, decentralized production, networks, franchising, subcontracting
8 Markets and customers	Domination of manufacturers over retailers, producers over users; one-way relations/mass advertising	Domination of retailing/ two-way relations between customer and manufacturer; firm rather than product advertising
9 Suppliers	Arm's length/stocks held 'just in case'	Two-way, relations/ stocks arrive 'just in time'
10 Competitive strategy	Compete by full capacity utilization and cost-cutting; tends to over production, stockpiling, mark downs	Compete by innovation; respond to falling market through diversification, innovation sub-contracting or lay-off

their production processes, through 'splitting up' their in-house production to geographically dispersed plants, and through 'putting out' aspects of production to subcontractors. This strategy in turn led to the development of a significant number of small, technologically advanced firms, often founded by skilled workers originally displaced from the large firm.

The second factor was the changing nature of market demand. As the market for standardized, mass-produced goods became saturated in the 1960s, two developments opened the way to FS. First, increased competition (both from other advanced countries and from the newly industrialized countries) forced large firms to cut costs (especially labour and fixed capital costs – with the splitting-up and putting-out strategies noted above). Second, consumers' tastes became more diverse as 'basic' needs were increasingly satisfied, and the resulting market differentiation enabled many 'First World' producers to profitably enter 'market niches' for low-volume, high-quality goods for which mass production was unsuited and for which high-wage, high-skill labour was an asset rather than a cost.

In addition to these two factors, the development of new technology – such as computer-aided design (CAD), computer-aided manufacture (CAM), computer numerical control (CNC), etc. – enabled small firms to produce efficiently in competition with large firms. Also, new technology enabled the integration of production, distribution and marketing to an extent previously unattainable. This was the basis of Benetton's success, for example. Finally, the success of Japanese producers in world markets, with their use of production methods such as just-in-time, total quality control, flexible work patterns and extensive use of subcontractors provided an example of a new form of manufacturing 'best practice' to which other firms should strive.

Three views about FS

There are a number of different views about the overall importance and 'progressiveness' of FS. For convenience, we can distinguish between three schools of thought: the optimists, the pessimists and the sceptics.

The 'optimists' regard FS as the new paradigm of production, which contains positive features for capital and labour (Brodner 1987; Brusco 1982; Friedman 1983; Hirschhorn 1987; Murray 1985; Piore and Sabel 1984; Sorge and Streeck 1988; Wobbe 1987; Wickens 1987). Many of them draw upon the experience of the clothing and engineering sectors in the so-called 'Third Italy', where regional clusters of small, innovative firms have been very successful in terms of increased growth, export performance, income and employment by the use of advanced computer technology in production, distribution and marketing. The optimists also include advocates of Japanese-style production methods and industrial relations (especially in vehicle manufacturing – the archetypal Fordist industry), with their emphasis on quality, low inventories, multi-skilling, etc.

The optimists see FS as challenging mass production, by providing opportunities for small companies (and regions based on clusters of such small firms, the so-called 'industrial districts') to compete with the large mass-production firms, and by allowing large firms to decentralize their operations and incorporate more skill, quality and variety into their organization of production so as to compete more effectively against low-wage mass producers in the Third World. They also consider 'niche' production as being of some potential to minority consumer groups, whose needs were neglected by the mass producers.

The 'pessimists' to a great extent share the views of the optimists about the significance of FS's challenge to Fordist production methods (Gough 1986; Holloway 1987; Hyman 1988; Mitler 1986; Murray 1987; Sayer 1986). However, by contrast, they regard the development with much more trepidation. Aware of its origins in the industrial relations struggles of the late 1960s, they see FS as having disproportionate benefits for capital, by dividing labour and intensifying the labour process more thoroughly than mass production ever did. They also doubt that small, innovative firms such as those highlighted by studies of the 'Third Italy' will necessarily be the dominant feature of an era of flexible production. Much more typical, they argue, are the dependent subcontractors, or homeworkers – 'sweatshop' labour with poor working conditions and low job security. In addition, the minority-tastes which FS caters to are likely to be luxury tastes, ignoring the needs of the majority.

The 'sceptics' doubt the significance of FS at all (Pollert 1988; Williams et al. 1987; Wood 1988). Some argue that, quantitatively, mass production is still very much more important than FS, which is at present confined to relatively few regions and industries. Also, mass production is much more 'flexible' than critics give it credit for – market segmentation and product choice in the 'Mature' consumer goods industries has increased markedly since the 1950s, under a mass-production regime. Others argue that the spread of Fordism itself has been exaggerated, and that FS is in fact more common in those sectors which were resistant to Fordism, such as batch engineering. Still others argue that the whole debate misses the point (Block 1985; Kuttner 1985). FS enthusiasts are manufacturing enthusiasts – but manufacturing is declining in significance and thus FS is not the wave of the future. However, although this concentration on manufacturing is true of some FS proponents, such as Piore and Sabel, it is not exclusively so. Poon, for example, in her work on the tourism sector, has argued that FS may in fact be even *more* applicable to services (as mass-production techniques are less prevalent there) (Poon 1988).

These schools of thought are by no means exclusive, of course. Many of the pessimists agree with the points raised by the sceptics – but they are still more alarmed by the threat of FS to organized labour. Many of the optimists are in fact 'guarded optimists', who recognize the negative potentialities of FS, especially if government support for labour is not forthcoming (Murray 1985). Piore and Sabel also emphasize the need for such support. And almost all optimists note that FS will flourish much better with growing market demand, to make the transition from mass production easier and to avoid competition between FS firms being based on cutting costs (and therefore wages), rather than on innovation (Piore and Sabel 1984; Brusco 1982). Many FS advocates are also coming to terms with some of the sceptics' arguments about the continued resilience of mass production. FS is increasingly regarded as 'a modifying factor for mass production which develops from the old, very conventional Ford style . . . into a new type that produces a range of high-quality products' (Wobbe 1987).

FS, WORK ORGANIZATION AND SKILLS

Work organization and skills are of special importance to the whole debate surrounding FS, for a number of reasons. First, the defining characteristic of mass production is seen by most as the hierarchically organized production process, with its extensive division of labour into fragmented and standardized tasks requiring a minimum of skills. FS, if it is a true alternative paradigm to mass production, should differ from it in this respect at least. Second, the different perceptions of the implications of FS for labour constitute the major dividing line between the optimists and the pessimists in their attitude towards FS.

For the optimists, FS offers an opportunity to reclaim the craft traditions of a bygone age. New technology and changed market conditions now enable the craft paradigm to reassert itself, offering more control over the labour process for workers, a renewed emphasis on skills, more job security, less alienation and better working conditions. For the pessimists, FS represents an intensification of work, further divisions of the workforce (and consequent problems for unions) and at best a neutral effect on workers' skills. Whether FS is seen positively or negatively, the issues of work organization and skills have major policy implications for government.

Before discussing these policy issues, the evidence from a number of industry sectors influenced by FS will be presented. At the outset, it should be recognized that the empirical evidence on the skill implications of FS is not yet very substantial. Most studies have either simply asserted the importance of skilled labour to FS, or instead concentrated on the effects of FS on unionization, work conditions, labour unity or left political strategy rather than on skills *per se*.

Clothing and textiles

Until recently, the clothing and textiles industry was considered to be 'the most mature of the mature industries' (Piore and Sabel 1984). Low-wage Third producers had increasingly outcompeted advanced industrial countries in producing low-cost, mass-produced garments for world markets. Any substantial industry left in the advanced industrial countries was either heavily protected through tariffs or quotas, or resembled Third World countries with sweatshop labour and low productivity. In short, it was the archetypal 'sunset' industry.

The success of the Benetton group (and of the Emilia-Romagna region of Italy in general), and of similarly organized companies in Britain such as Burton, Next and Richard, has altered this perception markedly (Murray 1985). High-quality innovative design and a new marketing and distribution system which reduces inventories to a minimum has enabled 'First World' producers to compete more effectively and to regain much of their lost market share. The 'Emilian model' is regarded as a prime example of an FS success story – high growth rates, high exports, low unemployment, a disproportionately high number of small firms, a low degree of vertical integration between firms, modern technology reliance on quality, customized goods produced in short series, etc. (Brusco 1982).

Assessments of the implications of this model for work organization and skills are generally enthusiastic. Brusco (1984), for example, considers it a certitude that this system is rich in opportunities for all, everyone *is* ultimately the 'master of his own fate'. Solinas (1982), though less rapturous, still considers that 'good jobs' predominate.

The evidence, however, is less clear cut. Both Brusco and Solinas acknowledge the existence of substantially different types of firms and conditions of work. Firms in the 'primary' sector – the vertically integrated, large batch producers – differ substantially from those in the 'secondary' sector – the small firms with small batch production. The former tend to be heavily unionized, to respect labour laws, to have stable employment, high wages, etc. They have a variety of skilled and unskilled workers.

The secondary sector is much less unionized, labour laws are commonly flouted (or do not apply) and it is much more flexible in its output, wage and employment levels. In fact, this flexibility is crucial as 'all attempts to impose rigidity on the secondary sector would immediately reverberate on the system as a whole' (Brusco 1982).

Within this secondary sector, at least three types of production unit are identified. Subcontracting firms undertake a single, intermediate stage of manufacture. 'Independents' are firms with access to the consumer market who produce individual styles and high-quality products (in fact, many only produce prototypes and subcontract out the production). Homeworkers have a similar function to the subcontractors, but work at home, often to evade taxes and to enable employers to avoid welfare payments. There are also the more seasonal and temporary workers, such as pensioners, students, moonlighters and married women.

The implications of this type of industrial structure for skills are ambiguous, and depend to a great extent upon which type of firm is being considered. Craft skills – the type most commonly associated with the 'Third Italy' – are not evenly distributed between firms, or between groups of workers. Artisans (who predominate in the 'independents' sector) are mainly older men, while production-line workers (who predominate in the subcontractor sector) and homeworkers tend to be women, younger men or newcomers to the region. Production-line workers in small firms tend to be more skilled than those in large firms, often as a result of fewer job demarcations which allow small-firm workers to acquire a wider variety of skills and to have more individual responsibility. However, opposing this is the lack of any real career structure within the small firm, and the greater degree of job insecurity (Solinas 1982).

(Solinas and Brusco also point out the extent to which 'good jobs' depend on strong product demand, which provides incentives for employers and employees to acquire skills. Should recession set in, the system would falter, as job mobility to higher skill opportunities would cease.

The situation outside the 'core' firms is quite different. Work by Mitter and the Greater London Council has shown the sweatshop nature of what remains of London's clothing industry, where skills are deemed to be 'inherent' in the (overwhelmingly) female (and immigrant) labour force and where training, job security and living wages are a rarity (Mitter 1987). Mitter argues that 'the rise of homeworking ... is currently playing an important role in the global restructuring of capital', and that any evidence of improved skills and conditions in, for example, Benetton are mirrored (and indeed dependent on) the decentralization of the less skilled parts of the production process to subcontractors. Thus, Benetton employs only 1500 workers directly, but another 10,000 indirectly – and the latter's job skills and conditions are unlikely to be comparable to those of the 'core' workers (Murray 1985).

The evidence from the clothing industry poses a number of crucial issues for FS. First, is the dualistic nature of the industry endemic or transitory? Piore and Sabel, for instance, argue that at the beginning of the FS movement the Italian small-firm sector *was* analogous to turn-of-the-century sweatshops. But, they insist, such dependence was not permanent: 'dependent subcontractors . . . used their collective capacities to devise innovative products and processes that gave them increasingly independent access to markets' (Piore and Sabel 1984). Solinas supports this interpretation by remarking that dependent, low-quality subcontractors are 'small in number and much less representative'. However, he then goes on to acknowledge that the subordination of other regions (which could include the UK producers discussed by Mitter) is a determining factor in providing the 'good jobs' in the core region (Solinas 1982).

Second, are the 'sweatshops' of the UK part of the FS production system, or of an old production system which is being *overrun* by FS? Mitter, to some extent, argues both. Without more quantification of the links and distribution of output, employment and skills between different types of firm, it is not possible to conclude definitively which is the case.

Third, the situation is not static. Purposive action by firms and governments can change things. Robin Murray, for example, and the GLC's *London Industrial Strategy*, argue that the London clothing sector (and others) could change from a vicious circle of low skills, low wages and low productivity to a more virtuous circle along Italian lines, with the aid of judicious investments in technology, and a different marketing and production strategy (Murray 1985; GLC 1987). Such a strategy would result in enhanced skills and training, but the problems of the overall impact on jobs and skills, and of the core-periphery dilemma would remain. For example, is the aim simply to shift London to the core, and by implication create other, peripheral workers elsewhere?

Machine tools and machine shops

The machine tool sector of the economy is distinctive because, despite its importance, it has traditionally been one of the least 'Fordist' in its production methods (Wood 1982). Small batch production has predominated and craft workers, often organized in strong unions, have maintained significant control over the production process.

The introduction of NC and CNC tools triggered a debate, begun by Braverman (Braverman 1974), about the extent to which the machine tool sector was becoming 'Fordist', in the sense of workers being de-skilled and losing control over production to management. The success of the Italian, West German and Japanese industries has led to speculation that principles of FS are supplanting any nascent tendencies towards de-skilling and the application of Fordist principles to the machine tool sector. For example, the Japanese machine tool industry (the most successful in the general-purpose machine market) comprises vertically disintegrated, specialized firms, able to shift quickly from one line of product to another using broadly skilled employees (Piore and Sabel 1984).

The craft skills of workers in the West German and Italian machine tool industries are also being used, in conjunction with the new technology, to transform production along FS lines with subsequent successes in international markets (Piore and Sabel 1984).

However, there are dissenting voices to this generally rosy picture. First, there are clear examples of where the new technologies have been used to de-skill workers in machine shops, rather than re-skill them, although the commercial wisdom of such a policy is being increasingly questioned. British industry has been singled out for this in many studies (Wood 1988). Second, there are those who criticize even the success stories. F. Murray, in his study of the Italian machine tool sector, echoes many of the criticisms of the 'Third Italy' clothing industry by noting the differentiated nature of skills and employment conditions between the élite workers (usually male) with skills and the rest of the workforce. Murray (1987) argues that alienated, low-skill labour is much more widespread than is commonly perceived.

Motor vehicles

The motor vehicle industry, in contrast to machine tools, constitutes mass production *par excellence*. 'Fordism', with its assembly line, strict subdivision of jobs and workers, and long production runs, was perfected in this industry. By the 1970s, however, the giant automobile manufacturers of the US and Western Europe were all faced with serious problems from a combination of changed consumer markets and tastes, government regulation and increased competition from Japan and other, Third World, producers.

The Japanese challenge was particularly significant because of its basis in a different philosophy of production organization. Concepts of total quality control and just-in-time production were utilized to achieve astonishing productivity improvements compared with traditional mass production. This Japanese strategy depended crucially on flexibility in all aspects of production (Friedman 1983).

The Japanese system of production is based, like that of Benetton, on a core-periphery distinction of firms and workers, with the latter bearing the major brunt of the risks in order to make the system suitably flexible. The 'core' firms, in order to maximize their own flexibility, ensure that their workers are sufficiently trained to undertake a variety of tasks. Life-time employment contracts are an important incentive for workers to acquire such skills.

The UK car industry, under threat from increased competition and with a long history of industrial relations problems, has now begun its own 'Japanization' strategy. Established companies like British Leyland and Ford have cut back on their 'core' workforce, reduced their inventories, begun to dismantle skill and job demarcations and, in general, have striven to instil flexibility and quality into their production processes. Nissan, which entered production in Britain unencumbered by existing work practices, has adopted Japanese production standards to an even greater extent (Holloway 1987; Wickens 1987).

Using a drastically reduced number of formal skill hierarchies, the trend is to combine teamwork and flexibility to establish a 'multi-skilled' workforce, organized by a one-union deal (as opposed to over twenty in Ford UK's plants) (Sayer 1986; Wickens 1987). The extent of such multi-skilling is, however, a moot point: critics argue that the job rotation and enlargement aspect of Nissan's operations are in reality forms of work intensification, in which downtime is reduced, and 'skills' can be acquired in a few days. As one worker put it, 'the jobs are just the same as before, you just do more of 'em' (Turnbull 1988). The control of the whole work process, meanwhile, is more effectively centralized in the hands of management away from the 'teams' who can only affect small parts of a plant's total production.

Printing

Printing provides an example of an industry where skill levels were maintained for a long time, despite the threats and intrusions from new technology and the potential of mass production. Print unions, in the UK at least, managed to hold onto their craft skills and their control of production until very recently, and also managed to extend this control virtually throughout the industry, despite the overwhelming numerical dominance of small firms.

However, recent developments in new print technology and the market offensive of print franchise companies have enabled a growing number of independent small companies to produce high (or acceptable) quality work without the use or sanction of skilled labour organized in trade unions. As such, instant print is being established 'as the "cutting edge" of an "alternative", non-union, printing industry' (Goss 1987). Goss's study of the instant print industry shows that the skill levels required in this sector are very low, and training is 'denied workers where possible'. Most workers are young, inexperienced, previously unemployed, and unable to withstand employer pressure. The success of instant print is regarded as important both in itself, as a growing sector of the total printing industry and as 'a model and a material asset' to employers in the wider printing industry, 'in the struggle to reassert control over labour' (Goss 1987).

SUMMARY

Perhaps the strongest impression to be gleaned about the effects of FS on skills and work organization from these brief industry case studies is that of confusion and uncertainty. This is the result of a number of factors. The first is that if we are moving into an era of FS, it is still very much in its early period, and the implications of FS for jobs, work organization and skills are by no means mapped out definitively.

Second, most empirical and theoretical discussion of the FS concept has been centred around private sector manufacturing industry. However, this sector employs a minority of workers. The application of FS to services and the public sector has received less attention and its prospects in these areas are also not yet clear. Because the Fordist or mass-production paradigm was developed for manufacturing industry, some critics have argued that FS is inapplicable to the services sector (Block 1985). Others argue, however, that the increasing use of 'flexible' workers, such as temporary and part-time staff, and the 'putting out' to specialist firms of many services formerly performed in-house (ranging from legal and insurance services to cleaning and catering) indicate otherwise. Hirschhorn's (1987) study of a large bank in the US tells a familiar tale, for example. He found that the bank 'broadened line jobs, . . . increased the sophistication of certain specialist jobs, [and] . . . increased its use of part-time workers'. Similar experiences were found in a recent study by the Institute of Manpower Studies of major UK service industry employers (Atkinson and Meager 1986). The role of the public sector has been even less scrutinized, although it has been argued that, in Britain at least, FS tendencies (in particular moves towards numerical flexibility [see below]) have been more prominent in the public than in the private sector (Pollert 1988).

Third, just as the extent to which particular industrial sectors and countries could be categorized as 'Fordist' differed quite markedly, so too it is likely that differences will appear in their tendency towards an FS regime (Piore and Sabel 1984). Countries and sectors with a stronger craft tradition and a ready supply of high-skilled labour (such as West Germany and the clothing regions of the 'Third Italy') are more likely to adopt FS principles than those steeped in Fordist traditions (such as the US and Britain). This has been demonstrated in a number of comparisons between West Germany and Britain, for example (Lane 1987, 1988; Sorge and Streeck 1988).

Fourth, and perhaps most importantly, the criteria of what constitutes an FS production system, or an FS firm, are far from settled. Small size, decentralized production, quality and design conscious products in niche markets, new technology, a skilled workforce – all have been cited, yet exceptions to each exist. An attempt to clarify terms has been made by

Atkinson and Meager with their distinction between numerical and functional flexibility. The former refers to the ability of a firm to adjust its employment levels to changes in the level of demand, while the latter refers to the ability of employees to perform a variety of tasks according to changes in the composition of demand.

Numerical flexibility gives a clearer idea of the core-periphery distinction. As reduction of the firm's exposure to uncertainty becomes the most important organizational motive (as distinct from the reduction of costs *per se*), workers and activities which are not deemed essential to the firm's core business are hived off to the periphery (Hirschhorn 1987). The growth in the number of temporary and part-time workers and of industrial services is given as evidence of this trend.

It is the notion of functional flexibility, however, that is central to the skills debate. Atkinson and Meager found, for example, that the most important occupational changes accompanying new forms of work organization were 'not the changing balance between occupational groups . . . but the changes to job content within occupational groups' (Atkinson and Meager 1986). It is in this context that many of the optimistic views about FS have been formed.

The claim that 'de-skilling' is an inevitable consequence of management strategy, and of technological change has been extensively debated and will not be reviewed here (Wood 1988; Hyman and Streeck 1988; Knights and Willmott 1988). However, there is an increasing consensus that, for 'core' workers at least, re-skilling is possible and in fact becoming more common. The growing need for flexibility in production in response to rapidly changing market demands has, especially in combination with the introduction of new computer-based technologies, resulted in a different perception on behalf of management about the skill requirements of the workforce (Atkinson and Meager 1986). It is becoming essential for all 'core' workers to have a 'better knowledge of the production process and more responsibility' (Heinz 1987). The distinction between blue- and white-collar work (the basis of the separation of the conception and execution of work) is becoming increasingly blurred and simple 'craft' notions of skill are being challenged (Wobbe 1987).

Efforts by firms to attain functional flexibility appear to involve an increase in the responsibility and skills of their 'core' workforce. In some cases, this has involved a vertical integration of skills, with workers undertaking tasks of a higher level of competence which had previously been done by a specialist, more highly-skilled group of workers. This has been the case with some multi-skilled machine operators. More common, however, has been a horizontal integration of skills, involving tasks at similar levels of competence – such as bricklayers becoming competent in joinery, plastering and painting (Atkinson and Meager

1986). This latter type of re-skilling is also more typical of the car industry (Turnbull 1988).

On the periphery, the picture is quite different. We can distinguish between two types of peripheral firms (and workers). The first is the relatively independent, specialist, skill-based firm providing quality goods to niche markets or 'producer services' to larger, 'core' firms. This type of peripheral firm corresponds to the 'independents' of the Italian clothing sector, the craft-based machine tool firms of Japan and Western Europe, and the growing number of software, computing, legal and other professional consultancy firms. Their skill profiles are, if anything, higher than those of the 'core' firms they service.

By contrast, there is a much larger 'poor periphery', represented by the dependent clothing subcontractors, the instant print shops, the growing part-time and temporary workforce composed mainly of domestically committed women, students and other minority or deprived groups, and of course homeworkers. In this part of the periphery, skills and training are not encouraged, employment security is minimal and wages variable.

It would appear, then, that both the 'optimists' and 'pessimists' of the FS debate have valid points to make. Some workers' skills *are* being enhanced – both at the core and in the specialist periphery. On the other hand, many people are being marginalized by being assigned to the 'poor periphery'.

The likely balance between these opposing tendencies is difficult to ascertain (giving support to the 'sceptics'!). As we have seen, the situation varies by region, country and industry and much more empirical work is required before any definitive conclusions can be made. The onus is on the proponents of FS (whether from an optimistic or pessimistic viewpoint) to produce stronger empirical support than they have up to now, to avoid the criticism that 'their vision of a future . . . dominates their analysis of the present' (Wood 1988).

One thing does seem fairly certain, however: 'core' jobs will not be the dominant mode of work in the future. Even FS proponents have noted how 'paradoxically, the better use production makes of the quality of labour, the smaller the quantity required' (Brodner 1987). Only a massive reduction in working hours, but with a maintenance of employment protection, can overcome the increasingly segmented nature of the labour market (Brodner 1987).

Within the periphery, the numerical balance between the specialist and the poor periphery *is* more problematic. The re-emerging craft paradigm, the basis of Piore and Sabel's FS thesis, is as yet restricted to only a few products and countries. Its ability to be extended appears constrained by FS's need for numerical flexibility, which implies a ready supply of low-skill, low-security labour. Indeed, even the specialist peripheral firms rely on a flexible labour supply to enable them to adjust to changing demand conditions (Brusco 1982).

Implications for training policy

Training policy is moving to the centre stage of political debate in many advanced industrialized countries (OECD 1983). The FS debate is likely to reinforce this, implying as it does the potential of a renewed demand for high-level skills. If it proves to be the case that we are moving towards an FS regime, the implications for training could be profound for management and government. They would also provide a strong challenge to trade unions.

For employers, the creation of a 'core' workforce has been accompanied by an increasing preparedness to provide resources for extensive retraining and upgrading of their workers' skills to ensure functional flexibility. However, as yet, most re-skilling (in Britain) has been add-on in nature and has not involved the definition of a new, core-skill requirement, reflecting the pragmatic rather than strategic attitude of most firms to their skill requirements (Atkinson and Meager 1986). This appears to be in contrast to the case in West Germany, where a much more integrated approach to skill training, work organization, investment in new technology and revised product market strategy has been taken (Lane 1988).

A longer-term problem for employers has been highlighted by Atkinson and Meager. Currently, core or peripheral status is normally allocated on the basis of posts, rather than postholders; yet most firms regard an individual (core) worker's behavioural characteristics as more important than the 'job' they are currently doing. In fact, the essence of a flexible workforce (and workplace) is that in principle everyone is capable of doing every job. The need to ensure that the core workforce is composed of the 'right' workers will require a new approach to recruitment, selection, training and severance policies (Lane 1988; Sayer 1986). The attraction of 'green field' start-ups, to overcome the rigidities and limitations of current practices, will also increase.

The in-house nature of training for core workers also means that skills acquired through training will become increasingly firm-specific, and their transferability on the external labour market will decline. Combined with the static or reduced number of positions within the firm, workers could find themselves 'trapped'. While some regard this as a 'feudalization' of the employment relationship (Heinz 1987), others are more positive, and cite the Japanese experience of life-time employment approvingly (Senker 1986).

For smaller firms, especially the skill-based, specialist firms, training represents a dilemma. The innovativeness and growth of these firms depends on a steady supply of skilled labour, but limited resources and competitive pressures make provision of the requisite training for current or future employees problematical. Government training assistance is vital to ensure the future provision of a skilled workforce (Piore and Sabel 1984).

The government's role is even more crucial in the case of peripheral workers, for whom firms are actively opposed to the provision of anything other than minimal training. The highly concentrated nature of workers in the peripheral sector (i.e. women, young people) also makes this a legitimate and pressing area for public policy, if such groups are to obtain access to the 'core' job market. Protection of peripheral workers' conditions of employment and assistance for the transitional costs of 'numerical flexibility' is also a state responsibility which has, however, been neglected or actively downgraded. If anything, current policy in Britain seems to be reinforcing peripheral status on young people through such schemes as the Youth Training Scheme (Goss 1987; Jarvis and Prais 1988). Atkinson and Meager (1986) also noted how large firms rarely use government Jobcentres for filling core-job vacancies.

CONCLUSION

Towards the end of their book, Piore and Sabel pose two possible scenarios for the future. One is a restricted FS regime, where 'isolated communities of producers . . . seek their fortune in disregard of the fate of their rivals, where an island of craftsmen, producing luxury goods . . . [is] surrounded by a subproletarian sea of misery'. The alternative is one where 'the local community structures [are] coordinated by national social-welfare regulation, and [where] the provision . . . of research facilities and training [is] . . . partly a public responsibility' (Piore and Sabel 1984). Given the failure of governments to ensure a more equitable distribution of core jobs and better conditions for peripheral workers, and (in Britain) the attacks on local government, this latter scenario of an 'artisans' republic' seems wildly optimistic. However, Piore and Sabel's insistence that the future is not determined is salutary in this context. Which scenario results will depend on a number of factors: government ideology and policies, the existing industrial structure, the corporate strategies of firms, evidence from successful examples else-where, etc. A potentially crucial factor will be the role played by the trade union movement. Any move towards FS will pose severe challenges to unions (Murray 1983; Rainbird 1988; Sayer 1986; Sorge and Streeck 1988; Wickens 1987). By establishing core-periphery relationships be-tween firms, FS threatens to further divide workers. By fragmenting production into smaller, dispersed units, it makes union organization more difficult. In Britain, these tendencies are aggravated by the structure of unions, organized as they are along craft and general union principles, rather than by industry. Multi-skilling and the general move towards functional flexibility threaten existing union boundaries and allow employers to play unions off against each other, as the recent debate over the proposed Ford Dundee plant indicates. Single union deals have become the yardstick of union flexibility, but are proving difficult to achieve. In such circumstances, even the work conditions of 'core' workers are threatened, either by non-unionization or by shifting production to other more 'amenable' countries.

The focus on teamwork, quality and innovation, and the new personnel policies inherent in FS, encourage identification by workers with the company. Placing responsibility on workers for production is a novel concept which blurs the lines between 'them' and 'us' and calls into question the traditional basis of British unionism (Turnbull 1988; Wickens 1987).

FS also highlights the need for unions to organize among peripheral workers and firms, to prevent exploitation. This will require a broader perspective and more solidarity to overcome barriers and conflicts between different groups of workers (Lash and Urry 1987).

Such a solidaristic and forward-looking strategy is more evident in unions in countries such as Sweden, West Germany and Austria than in Britain. It must be recognized that these countries enjoy a strong legislative basis conducive to consensual decision-making and 'holistic' industrial relations in the face of technological and organizational change. Such a favourable legislative backdrop is unlikely in Britain in the foreseeable future, and it is therefore imperative that unions adopt a more strategic approach to the challenge of FS than the 'confused and generally aimless' approach they have adopted so far (Atkinson and Meager 1986). The outcome of Britain's 'Second Industrial Divide' may depend on them.

REFERENCES

Atkinson, J. and Meager, N. (1986) *New Forms of Work Organization*, Institute of Manpower Studies.

Blackburn, P., Coombs, R. and Green, K. (1985) *Technology, Economic Growth and the Labour Process*, Macmillan.

Block, F. (1985) Economy and nostalgia, *Dissent* 32: 498–501.

Braverman, H. (1974) *Labor and Monopoly Capital*, Monthly Review Press.

Brodner, P. (1987) Towards an anthropocentric approach in European manufacturing, *Vocational Training Bulletin* 1: 30–9

Brusco, S. (1982) The Emilian model: productive decentralisation and social integration, *Cambridge Journal of Economics* 6 (2): 167–84.

Coriat, B. (1981) The restructuring of the assembly line: a new economy of time and control, *Capital and Class* 11: 34–43.

Friedman, D. (1983) Beyond the age of Ford: the strategic basis of the Japanese success in 35 automobiles, in Zysman, J. and Taylor, L. (eds) *American Industry in International Competition: Government Policies and Corporate Strategies*, Cornell University Press.

GLC (1987) *The London Industrial Strategy*, Greater London Council.

Gorz, A. (1982). *Farewell to the Working Class: An Essay on Post-Industrial Socialism*, Pluto Press.

Goss, D. (1987) Instant print: technology, and capitalist control, *Capital and Class* 31: 79–91.

Gough, J. (1986) Industrial policy and socialist strategy: restructuring and the unity of the working class, *Capital and Class* 29: 58–81

Heinz, W.R. (1987) The future of work, *Vocational Training Bulletin* 1: 13–18.

Hirschhorn, L. (1987) The post-industrial economy: labour, skills and the new mode of production, *The Service Industries Journal* 8(1): 19–38.

Holloway, J. (1987) The red rose of Nissan, *Capital and Class* 32: 142–64.

Hyman, R. (1988) Flexible specialization: miracle or myth?, in Hyman and Streeck 1988.

Hyman, R. and Streeck, W. (eds) (1988) *New Technology and Industrial Relations*, Blackwell.

Jarvis, V. and Prais, S.J. (1988) *Two Nations of Shopkeepers. Training for Retailing in France and Britain*, NIESR.

Knights, D. and Willmott, H. (eds) (1988) *New Technology and the Labour Process*, Macmillan.

Kuttner, R. (1985) The shape of things to come, *The New Republic*, 14: 8–96.

Lane, C. (1987) Capitalism or culture? A comparative analysis of the position in the labour process and labour market of lower white-collar workers in the financial services sector of Britain and the Federal Republic of West Germany, *Work, Employment and Society* 1(1): 57–83.

Lane, C. (1988) Industrial change in Europe: the pursuit of flexible specialisation in Britain and West Germany, *Work, Employment and Society*, 2(2): 141–68.

Lash, S. and Urry, J. (1987) *The End of Organized Capitalism*, Polity.

Murray, F. (1983) The decentralisation of production – the decline of the mass-collective worker?, *Capital and Class* 19: 74–99.

Murray, F. (1987) Flexible specialisation in the 'Third Italy', *Capital and Class* 33: 84–96.

Murray R. (1985) Benetton Britain: the new economic order, *Marxism Today*, November: 28–32.

Mitter, S. (1986) Industrial restructuring and manufacturing home work: immigrant women in the UK clothing industry, *Capital and Class* 27: 37–80.

OECD (1983) *The Future of Vocational Education and Training*, OECD.

Piore, M.J. and Sabel, C. F. (1984) *The Second Industrial Divide: Possibilities for Prosperity*, Basic Books.

Pollert, K. (1988) The 'flexible firm': fixation or fact?, *Work, Employment and Society*, 2(3): 281–316.

Poon, K. (1988) *Flexible Specialisation and Small Size – The Case of Caribbean Tourism*, SPRU.

Rainbird, H. (1988) New technology, training and union strategies, in Hyman and Streeck 1988.

Sabel, C.F. (1982) *Work and Politics: the Division of Labour in Industry*, Cambridge University Press.

Sayer, A. (1986) New developments in manufacturing: the just-in-time system, *Capital and Class* 30: 43–52.

Senker, P. (1986) The Technical and Vocational Education Initiative and economic performance in the United Kingdom: an initial assessment, *Journal of Education Policy* 1(4): 293–303.

Solinas, G. (1982) Labour market segmentation and workers' careers: the case of the Italian knitwear industry!, *Cambridge Journal of Economics* 6(4): 331–52.

Sorge, A. and Streeck, W. (1988) Industrial relations and technical change: the case for an extended perspective, in Hyman, R. and Streeck, W. (eds) *New Technology and Industrial Relations*, Blackwell.

Toffler, A. (1980) *The Third Wave*, Pan.

Turnbull, P.J. (1988) The limits to Japanisation: just-in-time, labour relations and the UK automotive industry, *New Technology, Work and Employment* 3(1): 79–81.

Webber, A.W. (1985) Socialization and its discontents, *Harvard Business Review* 63(3): 38–54.

Wickens, P. (1987) *The Road to Nissan: Flexibility, Quality, Teamwork*, Macmillan.

Williams, K., Cutler, T., Williams, J. and Haslam, C. (1987) The end of mass production? *Economy and Society* 16(3): 405–39.

Wobbe, W. (1987) Technology, work and employment – new trends in the structural change of society, *Vocational Training Bulletin* 1: 3–6.

Wood, S. (ed.) (1982) *The Degradation of Work? Skill, Deskilling and the Labour Process*, Hutchinson.

Wood, S. (1988) Between Fordism and flexibility: The US car industry, in Hyman and Streeck (1988).

Zysman, J. and Taylor, L. (eds) (1983) *American Industry in International Competition: Government Policies and Corporate Strategies*, Cornell University Press.

Chapter 7

The challenge of economic utility

C. Bailey

THE CHALLENGE SKETCHED

The view under consideration here takes either a purely instrumental view of education or places so much importance on the instrumental view as to seriously play down any liberal education element even when some form of balance between the two is being nominally advocated. The view has often been tacit or implicit, revealing itself most often in the criteria apparent in criticisms of the alleged shortcomings of the educational system or of its lack of relevance. For a pupil to complain that his education is not relevant to the job he wants to do, or fails to equip him to face unemployment, is to assume that education has a proper instrumental purpose that it has failed to fulfil. For a prime minister to chide the system for failing to produce the scientists and technologists the country needs is to assume that the education system has manpower provision responsibilities that it is neglecting. For a politician to complain that the education system allows pupils to leave school with unfavourable attitudes towards wealth creation or technological growth or competition, is to suggest that there are proper attitudes for an education system to foster.[1]

In recent years, however, the demand for at least a strong instrumental element in the curriculum of secondary education has become more overt, especially from government agencies and from employers or from institutions that speak for employers. This is so much the case that a recent HMI discussion paper on teacher training could open with the statement:

> It has in recent years become 'a truth universally acknowledged' that education should be more closely linked with the world of work and with the country's economic performance; and there has been increasing pressure on schools to assess the relevance of their curriculum to their pupils' future working lives.
>
> (Department of Education and Science 1982)

CRITICISM OF THE ECONOMIC UTILITY CHALLENGE

The assumptions of non-controversiality

Running through all the discussions of the economic utility model of education is an unspoken assumption of consensus about society, values and education. The assumed consensus is that of continually accepted technological change and development, strangely related to nineteenth-century conceptions of the undoubted good of 'progress', all taking place in the context of a competitive free market economy, and in a wider context of international competitive trade. Also assumed is the undeniable value of wealth creation, ostensibly as a necessary condition of all else that might be valued, but in fact by its emphasis seen as a value of and in itself. Education, in this model, becomes a commodity both for the individual person and for society as a whole, to be assessed like any other commodity in terms of its profitability or usefulness. The education favoured for the individual is one leading to a well-paid job; for the employer it is one producing well-disposed and capable workers and potential managers; and for the state it is one making the country strong in economic competitive power and united around simple ideas of patriotism. Some of these views are explicit in what I have been describing, but most of them are implied or taken for granted. Such a framework of assumed consensus is necessary to give coherence to all the claims and pressures.

That such a consensus exists as anything more concrete than an assumption or necessary presupposition is highly questionable. The value of continued technological growth, especially when dictated and operated by a profit mechanism, is challenged by many people. Not only does such a challenge come from the expected people: ecologists, conservationists and the anti-nuclear lobby, but also from groups like the Council for Science and Society which issued a report in 1981 entitled 'New Technology: Society, Employment and Skill'. The kind of questioning about the advance of technology I have in mind is evidenced by this comment in the CSS Report about the alleged benefits of automation based on computers:

> If we look at past experience, it seems likely that possibilities of this kind, if they can be realized profitably with the computer, will be implemented despite any protests by those concerned. To follow such a path of increasing automation usually requires an additional expenditure on capital equipment. Profitability then depends upon a reduction of employment for a given output, or at least the substitution of less-skilled, and so cheaper, labour for the more highly skilled. Both

courses reduce the demands which are made on human ability, and a classical economic argument sees this as the creation of new opportunity. The human resources set free are available for other needs of society, or to increase the production of goods. Moreover, an economic mechanism will automatically ensure that this opportunity is fully used. Yet the experience of the last fifty years does little to establish confidence in this self-regulating mechanism. The demoralising unemployment of the 1930s ended only with the beginning of the Second World War, and it is not clear that the depression would have ended without the war. The 1970s, against expectations, saw a renewed increase of unemployment. During the whole period a large proportion of those employed have done work below their capability. What is striking is that very great effort is expended upon the creation of the opportunity which unemployment or under employment represents, and in comparison almost none upon using that opportunity.

(Council for Science and Society 1981)

Such a lengthy quotation is necessary to show the kind of detailed critical argument about the benefits or otherwise of technological advance that is completely and naively absent from the statements of those advocating an economic utility model of education. Unemployment has, of course, become much worse since this report was written, and political commentators on unemployment consistently play down the very large technologically structural element within it, hoping instead for some miraculous upturn in international trade to remedy the situation.

The idea of the undoubted good of technological advance is not only thus questionable, it is actively questioned by many people and groups of people in technically advanced societies. Similar detail can be found in literature from the conservationist and anti-nuclear groups, represented as cranks in much of the establishment media, but actually producing complex, sustained and serious argument of a most disturbing kind for those prepared to read it.

It is no part of my present argument to claim that the views now being referred to are necessarily correct, though I believe many of them to be so. The argument here is that views about technological growth are far more controversial than could be inferred from DES documents, HMI documents and other sources referred to earlier. For educators to influence the minds of pupils in the sole direction of the economic utility model of education, in this and other respects, would be highly indoctrinatory and therefore inimical to the development of rational and moral autonomy which is the duty of the liberal educator.

Similarly, the background context of the free competitive market as the determinant of resource allocation is anything but a consensus view of how society should most desirably operate. The Green Paper (*Education in School: A Consultative Document*, 1977), issued by a Labour Party Secretary of State, talked of the mixed economy as the normal state which education must come to terms with, as we might have expected from a government largely in the hands of the right wing of the Labour Party. Conservative politicians and most industrialists are, of course, more stridently supportive of a larger, if not total, free market element, and more directly socialist members of the Labour Party and others too far to the left to be members of that organization would want to see more, or total, central planning of the economy. The numbers of people prepared actually to vote for one or other of these positions when dressed up in various guises in election manifestos varies over time. What is inescapable, however, is the controversial nature of the issue. Politicians and employers have every right in a democracy to argue their case; but it does not follow from this that any of them have the right, least of all in a democracy, to impose their particular view on the education system. Such a system, in so far as it tries to bring about political and economic understanding in the minds of the pupils entrusted to it, must treat controversial matters as controversial matters. The late Lawrence Stenhouse realized this when asked by the Schools Council to propose strategies for teaching the humanities, but the strategy his team constructed and tried so hard to introduce into schools is still only rarely seen in action. The suppression of student opinion in MSC sponsored courses, already mentioned, stands directly opposed to the thoughtful strategy of neutrality and impartiality advocated by Stenhouse and characteristic of all his work.

If consensus does not actually exist in these areas neither does it exist in the matter of judging the value of activities by their contribution to wealth creation. What this kind of emphasis leaves out of account is any consideration of what wealth is to be used for and how it is to be distributed. Even nineteenth-century utilitarians made happiness and not wealth creation the touchstone of value, and were thus concerned about how wealth was used and distributed, and contemporary political philosophers have consistently related these ideas to the justice and morality of the ends to which wealth is put and of its distribution.[2] None of these political theorists appears to believe that a society with more wealth-creation is, in any simple and unqualified way, necessarily better than one with less. It seems particularly one-sided to judge an educational system, or even particular educational practices, by the simple criterion of contribution to wealth-creation for two main reasons. First, because educators must be duty-bound to introduce pupils to controversial matters as controversial matters, as I have already said in connection with technological growth; and, secondly, because schools of liberal education must introduce pupils to those activities and practices which can be considered as worthwhile in themselves and therefore fit to be considered as ends rather than as means. To take small but illustrative examples of what I mean here: it would be pointless to judge the value of my listening to music, reading poetry, or even doing my gardening, by assessing their contribution to wealth-creation when these things are for me intrinsically valued ends; when they are, in fact, activities on which I use my wealth rather than means to increase it. It is true that for some people the issue becomes confused and wealth-creation becomes an end in itself; but that is but one of the peculiar perversions of modern capitalist society, destructive of justice, morality and a proper humanity, as Erich Fromm and others have pointed out (Fromm 1956). Education must be concerned with ends, and to the extent that it is so concerned it is improperly judged on the criterion of wealth-creation.

The last important controversial area in the economic utility model of education to be noted here is the emphasis on competition, both individual and national. A full discussion of the place of competition in education cannot be entered into here, but the point must be made that the place of competition, in both education and society at large, is controversial. Some people would favour a much more co-operative society and much more encouragement of co-operation in schools. Similarly some would favour much more international co-operation on trade instead of the present automatic assumptions about national competitiveness. Yet in the model I am criticizing competition is offered as a characteristic of the 'real' world, as though to question competition is like questioning the expansion of metals under heat or the necessity of moisture for growing plants; while co-operation for any other purpose than to defeat the other team, the other firm or the other country, is corrupting idealism, out of touch with the 'real' world. The assumption is as if Kropotkin had never written, the Co-operative Movement had never developed and fraternity had never been a political issue for which men and women had died on the barricades. Team spirit and loyalty have become transmogrified, as R.S. Peters puts it, into instruments of destructive competition instead of universal co-operation among all rational agents (Peters 1966).

The diversion of responsibility

This criticism of the economic utility model of education is directed to the appropriate allocation of responsibility. Certainly it cannot be denied that there must be efficient and appropriate vocational training in any community. The criticism made by the liberal educator is not against vocational training as such, only against the idea that such training is properly located in schools of general education, or that the needs of such training should dictate the curriculum content and methodologies of schools of general education.

The paradigm notion of training is to do with preparation for some activity of a relatively specific kind which, once trained for, a person will engage in for some time. Such were the reasonable assumptions, for example, of an apprentice; but apprenticeships were features of a craft-oriented economy which has now all but disappeared from the national scene. Preparing people, especially young people, for specific industrial tasks is difficult today for a number of reasons, but two are paramount: first, no one can guarantee that a young person will actually get a job in the task for which he or she has been trained; and, secondly, no one can guarantee that the technical requirements of a task will not change very quickly, even before the young person takes up a job. These difficulties operate profoundly at all levels, as the Council for Science and Society reports in the case of engineers:

> In the university training of engineers, the scientific content is again heavily, and increasingly, stressed. To teach the current technology and procedures of industry is more difficult and less rewarding because they evolve within industry and change rapidly. Only someone directly engaged in the activity can teach it, and what is learned will be rapidly outdated.
>
> (Council for Science and Society 1981: 89)

Yet employers still complain that graduates do not understand modern industry, and that school-leavers do not understand the particular aspects of work they find themselves in – if they do find themselves in work – as if this was solely the fault of the university or school. The very users of rapidly changing technologies, even the very makers of such technologies, show little signs of grasping these particular social implications, and education policy-makers can naively say that an aim of education should be 'to help pupils to acquire knowledge and skills relevant to adult life and employment in a fast changing world' (Department of Education and Science 1981: 3).

Because industry has been unable to cope with these problems itself, and because of the costs of frequently changing training needs, there have been increased demands for national patterns of training and increased blaming of schools for alleged failures to develop appropriate skills and attitudes in young school-leavers. Exactly what these appropriate skills and attitudes are does not appear to have been much discussed outside the literature of the Further Education Curriculum Development Unit, the MSC, and agencies serving them. Inside that literature, however, one finds a flowering of talk about generic skills, social skills and life skills which will have a vocational bias and provide vocational motivation while still being (allegedly) very wide in application. Much of this would not concern us here were it not for the fact that unemployment has brought many more 16- and 17-year-olds under the influence of these training philosophies, and because of the present government's intention to extend these techniques to the 14- and 15-year-old pupils in ordinary schools. In the next subsection I shall look more closely at the characterization of skills in this literature. Here I am concerned to make the point that the very agencies who should tackle the problems of industrial training in the context of modern technology and rapid change, namely the government and industry, have chosen to do so largely by attacking the general education base and attempting, not to put too fine a point on it, to take that base over for purely instrumental purposes. This is a grand passing of the buck and a lamentable shedding of blame and responsibility which has an effect that is doubly disastrous: it fails to provide adequate industrial training that is directly linked with jobs on the one hand, and frustrates, confuses and belittles attempts at a genuine liberal education for all pupils on the other.

Much has been made in some recent discussions on these issues of the need for school-leavers to be very adaptable in the present-day situation. The need is genuine, but there are no magic skills for adaptability. The best basis for adaptability is a liberal education which has encouraged a wide understanding and the development of reason and autonomy, in the fullest sense of those oft-misused words, without any early prejudging of how this understanding might later be put to vocational and career use. The very rate of technological change argues in favour of liberal education for all, and not against it; and only from such an education can come adaptability, if that is what is necessary, or the critical power to work for a social control of technology as that increasingly becomes necessary. Liberal educators should be left to their logically prior task, and only after that should those properly responsible for industrial training see that it is efficiently undertaken.

THE CHARACTERIZATION OF SKILLS

It is odd to note that most of the Further Education Curriculum Development Unit teaching material that is so favoured by the MSC attempts to characterize everything in terms of skills. These are not only skills like being able to use a screwdriver or an electric drill, which would be clear and comprehensible, but much more grandly named skills like 'life skills', 'social skills', 'interpersonal skills' and even 'generic skills' which are supposed to underlie all we do. The oddity comes from the contrast between this view that all that is necessary is to equip people with appropriate skills for work, leisure and life, and the comments on skill that we find in the Science and Society report on *New Technology: Society, Employment and Skill*. This report traces historically how the advance of technology has generally been accompanied by an elimination of skill:

> The historical evidence is not encouraging. Where it was possible to eliminate skill in the past, this was generally done. The opportunities which are being offered by the computer to remove skill from office work, printing, engineering design and other occupations, in general seem likely to be taken. . . . It will affect the majority of occupations up to and within the professional level. There will be a resistance to this development which will be strong and tenacious. . . . If it is unsuccessful, then the great majority of people will for the first time find themselves united in the misfortune of work which allows them no control or initiative.
>
> (Council for Science and Society 1981: 77)

Of course the report notes that developing technology generates a need for new skills, but these are for a smaller number of people, usually different people, from those who are de-skilled.

We seem, then, to have two different accounts. One seems to be saying that education does not concern itself enough with skills: 'We believe schools need to make a conscious effort to ensure that their pupils acquire skills, many of which may prove to have a life-long value' (Schools Council 1981: 22). The other appears to be saying that the trend of technological change is generally to make increasingly useless the skills that people have acquired.

Part of the confusion here arises from the way in which the word 'skill' is used. The Schools Council gives as examples of skills: initial reading and number skills, the ability to work alone and the ability to work with others (*ibid.*). These are among what I have called the serving competencies because they serve instrumentally the other aims and purposes within a liberal education. Whether they are appropriately called skills is questionable. Further skills mentioned by the Schools Council are: a knowledge of political processes, the ability to interpret scientific data and the ability to make judgements on environmental matters. What is gained by calling these abilities 'skills' is difficult to see. Most writers agree at a superficial level as to the components of a skill.

> A skill is more than knowing, and more than knowing how. It is action too. A skill involves the application of knowledge to achieve some anticipated outcome. It needs the capacity and the will to act, as well as knowledge. Skill without knowledge is inconceivable, but knowledge without skill has a long sad history.
>
> (*Ibid.*)

There are, however, interesting differences of emphasis. If the above quotation stresses the instrumentality of skills and their connection with

action and the will, the following, from the Council for Science and
Society report, emphasizes the knowledgeable control aspect of skill and
marks off two interesting limiting conditions:

> we should prefer to stress 'knowledgeable practice', and to emphasise
> the element of control without which skill does not exist. . . .
>
> Because control is essential for the exercise of skill, it follows that
> there can be no skill where everything is completely predictable.
> Screwing a nut onto a bolt demands at most dexterity, not skill. In a
> large measure, therefore, skill is a response to the unexpected and
> unpredictable. The blacksmith so places the red-hot iron on the anvil,
> and strikes it with such a sequence of blows, that its shape converges
> to the horse-shoe he desires, even though his actions will never be the
> same on two occasions.
>
> . . . On one side skill is marked off from more trivial accomplish-
> ments such as dexterity or 'knack'. On another it is distinguished
> from activities which are intended to affect people rather than things
> . . . 'managerial skill' has a manipulative sound if it is applied to the
> leadership of people. The 'skilled negotiator' or the 'skilled advocate'
> seem to contradict this rule, but reflection will show that both operate
> in situations where human contact is circumscribed and manipulation
> is sanctioned.
>
> (Council for Science and Society 1981: 23–4)

The suggested limiting conditions set in this quotation are, it seems to
me, sensible ones which accord with our normal usage of the term
'skill'. On the one hand, it accords with our intuitive idea that skills are
never merely manual and always have a strong cognitive determination
which is sometimes almost entirely determinant, as in the doctor's skills
of diagnosis which cannot be disassociated from his knowledge and
understanding of anatomy, physiology and pathology, as Ruth Jonathan
points out (Jonathan 1983: 9). On the other hand, the limiting conditions
accord with our unease when morality, personal relationships and even
certain features of communication are characterized as skills. People can,
of course, be skilfully manipulated by others. The point is that this has
usually been seen as a perverted side of human relationships, to be
spoken of in derogatory terms, and having nothing to do with those
humanistic aspects of morality, personal and social relations which
should be the concern of liberal educators. These concerns for life,
persons and society are, however, complex and are only to be understood
by the prolonged study of the kind of content discussed in chapter 7
(section s. 1) of my book *Beyond the Present and Particular* (Bailey 1984).
The advocates of a skill approach are obviously attracted by a simple
view of skills which they then project into matters too complex to make
the appellation appropriate. They seem to want the advantages of

simplicity which lend themselves conveniently to precise statements of objectives and easily manageable assessment and monitoring:

> In specifying the type and level of skill they intend their pupils to acquire teachers come near to setting themselves precise aims. Schools need to decide and state exactly what skills they do hope to develop in each of the main areas of experience they are concerned with. They could use statements of this kind as a basis for self assessment.
>
> (Schools Council 1981: 23)

Yet at the same time this simplicity and precision must be injected into complex areas like 'verbal skills as vehicles for thought, feeling and imagination' (*ibid.*) because the more complex realms of human action and reflection are clearly the most important and valuable.

Perhaps the fallacy of thinking that these complex areas can be characterized as skills arises from the fatal slip from the properly adverbial or adjectival to the improper substantive which is so ready a temptation of language. Because a person can be a thoughtful politician or an imaginative architect it is tempting to think that there are reifications like 'thought' or 'imagination' which can be readily identified, isolated and trained for. Similarly, because it is meaningful to talk of someone being a skilful thinker, or expressing their feelings skilfully, we are tempted to believe that there is a 'skill' to be identified, isolated and trained for. This reaches its maximum absurdity in notions like 'life skills', 'social skills' and 'generic skills', as if it were meaningful to think of people as skilful at life, in society or in some universal generic sense. These conceptions are either vacuous or pretentious names for isolated and relatively trivial abilities that might in some sense be subsumed under such titles, in the sense that blowing one's nose efficiently or cutting one's toenails adequately are 'life skills'. Ruth Jonathan puts it very well:

> It begins to look as if we have only to dub any desirable capacity or area of experience a 'skill' in order to suggest it can be easily identified and acquired. Advocates of the teaching of 'life skills' or 'survival skills' either have something utterly trivial in mind (like the ability to change plugs or walk through doorways), or something hopelessly vague (like the ability to be innovative or to work co-operatively) or are simply proffering glib new labels for the old educational aims of moral autonomy, rationality and aesthetic discrimination. If we are serious about the desirability of such goals we must look for advances in epistemology, psychology and ethical argument and be prepared to apply these insights in education, rather than following the blind alley of a behaviourist inspired skill-based approach.
>
> (Jonathan 1983: 8–9)

Other people are wary of the skills approach. Bernard Davies, writing for the National Youth Bureau, defends what he sees as a 'social education' orientation of youth workers against the pressure to go over to a skill-based approach. He rightly locates social education in the broad tradition of liberal education:

> advocates of social education who wish to resist the drift to social and life skills training may need to be looking for alliances with all those other educators now trying to defend the liberal and personalised traditions of education generally.
>
> (Davis 1979: 11)

He also shares my view, or appears to do so, of the importance of justifying and substantiating a liberal education philosophy if one is to be in any position to resist the encroachment of a crude skills approach:

> youth workers, teachers and others involved in social education need to regain their nerve – their conviction that some of the person-centred, critical and creative goals to which they have been committed are still valid. . . . If they cannot re-assert what is distinctive about the theory, philosophy and practice of their specialist field of work, they cannot hope to resist, still less to influence, the cruder, often highly mechanistic and behaviourist forms of social and life skills training now being foisted on so many young people.
>
> (*Ibid.*: 10)

It was noted in the previous subsection that only one immersed in the practice of a skill, properly so called, can train another person in that skill. This was the longstanding basis of apprenticeships and many other less thoroughgoing types of on-the-job training. If we are speaking of the skills of operating a lathe, a computer, a sailing dinghy or anything where particular processes and performances are to be explained and demonstrated by one person to another who then practises the processes under the eye of the expert, then this is an important part of the paradigm of skills. If it is, however, then even more doubt is cast on the idea of life skills, social skills, moral skills and the like. Who are those arrogant enough to claim the necessary expertise to train others in these areas? What qualifications should they possess and what experience should they have had? What is their ongoing practice of the expertise which trainees watch and then practise for themselves? What is the rationale of their explanations? How does it escape the controversy found in these fields for thousands of years by philosophers and other reflective persons? Perhaps it is simply ignorance of all these problems, arising from prolonged immersion in action and the assertion of the will.

I must end this subsection, and lead into the next, with what after all is the liberal educator's main complaint about the emphasis on skills. This is to do with the way in which any emphasis on skills divorces the instruments from their purposes, separates means from ends. Logically, of course, skills are not separable from purposes and ends. It is the characterisation of particular purposes that helps us to see the use of a particular skill – ball control in football, say – and there is no perform-ance that is just a skill in any isolated sense. To make this point, obvious though it may seem to be, is immediately to diminish the importance of instrumental skills relative to other considerations like being able to *choose our ends* in some understanding and informed way; like entering into an understanding of the *values* involved in different ends; like considering the *morality* of certain means rather than others, even when the ends are determined; and like *understanding* the varied and multitudi-nous practices of humankind which might or might not come to be valued ends for us. Ruth Jonathan again makes the point crisply when she says that 'education must logically equip children to make these choices before it equips them to carry them out' (Jonathan 1983: 8). Later in her paper she makes this point more fully:

> Formerly, individuals were either educated or trained. As social divisions became slightly more blurred, the vast mass of young people found themselves at the end of formal schooling neither educated nor trained. The answer does not lie in replacing education by training for all, but in acceptance that all young people require a general education which will open to them as many options of an intellectual, aesthetic and moral kind as they are capable of entertaining and society is able to support, followed by an appropriate period of generic training – not in imitative and obsolescent motor skills, but in the appropriate fundamental principles and general skills of particular technologies, whether industrial, commercial, scientific or service. The more specific our skills the shorter their useful life.[3]

With perhaps some room for negotiation as to where the former ends and the latter begins, few liberal educators would quarrel with that.

The belittling of knowledge and understanding

Knowledge and understanding, I have claimed, are proper terms for what a liberal education is trying to develop in pupils. These, however, are the very characterizations belittled by exponents of the economic utility model of education, in favour of characteristics like 'skill', largely of course because of the active and instrumental connotation of the latter as compared with the apparent passivity of the former. Part of the technique of advocating the utility model, whether used deliberately and consciously or not it is difficult to say, is to give false, Aunt Sally, conceptions of knowledge and understanding: 'able to understand but not to act', or 'knowledge without skill has a long sad history'. This polarity supposes there to be a kind of knowledge and understanding disconnected from action and purpose, and therefore easily characterized as 'useless' with all the derogatory force of that word in a mainly instrumental, acquisitive and materialistic society. I want to argue that the polarity is a false one. Not only can you not have skills, properly speaking, without knowledge and understanding, which seems to be grudgingly admitted by those who attack liberal education, but it is also nonsense to suppose there to be any knowledge and understanding that does not involve the appropriate exercise of skills. These skills may indeed be mental rather than physical in some, though not all, cases; but then so mainly are the skills of engineers, lawyers, doctors, politicians, business executives and other 'practical men and women'. The point is that to come to know and understand anything in the rich evidential sense I have been arguing for is anything but a passive and purely recipient business. To know and to understand in this sense is to be able to follow and to practise particular kinds of investigative procedures, weigh evidence, make judgements and decide what to believe and what not to believe; to decide how to see things and how not to see things. Being able to explain things to oneself in this kind of a way, with attention to consistency and coherence, is the first step to being able to explain them to others. Seen like this it is not at all surprising that the leaders of industry and commerce and their related services usually come from those who have had a rich liberal education, rather than from those who at an early age have been cut off from such an education and directed into narrow vocationalism emphasizing mainly motor skills.

The first complaint, then, against the attempted belittling of knowledge and understanding, is that these ideas are wrongly characterized. The decision-making that is so valued by the exponents of the utility model and by the 'capability' proponents is in fact both a necessary part of knowledge and understanding and would be pure unguided will without them.

The second complaint, also following directly from arguments made earlier in this work, is that only knowledge and understanding on a wide base can liberate a person from the particular restrictions of birth, social class and geography. Without such a base any choices are bound to be restricted because of the limited perspective brought to bear on them. To think that choices of career or life-style can be made solely on the basis of necessarily limited work experience, factory visits and similar experiences to be found in careers education courses, is clearly wrong. The number of places visited, the types of work experienced, the life-styles sampled, would need to be enormous for the choices to be made on that basis. The supposition that the evidence on which choices are made becomes more 'real' because of this kind of experience is a fallacy which might be dubbed the 'concrete fallacy'. Having a broken leg, being stuck in a front-line trench or being unemployed are not necessarily the best ways of gaining any extensive understanding of bone injury, war or unemployment; neither is working on a conveyor belt, learning to use a lathe or to prepare hotel meals the best way of getting an understanding of the so-called 'world of work'. The direct experience may well be sharp and penetrating, but because it is necessarily of such a limited aspect of what is to be understood its very force becomes a handicap rather than an asset. The emotive impact of an experience is no necessary measure of its contribution to understanding. The very detachment, lack of passion, and abstractness of much of the knowledge and understanding handled in a liberally educative way, which it is now so fashionable to attack, are essentials of a balanced, wide and liberating understanding.

A third complaint against the diminution of the extent of knowledge and understanding in a compulsory education, and its replacement by cruder training elements, is that such diminution reduces the liberating influence of education by reducing the pupil's opportunity to develop a critical framework of thinking. To be capable of critically viewing one's own position, one's own perspective, the demands being made upon one and the opportunities provided or not provided, it is necessary to be able to make comparisons and contrasts against a wide background of actual, possible and imaginable different conceptions of things and of how things might be. This kind of comparative complex is only to be gained by a reasonably extensive study of human practices as delineated in chapter 7 (section s. 1) of my book *Beyond the Present and Particular* (Bailey 1984). These practices included those that manifested themselves in economic, commercial and industrial institutions, and in art, craft and design; and the point was made that understanding these practices would necessarily involve some active participation, but that such participatory activities were to be directed to the end of understanding the practices and not towards training for a future in them. For example, I claimed that a pupil engaged in art at a school of general and liberal education is studying and practising with a different purpose from that of a student in an art school. In a school of liberal education we are not trying to produce an artist, but a human being who has some understanding of the arts as a great and pervasive human practice. I should add here that another characteristic of the place of art, or anything else, in a liberal education is that the particular practice is to be seen in the light of, and as shedding light on, all the other practices studied. What R.S. Peters called 'cognitive perspective' is an important aim of liberal education but does not seem to figure very largely in the economic utility model of education. To foreclose too soon on this process of a widening of cognitive perspective through an individual's growth of knowledge and understanding is to limit the growth of critical power which is a necessary part of individual autonomy.

It is perhaps wrong to claim that exponents of vocational training or emphasis within the period of compulsory education are deliberately seeking to curb critical power and attitude, though the references to MSC course censorship already made would lend weight to such a claim. Nevertheless, the result is the same whether deliberate or not, whether wished for or not. Those who seek to devalue knowledge and understanding, as compared with training, and those who seek to reduce the time involved in school concern for knowledge and understanding as against training, are devaluing the concern for developing the rational autonomy of the pupil which constitutes the main justification for compelling children to be in school at all.

CONCLUSION

In this chapter I have given a sketch and a criticism of what is perhaps the most overt and immediately pressing challenge which faces the view of liberal education. What I have sketched here is also, of course, an attack on the education system as it stands in this country today. It is important not to be confused here, since an attempt to develop a genuine liberal education for all pupils up to at least the age of 16 would also be an attack on the system as it exists today. To defend my view of liberal education against alternative conceptions giving emphasis to training and to vocational preparation is not to defend the present system. Conversely, arguments pointing to defects in the present system, in schools as they actually exist today, and there are many, are not necessarily arguments against the view of liberal education presented here. I happen to believe that a good deal of what goes on in our schools is liberally educating, but not enough of it is. There is not enough concern for evidential teaching and teaching for understanding, there is far too early a narrowing of curriculum spread; there is too much concern for relating the curriculum to career choice and there is too much emphasis on competition and not enough on collaboration. An exponent of the economic utility model of education that I have tried to characterize and criticize would no doubt turn these criticisms of the status quo on their head, claiming there to be too much concern about understanding and not enough concern about the 'realities' of competition, careers and the creation of wealth. Neither of us totally approves of the present system, but we would improve things in totally opposed ways. The debate is a real one.

At this historical moment (late 1983) there is little doubt that the economic utility model, supported by the government and the Manpower Services Commission as well as by powerful agencies of industry and commerce, is winning the power struggle if not the debate. The reason it is winning is mainly to do with the strength and alignment of political forces, but a powerful subsidiary factor is the failure of professional educators to first articulate, and then defend, a coherent view of liberal education.

There are those who would say that what is happening is no more than forces already and always at work in a capitalist democratic society becoming open about what they are always trying to do. The liberal education I am advocating would never stand a chance, these critics would say, because it could not be divorced from the productive and social relationships obtaining in a capitalist society. These critics raise profound problems about the relativity of knowledge, and about the relationship between knowledge and ideology, and to these difficult questions we must now turn.

NOTES

1 Mr James Callaghan, then Prime Minister, made such charges in his speech at Ruskin College Oxford, on 18 October 1976. The charge that schools pay insufficient attention to respect for industry and wealth creation was made by Mrs Shirley Williams, then Secretary of State for Education, in 1977 and more stridently by Conservative politicians and by groups like Understanding British Industry ever since.
2 To confirm this brief assertion, readers might look at: J. Rawls (1972) *A Theory of Justice* (Oxford: Clarendon Press); A. Gewirth (1978) *Reason and Morality* (Chicago: University of Chicago Press); and B. Ackerman (1980) *Social Justice in the Liberal State* (New Haven: Yale University Press).
3 Jonathan (1983: 9). The whole of Ruth Jonathan's paper is an excellent case against the trends criticized in this chapter. For another form of criticism against skills approaches see P. Atkinson, T.L. Rees, D. Shore and H. Williamson (1982) 'Social and Life Skills: The Latest Case of Compensatory Education', in T. Rees and P. Atkinson (eds) *Youth Unemployment and State Intervention*, London: Routledge & Kegan Paul.

REFERENCES

Bailey, C. (1984) *Beyond the Present and Particular*, London: Routledge & Kegan Paul.
Council for Science and Society (1981) *New Technology: Society, Employment and Skill*, London: CSS.
Davis, B. (1979) *From Social Education to Social and Life Skills Training: In Whose Interests?*, Leicester: National Youth Bureau.
Department of Education and Science (1981) *The School Curriculum*, London: HMSO,
Department of Education and Science (1982) *Teacher Training and Preparation for Working Life*, London: HMSO, p. 1.

Fromm, E. (1956) *The Sane Society*, London: Allen & Unwin.

Jonathan, R. (1983) 'The manpower service model of education', *Cambridge Journal of Education*, 13(2).

Peters, R.S. (1966) *Ethics and Education*, London: Allen & Unwin, pp. 225–6.

Schools Council (1981) *The Practical Curriculum*, Working Paper 70. London: Methuen Educational.

Chapter 8

Career trajectories and the mirage of increased social mobility

K. Roberts

DECADE OF OPPORTUNITY?

The 16–19 Initiative commenced in 1986 with the aim of identifying young people's main routes from education into the labour market, establishing which young people followed different career trajectories, and exploring the implications for their economic and political socialization, their self-concepts and subsequent prospects. In the event all mention of career routes and trajectories became controversial, especially the connotation of young people being somehow propelled along awaiting channels towards predetermined destinations. The researchers themselves became uncertain of whether these terms were helpful in analysing young people's movements towards, then into, the labour market. Indeed, Bates and Riseborough (1993) have contained much evidence of young people striving despite numerous obstacles to create paths for themselves towards their own goals. None of the groups studied in depth gave an appearance of moving passively towards destinations presented to them by the wider society. Beyond the research community, there was much talk in the 1980s about the social structure loosening and opportunities widening. Maybe earlier generations' paths into the labour market, and the jobs in which they would end up, had been clearly signposted. It was more debatable whether this still applied at the end of the 1980s. The virtual disappearance of youth employment in many parts of Britain had destroyed some former routes. It was possible to talk of school-leavers' prospects having deteriorated, though some young people, certainly the more enterprising among them, were supposed to be benefiting from new opportunities.

Enterprise became a buzz-word in the 1980s. Margaret Thatcher declared that there was no such thing as society, but we all knew that she did not intend to be taken literally. She meant that the shape of society was not the determinant so much as the outcome of the actions of individuals, families, businesses and other constituent groups. Her view was that people could and should be allowed to build their own lives and shape their society accordingly. Her successor, John Major, declared in favour of a classless Britain. Again, we all knew that he was not really advocating the abolition of socio-economic inequalities. He was arguing that his own biography, like his predecessor's, suggested that former barriers were being dismantled and would continue to be eroded. And this erosion was to be achieved by releasing capitalist market forces, not through socialist engineering. Margaret Thatcher was a grocer's daughter. John Major was a circus artiste's son. Neither of these prime ministers' careers followed an established trajectory. Nevertheless, the results of the 16–19 Initiative show that, for most school-leavers in the late 1980s, Britain was still a land of very unequal opportunities.

To begin with, the samples' prospects at age 16 had depended heavily on their prior education. Margaret Thatcher and John Major were both eleven-plus successes. They attended grammar schools. One wonders if their careers could have been built from secondary modern backgrounds. Of course, by the 1980s, the eleven-plus had been consigned to history in most parts of Britain, including all the areas covered in the 16–19 enquiries, though private schools continued to co-exist alongside local education authority (LEA) comprehensives, and, possibly more crucial to the present point, pupils from LEA schools were not being given equal starts in life. Comprehensive pupils were streamed and setted, entered for different examinations, and by age 16 had very different levels of qualifications. Since 1988, all pupils have been entered for GCSE examinations, but some follow relatively easy syllabuses that cannot lead to the higher grade passes demanded by most universities and employers who can offer 'good jobs'. So everyone can still be graded at age 16 according to their number of ABCs, and so on. As types of secondary school have ceased to be divisive, qualifications earned in secondary education have become increasingly important. This was evident in Bates and Riseborough (1993). The sixth-formers on A-level courses had good O-level passes, the BTEC students preparing for careers in catering and fashion design were from the next rungs down the qualification ladder, while the young people training on the YTS for jobs in care and building were on their schemes largely because they lacked useful qualifications. The importance of qualifications was confirmed in the quantitative evidence from the questionnaire surveys in all four areas. Indeed, qualifications earned by age 16 proved the best single predictor of the directions that individuals' careers would then take, particularly whether they would remain in full-time education and, if so, on which courses. However, qualifications also made a huge difference to the prospects of those who left full-time education at 16 (Roberts et al. 1991). Among those who entered the YTS, the better-qualified usually obtained training on employer-led schemes where there were prospects of being kept on. When individuals sought employment immediately on leaving school at 16, the better qualified were the most likely to obtain jobs and avoid unemployment. Qualifications earned earlier on remained important even at later career stages. When individuals became unemployed, those with the better qualifications stood the best chances of escaping quickly. When jobs were obtained, the better-qualified tended to be given the higher pay, the most training and the best prospects.

The ethnographies in this book illustrate how some young people's options were further limited to the opportunities in their home areas. The majority of the teenagers had not enjoyed the freedom to roam throughout the national labour market. They had all been sent to local schools, then proceeded to local colleges, training schemes or jobs. The majority could not afford to relocate, or even pay for the expensive public transport journeys given the lack of educational grants for most 16- to 18-year-olds and the modest allowances paid to youth trainees. In Liverpool, a representative sample of young blacks was studied alongside the main 16–19 Initiative sample (Connolly *et al.* 1991). The young blacks' opportunities were exceptionally restricted by a fear of venturing into most parts of their home city. The ethnographies in Bates and Riseborough (1993) have revealed how little scope for real choice many of the young people possessed, but they cannot portray how different their opportunities might have been had they lived in another part of Britain. The questionnaire findings from the area studies reveal the extent of these inequalities. Swindon, the one research area in southern England, was very different from all the others. A third of the Swindon sample made direct transitions from school into employment at age 16, whereas in Kirkcaldy, Liverpool and Sheffield only around one in ten made such 'traditional transitions'. Needless to say, unemployment was far lower in Swindon than in the other areas. Young people with just average or below-average educational attainments were the most affected by conditions in their local labour markets. The better-qualified could continue in education and eventually become part of the national labour market. Alternatively, if they sought jobs locally, their qualifications placed them at the head of the queues (Roberts *et al.* 1991). In Bates and Riseborough (1993) the privately educated girls studied by Debra Roker and the sixth-formers studied by John Quicke were earning qualifications that would give them above-average chances were they to enter their local labour market. However, these young people did not need to remain in their home area; they had wider options in higher education. Less-qualified teenagers normally faced the additional disadvantage of having to remain home-based, which was a particularly severe handicap where the local labour market was depressed. One wonders whether the teenage John Major would have found it as easy to move into merchant banking after a succession of stop-gap jobs had he lived in the provinces instead of London.

Sociologists are renowned for stressing the governing role of social class and this chapter will eventually prove true to type; its main argument is that the career propects of the young people studied in the 16–19 Initiative had depended mainly on their social class origins. One hesitates to say 'determined by', but the young people's educational attainments, and whether they attended private or LEA schools, were very much class related. At age 16, their immediate prospects varied greatly according to their social class backgrounds. A point to grasp is that focusing on individuals' success or failure at any particular career stage such as 16–19, then separating the different factors on which progress depends, inevitably obscures the influence of social class. This is because social origins do not directly determine adult positions but operate through a series of intermediaries – neighbourhoods, likelihood of attending a private school, qualifications earned whatever school attended, and so on. Also, the influence of social class is cumulative. Whether or not infants are well-prepared to make fast starts in infant school is class-related. Then, independently of prior preparation, so is progress within primary education. Then, whatever pupils' earlier attainments, so is progress in secondary education, and likewise from age 16 to 19, and then beyond. At each stage, social class may be well down the list of predictors of performance but its cumulative effects, gradually mounting over time, mean that its eventual hold on life chances proves considerable.

Even so, social class was certainly not the sole source of unequal opportunities among the young people studied in the 16–19 Initiative. Whatever their social class origins, the young people's subsequent opportunities had varied according to their achievements in school and places of residence. Ethnic divisions were also of huge importance, especially to members of minority groups. In Liverpool in 1988–89, approximately 20 per cent of the city's 18- to 19-year-olds were unemployed, while roughly a half held full-time jobs. Among the city's black youth, these proportions were almost exactly reversed: only a fifth had full-time jobs while a half were unemployed (Connolly et al. 1991). The greater part of this difference could not be accounted for in terms of educational attainments or the blacks' residential concentration in inner-Liverpool. Of course, the blacks were disadvantaged by the depressed state of the Liverpool labour market. White youth in Liverpool were likely to see this as their main problem, but for the young blacks racism was the main barrier of which they were all too painfully aware.

Sex had proved to be another great and persistent divider. There were only minor differences between the proportions of males and females in the 16–19 Initiative who remained in full-time education beyond age 16, entered the YTS, and who were employed and unemployed at different stages. However, there were huge sex differences in the courses followed by those in education, the occupations for which others were trained, and in which they were subsequently employed. Inge Bates and George Riseborough (1993) were being entirely naturalistic in selecting pairs of vocational courses and training schemes that recruited mainly girls and boys, respectively. Their ethnographies also reveal how each sex had gendered expectations and aspirations. Males' and females' life chances were structured differently, not only by the different opportunities to which they had access but also by the young people having largely internalized their society's expectations. The same applied to some extent to the different opportunities associated with places of residence and qualifications. Males and females who completed their secondary education with different levels of attainments were already partly pro-grammed so that they tended to avoid making choices which would have made it as plain to the individuals themselves as in our research evidence just how bounded their opportunities were, and how they were being propelled along awaiting career routes. It is true that some of the young people were attempting to break out. Some females were toying with aims untypical for their sex. Likewise, some of the less-qualified males and females were modestly ambitious and hoped to obtain appren-ticeships or to become nurses, for example. Yet they only had to attempt to enact these aims to discover all too painfully, in most cases, the boundaries which fenced their opportunities. During the 1980s in Britain, school-leavers' opportunities were restructured rather than destructured in ways that would have widened their options and left their futures more open.

NEW OPTIONS

The 1980s' 16-year-olds were certainly offered a range of wholly new options. From 1983 onwards, the YTS guaranteed quality training to all who left education and were unable to obtain suitable employment. The YTS was introduced at a time of high unemployment, but it was intended to become a permanent bridge between school and work. The Manpower Services Commission (MSC), the scheme's parent, insisted that this measure was not just another alternative to joblessness. It proclaimed that, first and foremost, the YTS was a training measure. The scheme replaced the Youth Opportunities Programme which had begun in 1978 as a temporary measure, and which offered, at best, a mere six months of work experience. The YTS was to be different. It was to deliver quality training leading to real skills and recognized qualifications. This scheme quickly became the normal next step for 16-year-old school-leavers in most parts of Britain. In three of the main 16–19 research areas – Kirkcaldy, Liverpool and Sheffield – approximately two-fifths of the samples entered the labour market through the scheme. Swindon was the sole area where more 16-year-olds made 'traditional transitions' straight into jobs at 16 (Roberts and Parsell 1990). The YTS began as a one-year scheme, and was extended to two years in 1986, just before the younger respondents in the 16–19 enquiry left school.

The 1980s' 16-year-olds also had new options in full-time education. The days were gone when schools had no places for 16-year-olds without the qualifications deemed necessary to attempt the A-levels in England and Highers in Scotland required for higher education. By the 1980s, 'new sixth-formers' were welcome in virtually all comprehensives. Many schools and colleges operated 'open enrolment' – a place for everyone. There were opportunities to retake or add to existing successes in O-levels and CSEs. Then, in addition, there were new courses leading to BTECs, the Certificate of Pre-Vocational Education (CPVE) and other vocational qualifications. Vocational education was not newly invented in the 1980s. National Certificates and Diplomas had been available since the 1920s, and City and Guilds and Royal Society of Arts qualifications since the nineteenth century. What happened in the 1980s was that many more part-time and full-time courses were introduced linked to a wider range of occupations than formerly, and catering for young people ranging from those with excellent academic qualifications to those with none at all. By the end of the 1980s, the dense 'jungle' of vocational credentials and courses was being systematized into a matrix of National Vocational Qualifications (NVQs). The launch of the YTS in 1983 was accompanied by a decline in the proportion of 16-year-olds remaining in full-time education, but by 1985–86 Britain's schools and colleges were once again retaining a rising proportion of the age group. So across all four areas in the 16–19 Initiative, 45 per cent of the older respondents who reached age 16 in 1985, but 54 per cent of the younger cohort who became 16 in 1987, re-enrolled in full-time education (Roberts and Parsell 1990). Many 16-year-olds must have been bewildered by their plethora of options in education and training. Even low-achievers discovered that their schools were keen to retain them. A crucial fact of this matter was that the schools needed the extra numbers to protect their rolls in a period when the size of the secondary school age group was declining. So sixth-forms and further education colleges began competing for young people at careers conventions. Meanwhile, television adverts told potential trainees that dozens of blue-chip companies, and even the England soccer team manager, were willing to train them.

A declared intention when these new opportunities were created was that they should be of greatest benefit to young people who were otherwise least advantaged. So the young unemployed were to be given the chance to learn skills that would equip them for the new technology jobs that were to come on stream. Young people who had not excelled on academic courses were to have the chance to acquire vocational knowledge and credentials. Those who did not thrive in classrooms were to be allowed to demonstrate their competence in real work situations. Unfortunately, there were serious hitches in these new opportunities. First, the chance of obtaining a real job at age 16 was not among them, and in 1988 most 16- and 17-year-olds lost the right to be unemployed and claim social security. Throughout the 1980s, it remained normal throughout Britain for young people to test the labour market as they approached the statutory school-leaving age. Even those who intended to stay on for A-levels would often submit job applications, just in case they failed to earn the grades required for their first choices. Many other 16-year-olds returned to education or joined the YTS only because they were unable to obtain jobs. If it had remained on offer, the likelihood is that many, possibly the majority, of these 16 year-olds would have grasped the old infinitely preferable opportunity of immediate employment. Most of the ethnographies in this book report on young people who either remained in full-time education or entered the YTS at age 16. Until the 1980s, such a selection could have been criticized as unrepresentative, but by the time of the research in the late 1980s, only approximately one in ten of all 16-year-olds in Sheffield, Liverpool and Kirkcaldy were obtaining full-time employment. It was necessity rather than choice that had pushed many other young people onto the YTS and retained others in education.

A second hitch was that the new opportunities did not have equal status. In terms of the likelihood of obtaining a good job by age 19, the best proposition was to continue along the academic mainstream earning A-levels. The second best options were other types of full-time education and employer-led youth training. Employer-led schemes had the clear advantage over other forms of youth training of there being at least a chance of being kept on. Despite the stated intention that the new opportunities should be most helpful to less advantaged 16-year-olds, individuals' chances of entering the pathways with the best prospects were governed by their existing qualifications. So, in Bates and Riseborough (1993), the girls who were training for care occupations and the boys on the college-based building YTS had not been offered the options of A-levels or even employer-led training.

A third hitch was that, when 16-year-olds were offered real choices, all the options often led to the same labour market destinations. Whether they sought employment immediately, stayed in full-time education or entered the YTS, poorly qualified 16-year-olds in Sheffield, Kirkcaldy and Liverpool were most likely to find themselves limited to non-skilled employment and competing for an inadequate number of jobs at age 18. In some cases, the different opportunities available at 16 amounted to little more than a variety of ways of postponing the risk of unemployment. It may tax the credulity of the relevant further education and training staff to be told that they were not improving the young people's labour market prospects. They are likely to have seen the majority of the teenagers who they taught or trained proceeding into employment, often in directly related fields, and would have assumed that the young people's progress was due to the education and training received. Yet the statistical evidence from the 16–19 Initiative is unequivocal. Particular schemes and courses may have focused young people's opportunities upon particular firms and occupations, but without necessarily raising the levels at which they were most likely to find employment. Trainers and teachers can never be certain of what would have happened if the young people in their charge had taken different paths. What would have happened if they had persisted in seeking jobs and declined all the alternatives at age 16? The survey evidence from the 16–19 Initiative answers this question. In the late 1980s, by age 18–20, young people overall would have had exactly the same likelihood of avoiding unemployment and holding jobs, and at precisely the same levels, as individuals who were equally qualified at age 16 and then opted for youth training or further education. In terms purely of their relationships to the labour market, that is, excluding any implications for personal and social development, the principal role of a great deal of the new further education and training created in the 1980s was 'warehousing'.

With the passage of time, this role is likely to be obscured by a ratchet effect. As more 16-year-olds enter further education or training, employers tend to switch their recruitment to an older age group, and before long it becomes necessary to proceed through more education or formal training in order to stand any chance of obtaining jobs that were once available at age 16. The point is that the main propulsive force behind this development in the 1980s was not a technical need for the young people concerned to receive further education or training prior to taking up employment, but a straightforward shortage of jobs. At the time there was much talk of a skills revolution, impending shortages, and of the economy needing young people to reach higher standards in skills and qualifications than in the past. One plain fact, however, was that much of the additional education and training was in low-level skills and qualifications that were not in increasing demand. Another fact of the situation was that there was far more hard evidence, as opposed to talk, of an abundance of labour and talent in relation to demand in the labour markets in most parts of Britain. These were the structural determinants of the actual role of much further education and training in the 1980s.

THE MAIN ROUTES

At the beginning of the 1970s, there were only two broad routes into Britain's labour markets. Academic high-fliers could remain in education at school or college until age 18 or later, whereas most other young people entered employment at age 16. This is not to say that everyone fell into one or the other of these groups. For instance, some took full-time vocational courses in further education. However, the majority of full-time students after age 16 were academic high-fliers, the remainder of the age group were most likely to start employment at age 16, and together these groups accounted for the vast majority of young people, whereas by the end of the 1980s the combined total of teenagers whose careers conformed to either of these types amounted to only a minority of the age group. There had been massive changes in 16- to 19-year-olds' opportunities. However, the new opportunities were stratified, and access was governed by the same predictors that had governed opportunities previously – sex, educational attainments – with social class origins lurking in the background – and places of residence. Beneath all the changes the old predictors remained in excellent working order. Perhaps even more remarkably, most of the new opportunities had been either absorbed within, or structured around, the longer-established routes – the academic mainstream, and employer-based experience and training from age 16.

One definite conclusion that can be drawn from the 16–19 Initiative's efforts to identify young people's main routes into the labour market is the impossibility of providing a definitive list. By the end of the 1980s, there were many possible ways of classifying young people's patterns of progression, or lack of progression, and which classifications worked best depended on the purposes. The ethnographies, rather than the statistical evidence from the questionnaires, describe 'real' trajectories and validate the concept. Every course and scheme selected for ethnographic study was drawing entrants from particular kinds of family and educational backgrounds, then pushing them irrespective of whether they went gently or were resistant, towards a specific set of labour market destinations. It is crystal clear from this evidence that there were definite links between young people's family and educational origins, their experiences from 16 to 19, and their subsequent employment prospects. The 'real trajectories' followed by the young people in the ethnographies were far narrower than categories such as 'vocational education' and 'YTS'; they were defined more precisely by the particular ranges of courses, schemes and subsequent jobs available to individuals of their sex, with their qualifications and in their localities. Throughout the UK, there would have been thousands of such trajectories defined by particular courses, schemes and local labour market conditions, though many of these unique routes shared a great deal in common. In analysing the Initiative's quantitative evidence, it was therefore possible to group the young people's transitional experiences to show how certain kinds of trajectory were occurring throughout the country and to highlight major differences.

An obvious grouping in the late 1980s was according to whether 16-year-olds remained in full-time education, entered the YTS, found jobs immediately, or obtained early experience of unemployment (Roberts and Parsell 1989b). This particular classification proved particularly useful for demonstrating how the young people's sources and levels of income, and therefore their consumption opportunities, varied according to their routes into the labour market. There were obvious possibilities for subdividing all the routes in this typology. Post-compulsory education could be split into academic and vocational segments, training schemes into those led by employers and the rest, and jobs according to the pay, security, prospects and training that were offered. However, on introducing such subdivisions, it became evident that in terms of the types of young people recruited and their subsequent prospects, some varieties of youth training had more in common with certain types of jobs and educational programmes than other branches of the YTS. Hence the possibility of a further reclassification.

Different typologies served different purposes, and for revealing how 16-year-olds were being propelled along pre-set trajectories, with each step onwards increasing the probability of them reaching what had always been their most likely destinations, *the most useful classification identified just three main routes* − only two of which led towards the types of employment that virtually all the young people had hoped to enter prior to leaving school. These two routes had not been newly constructed during the 1980s. They were long-established and were absorbing or otherwise defining niches for, rather than being obliterated by, the new schemes and courses that had recently become available. One route was based on academic success, which secured entry to jobs with training and encouragement to earn further qualifications, leading eventually to professional, management and other high-level employment. It was possible to make the transition from education into this career stream at age 16, but it was more common for high achievers to remain full-time students at least up to A-levels and often through higher education. The second route was into 'good jobs' but not 'top jobs', whether manual or white-collar, which offered average or better security and pay. Access was by gaining experience in, and proving one's worth within, the firms that had such jobs to offer. The initial in-firm training could be in regular employment or under the YTS, but it had to be within a firm that could offer a 'good job' at the end. Vocational skills and qualifications from colleges and training schemes were doing little to strengthen their holders' chances in external labour markets (Roberts and Parsell 1989a).

Now these same routes were identified by Ashton and Field (1976) in the 1970s. They divided beginning workers at that time into those who embarked on extended and short careers. The main changes on the extended career route by the later 1980s were, first, that the path had broadened due to changes in the occupational structure with the proportion of high-level jobs having increased at the expense of low-level employment and, secondly, that well-qualified young people were more likely to remain in full-time education until age 18 or later, so the transition into employment was normally at a later age than formerly. On the short career route, the main changes had been, first, that some of these transitions had been prolonged by the insertion of a YTS stage and, secondly, that qualifications had become more important in gaining entry. This was a result of the growth in the proportion of school-leavers, especially among those with average and below-average academic ability, who could offer paper qualifications, and the importance attached to this signal of potential in employers' selection procedures.

However, the main change since Ashton and Field's research had undoubtedly been in the prospects of young people who failed to gain entry even to short careers. From the Second World War until the 1970s, they were able to obtain non-skilled jobs and to move between a succession of such jobs if they so desired. The compensation for lack of long-term prospects was 'good money' at a young age. The lads in Paul Willis' *Learning to Labour* (1977) had seized such employment enthusiastically, but by the end of the 1980s most of these jobs had either been wiped out by economic and occupational restructuring or were filled by adults. So school-leavers and scheme-leavers who failed to progress to 'good jobs' were likely to move between unemployment, insecure low-paid jobs and temporary places on schemes such as the Community Programme up to 1988 and Employment Training subsequently. Needless to say, these individuals were at risk of longer-term unemployment. They were unable to save for deposits to purchase houses, or even to furnish rented accommodation and thereby cross other normal thresholds in the transition to adulthood.

The divisions between these three trajectories were clear in the survey evidence from the 16–19 Initiative, though not necessarily to the young people themselves. There were several reasons for this. First, individuals in all social locations tend to be most aware of, and sensitive to, the differences between their own and adjacent rather than more distant positions. So youth trainees were tending to judge their own experiences against those of friends on similar schemes. Those who failed to gain even non-skilled jobs typically compared their own lack of luck with individuals who managed to gain and hold on to such employment.

Secondly, a norm of optimism prevailed among the young people, and possibly throughout adult society. Even those in the least advantaged positions seemed to believe that eventually they would overcome their difficulties; to have felt otherwise would have betrayed a lack of confidence in themselves. Thirdly, and related to the need to be optimistic and to feel in control, the young people seemed to have accepted that their futures were their own responsibility rather than dictated by society. To this extent, they had absorbed the enterprise culture. Fourthly, in the post-16 career stage, the young people were not only being channelled towards, but were typically experiencing further socialization which was adjusting their aspirations to their actual prospects. So the girls being trained in care in Bates and Riseborough (1993), for example, were learning to hope for and to seek jobs with care organizations.

CLASS ORIGINS AND TRAJECTORIES

A further classification of the samples' career development was according to individuals' success or failure at three successive stages: before age 16, from age 16 to 18, and thereafter. First, the samples were divided according to whether their examination performances at age 16 were above or below average. In the second stage, the young people were rated as making successful transitions between 16 and 18 if they remained in full-time education throughout or if any youth training was employer-led, and if they avoided unemployment whatever their ages on entering the labour market proper. In the third stage, individuals were judged to have reached successful destinations at 18–20 if they either entered and remained in higher education, or if they obtained skilled manual or white-collar jobs and avoided unemployment completely.

It will be clear by now that this was just one of many ways in which the samples' career development could be and was analysed, but the scheme now being described was particularly useful for highlighting differences by social class origins. Young people from middle-class families were twice as likely as those from working-class homes to experience continuous success. Indeed, this was not just the most common but the majority pattern of career development for such young people. Seventy per cent were 'successful' as defined above at all three career stages. Transitions for young people from middle-class backgrounds had normally been relatively smooth. They had mostly been successful in their secondary schools. Subsequently, they either stayed on to take A-levels (Highers in Scotland), obtained good jobs immediately or proceeded to good jobs through employer-led youth training. A middle-class home background was not only a good predictor of educational success, but was also independently related to young people making the best possible use of their qualifications at later career stages.

Pat Allatt's discussion of the relationships between middle-class parents and their teenage children in Bates and Riseborough (1993) provides insights into how this was occurring. The parents not only wanted but expected their children to succeed, and by age 16 the young people had internalized these aspirations. Also, the parents could advise their children knowledgeably and confidently, and could use their own contacts if necessary, in order to ensure that the young people were given the opportunities that they wanted and were deemed to deserve. Debra Roker (op. cit.), discussing girls at a private school, describes how anyone contemplating dropping-out prior to *higher* education was considered a 'weirdo'. It is likely that anyone from this school whose examination performance was below-average for the entire age group, or who entered any branch of youth training, would have been a grave disappointment to the parents and teachers concerned. Even in LEA comprehensives, young people from middle-class homes were typically surrounded by social and cultural support systems which carried them across all the hurdles *en route* to good jobs. Succeeding did not appear to demand exceptional effort or enterprise from most of the young people themselves. Rather, dropping-out must have required the greater initiative and willingness to face censure from parents, teachers and also from friends.

The normal pattern of career development among young people from working-class homes was not continuous failure. Only 12 per cent of those from manual families in the questionnaire samples had below-average success at secondary school, followed by unemployment or low-status youth training between 16 and 18, then unemployment or poor quality jobs between 18 and 20. However, two-thirds of the respondents from working-class backgrounds had experienced failure at one or more stages. Major setbacks had been normal experiences for these young people, and it was this that set them apart from their middle-class contemporaries. The working-class child who rose smoothly to a good job or higher education by 18–20 was the exception rather than the norm within his or her peer group. In former years, the 11-plus was a major hurdle, but none of the children in the 16–19 Initiative's areas had faced this particular obstacle. Nevertheless, in their comprehensive, the pupils from working-class homes had typically found themselves in the lower streams or sets, and had achieved only lower-grade passes in the 16-plus examinations. It is true that very few had left school without any qualifications at all, but some with graded passes considered that their qualifications were useless – indications of failure rather than success. The interviews with 16- to 18-year-olds on the lowest status trajectories – the care girls and the lads on the building course in Bates and Riseborough (1993) – revealed several cases where individuals simply did not know what their school-leaving qualifications were; they had not bothered to find out and had assumed that any lower graded passes that they had achieved would be worthless.

Some recovered from poor performances at age 16 by staying on to repeat exams or to earn vocational qualifications. Others managed to obtain good jobs or places on employer-led training schemes, despite their lack of impressive educational attainments. However, lack of such qualifications placed the individuals concerned at high risk of allocation to non-employer-led training, or unemployment if they sought jobs without passing through the YTS. Working-class teenagers with above-average educational attainments were more likely to fail during the 16–18 stage than similarly qualified young people from middle-class families. This seemed to be because, as indicated previously, the latter had internalized greater self-confidence and higher aspirations, and their families and friends were more likely to have useful contacts in education and industry. The case studies (*op. cit.*) of young people pursuing BTEC qualifications in the hope of embarking on careers in hotels and catering, and fashion design, draw attention to the importance of the financial support that the students' families could or could not offer. Some, but not all, of the students, felt that they needed to do one or more part-time jobs alongside their full-time studies. So a working-class background increased the likelihood of individuals failing in secondary school, and also at 16–18. Of course, recovery was still possible, but for those with records of repeated failure up to age 18, further difficulties were probable. Even beyond age 18 individuals from middle-class homes were continuing to benefit from the support, encouragement, aspirations and social networks that they had inherited. By this stage, some young people, mainly from working-class homes, were scarred by repeated experiences of failure.

A successful transition for young people from working-class backgrounds meant surviving though difficulties and failures. It would be wrong to create an impression that most respondents from working-class homes either regarded themselves as failures or were reconciled to whatever labour market fates awaited them. Many were not following their career trajectories enthusiastically or even passively. Some were non-compliant. Some were determined to break-out and get on, but ambitions alone were no guarantee of success. Moreover, working-class teenagers tended to measure their own success or failure against the norms for their own social groups. In general, the young people were optimistic about their prospects. In every wave of the questionnaire surveys, they collectively over-estimated their chances of being in jobs and under-estimated their risks of unemployment 12 months forward. Their self-confidence and belief in their ability to obtain suitable jobs eventually were normally surviving setbacks. However, the ethnographies illustrate how individuals were often adjusting their sights in line with their most likely opportunities. So 'the lads' studied in Bates and Riseborough (1993) knew that they could expect nothing better than labouring jobs, and the 'care girls' (*op. cit.*), were eventually delighted if and when they were kept on by the employers with whom they were placed for training. Very few had felt this way about care jobs on starting their training scheme. Their experience on the YTS appeared to be teaching these groups of young people to be grateful for the chance to prove their worth to an employer, and to consider themselves successful if offered permanent employment. The girls at Debra Roker's independent school and the sixth-formers studied by John Quicke (op. cit.) judged success using very different yardsticks.

THE MIRAGE

The volume of social mobility revealed by the questionnaire surveys was far from trivial. Just over a third of the young people from working-class homes were experiencing continuous success as they moved through the 16-plus examinations, further education or training, then into higher education or good jobs. Only a minority of the privately educated girls in Debra Roker's study (op. cit.) – generally those benefiting from assisted places – were from working-class families, but such origins were much in evidence among the LEA sixth-formers discussed by John Quicke (op. cit.).

The 16–19 Initiative was insufficiently longitudinal to study trends over a generation or more, but there can be little doubt that in the 1980s the proportions of children from working-class homes who were succeeding in secondary school, proceeding to higher education, and entering skilled and other high-level jobs were higher than in the 1950s and 1960s. Other things had only to remain equal for this to result from the expansion of post-compulsory education and the parallel increase in the proportion of professional and management jobs at the expense of manual employment. Increased upward mobility forced or facilitated by structural changes is a long-running trend in Britain. The 1944 Education Act increased the chances of working-class children receiving a grammar school education and, by the 1950s, across the country, approximately a half of all grammar school pupils were first-generation from working-class homes. Such figures and trends easily create an appearance of Britain becoming a more open and fluid society. The reason why this appearance is just a mirage is that the same developments that have drawn more working-class young people up the educational and occupational ladders have simultaneously reduced the chances of middle-class children descending. The net result, following the 1944 Education Act, was that relative inequalities in life chances, the greater likelihood of middle-class than working-class children reaching middle-class destinations, remained virtually unchanged (Goldthorpe *et al.* 1980; Halsey *et al.* 1980). This was probably happening during the 1980s when, according to the evidence from this research, just over a third of young people from working-class backgrounds, but over two-thirds from middle-class homes, were experiencing continuous success. This was a glaring flaw in the open society scenario.

Another was that only some of the young people in post-compulsory education and training had good prospects. From afar, from Westminster and London newspaper editorial suites, it may have been possible to believe that all young people who were being given new opportunities in further education and training were benefiting from enhanced life chances. Actually, the students with good prospects were generally those who had achieved good qualifications at age 16, especially those who then proceeded down the traditional academic route. The youth trainees with good prospects were mostly those with good enough qualifications to have won selection by employers offering high-quality training with prospects of retention and progressive careers to follow. The most likely sequels to other courses and training schemes were far less attractive. Upward mobility from the working class, when in process, was normally based on good performances at secondary school, as in the past, and the most common subsequent mobility channel was the traditional academic mainstream. A substantial proportion of those following this route were from working-class families and it is tempting to applaud both the young people's success and the educational route that they were following for enabling individuals from less advantaged backgrounds to prove their capability and get on. However, such approval simultaneously legitimizes the procedure and channels that were safeguarding middle-class youth from descent and excluding the majority with working-class origins.

The 1980s did create more opportunities for working-class young people to ascend. These opportunities were mostly constructed not from the enterprise initiatives that Robert MacDonald has described in Bates and Riseborough (1993), but by the expansion of high-level employment and the academic mainstream. However, from a working-class perspective, an equally significant change during the 1980s was the increased risks of descent. Young people who failed to enter short careers and reasonably secure jobs stood real risks of unemployment and survival on poverty incomes with no escapes in sight. For certain groups of young people, the risks of long-term unemployment, or joblessness broken only by low-paid, short-lived jobs and schemes, were considerable. At age 18–19, a half of all young blacks in Liverpool were unemployed, more than twice as many as held full-time jobs, and most of their jobs were from the bottom of the labour market. The YTS lads who spoke for themselves (op. cit.) knew that unemployment following their training was a real possibility, as did the 'care girls' in Inge Bates' study (op. cit.), though their labour market problems were likely to be concealed by withdrawal into domesticity, as happened among earlier generations of young women. Young people who proceeded through the lower status branches of post-compulsory education and youth training were then at risk of unemployment, whereupon they became candidates for the Community Programme, subsequently Employment Training, and the other enterprise initiatives that Robert MacDonald described in Bates and Riseborough (1993). Most of the young adults in his study who were trying to embark into self-employment were doing so only because of their inability to obtain 'proper jobs'. Working-class striving was being sustained as much by a real fear of descent from the 'respectable' into the 'rough' as by the prospect of joining the middle classes.

Whenever social mobility is discussed, it tends to be the upward variety that commands attention. Education and training policies are presented as creating more opportunities for working-class youth to get ahead. How to promote more descents from the middle class is rarely considered, though this would be an inevitable aspect of a more open, fluid society. One has only to raise this problem to recognize why increased social fluidity proves so difficult to achieve. Downward mobility appears to be unacceptable in our society. Individuals will resort to all manner of social and psychological strategies to deny that it has happened or is happening to them (Roberts *et al.* 1977). Downward mobility was not a fate to which the working-class respondents in this research could be easily reconciled. They all preferred to think of their futures in terms of overcoming immediate difficulties. Yet many knew that unemployment was a genuine risk. This was why the working-class teenagers and their parents could regard mere survival in the labour market as success. The working-class young people in Sheffield, Liverpool, Kirkcaldy, Durham and Teesside all had acquaintances if not close friends or family members with direct recent experience of unemployment. The increased risk of downward mobility from the working class was being obscured by the young people's own hopes and optimism, and by the training and education to which they had immediate access. For the middle classes long-range descent was a remote possibility. The contraction of manual employment was forcing more working-class young people upwards than in previous generations, but it was also threatening greater numbers with descent. For middle-class youth, the expansion of professional and management jobs meant that their positions were less vulnerable than before. Their typical problem was to choose between the widening range of occupations at, and routes towards, this level. For working-class youth, beneath the mirage of wider opportunities, descent into unemployment was the main new career trajectory created by trends in the 1980s.

REFERENCES

Ashton, D.N. and Field, D. (1976) *Young Workers*, London: Hutchinson.

Bates, I. and Riseborough, G. (1993) *Youth and Inequality*, London, Routledge & Kegan Paul.

Connolly, M., Roberts, K., Ben-Tovim, G. and Torkington, P. (1991) *Black Youth in Liverpool*, Culemborg: Giordano Bruno.

Goldthorpe, J.H., Llewellyn, C. and Payne, C. (1980) *Social Mobility and Class Structure in Modern Britain*, Oxford: Clarendon Press.

Halsey, A.H., Heath, A.F. and Ridge, J.M. (1980) *Origins and Destinations*, Oxford: Clarendon Press.

Roberts, K., Clark, S., Cook, F. and Semeonoff, E. (1977) *The Fragmentary Class Structure*, London: Heinemann.

Roberts, K. and Parsell, G. (1989a) 'The stratification of youth training'. Occasional Paper 11, ESRC 16–19 Initiative, London: City University.

Roberts, K. and Parsell, G. (1989b) 'Recent changes in the pathways from school to work in Great Britain', in K. Hurrelman and U. Engel (eds) *The Social World of the Adolescent: International Perspectives*, New York: De Gruyter.

Roberts, K. and Parsell, G. (1990) 'Young people's routes into UK labour markets in the late-1980s'. Paper presented to the *Conference on Understanding Unemployment*, Department of Employment/University of York.

Roberts, K., Parsell, G. and Connolly, M. (1991) 'Young people's transitions into the labour market', in M. Cross and G. Payne (eds) *Work and the Enterprise Culture*, London: Falmer Press.

Willis, P. (1977) *Learning to Labour*, Farnborough: Saxon House.

Chapter 9

Training credits

The pilot doomed to succeed

L. Unwin

INTRODUCTION

By 1996, every 16- or 17-year-old leaving full-time education in England, Wales and Scotland will be entitled to receive a training credit to pay for part-time vocational education and training (VET). First announced in March 1990 by the then Secretary of State for Employment, Michael Howard, training credits were to be initially piloted by ten Training and Enterprise Councils (TECs) and one Local Enterprise Company (LEC). As Howard stated in 1990:

> There has been widespread interest in individual training credits as a means of motivating young people to participate more effectively in the training market. . . . The approach is, however, untested. I have therefore decided that there should be pilot schemes at local level.
>
> (ED 1990)

Nevertheless whilst the original pilots were still being evaluated, the 1991 White Paper *Education and Training for the 21st Century* revealed that the scheme was to be extended to a further seven TECs and two LECs in 1993 and would have national coverage by 1996. Known colloquially as the pilot 'doomed to succeed', training credits represent yet another intervention by the Conservative Government to transform post-16 VET. Like previous initiatives, and most notably the Youth Training Scheme (YTS), training credits have been launched as the answer to this country's youth training problems.

Much of the material for this chapter was gained through an evaluation of the first year of South and East Cheshire TEC's pilot. Each of the 11 original pilots underwent similar local evaluations, all commissioned by the Employment Department (ED) and completed by January 1992. In addition, Her Majesty's Inspectorate, the Careers Service Inspectorate and the ED's Training Standards Inspectorate carried out their own evaluations of each first round pilot. Despite this considerable amount of evaluation, however, it was not until summer 1992 that the ED published a summary report of the findings, some ten months after second round pilots had begun developing their operational models.

The chapter begins by examining the government's approach to credits and draws on the experience of the implementation models adopted by the original pilots. It then turns to the operational issues faced by pilots using illustrations from South and East Cheshire TEC in particular to show how credits were working at local level by mid-1992. A significant difference between training credits and previous youth training initiatives is the extent to which local groupings other than the young people themselves have been involved at both the planning and operational stages of the pilot. The way in which those groupings – school teachers, careers officers, employers, college staff and training providers – have responded to credits is explored in this chapter, along with the reactions of the young people themselves. In so doing, questions are raised in relation to VET funding, employer recruitment policies, the provision of careers education and guidance, and the extent of the TECs' influence and acceptance within their local communities. The chapter concludes by considering the long-term viability of training credits given the increasing numbers of young people staying in full-time education after 16 and the continuing impact of economic recession on the availability of jobs for school leavers.

BACKGROUND TO CREDITS: VET IN THE MARKETPLACE

> I've been given this Prospects card to buy a course at college but first I've got to find an employer who will let me use the card. There aren't many jobs round here so I'll be lucky to find anything decent. What happens when I get to the interview and the employer says I've got the job but doesn't mention anything about going to college? The woman from the TEC said we were supposed to tell the employer that we had the right to go to college and this card would pay for the cost. What if he says he's not interested in any card and I can take the job or leave it?
>
> (16-year-old school leaver, Crewe 1992)

In 1989, the Confederation of British Industry (CBI) called for the introduction of individual education and training credits as a key step in what it termed the 'skills revolution'. Such a credit would pay for courses leading to NVQ level 3 or advanced (A) levels. The CBI stated that six benefits would result from creating 'a training market where individual choice can be exercised' (CBI 1989). It is worth considering what the CBI was claiming for its credits model before moving on to examine the government's policy response.

- It provides all young people with an entitlement and greater control over their own development, giving a clear signal of the importance society attaches to skills and the rewards which learning can bring.
- It treats all young people equally, bridging the education and training divide and raising the status and profile of vocational education and training to young people. Consequently it would increase participation.
- It forms the basis for a market for vocational education and training with the individuals as buyers and the providers competing to meet their needs. It would avoid the inadequacies of national manpower planning.
- By providing an entitlement separate from wage or income support and by encouraging the employer to supply the latter it should be more relevant to most young people and employers at a time when demographic change is making traditional YTS less attractive. 'A job or training' becomes 'a job and training'.
- It would act as an incentive to employers because it is directly relevant to their normal employment needs and will draw in additional business investment.
- Giving the credit to the individual would be a powerful influence on persistent non-training employers. Young people in short supply would simply go to other employers offering training.

The CBI's context here is that of the 1980s expanding economy and a decline in the numbers of 16- and 17-year-olds who, it was thought, could pick and choose relatively well-paid jobs but who were not necessarily motivated by the thought of training to ensure career enhancement. Lack of motivation on the part of young people to train coupled with their lack of preparedness for the workplace have been offered as key contributors to this country's skills crisis and qualifications record since James Callaghan's 'Great Debate' speech in 1976. Stronach and others have argued strongly against this shifting of blame from economic reality to young people and their teachers (Stronach 1989). Nevertheless, the rationale of the YTS, the Technical and Vocational Education Initiative (TVEI) and, latterly, the Enterprise in Higher Education Initiative has been the same – to develop personal and social skills and an understanding of the workplace to make young people more attractive to employers. The rationale of credits comes at the problem from a different angle, however. It suggests that by giving young people purchasing power, not only will this motivate them to seek jobs with training but it will also encourage employers to create such jobs.

The government responded within eight months to the CBI's suggestion and in March 1990 announced that it would set up 11 pilot credit schemes to operate from April 1991. The CBI's call for credits to purchase post-16 education as well as training was rejected, however, lest it revive the controversy surrounding the early Thatcher administration's enthusiasm for education vouchers. Credits were now to pay for vocational training to a minimum of NVQ level 2, undertaken by young people who had left full-time education to be either directly employed or to join a YT programme. TECs and LECs were invited to bid for pilot status and out of the 32 which submitted proposals, 17 were given development funding of up to £10,000 to prepare detailed bids. In August 1990, the ED announced that the 11 successful pilots were: Birmingham, Bradford, Devon and Cornwall, Grampian, Hertfordshire, Kent, North East Wales, Northumberland, South and East Cheshire, SOLOTEC in South London and Suffolk.

In its prospectus to TECs and LECs, the ED stated that the main purpose of training credits 'is to expand and improve the training of young people', and that credits had the potential to:

- strengthen the motivation of the individual to train, and to heighten standards;
- help to establish an efficient market in training;
- make training which is relevant to employer's needs an accepted part of normal working life (ED 1990).

The prospectus went on to stress that:

> It will be a requirement for all pilots that they increase participation in training; raise the level of skills attained; and generate more jobs with training for young people. They will also have to ensure appropriate arrangements for careers advice, working wherever appropriate through the Careers Service and careers teachers. Whether through the credits arrangements or otherwise, all TECs running pilot schemes will have to ensure that, in their area, they meet the Government's Guarantee of a training place up to the age of 18 for all young people who have left full-time education and are unable to find a job.
>
> (ED 1990)

The prospectus acknowledged that TECs and LECs might also have their own additional objectives in operating a credits pilot '. . . such as raising general awareness of training for young people in their area, tackling key skill needs, or increasing training in small companies'.

Despite the enormity of the task facing the first round pilots, they had about six months to develop their systems and procedures in order to be ready to issue credits from April 1991.

MODELS OF DELIVERY

The basic credits idea is a simple one which presupposes the following context: school leavers find employment, which could be on the basis of trainee status, and use the credit to purchase a training course leading to a minimum NVQ level 2 from a provider of their choice; the enhanced vocational guidance they received before leaving school coupled with their developed negotiation and decision-making skills will have enabled each young person to persuade their employer to release them for training; in return, the TEC/LEC or the training provider supplies the young person with regular statements showing how the credit is being spent having been encouraged to treat young people as valued customers; if the young person and/or their employer is unhappy with the service, they can transfer the credit to a different provider or use their purchasing power as a weapon to force providers to improve; the concurrent expansion of a unit-based qualifications system is intended to facilitate the transfer of students' credits between providers.

In reality, of course, credits were launched into a very different context. Pilots have, therefore, had to tackle several interrelated deficiencies in terms of VET provision when developing their own models of credit delivery. Indeed, by working in partnership with local education authorities (LEAs), colleges, schools and the Careers Service, credits pilots have given a higher profile to the need for improvement across the VET infrastructure. Provision of vocational guidance has, for example, been considerably strengthened in pilot areas with credit funding being used to appoint extra careers officers whose role involves preparing Individual Action Plans for all Year 11 pupils. As a consequence, careers officers have spent more time in schools helping careers teachers to promote the need for careers education, often the poorest relation when it comes to curriculum priorities. Teachers in South and East Cheshire reported that credits had 'put careers education on the curriculum map' and had made both them and their pupils address the concept of post-16 entitlement to training and further education in a fresh way. At the same time, teachers and careers officers were wary of the fact that credits could become yet another short-term measure to boost youth training. They questioned how far employers were being encouraged to play their part in the initiative and were concerned that employers had, for some time, showed signs of 'initiative fatigue'.

Eight of the original pilots decided to make credits available to all school leavers – including those with special needs – seeking work in any occupational sectors, whilst two pilots (Birmingham and Kent) restricted the scheme to certain sectors in which there were skill shortages. Grampian LEC placed no restriction on occupational sector but required any credit holder to be properly employed before they could use the credit. First round evaluation showed that the selective model of delivery was prone to considerable difficulties. Two further ways in which pilots differ concern the age range within which a credit is valid and whether or not to include young people who live outside the TEC area but who enter that area for employment. Subsequently, due to low take-up, some pilots have extended their eligibility criteria. Hertfordshire TEC, for example, has opened its scheme to 18–24-year-olds employed in the county, whilst Kent includes 18–20-year-olds who are in a job which previously did not offer them the chance to gain a qualification. All first round pilots have made special provision to try and meet their YT guarantee of a training place for any unemployed school leaver. Such arrangements include allowing the credit to pay for full-time courses at further education colleges and for full-time training programmes with private providers who 'mind' the young people until they find places with employers. The numbers of young people using their credits under these special arrangements could be considerable in areas where youth unemployment is rising. As such numbers are counted in the overall totals for the take-up of credits, the true take-up figure, which should reflect the number of young people using their credit in employment, is distorted.

The packaging of the credit varies among the pilots with the majority opting for some sort of 'credit card' format. Four pilots opted for a local brand name (South and East Cheshire – *Prospects*; NE Wales – *Career Link*; Grampian – *SkillSeekers*; SOLOTEC – *Training Accounts*) – in order to create both a fresh image for credits and one that was distinctly different from previous government-led youth training schemes. In South and East Cheshire TEC, for example, early market research revealed that young people were very wary of any scheme using the term 'credit' as they associated this with potential debt. The TEC was also concerned about the poor image of YT in its area and decided to launch credits under the new title *Prospects*. The term YT has been replaced by Traineeship for placements with employers and Careership for placements which have employed status with the TEC's intention being to place the majority of young people on Careerships. Evaluation findings from this TEC's pilot subsequently bore out the TEC's concern for nomenclature for they showed that young people not only distrust the word 'credit', but associate the term 'training' with low-skilled, manual jobs and see it as having no relevance to anyone staying in full-time education after 16. Comments to this effect from young people included:

'I am doing "A" levels; I do not intend to do any training.'
'I am not going into a career that needs training' (nursing, radiography, teaching).
'I am going to college to do business studies and I'm not sure I'll need training for the sort of job I'm going to do.'
'I am going into a job where training isn't important – where you learn from experience, not training'

(Care sector)

It is ironic to discover that the main achievement of some sixteen or so years of government-led youth training schemes has apparently been to embed a negative view of 'training' in the minds of young people.

Finding a suitable name for credits schemes becomes more problematic as new regions become involved. The ED appears to want TECs and LECs to use the universal branding 'Training Credits' to avoid confusion as the initiative grows. There is, however, a much more fundamental issue than language at stake. Evaluation findings from South and East Cheshire showed that the vast majority of young people, regardless of their post-16 destination, welcomed the idea of an individual credit for which they would be personally responsible. Those who had decided to stay in full-time education felt they should be able to use the credit just as much as those who were leaving to seek work. They may have distanced themselves from 'training' but they clearly wanted to have more control over their post-16 futures and saw their *Prospects* card as the key to this. Nevertheless, if credits are only available for young people who leave full-time education at a time when the majority are choosing to stay at school or college, they are likely to become tainted in the same way as previous youth training initiatives. South and East Cheshire, in an attempt to maintain the interest of young people who stayed in full-time education and avoid such negative connotations, have introduced individual *Prospects* awards so that young people on full-time courses can use these to pay for experiences such as for field trips, university taster programmes and special projects for A-level.

The way in which a young person acquires their training credit varies across the pilots. In South and East Cheshire, the Careers Service is responsible for distributing *Prospects* cards and information packs to young people before they complete Year 11 of schooling. This distribution forms part of an extensive marketing campaign in which TEC staff and careers officers give presentations, including the use of video, to pupils, teachers, parents and college staff. Young people are also given a registration form which they are asked to complete once they have made a definite decision about their post-16 destination. If they are seeking work, they are asked to wait until they have found a job, be it Traineeship or Careership, before completing their form which they return to the TEC. On receipt of the form, the TEC sends the young person a cheque for £15 which can be spent in any way the young person chooses. Given that there are just under 4,000 eligible school leavers in the TEC area, the decision to hand over £15 per person was criticised by many teachers who felt the money could have been used by schools. The TEC's registration system, however, is central to the operation of its credits model for it provides the TEC with a means of tracking every eligible school leaver in South and East Cheshire recorded on its registration database. Cheshire Careers Service and the LEA have both praised the registration system for providing destination data more quickly than the existing Careers Service system. It has also, for the first time, provided the LEA with details of the type of courses young people are taking in colleges outside the LEA boundary.

Those young people who return cards showing they have taken jobs without training are visited by a TEC training adviser who attempts to persuade the employer to activate the credit by allowing the young person to attend a course offered by a college or a private provider. Similarly, young people who remain unemployed are sent details of vacancies and Traineeships. In the first year of its pilot, the registration system enabled the TEC to convert many jobs into Careerships and, therefore, to become one of the few TECs to reach its target for credits take-up.

RECYCLING RESOURCES TO FUND CREDITS

Training credits funding is made up from the following three sources:

- planned provision for YT in each TEC or LEC;
- a proportion of the Revenue Support Grant (RSG) allocation for part-time VET currently controlled by local education authorities and previously given direct to colleges;
- a further £12m (in 1990/91) from existing Government expenditure plans to be spent on enhanced careers guidance and to be used as top-up to deliver higher levels of training.

In addition, the first round pilots received £4.8 million in development money. The bulk of the available funding, therefore, was to be recycled from existing YT programmes. Procuring and managing the RSG element, though much smaller than the YT budget, has proved to be highly problematic both at the initial planning stage and subsequently when young people began cashing their credits. Clearly, the TECs and LEC had to work in partnership with their LEAs, whose colleges were to act as training providers. For some of the larger pilots, this meant making arrangements with more than one LEA as TEC/LEC boundaries do not equate to LEA boundaries. In all pilots, it also meant ensuring that financial provisions was made to ensure some credits could be cashed at colleges outside the TEC/LEC boundary but to whom young people and employers had traditionally gone for reasons of quality and/ or choice. The second round pilots will have the added complication of making new arrangements with the Further Education Funding Council for transfer of whatever equates to the RSG element in the new independent world of further education institutions.

In attempting to create effective and workable financial structures within which credits can be delivered, TEC/LEC managers, their local authority partners and, indeed, ED civil servants, have found themselves at the mercy of the arcane and obscurely complicated world of VET funding. Myriad locally agreed pricing arrangements have developed over the years between colleges, private training providers and employers. The RSG funding is supposed to cover further education costs for all 16–18-year-olds, apart from those on YT, thus in theory making it possible for any employer to send a young person for day-release classes at no cost. In practice, most employers have always paid towards that training, usually in the form of a locally agreed subsidy of around 70 pence per student hour or through their association with an industrial training board. Colleges have been cushioned by the automatic annual payment of RSG monies and work-related further education funding, amounting to some 5 per cent of a college's overall budget, direct from the ED. In addition, since the late 1970s, colleges have either run their own YT schemes or serviced others and received payment for this on the basis of a minimum number of students in any one group. This mixture of funding arrangements has meant that the true cost of supporting a student in the further education sector has never been decisively calculated and colleges have been able to transfer money from one pot to another in order to subsidise courses which fell below projected numbers or which required extra support. The credits concept challenges the group-based approach to costings and, importantly, presupposes that every course is clearly costed in order that an appropriate value can be assigned to each credit, taking into account, for example, that an engineering course costs far more than one in business administration. As such, assigning a meaningful value to the credit has proved to be impossible as the true costs of training vary so much according to occupational area and chosen qualification. South and East Cheshire's *Prospects* card states that it is worth a minimum of £750 whilst Northumberland's and SOLOTEC's cards have face values of £1500. Such values are misleading as they relate to training costs only and do not reflect items such as travel and equipment expenses and employer contributions to trainees' weekly allowances.

The RSG figures themselves have also caused problems for credits pilots. The Department for Education (DFE) calculates the RSG from the annual Further Education Statistical Return (FESR) it receives from the LEAs. This meant that TECs and LEAs based their credits take-up figures on DFE statistics which would be two years out of date by the time the pilots began operating. Crucially, for the original pilots, those statistics reflected a pre-recessionary situation in which part-time numbers were quite buoyant. As the recession started to bite, TECs and LEAs realised that colleges were likely to lose out on the RSG transfer as part-time numbers fell. In order to protect colleges' income, some pilots developed special procedures for ensuring the RSG was paid back, procedures which look set to continue as part-time numbers fail to reach their pre-recession levels. The most notable procedure in this regard has been arrangements which allow colleges to receive credits as payment for new full-time courses supposedly set up specially for unemployed school leavers. Private training providers have, quite naturally, been complaining that such procedures are a direct contradiction of the credits' objective to create a customer-led training market and that they simply maintain the *status quo* in further education.

PRIVATE VET PROVIDERS AND CREDITS

As they prepare for independent status in 1993, colleges are likely to reappraise their participation in government-led initiatives. Some have never been happy servicing youth training schemes and may decide that they prefer to recruit students from the cosier and more profitable markets of adult business studies courses, full-time 16–18 A-level programmes and franchising arrangements to deliver degree courses in conjunction with local higher education institutions. Some, however, may find they are under political pressure to join credits pilots as TEC board members may also be college governors and/or influential local employers.

Involvement with a credits pilot should, in theory, make many demands on colleges. It presumes, for example, that they are able to identify the exact source of funding for every student they enrol. In a typical college with several thousand students on the books and classes containing students funded by a variety of sources, such identification can take several months after initial enrolment. Many young people, for example, arrive at college unsure as to whether they are on YT or directly employed. Under credits, young people should be arriving at college with an action plan ready to negotiate entry to an appropriate course and have access to tutors and student support staff who fully understand and appreciate that they are now dealing with a customer. In the first round pilots, young people found their purchasing power to be illusory. Their credit card was simply regarded as yet another form of funding to be noted on the appropriate form. The following comments reflect the views of many young people in South and East Cheshire:

> I keep my card in my pocket in case anyone wants to see it and in case I can use it but so far it's stayed in its plastic wallet. I still think it's a good idea but I'm not sure the college knows what to do with it.

> All the college did when we enrolled was use the card to get our number. I thought we'd use the card once a week and have to plan how we spent the money.[1]

To the same extent, credits have offered little incentive to the private training provider to become more customer-oriented. Contracting arrangements between the host TEC/LEC and providers vary across the pilots with a few, including South and East Cheshire, having dismantled the existing Managing Agent structure in order to deal directly with employers recruiting school leavers. In these cases, private providers operate like colleges in that they provide the off-the-job training. In contrast, private providers are vital when it comes to meeting the YT guarantee as they can house young people until placements are found with employers. Payment of the output related funding (ORF) – a requirement of all ED training credit contracts and a sum which can represent as much as 25 per cent of the credit value – also varies according to how much is paid to the young people on achievement of their NVQ and how much to their employer or training provider. A major anomaly in terms of the ORF, however, is that it does not categorise the gaining of a job as a positive outcome so that those agencies which place young people as trainees with employers are not penalised financially if they do not make efforts to convert Traineeships into real jobs.

EMPLOYERS: ACTIVE PLAYERS OR PASSIVE RECIPIENTS?

That a major attitudinal change on the part of employers is needed when it comes to releasing employees for training has been well documented elsewhere (see Finegold and Soskice 1988; Steedman and Wagner 1989). Evidence from the first round pilots shows that Training Credits have not only had little impact on that attitudinal change, but that the understanding and awareness of employers of credits themselves was very disappointing. It has already been noted that credits were launched during a severe economic recession when many employers, including the largest, had frozen recruitment of young people. For some time, the ED has been relaxing the administrative burden placed on employers by the early youth training schemes and credits pilots have sought to keep the new initiative as simple as possible for employers to understand.

There is evidence to suggest that where employers have understood the rationale of credits, they have welcomed the initiative, particularly with regard to its insistence on young people achieving qualifications. There are two major problems, however, related to the link between credits and NVQs, the qualifications to which the government and TECs are commited. Firstly, understanding and awareness of NVQs is very limited among employers of all sizes and in all sectors. Secondly, when employers do have experience of NVQs they often criticise their applicability to local labour market need and the slowness with which they are being introduced. Employers also still harbour deep-seated prejudices about the basic and social skill abilities of school leavers.

In South and East Cheshire, which has a fairly strong labour market even in recession, employers who wish to participate in credits have to become members of both the TEC and its Business Education Partnership which manages the credits pilot. Here, young people are recruited to Traineeships or Careerships under TEC contract but paid a wage directly by the employer and only employers who take young people with special needs are given extra support towards the trainee's weekly allowance. SOLOTEC, on the other hand, has had to reintroduce a system of paying the weekly allowance to encourage employers to recruit young people during the recession, whilst in Kent small employers (less than 25 employees) now receive a supplement of £100 per quarter, per employed trainee. It seems highly likely that some of the 1993 pilots, for example Merseyside, will also have to offer a substantial allowance to employers and create their own work placements. Under such arrangements, credits funding simply becomes YT funding under a new name.

All first round pilots reported that they were having to put far more time and resources into marketing credits to employers than had been envisaged and that special funding arrangements would definitely continue for the foreseeable future as there were no signs of an improvement in their local economies. Ironically, however, at their annual national conference in July 1992, TECs were told by Gillian Shepherd, Employment Secretary, that public spending on youth training was unlikely to rise and could be cut (*The Guardian*, 3 July 1992). This news came despite the fact that TECs had been telling the government for some time that, due to funding cuts, they were finding it increasingly difficult to meet their youth training guarantee of a place for every 16–18-year-old who could not find employment. The TECs' problems were supported by a report from the leading youth charities which showed that nationally there were too few places available in 1992 to enable TECs to deliver the youth training guarantee (Youthaid 1992). A further problem for medium and large sized employers who deal with more than one TEC or LEC is that they are faced with varying administrative procedures which means employing someone specifically to deal with the paperwork. Meanwhile, the very employers upon whom the success of credits depends and who sit on the boards of TECs are becoming more vociferous in their dealings with Government and some, notably in London, are delaying signing their annual contracts in an attempt to secure better funding.

YOUNG PERSON AS CONSUMER

A small employer in the 25–50 employee band in South and East Cheshire encapsulated the burden placed on the credit-carrying young person:

School leavers need to present themselves to employers properly and be prepared to explain that they now come with a package of benefits – *Prospects*, Action Plan, Record of Achievement and so on. We employers need school leavers to help us understand these new initiatives.

The lack of coherence and co-ordination concerning a range of school-based initiatives adds to the confusion young people feel about processes and products which are, in theory, supposed to be for their benefit. In many schools, careers education, which often does not begin until Year 10, has to be squeezed into an already small timetable slot for personal and social education. At the same time as they are preparing for their GCSEs, pupils are taking time out for work experience, to complete progress charts for their record of achievement, to attend guidance interviews with careers officers and to make an Action Plan. In schools where there are still sixth forms, pupils may be coming under increasing pressure to stay on regardless of whether they are traditional A-level candidates as schools compete for the declining pool of 16-year-olds. The number of schools offering Business and Technology Council (BTEC) First Certificate courses and the willingness of others to pilot general national vocational qualifications (GNVQs) as alternatives to A-levels is testimony to their need to increase their post-16 numbers. At the same time, in areas where a tertiary system operates, schools may work in conjunction with colleges to increase staying-on rates as they are now themselves in the marketplace for pupils.

Training credits sit awkwardly alongside the government's drive to increase staying-on rates for they are the mechanism via which young people who do not want to pursue an academic route post-16 can combine workplace learning and vocational education. This mixture was, of course, the basis of apprenticeships and was continued in the better youth training schemes. The mixed-model of post-16 VET has, however, been severely damaged by the poor performance of many youth training schemes which failed to convert placements into real jobs or to provide young people with nationally recognised qualifications. In addition, the introduction of a competence-based model for vocational qualifications, the very reform which was supposed to inject real quality into workplace learning, has also been heavily criticised for the narrowness of its approach, the complexity of its assessment procedures and the disparity between the lower and higher level qualifications (see Steedman and Wagner 1989; Raggatt 1991; Unwin 1990a,b).

Nevertheless, the following case studies from South and East Cheshire illustrate how appropriate the mixed-model can be when enlightened employers offer work-based training and access to meaningful qualifications:

Ian was persuaded to stay at school by his parents and teachers even though the school did not offer information technology, his main interest, in the 6th Form. He began two A-level courses – geography and French – and was trying to improve his GCSE grades in science and human biology. After six months, Ian decided academic study was not for him and, using his training credit (*Prospects*), took up a Traineeship with a local building society. He is now (1992) attending his local further education college one day a week studying for his BTEC National in computing technology. He said: 'I'd kept the *Prospects* card in my wallet all the time I was in the 6th Form. I knew all along school wasn't right for me but my parents wanted me to get a good qualification. The card made me realise I had a say in my future and I'm now getting what I wanted in the first place.'

Susan has always wanted to be a primary school teacher but by the middle of Year 11 felt that she had had enough of school. During her guidance interview, she discussed with her careers officer the possibility of leaving school to start work in a company which would allow her to study for qualifications which give her access to higher education at a later stage. In her school's eyes, Susan was an automatic A-level candidate and teachers were, naturally, concerned that she might never make the switch from employment to higher education. An offer of a Careership with a large manufacturing company persuaded Susan to leave school and she is now combining work in the marketing department with study for a BTEC National Diploma in Business and Finance. She is also taking French A-level at her local college in the evening. Susan said: 'I still want to teach eventually but working has made me more confident and I love the atmosphere. The *Prospects* card was like a passport to a different future for me.'

In the light of current levels of youth unemployment, Ian and Susan are doubly privileged, first in that they found employment and, second, in that they were academically gifted enough to have succeeded in full-time education. Both, however, challenge the growing consensus that full-time education should be the norm post-16.

The next case study demonstrates the reality of staying on at college for many young people, who may come out after one or two years with a level 1 or 2 qualification but who will not, necessarily, have gained enough credits to progress to a level 3:

Gary enjoyed school but his predicted GCSE grades were very low. During his two week work experience in Year 10, Gary discovered an interest in catering and decided he would like to work in hotels. Gary's school does not have a sixth form so pupils transfer to the local tertiary college. When it came to deciding which route to take,

Gary found that most of his closest friends were going to college to do general courses which did not require GCSE passes. He was offered the chance of a Traineeship with a local restaurant but decided to follow his friends to college where he is taking a food-related Diploma in Vocational Education. Gary said: 'the Traineeship was only going to pay me £29 a week but I can get £20 working three nights in the fish and chip shop where I live. All my mates were going to college and I wanted to stay with them. My dad said it was better to stay-on.'

For young people like Gary, full-time education is replacing a locally available youth training scheme as the new post-16 rite of passage.

Young people in South and East Cheshire interviewed after they had left school said that much of their careers education and vocational guidance had been wasted either because they were too concerned with GCSE work or because they found it difficult to project themselves beyond the school leaving date. Now that they had left, they felt ready to listen and think through the options available. Those in work said that they were better able to understand the relevance of the credit but that neither their employer nor their college tutor regarded it as a mechanism for facilitating individual career progression.

The Careers Service only has a statutory duty to provide vocational guidance to eligible school leavers, though in some areas a limited service is available to Year 12 pupils and full-time college students. In the light of the increased numbers of young people staying in full-time education, many of whom will leave to seek work rather than enter higher education, there is an urgent need for independent vocational and educational guidance to be available to all young people up to the age of 18. To be worthwhile, Records of Achievement and Individual Action Plans must become meaningful products which support young people as they progress to the next stage of education and training and be used to inform those professionals whose job it is to create education and training plans for each young person. Young people also need the opportunity to develop the skills which will enable them to participate fully in the guidance process and then act on their decisions. At the same time, employers have to be aware of the benefits to them of allowing their employees to activate the credit.

Although all TECs and LECs operating training credits have to conform to ED guidelines, they have been given considerable freedom to design local models of delivery, a freedom which has continued for the second round of pilots. This diversity of process and practice has led to a complex web of local funding arrangements and eligibility criteria. For the young person, now supposedly newly empowered to purchase the training of his or her choice, that empowerment and choice will differ significantly from one county to the next. Employers, too, will find that they are wooed in different ways according to their TEC or LEC area, whilst the providers of training, whether they be private agencies or colleges of further education, will be paid at different rates and be expected to meet varying requirements for each credits scheme with which they are involved. Such diversity poses problems in trying to evaluate training credits in the context of national policy objectives and in attempting to make meaningful comparisons between the different pilots. Moreover, there is a danger that the detailed reality of credits delivery could be hidden from the public scrutiny applied to, say, YTS which, though delivered locally, was prescribed by a nationally designed operating framework.

JUST ANOTHER INITIATIVE? THE FUTURE FOR CREDITS

Responding to the fact that fewer than half of the 27,000 training credits offered to young people who left school in 1991 had been taken up by November of that year, Michael Howard referred to the increase in staying-on rates. At the same time, the TECs and LEC involved were blaming the recession. Undoubtedly, the training credits initiative could not have been launched at a worse time, as employers of all sizes and in all sectors stopped recruiting young people. To what extent the concurrent rise in staying-on rates is a consequence of the recession is difficult to measure but it is certain that many young people will only remain in full-time education for one year. An important credibility test for training credits will be to see how many of those 17-year-olds take up their entitlement.

Both factors – the recession, the effects of which will haunt training credits pilots for some time to come, and increased staying-on rates – present TECs and LECs with practical problems. In terms of their impact on national training policy, they each represent a paradox. If the main purpose of training credits is, in the words of the government, 'to expand and improve the training of young people', how can this be achieved, recession or boom, if credits are reliant on employers recruiting young people to jobs with training? At the same time, the government appears to be succeeding in encouraging schools and tertiary colleges to retain as many students beyond the age of 16 as possible, thus promoting the status of full-time student over that of part-time trainee.

New initiatives are useful in that they often expose weaknesses in the current system. Despite all the problems with NVQs, for example, the shift to a competence-based approach to qualifications is exposing the cosy world in which awarding bodies annually rubber-stamped college provision, the reliance on written tests for assessment purposes regardless of the need to assess practical skills, and the disparity between educationally derived curricula and the working practices in modern industry and commerce. Similarily, and perhaps ironically for the government, training credits are serving to expose even further the weaknesses of this country's VET infrastructure.

For young people in South and East Cheshire, the training credit has made them, their parents and teachers aware of their entitlement to receive vocational education and training after the age of 16. A credit represents, quite simply, the key to unlock that entitlement even though, in practice, the credit currently unlocks a choice of events some of which are empowering for the young person whilst others, often according to local labour market conditions and the TEC's credit model, offer no choice of education and training route.

Credits have been launched into a hostile economic environment in which youth unemployment is rising and the funding of educational institutions is becoming increasingly dependent on the numbers of full-time students they retain. Moreover, empowered young people pose a big problem to educational institutions. They demand course combinations which upset the smooth operation of the timetable and if an astute employer is involved, colleges may increasingly face demands for flexibility in terms of the start and finish dates of courses.

Yet whilst upsetting the educational apple cart would seem to fit quite happily with the Conservative Government's and the ED's agenda during the 1980s and early 1990s, other circumstances are combining to make the use of credits far from easy. Specifically, unless training credits are upgraded to become the key which unlocks a young person's entitlement to both further education and vocational training regardless of full or part-time status, then they will be by-passed by the majority of eligible school leavers in the 1990s. Those in the minority who choose to leave full-time education to seek work may find that the credit merely buys them a re-vamped youth training place. This polarisation of youth reflects the seemingly different and conflicting policy agendas of the Employment Department and the Department for Education (DFE). On the one hand, the ED is attempting, via a funding mechanism which routes funds through individuals rather than providers, to increase the numbers of young people entering jobs with training and, hence, the numbers of part-time students in further education. On the other hand, the DFE continues to route funds through institutions and to promote full-time 16–18-year-old provision over part-time. The grand design of the CBI referred to at the start of this chapter and the ED's claims that credits would 'expand and improve the training of young people' appear to be a long way from being realised.

NOTES

* Since this article was first published training credits have been re-named youth credits.
1 These and other comments by those involved in training credits in South and East Cheshire form a part of my local, unpublished evaluation of the initiative for the TEC.

REFERENCES

CBI Task Force (1989) *Towards a Skills Revolution*, London: Confederation of British Industry.

ED (1991) *Education and Training for the 21st Century*, HMSO.

ED (1990) *Training Credits Prospectus for TECs and LECs*, Sheffield: Employment Department.

Finegold, D. and Soskice, D. (1988) 'The Failure of Training in Britian: Analysis and Presctiption', *Oxford Review of Economic Policy*, 4(3).

Raggatt, P. (1991) 'Quality Assurance and NVQs', in Raggatt, P. and Unwin, L. (eds) *Change and Intervention: Vocational Education and Training*, London: Falmer Press.

Steedman, H. and Wagner, K. (1989) 'Productivity, Machinery and Skills: Clothing Manufacture in Britain and Germany', *National Institute Economic Review*, May 1989.

Stronach, I. (1989) 'Education, Vocationalism and Economic Recovery: the Case Against Witchcraft', *British Journal of Education and Work*, 2(1): 5–31.

The Guardian, 'Crisis-hit Training Councils face New Cuts, Minister says', 3 July 1992.

Unwin, L. (1990a) 'The Competence Race: We Are All Qualified Now', in Corbett, J. *Uneasy Transitions: Disaffection in post-compulsory education and training*, London: Falmer Press.

Unwin, L. (1990b) 'Staff Development, Competence and NVQ', *Journal of Further and Higher Education*, 14(2).

Youthaid and the Children's Society (1992) *A Broken Promise – the Failure of Youth Training Policy*, London: Youthaid.

Part III

Ideologies in conflict

Chapter 10

The Ruskin College speech

The Rt Hon. J. Callaghan

I was very glad to accept your invitation to lay the foundation stone for a further extension of Ruskin College. Ruskin fills a gap as a 'second chance' adult residential college. It has a special place in the affections of the Labour movement as an institution of learning because its students are mature men and women who, for a variety of reasons, missed the opportunity to develop their full potential at an earlier age. That aspect of the matter is a particular interest of my own.

Ruskin has justified its existence over and over again. Your students form a proud gallery and I am glad to see here this afternoon some of your former students who now occupy important positions. They include leading academics, Heads of State of Commonwealth countries, leaders of the trade union movement and industrial life and Members of Parliament. Indeed, eleven of the present Labour Members of Parliament graduated from Ruskin and five of them are either in the Government or have served there, including one present member of the Cabinet: Eric Varley, the Secretary for Industry.

Among the adult colleges, Ruskin has a long and honourable history of close association with the trade union movement. I am very glad to see that trade unions are so strongly represented here today because you are involved in providing special courses for trade union officials and I hope that this partnership will continue to flourish and prosper.

The work of a trade union official becomes ever more onerous, because he has to master continuing new legislation on health and safety at work, employment protection and industrial change. This lays obligations on trade unionists which can only be met by a greatly expanded programme of education and understanding. Higher standards than ever before are required in the trade union field and as I shall indicate a little later, higher standards than in the past are also required in the general educational field. It is not enough to say that standards in this field have or have not declined. With the increasing complexity of modern life we cannot be satisfied with maintaining existing standards, let alone observe any decline. We must aim for something better.

I should also like to pay tribute to Billy Hughes for his work at Ruskin and also for his wider contribution to education as Chairman of the Adult Literacy Resource Agency. This has been a strikingly successful campaign for which credit must go to a number of organisations, including the BBC. It is a commentary on the need that 55,000 students were receiving tuition this year with a steady flow of new students still coming forward. Perhaps most remarkable has been that 40,000 voluntary teachers have come forward to work, often on an individual, personal basis with a single student. When I hear, as I do in so many different fields, of these generous responses to human need, I remain a confirmed optimist about our country. This is a most striking example of how the good will, energy and dedication of large numbers of private persons can be harnessed to the service of their fellows when the need and the opportunity are made plain.

There have been one or two ripples of interest in the educational world in anticipation of this visit. I hope the publicity will do Ruskin some good and I don't think it will do the world of education any harm. I must thank all those who have inundated me with advice: some helpful and others telling me less politely to keep off the grass, to watch my language, and that they will be examining my speech with the care usually given by Hong Kong watchers to the China scene. It is almost as though some people would wish that the subject matter and purpose of education should not have public attention focused on it; nor that profane hands should be allowed to touch it.

I cannot believe that this is a considered reaction. The Labour movement has always cherished education: free education, comprehensive education, adult education. Education for life. There is nothing wrong with non-educationalists, even a Prime Minister, talking about it again. Everyone is allowed to put his oar in on how to overcome our economic problems, how to put the balance of payments right, how to secure more exports and so on and so on. Very important too. But, I venture to say, not as important in the long run as preparing future generations for life. R.H. Tawney, from whom I derived a great deal of my thinking years ago, wrote that the endowments of our children are the most precious of the natural resources of the community. So I do not hesitate to discuss how those endowments should be nurtured.

Labour's Programme '76 has recently made its own important contribution and contains a number of important statements that I certainly agree with. Let me answer the questions: 'What do we want from the education of our children and our young people?' with Tawney's words once more. He said: 'What a wise parent would wish for their children, so the State must wish for all its children.'

I take it that no one claims exclusive rights in this field. Public interest is strong and legitimate and will be satisfied. We spend £6 billion a year on education, so there will be discussion. But let it be rational. If everything is reduced to such phrases as: 'educational freedom versus State control', we shall get nowhere. I repeat that parents, teachers, learned and professional bodies, representatives of higher education and both sides of industry, together with the Government, all have an important part to play in formulating and expressing the purpose of education and the standards that we need.

During my travels around the country in recent months, I have had many discussions that show concern about these matters.

First let me say, so that there should be no misunderstanding, that I have been very impressed in the schools I have visited by the enthusiasm and dedication of the teaching profession, by the variety of courses that are offered in our comprehensive schools, especially in arts and crafts as well as in other subjects; and by the alertness and keenness of many of the pupils. Clearly, life at school is far more full and creative than it was many years ago. I would also like to thank the children who have been kind enough to write to me after I visited their schools: and well-written letters they were. I recognise that teachers occupy a special place in these discussions because of their real sense of professionalism and vocation about their work. But I am concerned on my journeys to find complaints from industry that new recruits from the schools sometimes do not have the basic tools to do the job that is required.

I have been concerned to find that many of our best trained students who have completed the higher levels of education at university or polytechnic have no desire to join industry. Their preferences are to stay in academic life or to find their way into the Civil Service. There seems to be a need for a more technological bias in science teaching that will lead towards practical applications in industry, rather than towards academic studies. Or, to take other examples, why is it that such a high proportion of girls abandon science before leaving school? Then there is concern about the standards of numeracy of school leavers. Is there not a case for a professional review of the mathematics needed by industry at different levels? To what extent are these deficiences the result of insufficient co-ordination between schools and industry? Indeed, how much of the criticism about basic skills and attitudes is due to industry's own shortcomings, rather than to the educational system? Why is it that 30,000 vacancies for students in science and engineering in our universities and polytechnics were not taken up last year, while the humanities courses were full?

On another aspect there is the unease felt by parents and others about the new informal methods of teaching which seem to produce excellent results when they are in well-qualified hands but are much more dubious when they are not. They seem to be best accepted where strong parent/teacher links exist. There is little wrong with the range and diversity of our courses. But is there sufficient thoroughness and depth in those required in after life to make a living?

These are proper subjects for discussion and debate. And it should be a rational debate based on the facts. My remarks are not a clarion call to Black Paper prejudices. We all know those who claim to defend standards but who in reality are simply seeking to defend old privileges and inequalities.

It is not my intention to become enmeshed in such problems as whether there should be a basic curriculum with universal standards – although I am inclined to think that there should be – nor about other issues on which there is a divided professional opinion such as the position and role of the Inspectorate. Shirley Williams, the new Secretary of State, is well qualified to take care of these issues and speak for the Government. What I am saying is that where there is legitimate public concern, it will be to the advantage of all involved in the education field if these concerns are aired and shortcomings righted or fears put to rest.

To the critics I would say that we must carry the teaching profession with us. They have the expertise and the professional approach. To the teachers I would say that you must satisfy the parents and industry that what you are doing meets their requirements and the needs of our children. For if the public is not convinced then the profession will be laying up trouble for itself in the future.

The goals of our education, from nursery school through to adult education, are clear enough. They are to equip children to the best of their ability for a lively, constructive place in society and also to fit them to do a job of work. Not one or the other, but both. For many years, the accent was simply on fitting a so-called inferior group of children with just enough learning to earn their living in the factory. Labour has attacked that attitude consistently, during 60 or 70 years and throughout my childhood. There is now widespread recognition of the need to cater for a child's personality, to let it flower in the fullest possible way.

The balance was wrong in the past. We have a responsibility now to see that we do not get it wrong in the other direction. There is no virtue in producing socially well-adjusted members of society who are unemployed because they do not have the skills. Nor at the other extreme must they be technically efficient robots. Both of the basic purposes of education require the same essential tools. These are basic literacy, basic numeracy, the understanding of how to live and work together; respect for others; respect for the individual. This means acquiring certain basic knowledge, and skills and reasoning ability. It means developing lively inquiring minds and an appetite for further knowledge that will last a lifetime. It means mitigating as far as possible the disadvantages that may be suffered through poor home conditions or physical or mental handicap. Are we aiming in the right direction in these matters?

I do not join those who paint a lurid picture of educational decline because I do not believe it is generally true, although there are examples which give cause for concern. I am raising a further question. It is this. In today's world higher standards are demanded than were required yesterday and there are simply fewer jobs for those without skill. Therefore we demand more from our schools than did our grandparents.

There has been a massive injection of resources into education, mainly to meet increased numbers and partly to raise standards. But in present circumstances, there can be little expectation of further increased resources being made available, at any rate for the time being. I fear that those whose only answer to these problems is to call for more money will be disappointed. But that surely cannot be the end of the matter. There is a challenge to us all in these days and a challenge in education is to examine its priorities and to secure as high efficiency as possible by the skilful use of the £6 billion of existing resources.

Let me repeat some of the fields that need study because they cause concern. There are the methods and aims of informal instruction; the strong case for the so-called 'core-curriculum' of basic knowledge; next, what is the proper way of monitoring the use of resources in order to maintain a proper national standard of performance; then there is the role of the Inspectorate in relation to national standards; and there is the need to improve relations between industry and education.

Another problem is the examination system – a contentious issue. The Schools Council have reached conclusions about its future after a great deal of thought, but it would not be right to introduce such an important change until there has been further public discussion. Maybe they haven't got it right yet. The new Secretary of State, Shirley Williams, intends to look at the examination system again, especially in relation to less-academic students staying at school beyond the age of 16. A number of these issues were taken up by Fred Mulley and will now be followed up by Shirley Williams.

We are expecting the Taylor Committee Report shortly on the government and management of schools in England and Wales that could bring together local authority, parents and pupils, teachers and industry more closely. The Secretary of State is now following up how to attract talented young people into engineering and science subjects; whether there are more efficient ways of using the resources we have for the benefit of young people between the ages of 16 and 19 and whether retraining can help make a bridge between teacher training and unemployment, especially to help in the subjects where there is a shortage.

I have outlined concerns and asked questions about them today. The debate that I was seeking has got off to a flying start even before I was able to say anything. Now I ask all those who are concerned to respond positively and not defensively. It will be an advantage to the teaching profession to have a wide public understanding and support for what they are doing. And there is room for greater understanding among those not directly concerned of the nature of the job that is being done already.

The traditional concern of the whole Labour movement is for the education of our children and young people on whom the future of the country must depend. At Ruskin, it is appropriate that I should be proud to reaffirm that concern. It would be a betrayal of that concern if I did not draw problems to your attention and put to you specifically some of the challenges which we have to face and some of the responses that will be needed from our educational system. I am as confident that we shall do so as I am sure that the new building which will rise here will house and protect the ideals and vision of the founders of Ruskin College so that your future will be as distinguished as your past and your present.

Chapter 11

Public versus private provision

S.R. Dennison

THE BASIC ECONOMIC ANALYSIS

It has now become an almost unquestioned faith that many services should be – indeed, can only be – provided by government, preferably by a monopoly. Private provision is regarded as inferior, 'divisive', and 'at the expense of' those dependent on state provision. Any development in the private sector is an 'attack' on the state sector. . . . Far from provision by the state being necessary, a market is usually superior in meeting the wants of individuals as they themselves judge them in the light of their own circumstances; and the market does so with economy and efficiency in the use of scarce resources. Further, in meeting the genuine wants of individuals, 'social' objectives are more likely to be achieved than by imposing *political* objectives administered by bureaucrats. Finally, state provision, especially if a monopoly, creates problems which profoundly affect not only the operation of the service but also the whole political, economic and social structure.

Attacks on the market usually confuse its operations as a mechanism for allocating scarce resources with the allocation which results because of other factors, such as the distribution of income or the preferences of consumers which differ from the aims of political planners. The most common objection is that freedom of choice is limited by income – 'rationing by the purse'. This fact is neither a criticism of the market as a mechanism nor a justification for provision of services by the state. At most, it is a criticism of a particular distribution of income, and it suggests that there should be help for the less well-off to purchase in the market what they wish.

In contrasting the alleged evils of the market with the alleged benefits of state provision, the fundamental element which is ignored is that in both cases the services have to be paid for. It is simply *assumed* that in the market there is 'rationing by the purse' but that state services are provided 'free'. However, nothing in this imperfect world is 'free'. Services provided by government use scarce resources which are consequently not available to meet other wants, and have to be paid for through taxation. There is a shifting of decisions on the use of their incomes from individuals to politicians, pressure groups and bureaucrats.

When state provision absorbs a large part of the national income even people with low incomes have to be heavily taxed, paying for services whether they use them or not, and often getting poor value for money when they do, or try to, use them. There is a vast apparatus for shuttling money around, which is costly and inherently wasteful, with indeterminate results on the relationship between the charges to an individual and the benefits he receives. On balance, everyone is worse off, except employees in the state services who receive higher incomes than they would in a free market . . .

Three cases for government intervention

When it was possible to examine these matters more or less dispassionately, instead of in terms of political dogma, three cases were usually advanced in which government intervention in market operations could be beneficial. None was regarded as requiring state *provision* of the service, but merely ground for some form of indirect control, such as subsidies or taxes.

The first is that of 'public goods', for which it is believed that private initiative will not make adequate provision, because individual benefits cannot be assigned and therefore a market cannot operate effectively. The classic examples are defence and policing.

The second is 'externalities', 'neighbourhood' or 'spill-over' effects. In the language of the original welfare economics, if there is divergence between private and social marginal net products, the state should intervene (by tax or subsidy) to redress the balance. Thus, the classic case, damage to third parties caused by pollution, should be paid for by the producer responsible for it, or the consumers of his product. In the reverse case of benefits accruing to people other than those paying for the good or service, the producer should be subsidised to produce more. This is the basis of much of conventional welfare economics (now becoming outdated), with its complex models of hypothetical compensations and penalties, which at best are of no practical significance and at worst are positively misleading (Cheung 1978). It is also the basis for much of the pseudo-science of cost-benefit analysis (Peters 1966), which again inflicts more damage than it sheds light (e.g. the Maplin Airport case) (Foster *et al.* 1974).

Third, there are economies of scale which cannot be realised in a 'fragmented' competitive market and require government intervention to ensure the creation of productive units sufficiently large to realise all the economies. This was always a weak case. Nevertheless, it has been highly influential, and a potent factor behind considerable economic and industrial damage in the 'rationalisation' movement of the inter-war years, the 'New Deal' in the United States, the establishment of national-ised industries, and post-war creations of new giants through the National Enterprise Board and other means.

None of these three arguments remotely justifies state provision of education. Professor Blaug has reached the same conclusion (Blaug 1967). After examining the three possible grounds advanced by econo-mists ('classical' and 'modern'), he decides that 'we have not so far produced a single argument in favour of state-administered education'. What is shown is, at best, a case for subsidy. Nevertheless, he favours a state monopoly rather than a 'mixed system of private and state schools', and condemns 'subsidies' for private schools. The only reason he adduces (advanced only as 'possible') is that it promotes 'social cohesion'. As this term is not defined and there is no attempt to show how it would be promoted by a state monopoly, discussion of it is unnecessary as well as impossible.

HISTORICAL CONSPECTUS

The present near-monopoly in schooling in Britain, which goes much further than in most European countries, is of recent origin. The history of schooling has long been misrepresented. The popular view is that until Forster's Act of 1870, which provided 'free education for all' (Trevelyan 1944) (it did not), few children went to school and the population was largely illiterate. Nothing could be further from the truth. More recent historians have examined the evidence rather than relying on popular myths (West 1965, 1975). Private provision of schooling goes back for centuries, whereas 'free' provision by the state goes back for less than half a century, with some state support for less than a century before.

Rapidly growing private education sector in the nineteenth century

From the Middle Ages (and even before), schools were founded and supported by individual benefactors and religious bodies. Many survived the Reformation, many others were established. By the beginning of the nineteenth century a substantial proportion of children were receiving schooling, though boys rather than girls. In 1818 the number of children in schools was 478,000. Together with the number of schools, it was rapidly increasing, entirely through private initiative and often by charit-able organisations. The first state support did not come until 1833, with a grant of £20,000 to two voluntary bodies. By that date, the number of children in schools was 1,294,000, and the population largely literate. The Census of 1851 commented on 'the existence of much modern zeal', with 'a very considerable number' of new schools established and old ones enlarged in the previous 10 years. Professor West has suggested that, when it did start to support schools, the government 'jumped into the saddle of a horse that was already galloping' (West 1965).

An equally false belief is that the schools were appallingly bad. This, like much other misleading social history, derives mainly from Victorian novelists, especially Dickens and his infamous Dotheboys Hall. Although it had a slim factual basis, it was more a product of the novelist's imagination than a valid account of the general state of the schools. There was then, as now, a wide variety of schools, from the very good to the very bad. It is, moreover, essential to try to judge them in the light of their *contemporary* environment. Although buildings were often of a kind that would now be condemned, so were the homes of most of the pupils. Many of the schools established after 1870 with state support were no better, and some worse, than the private schools they eased out. Britain was still a relatively poor country, with real income per head of population perhaps about one-tenth of what it is now; poverty for the majority of the 'working classes' was a grim reality rather than a sociological construct based on averages. Yet expenditure on education in 1870 amounted to about 1 per cent of the national income, at which figure it remained until after 1945, when the great expansion began, to raise it to about 2 per cent by 1965.

There was not much completely free schooling; even the charitable foundations charged fees of a few pence a week. In 1870, Forster estimated that the cost of schooling was met about equally from fees paid by parents, voluntary contributions (from charities) and government grants. His Act envisaged the continuation of this tripartite arrangement. From incomes of perhaps a pound a week, working-class parents were finding two or three pence for fees, as well as keeping their children, even if often ill-nourished and ill-clad. It is true that schooling was often limited to three or four years (though this period was steadily rising) and that there was frequent absenteeism. But this was the result of poverty, not parental neglect or incompetence. Working-class parents were as anxious to do their best for their children (to 'buy privilege') as are the 'wealthy' today; indeed, the evidence shows a high degree of discernment in choice of schools, and severely questions the view of present-day sociologists, etc., who insist that working-class parents would choose schools badly.

Far from providing 'free' schooling for all and ushering in a new age of universal literacy, Forster's Act merely filled in some of the gaps in the voluntary system, by providing financial support for new schools established by local School Boards. These schools were still to charge fees, although with provision for 'free' places – as indeed there were at voluntary schools. Fees at the Board Schools were abolished in 1891. The voluntary schools had already been discriminated against in the apportionment of state aid, and were being eased out by Board Schools with lower fees. Abolition of fees for the Board Schools accelerated this tendency.

In 1902, the Schools Boards were abolished and schools came under the control of local authorities, which were then able to provide secondary schools for children aged 11 to 18, above the leaving age for primary schools. They charged fees, usually around £2 or £3 a term, about equivalent, relatively to working- and lower-middle-class incomes, to the few pence a week of the nineteenth-century primary schools. There were substantial numbers of free places, awarded on competitive examination. Fees were not abolished until 1945. The development of these schools, together with the growth of the grammar schools and the introduction of Direct Grant, was perhaps the most significant feature of the half century, and a potent factor in promoting economic and social mobility, and breaking down barriers of 'class'.

SOCIAL COSTS AND BENEFITS

The historical evidence demonstrates that education is not a 'public good' in the sense that it will not be provided unless the state intervenes. The second ground for state intervention – a possible divergence between private and social marginal net products – is equally defective. As usual, problems of measurement are insuperable, especially of the more remote effects. It is an interesting fact that nineteenth-century supporters of state assistance often justified it by its supposed effects in reducing crime, drunkenness, etc. They were about as wrong as the advocates of comprehensive schools as a means of reducing 'divisiveness'. The matter is one of subjective judgement, not measurable objective fact; almost any desired answer can be reached by manipulating the assumptions. But the allegation that private education benefits individuals 'at the expense of' the state schools and of society in general (or 'the people as a whole') – or even other individuals – is without foundation . . . Although benefits and costs cannot be even approximately assessed, there is a strong presumption that in general the benefits to society of the development of the talents of above-average children, and especially the gifted, are at least as large as those which they themselves derive, and often considerably larger.

DISECONOMIES IN PUBLIC PROVISION

The third ground, economies of scale which cannot be obtained unless the state intervenes, is probably the weakest of the three. Small schools can achieve high standards and be 'cost-effective', while even moderately large size, say above 1,000 pupils, brings diseconomies and can threaten standards. It is in the education service 'as a whole' that real diseconomies appear. The organisation of the service requires a vast administrative machine, which is costly and often either ineffective or pernicious.

An analysis of the figures for 1981–82 of local authorities shows an enormous range of costs per pupil for support staff in schools and 'central' costs of administration. The ILEA stands out as the most costly under both heads: £89 per pupil in the schools and £115 at the centre – a total of £204. For Outer London, with 20 authorities, the figures were £44 and £59, a total of £104, about one-half of that for the ILEA. Differences in local conditions must, of course, result in some differences in costs, but a general disparity of this order suggests prodigality and mistaken policies, as well as diseconomies of scale.

For Metropolitan Districts, the average 'school' costs were £30.50 and central costs £41.25 – a total of £72. Non-Metropolitan Counties had similar averages: £29.50, £41 and a total of £70.50. Both of these categories thus come out at a little over one-third of the ILEA. There was also a wide range among different authorities in the same group. In Outer London there is what seems one 'freak' result, in Harringey: school costs of £65 and central costs of £137, a total (£202) close to that of the ILEA. The others have ranges of £31 to £63 for school costs and £29 to £80 for central costs. In the Metropolitan Districts, for schools costs there is a range of £15 (Bradford) to £45 (Coventry, with Manchester at £44), and central costs £24 (Kirklees, West Yorkshire) to £63 (Bradford). Non-Metropolitan Counties do not show such large differences.

Some differences could result from different allocations of functions. Bradford stands out, with the lowest school costs and the highest central costs, to give a total about average. But it is exceptional. By and large, authorities with high school costs also have high central costs. There is also a general feature that, in all cases except two, central costs are higher (often much higher) than school costs. This could result from apportionment of functions, but its consistency suggests another explanation: that, in the allocation of resources, the bureaucracy is more influential than the toilers at the 'coal face'; in other words, the closer to the pork barrel the better.

There are no comparable data for the private sector. I shall therefore take only the Royal Grammar School, Newcastle upon Tyne, which can be regarded as more or less typical, though with several elements which involve more administration – large size (over 1,000 boys), wide catchment area, very large range of extra-curricular activities, participation in the Assisted Places Scheme, etc. In 1981–82, the average school cost of administrative, clerical, etc., staff was £55. There were, of course, no 'central' costs, apart from subscriptions to outside bodies, which were almost negligible. For £55 a year per pupil, the school was providing more services than those provided by the local education authority (LEA) in which it is situated at an average of £72 a year per pupil. Thus, as well as the appointment and payment of staff – including PAYE, National Insurance and pensions – the purchase of supplies and the organisation of maintenance, the school was also collecting fees, operating selection on a much more sophisticated basis, awarding scholarships and bursaries, and operating the Assisted Places Scheme. It was doing all that, and much more than is done by the school support staffs in the state sector, and with no central costs. The difference is that it did not have to perform the functions generated in a state system (but not in the private market).

STATE PROVISION CREATES INSOLUBLE PROBLEMS

The traditional grounds for state provision of a service do not have even remote application to education. Even more important are its disadvantages and virtually insoluble problems. Many arise from the absence of the disciplines of the market, and the replacement of consumers' choice by political and administrative decisions. When services are 'free', there is no limit to potential demand, and some form of control (such as quantitative rationing) has to replace price. This is often exacerbated by the impossible expectations aroused when the service is established. In education, the aim of providing a national system which will be 'genuinely fair to the talents, aspirations and needs of every child' presumably implies that the best facilities will be freely available to all children.

On the supply side, the lack of the signals provided by a market means that the main incentive to respond to genuine consumer demand is removed. This is more than a matter of consumer choice (important though that is); it profoundly affects the allocation of resources among competing ends. Instead of reflecting the wishes of consumers, it is determined by politicians and bureaucrats, influenced by innumerable pressure groups, with a continuing struggle among vested interests. Further, the incentive to use resources economically is seriously weakened.

In these conditions, the fundamental problem of scarcity is often not merely swept to one side, but denied . . . There seems to be an inbuilt presumption that expenditure on any service can only rise, and never fall, whatever might be the conditions under which it operates. In a state monopoly this is not far short of reality, whereas in a market a fall in the demand for a service would result in the release of resources for use in entirely different ways. Thus a fall in the number of children requiring education would reduce demands on parental incomes and enable them to purchase other goods and services in infinite variety and quality according to their own preferences . . .

More does not mean better

Another basic tenet is that, however large the expenditure, and however fast it has been rising, it is never enough; the services are 'starved'; and, if standards are to be maintained, let alone improved, massive injections of cash are necessary. This is particularly important in education because the shortcomings (to use the mildest description) of state schools are attributed entirely to inadequate funding and to the 'savage cuts' imposed in the last couple of years. Expenditure per pupil in real terms in 1980 for pupils in state secondary schools was 44 per cent higher than in 1960; for primary schools 60 per cent. In spite of the 'cuts' of the past two or three years, there has been no fall in expenditure per pupil. This has been partly the result of the fall in the numbers of pupils. Adjustment must take time (in a state system a very long time), but it certainly suggests hollowness in the protests. The majority of independent schools manage well, and achieve high standards, on levels of funding no better than those of many state schools and certainly without increases of the order the latter have enjoyed in recent years.

It is abundantly clear that increased expenditure has not resulted in higher standards. In October 1982, Dr Rhodes Boyson, then Parliamentary Under Secretary at the Department of Education and Science, had the temerity to suggest that there was no necessary connection – partly on the basis of an analysis of the expenditure by different local authorities and the results achieved by their schools. Some of the highest spenders had the worst examination results (the ILEA is the paradigm), while very good results were often achieved by schools controlled by authorities well down the league table of spending. He commented that he gave the figures

> not to indicate that LEAs should spend less or more on education, but simply that there is no automatic link between financial output and academic results in school education. Good results come from good teaching, good discipline, and a sense of purpose in a school.

This eminently reasonable statement was greeted with the usual abuse from the teachers' unions and other groups . . .

THE JUGGERNAUT OF RISING EXPENDITURE

There are strong reasons for expecting that a state-provided service will generate increasing expenditure. There are three main ways in which this effect operates. Two have been elaborated in the analysis of 'public choice', or the 'economics of politics' (Tullock 1976; Buchanan *et al.* 1978) (developed mainly by American economists from the original conception of the British economist, Duncan Black) (Black 1958) which – on the basis of empirical evidence as well as logic – provides a convincing case that politically-controlled bureaucracies are less likely to benefit the public than voluntary enterprise operating through markets. They provide, at excessive cost, inferior services, often not wanted by, and at times not even available to, those who have to pay for them – with the further result that other services which consumers do want cannot be afforded.

Vote-catching

The first element is vote-catching by the politicians, bribing sections of the electorate. There is abundant evidence from the United States, but it is not wanting in Britain. (The General Election of 1983 provided an *embarras de richesses*, the Labour Party promising every conceivable group additional hand-outs while the Conservatives defended their record as purveyors of increased benefits.) The danger is that the costs of subsidising any group are diffused throughout the community, through small increases in taxation or inflationary borrowing, thereby obscuring the link between benefits and costs. The fallacy, and the danger, lies in the proliferation of largesse, so that the total becomes unbearable.

Expansive state bureaucracies

Secondly, state bureaucracies by their very nature are expansive. The remuneration, status, career prospects, and even jobs of the bureaucrats who control them (subject to political oversight) depend on the size and functions of the organisation. However public-spirited the head of a service (or the many officers under him) might be, it is difficult to imagine their seeking to *reduce* their functions. Indeed, the more public-spirited they are, the more the danger, as they will constantly be perceiving new 'needs', new ways of serving their fellow-citizens, new ways of 'improving' the service, all of which demand increased resources. Further, they do not have to satisfy customers by supplying a service they want at a price they are willing to pay, but only to convince other bureaucrats or vote-catching politicians. Without any acceptable measure of output, as measured by subjective consumer satisfaction, financial input created in the political process becomes the criterion of success. A programme has been 'achieved' if the money allocated to it has been spent; if there is a shortfall, then some 'need' or other cannot have been met. And if there should be any inadequacy of provision, or some 'need' not met, it can only be the result of insufficient money having been allocated.

Bilateral monopoly

The third element is that national monopoly of provision of a service is usually accompanied by trade union monopoly of the supply of labour. The literature of economics over more than a century is littered with argument about the operations of bilateral monopoly; the main conclusion is that the outcome is indeterminate in the sense of failing to lead to an equilibrium between demand and supply in which consumers get services in the quantities they want, at prices they are willing to pay, and suppliers are willing to provide at opportunity costs which represent the most efficient use of scarce resources. There is instead a struggle between different interests, the outcome depending on their relative bargaining strengths and other adventitious circumstances, including political and other pressures. This is now the situation in various state services . . .

The unions regard their functions as going well beyond the negotiation of conditions for their members, and ensuring that as many will be employed as possible . . .

DANGERS OF MONOPOLY

The major danger of a state monopoly is that it will pursue objectives which are politically determined and removed from the wishes of the consumers who are forced to pay for it. This is, indeed, its purpose. This result can be seen not only in the attack on independent schools as enabling parents to opt out of the state system, but also in hostility to all freedom of choice within the state system itself. It is a commonplace of NUT dogma that, in any sphere, the wishes of consumers cannot be allowed to frustrate the decisions of planners. As it observed in 1970, 'parental choice should not be exercised contrary to public policy'. In this case, 'public policy' was that each school should have 'a representative cross-section of the full ability range' (one of the comprehensive principles), so that children would be allocated to schools by bureaucrats, not to schools chosen for children by their parents. Or, Professor Brian Simon, in 1980, demanded the extirpation of 'covert systems of selection through the operations of "parental choice"'. In 1978, Barbara Bullivant, at one time national secretary of the Campaign for the Advancement of State Education (CASE), saw 'grave dangers in unrestricted right of choice', which could 'operate against a particular school in favour of a particular school'. She suggested that parental choice could be even worse ('less fair') than the 11-plus (Bullivant 1977). A major element was the belief that parents are generally incompetent, wrong-headed and incapable of making correct choices. We could multiply the examples, but these should be sufficient.

REFERENCES

Black, D. (1958) *The Theory of Committees and Elections*, Cambridge: Cambridge University Press.

Blaug, M. (1967) 'Economic Aspects of Vouchers in Education', in *Education: A Framework for Choice*, IEA Readings No. 1, London: Institute of Economics Affairs.

Buchanan, J.M. *et al.* (1978) *The Economics of Politics*, London: IEA.

Bullivant, B. (1977) 'Parental Choice and its Dangers', *Comprehensive Education*, No. 37.

Cheung, N.S. (1978) *The Myth of Social Cost*, Hobart Paper 82, London: Institute of Economic Affairs.

Foster, C. *et al.* (1974) *Lessons of Maplin*, London: Institute of Economic Affairs.

Lord, R. (1983) 'Value for Money in the Education Services', *Public Money*, September.

Peters, G.H. (1966) *Cost-benefit Analysis and Public Expenditure*, Eaton Paper 8, London: Institute of Economic Affairs.

Trevelyan, G.M. (1944) *English Social History*, London: Longman.

Tullock, G. (1976) *The Vote Motive*, London: IEA.

West, E.G. (1965) *Education and the State*, London: IEA.

West, E.G. (1975) *Education and the Industrial Revolution*, London: Batsford.

Chapter 12

Markets or democracy for education

S. Ranson

CHUBB AND MOE ON MARKETS AND DEMOCRATIC CONTROL

By removing the local education authority from its constitutional role and by abolishing the requirement to establish an education committee, the 1993 Education Act brings into question the role of local democracy in education.[1] If the reason for this strategy has been left implicit by our legislators, it is revealed in Chubb and Moe (1990) whose advocacy of markets against direct democratic control has purportly been made prescribed reading by Ministers of Education for their civil servants.[2]

Chubb and Moe argue that a generation of reforms to American schools failed because the underlying cause – the institutions of direct democratic control – were not identified. Schools fail because the 'game of local democracy' constitutes a perpetual struggle for power that creates winners and losers with the victors imposing their higher order values ('sex education', 'socialisation of immigrants', 'the mainstreaming of the handicapped', 'bilingual education', 'what history to teach') on schools by bureaucratising control. Democracy is coercive, stifling the autonomy of schools and demotivates the teachers. Institutions work when people choose them. The key to better schools lies, thus, in institutional reform creating markets in which consumers influence schools by their choices. Markets promote autonomy by enabling all participants to make decisions for themselves; markets are myopic, offering what people want. Because markets also select and sort, if schools are to be successful they will need to find a niche – a specialised segment of the market to which they can appeal and attract support: targeting particular values and learning – discipline, religion, socio-economic and ethnic make-up of students. Although markets have imperfections, these are preferable to those of local democracy. Thus the institutional conditions for effective schools require the de-democratisation of institutional settings and the creation of market settings entailing de-centralisation, competition, choice, autonomy, clarity of mission, strong

strong leadership, teacher professionalism and team cooperation. This belief that strong markets, together with increased internal professional control, will secure improved schooling finds its expression in this country in the writing of Tooley (1992a, b, 1993).

THE MACHINERY OF THE MARKET: AN INTERPRETIVE ANALYSIS

The Conservative Government in the UK has over time introduced complex administrative regulations designed to create a highly structured market of educational choice. In this section an interpretive analysis is developed[3] which argues that the mechanism of the market is intrinsically flawed as a vehicle for improving educational opportunities: it can only radically contract them. Rules and relationships within education markets develop with inexorable force to erode local democracy and to reinforce a segmented social structure. So, while appearing to liberate consumers, the education market in fact entrenches most in a deeper and less accountable structure of control.

An atrophied psychology of possessive individualism

The organising principles of the market make assumptions about the public, about their orientation, capacities and resources. When individuals pursue their own interests, it is claimed, they will benefit society as much as themselves: 'I have never known much good done by those who affected to trade for the public good' (Adam Smith in Pack 1991: 34). Conceiving the public alone as self-interested consumers or 'possessive individuals' (Macpherson 1973) presents, however, a degraded and distorted psychology of human nature. Not only does it mistake the diversity of qualities which inform individual motivation (making unintelligible Titmuss' (1971) illustration of blood doning as the paradigm of civic virtue), it also misconstrues the nature of individuality itself. It is to assume that my purposes, my development, must always be at the expense of someone else's. The point is not that individuals are by nature possessively self-interested, but that the institutions of the market make them so. The institution of the market demands a singular currency of transaction.

The institutionalising of instrumental rationality

The market normally assumes that all goods and services are unchanging products. My purchase of a cassette has no effect on the product although pressure may be placed upon production or delivery. But in education the market has chameleon-like qualities which can actually change the characteristics of the goods being purchased. My preference for a school, privately expressed, together with the unwitting choices of others can transform the product. A small school grows in scale with inevitable consequences for learning style and administrative process. The distinctive ethos which was the reason for the choice may be altered by the choice.

These seemingly unpredictable collective outcomes of private choice can create for any individual the disturbing effect of bringing into question the very rationality of action in the education market place. Rational agency implies that an actor is able to calculate the means necessary to realise defined purposes. The actor is able to formulate intentions *ex ante* with the reasonable expectation that preferences can, other things being equal, translate into actions. But in markets like education 'things' are not equal. The unintended consequences of multiple and independent transactions leaves any and every actor completely in the dark about what it is rational to believe is being chosen. In principle, therefore, outcomes are chronically unpredictable, literally out of anybody's control. This anarchic quality of markets is one of the characteristics which critics emphasise (Callinicos 1993). Markets can thus appear to be beyond rational decision and influence.

Markets also leave actors having to base their actions on extrinsic considerations, on judgements about the context they are in, or the outcome of others' transactions, rather than considerations that are internal to their own value informed purposes. The actor is continually constrained to react, to judge *ex poste* what it is best to do. For example, a number of schools have not wished to opt out and seek grant-maintained status, disagreeing with the assumptions on which that policy is based. Yet a moment can arrive when the governors and the headteacher feel constrained to judge, in a context of changing admissions and resources, that if the interests of the institution (to survive) are clarified then a conclusion to opt out is inescapable. Yet this begins to illustrate the underlying rationality of market transactions. If exchange drives out values based on purposive action, it nevertheless reinforces instrumental rationality. Action in the market is driven by a single common currency: the pursuit of material interests. . . .

The paradox of this process is that consumer choice empowers the producers. The evidence grows in education, as much as in other competitive markets, that producers select consumers or, more subtly, some producers and consumers search each other out in a progressive segmentation of the market. Schools begin to differentiate themselves to fit specific niches in the educational market – perhaps as an 'academic' school, or a 'technology' school. The institutions begin to market what they believe to be their distinctive image, qualities and achievements. A hierarchy of distinction and public esteem emerges (Tomlinson 1988). It is likely in an education market, therefore, that the intention of increasing choice results not only in the product being altered but choice itself being reduced or eliminated. This paradox does not emerge by chance but from the principles which emerge to govern interaction in the market. . . .

The commodification of education

Because education is an institution which society may use to 'screen' or 'filter' individuals into privileged occupations, competition intensifies as individuals aspire to acquire qualifications with the highest exchange value. Education, like original works of art or a house by the sea, can become a 'positional good' (Hirsch 1977), by definition in scarce supply. Where the good, like education, is subject to congestion or crowding, it is relative advantage for which each strives, necessarily at the expense of others (Jonathan 1990). When competition intensifies for positional goods with limited supply their price rises relative to other goods thus choking off any excess demand: 'the price mechanism is the basic regulator containing demand within the limits of inherently restricted supply. Allocation proceeds in effect, through the auction of a restricted set of objects to the highest bidder' (Hirsch 1977: 28). The currency of this commodity market is unmistakably social status: the search on the part of schools and parents to enter into the mutual creation of an exclusive institution. The price paid by consumers for entry into privileged market niches is one manifestation of cultural capital.

Reinforcing a class divided society

The educational market becomes the social manifestation of Darwinian natural selection. It is assumed that all parents have the resources available to them to facilitate choice: the time to travel in search of a school and in transporting a child over any distance; the availability of cars, childcare support and, in the last resort, the capacity to move house. Choice imposes costs which are likely to be prohibitive for many families. As emerging evidence indicates, for many families, certainly in rural areas, the promise of choice is regarded cynically as empty rhetoric. To lack resources is to be disenfranchised from the polity of the market.

Thus, whatever commodities are exchanged, it is the unique social functions of the market which are of fundamental importance. The market is formally neutral but substantively interested. Individuals come together in competitive exchange to acquire possession of scarce goods and services. Within the market place all are free and equal, only differentiated by their capacity to calculate their self-interest. Yet, of course, the market masks its social bias. It elides, but reproduces, the inequalities which consumers bring to the market place. Under the guise of neutrality, the institution of the market actively confirms and reinforces the pre-existing social class order of wealth and privilege. The market is a crude mechanism of social selection. It can provide a more effective social engineering than anything we have previously witnessed in the post-war period.

Why is it that individuals are trapped into acting within the rules of a game which they did not produce, which they cannot influence, and even though enacting the rules can only disadvantage them? A system of spiralling disadvantage and advantage ensues which contracts the extent and scope of choice and opportunity. What is an anarchy for all but a few individuals necessarily becomes a certainty for just those few: for only those with accumulated 'capital' can succeed. The paradox of a system designed to enhance choice yet producing constraint derives, so it is argued, from the internal contradictions of the education market: its institutional and social limits create a 'prisoner's dilemma' for its participants (Jonathan 1990; Miliband 1991).[4] Individuals are trapped into diminishing their own welfare because the mechanism prevents them from purposively coordinating their preferences to mutual advantage. Self-interest is self-defeating, and private choice irredeemably diminishes public welfare. Does the institutional mechanism of market competition interact with the purported nature of education – as a positional good – to create a social system beyond repair? The institutional and social characteristics of markets are, on the contrary, not fixed and unalterable but *chosen* to serve social and political purposes. The market is not a neutral mechanism but constituted to alter the relations of power in order to change society.

The polity, the market and civil society

The market is a political creation, designed for political purposes, in this case to redistribute power in order to redirect society away from social democracy and towards a neo-liberal order. The market in education is not the classical market of perfect competition but an administered market carefully regulated with stringent controls. It is an institution constituted by government and underwritten by legislation to define the relative powers and contractual responsibilities of participants. Thus the administered market in education seeks to fetter local elected representatives and professionals, as the bearers of the old order, and emancipate the middle class as the bearers of the new.

While some of the intended changes result directly from introducing market procedures within the public domain of education, other purposes emerge indirectly as a consequence of the unfolding interactions of competition. As power shifts and relationships alter the old polity becomes unrecognisable and a distinctively different political order emerges. 'Exit' replaces 'voice' as the mechanism by which a society takes allocative decisions (Hirschmann 1970). Collective 'choices' arise from the aggregation of emergent private choices. Exit becomes, by implication, a form of political choice. The market, by determining the distribution of winners and losers in exchange, is in effect making policy decisions about the allocation of resources, services and power through uncoordinated, piecemeal decisions of private individuals. Policy is whatever people do, how they behave. If consumers dislike something their views can only be expressed implicitly but unmistakably through exit and an alternative purchase – if such is available or accessible.

The market as a result places public policy and collective welfare beyond the reach of public deliberation, choice and action: in other words, democracy. It uses exit to hold voice at bay, substituting the power of resources in exchange for the power of better reasons in public discourse. In principle, a community is denied the possibility of clarifying its needs and priorities through the processes of practical reason, in which judgements are formed about what is in the public good based on reasoned argument that leads towards practical collective choices that are monitored, revisable and accountable to the public. In particular, the disadvantaged are denied the possibility of deliberating upon and determining their life chances. By removing the pattern of social relationships and the emergent structures of power and wealth from the possibility of critical scrutiny, civil society is separated from the polity. The market entrenches the powerful beyond control. A community, therefore, which inserts exit in place of voice in the public domain and so narrows the scope of its democratic discourse to the negative freedoms of the market place is more truly, *pace* Hayek, on 'the road to serfdom'. . . .

The market polity colludes in promoting the agency and choice of the public while actually extinguishing it. While indicating radical change, it actually entrenches a traditional order of authority and power. Why does the public appear to collude in its own downfall? The answer seems to be that the market can parade under the guise of neutrality while any ensuing inequality can hide beneath the illusion that, because the agents have acted, they must also have assented (Jonathan 1990). The market polity, by reinforcing only the interests of a minority, rests on a limited and thus vulnerable legitimacy. The emphasis upon rights and an ensuing order of natural selection reveals the struggle to clothe the polity with a legitimating moral authority while removing the social order from democratic scrutiny (Hayek 1994; Oakeshott 1962; Anderson 1992).

The New Right in espousing these organising principles of competitive exchange is, therefore, either naive or dishonest. Either it is ignorant of all the evidence that markets inescapably create inequality or understands perfectly the effects of competition and has developed a rhetoric of choice to bamboozle a supposedly unwitting public. In a more open moral order there would be debate about the possibility of reconciling the purported virtues of the market – in its responsiveness, flexibility, decentralised knowledge – with the recognition of its vices in creating inequality. . . .

Markets cannot resolve the predicaments we face: indeed they ensure that we stand no chance of solving them. Those problems – the restructuring of work; environmental erosion; the fragmentation of society – present issues of identity, well-being, rights, liberty, opportunity, and justice which cannot be resolved by individuals acting in isolation, nor by 'exit' because we cannot stand outside them. Markets merely exacerbate these problems which are public in nature and, because they confront the whole community, we all have a right to contribute to their analysis and resolution. Deliberation, judgement and public choice are inescapable. Only the democratic processes of the public domain can enable members of a locality to articulate and reconcile the different values and needs which they believe to be central to the welfare of the communities in which they live. . . . The challenge for our time is to reconstitute the conditions for a learning society in which all are empowered to develop and contribute their capacities.

TOWARDS EDUCATION FOR DEMOCRACY: THE LEARNING SOCIETY

This theory of the learning society builds upon three axes: of presupposition, principles, and purposes and conditions. The *pre-supposition* establishes an overarching proposition about the need for and purpose of the learning society; the *principles* establish the primary organising characteristics of the theory; while *purposes* and *conditions* establish the agenda for change that can create the values and conditions for a learning society.

Presupposition

There is a need for the creation of a learning society as the constitutive condition of a new moral and political order. It is only when the values and processes of learning are placed at the centre of the polity that the conditions can be established for all individuals to develop their capacities, and that institutions can respond openly and imaginatively to a period of rapid and radical change. A learning society, therefore, needs to celebrate the qualities of being open to new ideas, listening to as well as expressing perspectives, reflecting on and inquiring into solutions to new dilemmas, cooperating in the practice of change and critically reviewing it.

Principles

Two organising principles provide the framework for the learning society: that its essential structure of *citizenship* should be developed through the processes of *practical reason*. Citizenship establishes the ontology, the mode of being, in the learning society. The notion of being a citizen ideally expresses our inescapably dual identity as autonomous individuals and responsible members of the public domain. Citizenship establishes the right to the conditions for self-development but also a responsibility that the emerging powers should serve the well-being of the common-wealth. Citizenship involves membership of national and local communities which thereby bestow upon all individuals equally reciprocal rights and duties, liberties and constraints, powers and responsibilities (Held 1989). Citizens express the right as well as the obligation to participate in determining the purposes and form of community and thus the conditions of their own association.

Practical reason, on the other hand, establishes the epistemology, mode of knowing and acting of the citizen in the learning society. Practical wisdom . . . describes a number of qualities which enable us to understand the duality of citizenship in the learning society: knowing what is required and how to judge or act in particular situations; of knowing which virtues should be called upon. Practical reason, therefore, presents a comprehensive moral capacity because it involves seeing the particular in the light of the universal, of a general understanding of what good is required as well as what proper ends might be pursued in the particular circumstances. Practical reason, thus, involves deliberation, judgement and action: *deliberation* upon experience to develop understanding of the situation, or the other person; *judgement* to determine the appropriate ends and course of action, which presupposes a community based upon sensitivity and tact; and learning through *action* to realise the good in practice.

Purposes and conditions

To provide such purposes and conditions, new values and conceptions of learning are valued within the public domain at the level of *the self* (a quest of self-discovery), at the level of *society* (in the learning of mutuality within a moral order), and at the level of the *polity* (in learning the qualities of a participative democracy). These conditions for learning within the self, society and the polity are discussed in turn.

CONDITIONS FOR A LEARNING SELF

At the centre of educational reform within the inner city as well as debate on policy within the polity itself is a belief in the power of agency: only an active self or an active public provides the purposes and condition for learning and development. Three conditions are proposed for developing purpose within the self: a sense of agency; a revived conception of discovery through a life perceived as a unity; and an acknowledgement of the self in relation to others.

The self as agent

Learning requires individuals to progress from the post-war tradition of passivity, of the self as spectator of action on a distant stage, to a conception of the self as agent both in personal development and active participation within the public domain. Such a transformation requires a new understanding from self-development for occupation to self-development for autonomy, choice and responsibility across all spheres of experience. The change also presupposes moving from our prevailing preoccupation with cognitive growth to a proper concern for development of the person as a whole – feeling, imagination and practical/social skills as much as the life of the mind. An empowering of the image of the self presupposes unfolding capacities over (a life) time. This implies something deeper than mere 'lifelong education or training'. Rather, it suggests an essential belief that an individual is to develop comprehensively throughout his or her lifetime and that this should be accorded value and supported.

The unity of a life

We need to recover the Aristotelian conception of what it is to be and to develop as a person over the whole of a life and of a life as it can be led (MacIntyre 1981).[5] This has a number of constituent developments. First, perceiving life as a whole and the self as developing over a lifetime. Second, therefore, a conception of being as developing over time: life as a quest with learning at the centre of the quest to discover the identity which defines the self. Third, seeing the unity of a life as consisting in the quest for value, each person seeking to reach beyond the self to create something of value, which is valued. Fourth, developing as a person towards the excellences; perfecting a life which is inescapably a struggle, an experience of failure as well as success. Fifth, accepting that the struggle needs to be guided by virtues and valued dispositions which support the development of the self. Lastly, acknowledging that the most important virtue is that of deliberation, a life of questioning and inquiry committed to revising both beliefs and action; learning from being a means becomes the end in itself, the defining purpose creatively shaping the whole of a life.

The self as persons in relation

We can only develop as persons with and through others; the conception of the self presupposes an understanding of how we live a life with each other, of the relationship of the self to others; the conditions in which the self develops and flourishes are social and political. The self can only find its moral identity in and through others and membership of communities. Self-learning needs to be confirmed, given meaning by others, the wider community; what is of value will be contested; therefore we need to agree with others what is to be considered valuable; to deliberate, argue, provide reasons.

THE SOCIAL CONDITIONS FOR LEARNING

The unfolding of the self depends upon developing the necessary social conditions which can provide a sense of purpose within society both for the self and others. These conditions are civitas, active participation in creating the moral and social order, and a capacity for interpretive understanding.

Virtues of civitas: the civic virtues of recognising and valuing others, of friendship

The conditions for the unfolding self are social and political: my space requires your recognition and your capacities demand my support (and vice versa). Jordan (1989) emphasises the importance of mutual responsibility in developing conditions for all individuals to develop their unique qualities. It recalls Aristotle's celebration of civic friendship – of sharing a life in common – as being the only possible route for creating and sustaining life in the city. . . .

Creating a moral community

The post-war world was silent about the good, holding it to be a matter for private discretion rather than public discourse. But the unfolding of a learning society will depend upon the creation of a more strenuous moral order. The values of learning (understanding) as much as the values which provide the conditions for learning (according dignity and respecting capacity) are actually moral values that express a set of virtues required of the self but also of others in relationship with the self. The values of caring or responsibility upon which can depend the confidence to learn derive any influence they may have from the authority of an underlying moral and social order. The civic virtues, as MacIntyre (1981) analyses, establish standards against which individuals can evaluate their actions (as well as their longer 'quest'): yet particular virtues derive meaning and force from their location within an overall moral framework (what MacIntyre calls a 'tradition'). A moral framework is needed to order relationships because it is the standards accepted by the moral community which provide the values by which each person is enabled to develop.

Yet a moral order is a public creation and requires to be lived and recreated by all members of the community. Each person depends upon the quality of the moral order for the quality of his or her personal development and the vitality of that order depends upon the vitality of the public life of the community. . . . The development of a moral community has to be a creative and collaborative process of agreeing the values of learning which are to guide and sustain life in the community. . . .

Interpretive understanding: learning to widen horizons

Taylor (1985) has argued that the forms of knowing and understanding, as much as or at least as part of, a shared moral order are the necessary basis of civic virtue. Historically conditioned prejudices about capacity, reinforced by institutions of discrimination, set the present context for the learning society. The possibility of mutuality in support of personal development will depend upon generating interpretive understanding, that is, on hermeneutic skills which can create the conditions for learning in society: in relationships within the family, in the community and at work. In society we are confronted by different perspectives, alternative life-forms and views of the world. The key to the transformation of prejudice lies in what Gadamer (1975) calls '*the dialogic character of understanding*'. Through genuine conversation the participants are led beyond their initial positions, to take account of others, and move towards a richer, more comprehensive view, a 'fusion of horizons', a shared understanding of what is true or valid. Conversation lies at the heart of learning: learners are listeners as well as speakers.

The presupposition of such agreement is *openness*. We have to learn to be open to difference, to allow our pre-judgements to be challenged; in so doing we learn how to amend our assumptions, and develop an enriched understanding of others. It is precisely in confronting other beliefs and presuppositions that we are led to see the inadequacies of our own and transcend them. Rationality, in this perspective, is the willingness to admit the existence of better options, to be aware that one's knowledge is always open to refutation or modification from the vantage point of a different perspective. . . .

Reason emerges through dialogue with others through which we learn not necessarily 'facts' but rather a capacity for learning, new ways of thinking, speaking, and acting. . . . The conditions for this depend upon the creation of arenas for public discourse – the final and most significant condition for the creation of the learning society.

CONDITIONS IN THE POLITY

The conditions for a learning society are, in the last resort, fundamentally political, requiring the creation of a polity which provides the foundation for personal and collective empowerment. The personal and social conditions, described above, will be hollow unless bedded in a conception of a reformed, more accountable, and thus more legitimate, political order. The connection between individual well-being and the vitality of the moral community is made in the public domain of the polity: the good (learning) person is a good citizen. Without political structures which bring together communities of discourse, the conditions for learning will not exist for it is not possible to create the virtues of learning without the forms of life and institutions which sustain them. The preconditions of the good polity are:

Justice: a contract for the basic structure

The conditions for agency of self and society depend upon agreement about its value as well as about allocating the means for private and public self-determination. Freedom rests upon justice, as Rawls (1971, 1993) and Barry (1989) argue. But this makes the most rigorous demands upon the polity which has to determine the very conditions on which life can be lived at all: membership, the distribution of rights and duties, the allocation of scarce resources, the ends to be pursued. The good polity must strive to establish the conditions for virtue in all its citizens. These issues are intrinsically political and will be intensely contested, especially in a period of transformation that disturbs traditions and conventions. If decisions about such fundamental issues are to acquire the consent of the public then the procedures for arriving at those decisions will be considered of the greatest significance for legitimate authority of the polity. The process of making the decisions – who is to be involved and how the disagreements that will inexorably arise are to be resolved –will be as important as the content of decisions themselves.

Participative democracy

Basing the new order upon the presupposition of agency leads to the principle of the equal rights of citizens both to participate in determining what conditions the expansion of their powers and to share responsibility for the common good. The political task of our time is to develop the polity as a vehicle for the active involvement of its citizens enabling them to make their contribution to the development of the learning society. There is a need, in this age of transition, to fashion a stronger, more active democracy than the post-war period has allowed. The post-war polity specialised politics and held the public at bay except periodically and passively.

The constitutive conditions for citizenship within a more active democracy is a polity that enables the public to participate and express their voice about the issues of the transition, but also a polity that will permit public choice and government. The politics of public expression, but also the government of choice and action, is the challenge for the new polity. Within such a polity the procedures for involving the public and for negotiating decisions will be important. Even so, it is through the prerequisites of procedural justice (Habermas 1984; Haydon 1993; Hampshire 1989) than an educated public of citizens can emerge. Citizens need to acquire the dispositions of listening and taking into account as well as asserting their view. . . .

By providing forums for participation the new polity can create the conditions for public discourse and for mutual accountability so that citizens can take each other's needs and claims into account and learn to create the conditions for each other's development. Learning as discourse must underpin the learning society as the defining condition of the public domain.

Public action

A more active citizenship, Mill believed, would be a civilising force in society. Through participation citizens would be educated in intellect, in virtue and in practical activity. The upshot of participation should now be public action based upon deeper consent than that obtained from earlier generations. For Sen (1990; Dreze and Sen 1989) the possibility of producing a fairer world, one which will enrich the capacities and entitlements of all citizens, depends upon the vitality of public, democratic action. The creation of a learning society expresses a belief in the virtue of the public domain and will depend upon the vitality of public action for its realisation.

If these principles of local participation and responsive action in the learning society are to be firmly established then reforms will be needed to the local governance of education. In addition to a strategic, enabling local education authority and strong institutions, three mechanisms could be developed to strengthen the 'periphery' of local education by identifying local needs, facilitating participation and supporting the coordination of schools and colleges in a new community perspective. These are:

(a) *Community forums*: some schools have in the past introduced such forums to extend community participation, and in some authorities forums have been established for specific purposes, for example to review proposals for school reorganisation or, more generally, to consider educational issues. A stronger democracy suggests the need for community forums with a wider remit to cover all services enabling parents, employers and community groups to express local needs and share in decision making about provision to meet them.

(b) *Grant-giving capacity*: public dialogue about change in the community is properly a primary responsibility of local forums but they should be able to exert influence. This could be achieved by a limited resource giving capacity (delegated by the local authority) to support the learning needs of individuals and groups within the community. This would be an important strategy in enfranchising and empowering community education and reinforce service providers' responsiveness to local needs.

(c) *The enabling role of an area officer*: Mutual cooperation in services will sometimes happen spontaneously. It is likely to be accelerated with the support of an area officer or adviser who encourages parental and group involvement in identifying learning needs and in deciding upon and organising appropriate development projects. Monitoring and evaluating progress, enabling the dialogue of accountability are crucial activities in the role. It is a networking role, in which the officer, or local community representative, works to link up the parts of the service so that the LEA and its institutions can make an integrated response to the needs of parents and the community. The role becomes the 'animateur' of the community as an educational campus.

CONCLUSION

An internal educational market will ensure selection to match a pyramidal, hierarchical society (the hidden curriculum of which is learned very early by young people). It is underpinned by a political system which encourages passive rather than active participation in the public domain. A different polity, enabling all people to make a purpose of their lives, will create the conditions for motivation in the classroom. Only a new moral and political order can provide the foundation for sustaining the personal development of all. It will encourage individuals to value their active role as citizens and thus their shared responsibility for the common-wealth. Active learning in the classroom needs, therefore, to be informed by and lead towards active citizenship within a participative democracy. The learning society thus can only be sustained by a strong *system* of reformed local democracy. For learning is inescapably a process which cannot be contained within the boundaries of any one institution. Discovery and understanding occur at home, in the community, on a scheme of work experience as well as in college or school. Education needs to be a *local* system of management so as to ensure understanding of local needs, responsiveness to changing circumstances, and efficiency in the management of resources within geographic boundaries consistent with identifiable historical traditions. Such local systems need to be properly accountable and this requires location within a local democratic system. Education needs to be a local *democratic* system because it must be a public service responsive and accountable to the community as a whole in which local people express their views and participate actively in developing its purposes and processes. A participatory model of governing local education rather than a market model can establish the democratic foundations for the learning society.[6]

NOTES

1 During the passage of this Act a new clause I was introduced which removes the reference in S.1 of the 1944 Education Act to national policy being secured by LEAs under the 'control and direction' of the Secretary of State for Education. In so doing the 1993 Act not only withdraws the LEA from its pre-eminent position in the provision of state education, it terminates what was, in its introduction, a constitutional settlement between central and local government of education (cf. Morris and Fowler 1993).
2 As reported by a senior civil servant at a public seminar in Birmingham.
3 This analysis builds upon: Dworkin 1983; Sen 1985, 1990; Ranson 1988; Jonathan 1990; Whitty 1990; Levačić 1991; Miliband 1991; Ball 1992a, b; Bowe and Ball 1992; Edwards and Whitty 1992; Walford 1992.
4 Although Tooley (1992a) argues that *some* educational contexts cannot be modelled using the Prisoner's Dilemma game, his many reconstructions fail, in my view, to model the precise dilemmas described by Jonathan, the point of which can be illustrated using a number of metaphors (see Parfit 1984).
5 Compare Archbishop Temple's speech in 1942 ('. . . are you going to treat a man as what he is or what he might be? That is the whole work of education') quoted in Butler (1982).
6 See also: Ranson 1992b and 1993b.

REFERENCES

Anderson, P. (1992) 'The intransigent Right at the end of the century', *London Review of Books*, 24 September.
Ball, S.J. (1990a) *Politics and Policy Making in Education: Explorations in Policy Sociology*, London: Routledge.
Ball, S.J. (1992a) Schooling, enterprise and the market, American Education Research Association symposium paper, San Francisco, April.
Ball, S.J. (1992b) *The Worst of Three Worlds: Policy Power Relations and Teachers' Work*, Keynote address to BEMAS Research Conference, University of Nottingham, April.

Barber, B. (1984) *Strong Democracy: Participatory Politics for a New Age*, Berkeley: University of California Press.

Barry, B. (1989) *Theories of Justice: Volume 1: A Treatise on Social Justice*, London: Harvester Wheatsheaf.

Bowe, R. and Ball, S.J. with Gold, A. (1992) *Reforming Education and Changing Schools*, London: Routledge & Kegan Paul.

Butler, R.A. (1982) *The Art of Memory*, London: Hodder & Stoughton.

Callinicos, A. (1993) Socialism and democracy. In D. Held (ed.) *Prospects for Democracy*, Oxford: Polity.

Chubb, J. and Moe, T. (1990) *Politics, Markets and America's Schools*, Washington: Brookings Institution.

Dreze, J. and Sen, A. (1989) *Hunger and Public Action*, Oxford: Clarendon.

Dworkin, R. (1985) *A Matter of Principle*, Oxford: Clarendon.

Edwards, T. and Whitty, G. (1992) 'Parental choice and educational reform in Britain and the United States', *British Journal of Educational Studies*, 40(2), 101–17.

Elster, J. (1979) *Ulysses and the Sirens*, Cambridge: Cambridge University Press.

Elster, J. (1983) *Sour Grapes*, Cambridge: Cambridge University Press.

Elster, J. (1992) *Local Justice: How Institutions Allocate Scarce Goods and Necessary Burdens*, Cambridge: Cambridge University Press.

Gadamer, H.G. (1975) *Truth and Method*, London: Sheed & Ward.

Habermas, J. (1984) *The Theory of Communicative Action: Volume One: Reason and the Rationalization of Society*, London: Heinemann.

Hampshire, J. (1989) *Innocence and Experience*, London: Allen & Unwin.

Haydon, G. (1985) 'Towards a framework of commonly accepted values.' In G. Haydon (ed.) *Education for a Pluralist Society*, London: University of London Institute of Education.

Hayek, F.A. (1944) *The Road to Serfdom*, London: Routledge & Kegan Paul.

Held, D. (1989) *Political Theory and the Modern State*, Oxford: Polity.

Hirsch, F. (1977) *The Social Limits to Growth*, London: Routledge & Kegan Paul.

Hirschmann, A.O. (1970) *Exit, Voice and Loyalty, Responses to Decline in Firms, Organisations and States*, Cambridge: Harvard University Press.

Jonathan, R. (1990) 'State education service or prisoner's dilemma: the "hidden hand" as a source of education policy', *Educational Philosophy and Theory* 22(1): 16–24.

Jordan, B. (1989) *The Common Good: Citizenship, Morality and Self-Interest*, Oxford: Blackwell.

Levačić, R. (1991) 'Markets and government: an overview.' In G. Thompson, J. Frances, R. Levačić and J. Mitchell (eds) *Markets, Hierarchies and Networks: The Coordination of Social Life*, London: Sage.

MacIntyre, A. (1981) *After Virtue: A Study in Moral Theory*, London: Duckworth.

Macpherson, C.B. (1973) *Democratic Theory: Essays in Retrieval*, Oxford: Clarendon.

Miliband, D. (1991) *Markets, Politics and Education: Beyond the Education Reform Act*, London: Institute for Public Policy Research.

Morris, R. and Fowler, J. (1993) *Beyond Clause Zero: The Education Bill 1992–93*, London: Association of Metropolitan Authorities.

Mouffe, C. (1992) *Dimensions of Radical Democracy: Pluralism, Citizenship, Community*, London: Verso.

Oakeshott, M. (1962) *Rationalism in Politics and Other Essays*, London: Methuen.

Pack, S. (1991) *Capitalism as a Moral System: Adam Smith's Critique of the Free Market Economy*, Aldershot: Edward Elgar.

Parfit, D. (1984) *Reasons and Persons*, Oxford: Oxford University Press.

Ranson, S. (1988) 'From 1944 to 1988: education, citizenship and democracy', *Local Government Studies*, 14(1): 1–19.

Ranson, S. (1992a) 'Towards the learning society', *Educational Management and Administration* 20(2): 68–79.

Ranson, S. (1992b) *The Role of Local Government in Education: Assuring Quality and Accountability*, Harlow: Longman.

Ranson, S. (1993a) 'Public education and local democracy'. In H. Tomlinson (ed.) *Education and Training: Continuity and Diversity in the Curriculum*, Harlow: Longman.

Ranson, S. (1993b) *Local Democracy in the Learning Society: A Briefing Paper*, London: National Commission on Education.

Ranson, S. (1994) *Towards the Learning Society*, London: Cassell.

Rawls, J. (1971) *A Theory of Justice*, Oxford: Clarendon.

Rawls, J. (1993) *Political Liberalism*, New York: Columbia University Press.

Sen, A. (1982) *Choice, Welfare and Measurement*, Oxford: Blackwell.

Sen, A. (1985) 'The moral standing of the market', *Social Philosophy and Policy* 2(2): 1–19.

Sen, A. (1990) 'Individual freedom as social commitment', *New York Review of Books*, 14 June.

Sen, A. (1992) 'On the Darwinian view of progress', *London Review of Books*, 5 November.

Taylor, C. (1985) *Philosophy and the Human Sciences: Philosophical Papers 2*, Cambridge: Cambridge University Press.

Taylor, C. (1992) *Multiculturalism and 'The Politics of Recognition'*, Princeton: Princeton University Press.

Titmuss, R.M. (1971) *The Gift Relationship: From Human Blood to Social Policy* London: George Allen & Unwin.

Tomlinson, J. (1988) 'Curriculum and the market: are they compatible?' In J. Haviland (ed.) *Take Care Mr. Baker!*, London: 4th Estate.

Tooley, J. (1992a) 'The prisoner's dilemma and educational provision: a reply to Ruth Jonathan', *British Journal of Educational Studies* 40(2): 118–33.

Tooley, J. (1992b) 'The "Pink Tank" on the Education Reform Act', *British Journal of Educational Studies* 40(4): 335–49.

Tooley, J. (1993) *A Market-led Alternative for the Curriculum: Breaking the Code*, London: The Institute of Education.

Walford, G. (1992) *Selection for Secondary Schooling*, London: National Commission on Education.

Whitty, G. (1990) The New Right and the national curriculum: state control or market forces?' In M. Flude and M. Hammer (eds) *The Education Reform Act 1988: Its Origins and Implications*, London: Falmer.

Chapter 13

Explaining economic decline and teaching children about industry

Some unintended continuities?

J. Ahier

... What I want to do here is to criticize the cultural explanations of national economic decline and to show, by comparison with some other types of explanation, that they have a kind of affinity with discourses within state schooling. In spite of being mistaken these cultural explanations can be used to justify certain educational developments in a direct and simple way, and their rhetoric can be easily assimilated into contemporary educational debate. Other kinds of explanation create interesting dilemmas and problems for educators which I shall attempt to eludicate.

The text which may have had the most effect in developing and sustaining the cultural explanation of economic decline is Martin Wiener's (1981) *English Culture and the Decline of the Industrial Spirit, 1850–1980.* ... Subsequently Wiener's thesis has been used by many political commentators and academics.

In his book Wiener documents numerous instances of anti-industrialism and anti-urbanism from a whole range of cultural practices, arguing that these sentiments and values are particularly English. From the Gothic revival onwards he sees English culture continually expressing a deep suspicion of industry and commerce. Dickens, for example, rejected the values of commercial society, as did Ruskin and Arnold. The very image of the nation – Old England – he saw as constructed after 1900 by nostalgic reference to thatched cottages and rural existence, and village life was consistently idealized. Middle-class English suburban architecture provided mostly farmhouses and yeomen's cottages, and the politicians from Baldwin to Churchill played upon a popular nostalgia. Wiener considers that, by the First World War, fascination with the old country life had spread throughout the middle class and anti-industrialism had invaded all of the national culture.

In the second half of the book Wiener goes on to show the effects of this development. It has meant that a set of values has ensured that low status has been given to industrialists, who lost confidence and had to suffer, not only the attacks from the political Left, but also the condescension of both the learned professions and the City (Wiener 1981: 129).

Those who stayed in industry lacked commitment to business and tried to live the lives of country gentleman.

Wiener explains this apparent national cultural aberration by tracing it back to what has been called Britain's 'exceptionalism' (Ingham 1984: 3). To blame was the fact that, in this country, a bourgeois, industrial élite never really triumphed. Instead an accommodation was reached between the aristocracy and bourgeoisie, with the old rentier aristocracy holding on to cultural hegemony. This meant that the very class which should have been pressed on with the entrepreneurial spirit became compromised, as did the whole nation.

In reading Wiener one cannot escape some of the great similarities between his arguments and an earlier Left critique of the national culture by Perry Anderson (Anderson 1964, 1968). Indeed Wiener acknowledges how this form of cultural criticism knows no political boundaries by including Anderson with some Right wing commentators like Joseph and Worsthorne (Wiener 1981: 8). If some of the Right have thought that the original class compromise failed to make this country safe for successful capitalism, Anderson and others on the Left bemoaned the fact that it inhibited the production of a true, holistic, bourgeois world view which could only be challenged by a home-produced Marxism (Anderson 1968).

All this may seem both confusing and possibly inconsequential were it not for the fact that over the last ten years institutional changes have been brought about, the rationale for which is to be found on the Right hand side of this interpretation of cultural history. Attempts to turn educators into market calculators, to bring enterprise culture into schools and colleges and to replace state dependence with entrepreneurial vigour are the Right's political answers to a nation seen to be in decline.

It is timely, therefore, to consider critically this social explanation of an economic fact and to ask what light it can throw on the study of education and contemporary curriculum change.

To begin with, the social and cultural history which is presupposed in the Wiener thesis and others like it is highly problematic. Over 20 years ago E.P. Thompson suggested some serious problems with Anderson's work (Thompson 1965) but Wiener took little notice. The latter uses concepts like 'accommodation', 'adaptation', and 'absorption' (Wiener 1981: 9–10) to describe the relationship between the cultures of the aristocracy and bourgeoisies, thus presuming that there were at a crucial point in the nineteenth century two quite distinct and essential sets of values and ways of life. It is interesting that this is not the first time that writers who have sought to describe the national personality have been drawn by this human metaphor to find in history two parents for their creature. In more confident times it was thought that the English character was the ideal product of the freedom-loving Anglo-Saxons and the discipline of the Normans (Fletcher and Kipling 1911). Such approaches require both the simplistic reduction of a group's culture to a set of values and a belief that one group's apparently predominant values were set and generated internally before contact with the other.

Problems with any notions of economic class categories as agents with their own internal cultures have been well rehearsed in theory. . . .

If recent research is opening up the presuppositions about the middle-class culture which informed Wiener's book then there has already been considerable doubt thrown on the characterization of what may be called the other side. Thompson, among others, has shown fairly conclusively that the landed aristocracy, if it had ever been un-capitalist or anti-capitalist, had certainly moved more than half way towards embracing capitalist methods and ideals by the mid-nineteenth century; hence it is misleading to argue that the drive towards landed status, and the adoption of gentlemanly values, inevitably sapped 'the industrial spirit . . .' (Thompson 1984: 208). . . .

Wiener's actual social analysis is concerned with identifying an all-powerful social élite, born of the rentier aristocracy and the industrial bourgeoisie, which was completely homogeneous in terms of culture, values and education by the end of Queen Victoria's reign. In his book, however, this élite is vaguely defined, at one time tautologically becoming all those who espoused the values of the élite (Wiener 1981: 159), at another time being defined by sources of income, by wealth, occupation and education (*ibid.*: 158). Other studies of the élites have usually been concerned with the empirical investigation of the degrees to which various groupings are interconnected, the extent of élite coherence and so on (Stanworth and Giddens 1974), but Wiener deals in holisms, more associated, perhaps, with forms of Hegelian Marxism. His élite has a 'world view' (the title of Part II of his book), with all the presuppositions of unity. It is this world view which became the unchallenged cultural essence of the nation via what might be called a 'seepage' theory of élite influence. His approach is perfectly expressed in the following quote:

> Elites have disproportionate influence upon both the effective climate of opinion and the conduct of affairs. The values of the directing strata, particularly in a stable, cohesive society like modern Britain, tend to permeate society as a whole and to take on the colour of national values, and of a general mentalité. (Wiener 1981: 5)

The role of educational institutions in such an implicit society theory is clear. They both consolidate the elite and diffuse its values throughout society. Wiener sees the public schools as devoted to separating the sons of the industrial middle class from their economic roots by assimilating them into the ways of the leisured, landed gentlemen via a liberal, non-scientific, anti-industrial curriculum (*ibid.*: 16–22). Subsequently the grammar and state schools came to emulate these high status institutions because they were developed, after 1902, by the products of that public school system. Recently this aspect of Wiener's work has been extended to show that the present attempts to change the educational system towards commercial awareness and a pro-industry stance is bound to fail because the system has always embodied and perpetuated 'the values of British society's dominant elites' (Mathieson and Bernbaum 1988: 127). . . .

What approach to the content of school curricula does the Wiener thesis suggest? His means of establishing the existence of an anti-industrial and anti-urban world view was to itemize numerous examples of the essential sentiments. If we were to substantiate his theory as far as education was concerned we would have to study the content of various school curricula to detect the presence of these sentiments, looking, for example, at how industry was portrayed, and, indeed, whether it was referred to at all. In his inimitable style this is exactly what David Marsland did in his critical analysis of introductory sociology textbooks (Marsland 1988). Following exactly Wiener's explanation of economic decline (pp. 23–4) he vigorously pursued what he considered to be a whole set of biases in these books, and he did this by considering what it omitted, what is given insufficient emphasis or a negative evaluation, and what is unfairly described. Thus he found a constant neglect or negation of enterprise, competition, advertising, property and profit, and students got no contact with 'economic reality' (p. 50).

In some ways Marsland makes a number of telling points. In much of popular sociology there has been very little concern for such things as economic policy, the different nature of economic institutions in various states which may account, in part, for their different economic performances, and other important areas of economic understanding. It is the case where there has been a tendency to consider economic structures only from the point of view of their class-producing functions (Ahier 1983: 12). But his points are not really made to correct imbalances within an academic discipline or even to encourage the economic education of students of social science, but to promote one bias against another, and to instil respect for Britain's 'established and requisite economic and political institutions' (Marsland 1988: 29). Marsland wants the textbooks to give 'a positive account of British society and its economic institutions which is powerfully justified by all the relevant facts' (*ibid.*: 58). This is indeed an extreme version and interpretation of the Wiener thesis. Anyone with a concern about national economic performance – and Marsland himself admits there has been a 'drift towards national bankruptcy' (*ibid.*: 25) – could hardly be serious in thinking that the causes of that economic performance have been the anti-enterprise values as found in sociology textbooks. It is a sign of the level of the debate represented in this book, and currently within the popular press, that Marsland can suggest that we should study 'the market' in sociology because it is the 'primary institution of the economy of liberal-capitalist societies' (*ibid.*: 45). Studying 'the market' as a single institution is likely to be as unpromising as studying 'the state' as a single unified body or 'the people' as the undifferentiated beneficiary and supporter of socialism.

What is mistaken in this whole enterprise is the belief that you can track down some socially damaging cultural element, be it racism or ruralism, by the content analysis of educational or other texts, and then put it right by rewriting the books, reversing the values and including the excluded. Marsland ends his attack with the inevitable check lists, very similar, in their way, to the ones produced by those who have pursued racism and sexism by the same methods. More sinister is Marsland's reliance on an implicit state power for inspection and enforcement (*ibid.*: 197).

If the belief that English culture had become generally imbued with elements of anti-industrialism over a long period was correct, and if one thought that content analysis was a satisfactory means of investigating texts, then one might well expect to find these elements in the textbooks of the nation's schools. Given that sociology is a recent and perhaps temporary visitor to the English secondary school curriculum one might look at the texts of two established subjects which could be relevant, history and geography.

When looking at history books used in elementary schools, and later in the primary schools in England from the 1900s to the 1960s such a reading of these books will certainly provide evidence for the Wiener thesis. On the other hand it will also provide hints that the thesis is at fault and that the other ideological tasks performed by schools were contradictory in appearance and ambivalent in outcome.

In these books one can find substantial support for the existence of one aspect of anti-industrialism. They abound with ruralist sentiments and generally portray urban life, especially in industrial cities, as dirty and miserable. By way of contrast the Anglo-Saxon period was presented as a particularly favourable time, when original English people could farm and enjoy country pleasures. Children were so often told that it was the 'country air' which was so beneficial compared with 'town air', which, regardless of period or place, was always foul. When visual images of town and country were used the rural scenes were viewed from above, with villages, fields, cottages and domestic life spread out below. The towns, by contrast, were represented from street level, with all their inhospitable dirt and vulgar business. Thus, when it comes to explaining to the child reader the complex process of industrialization, the key indicator used was a particularly regrettable *loss*, of air, land and homeliness.

Significantly the contrasts between the rural past and what came after it were most extreme when the texts compared the lives of children in the two periods and localities. Quite ignoring the facts of rural child labour they described the idyllic life of rural children and contrasted it with that of town children in factories and streets, whose only hope was the coming of Lord Shaftesbury and the state schools in which these textbooks came to be used (Ahier 1988: 112–13). There is no support here for industrial–urban life. Indeed, in the books written and used after the Second World War it is as though the urban–industrial period of British history was over, and the key signs of modern Britain were taken to be the New Towns and suburbs of a planned landscape. New domestic scenes were depicted, safe and at ease in the housing estates of social democratic England.

Surely these images found in English history textbooks could be taken as undeniable evidence of the anti-industrial culture which they expressed and into which they initiated the child-readers? There are, however, other ways of reading these texts. First, the way industrialization is explained may be mistaken, yet it does hold up for adulation all the virtues of enterprise and inventiveness. In fact the whole process of industrialization has been explained in terms of the hard work and diligence of individual men. If squires, farmers and yeomen were the heroes of rural life, Arkwright, Stephenson, Cartwright, Hargreaves and Watt were the men who brought us strength, wealth and employment. These explanations, together with their descriptions of the machines which were thought to be so important, may not have given children any adequate understanding of the economic, social and political process of industrialization. They might have given magical accounts of wealth creation as the business of individual men, yet in that respect they are quite consistent with the presuppositions of the advocates of an enterprise culture.

It could still be argued that this adulation of the enterprising inventor stands out simply because there is so much appreciation of rural figures and rural settings. There are, however, other ways of understanding the predominance of the latter besides seeing them as cumulative expressions of national anti-industrialism. There are what might be called *internal* reasons for presenting the past in the ways the books have done. For example, one cannot escape the feeling that rural, domestic life was described in the way it was because it was thought to suit the minds and inclinations of child-readers. Many of the books were organized in series to be followed chronologically, and the chronology of the nation was linked to pre-given notions of the stages of children's development. Because it has been thought for so long that children below a certain age could not, and should not, grasp the abstractions of money, markets, capital, investment and profit, the development of capitalism has had to be 'belittled' for them and made concrete by the images of urbanization and invention. Mathieson and Bernbaum (1988), in their extension of the Wiener thesis, thought that educational progressivism was tainted by English anti-industrialism, but the most effective development of progressivism took the form of a child-centredness which was built on notions of the nature of childhood and its stages, and so many writers on children's development have thought that they are best nurtured in direct contact with nature. The peculiarity of these histories for children appear to have more to do with the gentility of the child-centred pedagogue than with the ruralism of a whole national culture.

More doubt still is cast upon the notion of the school curriculum expressing the national culture as characterized by Wiener if one considers the textbooks of another subject. In geography books we find an emphasis on the 'natural' ways of teaching children the subject by contact with nature. Much is made of observing the weather and walking in the countryside (Ahier 1988: 129–30). When considering what was often called 'the homeland' the greatest prominence is given to the farmer, but the books also went to great lengths to present the nation as the 'workshop of the world'. When children have been introduced to the differences between 'us' and 'them', 'here' and 'there', it is the urban and industrial which has been taken as the positive distinguishing quality of the nation. Children in the past have been told frequently that the natural gifts of a temperate climate and adequate supplies of coal have made 'us' what we are – a powerful, civilized, *industrial* country. The travels of imaginary child-characters in many of the books include visits to coal mines, steel works and cotton factories, as well as farms, all interconnected within a national homeland, a national division of labour and an exchange of equivalents.

When a world geography was presented to children, a set of contrasts played upon 'our' industrialization and 'their' primitiveness. Again, because of certain internal educational commitments to a regional geography and its climatic determinations, and because it was thought that children would be fascinated by the odd and the different, it was other countries which were always represented by their agriculture and other people who were seen as close – too close – to nature. Certainly the idea that Britain was the only industrialized society, or that other countries were only too happy to 'help' us by sending us their produce, was a gross misunderstanding of the evolving place of the British economy during the long period when these books were in use, but one could hardly see such representations of 'us' and 'them' as springing from any essential anti-industrialism.

The problems found with the Wiener thesis and its application to school knowledge can be used to make three more general points with regard to the study of contemporary curricula and their associated texts and materials.

First, it would appear difficult, if not impossible to maintain any notion of a singular curriculum as an expression of a culture, whether of a nation or a social class. (Wiener's thesis depends on the former becoming the latter.) The difficulty cannot be solved by merely adding other influences, or by seeing the curriculum as an arena of cultural conflict between groups differentiated outside of schools and education. Such an approach may throw light on contemporary struggles between those who seek a more 'practical' curriculum and an 'education for capability', and those who want to preserve the national culture via traditional standards, but it tends to ignore factors internal to pedagogy and the institutions of schooling. The chronological organization of children and the related theories of cognitive development which have been integral to the enterprise of state schooling must be seen as crucially determining what can be taught, how, in what order and to whom. Thus what might be seen as elements of a national anti-urbanism at one level may also be considered as attempts to charm the innocent and natural young child and use their innate curiosity. In a similar way, the persistence of certain images within the textbooks used in the nation's schools may have more to do with the way internal pedagogic conventions of representation appear to be sustained by educational publishing practices than by any national cultural lag or lasting aristo-cratic embrace. In school publishing the standard texts and original images have been in use, with minor revisions, for very extended periods of time. It is not only because this is profitable for the publishers, but also because of the way conceptions of the child-reader, in a sense, *polices* the texts which can be produced. Thus, for example, although there has been some considerable support recently for teaching primary schoolchildren about industry and work, the materials to help teachers do this have been very limited, and few have been able to present even the simplest economic concepts to a young readership.

Second, if the curriculum and curricular materials *express* no unity then we should not expect that they *address* any unity either. So often critical analysis of educational knowledge presumes that certain materials will have similar effects on all children. When different effects are admitted, then those will be accounted for purely in terms of the relevance or irrelevance of the materials and ideas to children of different classes, races or localities. For example, one of the most public criticisms of the so-called traditional curriculum in the 1970s by educationalists like Midwinter (e.g. Midwinter 1971) was that the content was quite inappropriate for children of the inner city. It was argued that the issues dealt within, say, English or history were unrealistic, even whimsical, and too distant from the everyday lives of the children from the urban working class. Following significant developments in the analysis of the relationship between author, reader and text we can no longer accept, either that curriculum content has any necessary direct effect upon pupils conceived as passive recipients in the ways previously presumed, or that the closer the content is to the everyday life of the child-subject then the more effective it will be. Research on the way comics and school stories work for girls (Walkerdine 1984; Frith 1985) suggest that the content of school subjects may be highly unpredictable in its effects on different pupils. Furthermore, such content may not be understandable by any critique based on charges that the content lacks relevance or realism. We would have to consider instead how children from various cultural, geographical and economic backgrounds can locate themselves in the different narratives found within the school subjects, and whether they accept, reject or re-interpret the positions offered them as learners.

Third, following on from this, we must ask what the form and content of curricula do for us, the adults and teachers, and what is involved in the production of curriculum materials for children. Jacqueline Rose's work on Peter Pan (1984) looked at the psychological functions which may be served by writing fiction for children, but, as far as I am aware, similar issues have rarely been explored in the study of non-fiction elements of the curriculum. In my own study of earlier history and geography books for younger children it was difficult to avoid the conclusion that writing and using these books secured for adults a world safely ordered both in time and space. Among more recent attempts to teach children about industry there is evidence of the way in which making economic matters amenable to the children can also make them acceptable to the adults. In some reports on industry projects in primary schools, for example (Jamieson 1985; Smith 1986, 1988) the 'world of work' can appear repossessed by adults in education, making it secure, integrated, rational and even playful.

If it is useful to consider why certain curriculum materials and programmes satisfy or appeal to teachers and other adults, it may also be important to look at what it is about the Wiener thesis itself, and others like it, which appeals to some politicians, industrialists, and some educationalists.

One could begin by seeing a similarity between the blaming of a nation's culture for its economic difficulties, and earlier attempts to blame the culture of working class parents for the comparative failure of their children in schools. Perhaps the national culture can be seen as deformed in the way that those parents' culture was deprived. As was so frequently pointed out at the time when cultural deprivation arguments were so popular, such ideas served only to redirect attention away from the teachers and the schools at which these children so persistently failed. In a somewhat conspiratorial sense it is possible to argue that blaming the culture and, more specifically, the agencies of cultural transmission for economic problems was an excellent way for industrialists to defend their autonomy and freedom to carry on as before. John Beck has shown how, against a background of political attempts in the 1970s to make British industrialists more accountable to their employees and to the state, they turned such demands on to the teachers (Beck 1983). In that paper it is also suggested how linking education to industrial policy had certain political advantages for the Labour Government of the time. It showed it to be doing something in response to attacks on education by the Conservatives, it had the appearance of an industrial strategy, and it could be held up as a significant area of co-operation between government, unions and employers. If there could be no co-operation on prices, incomes, or any other vital aspects of national economic regeneration or control, the Government could at least launch the Schools Council Industry Project. . . .

I want to explore the particular difficulties of introducing to younger pupils a central family of concepts for contemporary citizenship when linked with industrial or economic awareness.

One of the difficulties of even starting to equip young people with the conceptual tools for citizenship arises, not because of the problems associated with teaching so-called controversial issues, but because there is a conceptual hole in the very middle of contemporary educational discussion about political, economic and social education itself. That hole is the space which was once occupied by 'the nation' in the conventional history and geography curriculum. As Jeffs points out, after the Second World War opposition to political education was much less pronounced because it was thought that any development of political or social awareness would necessarily preserve and further 'the British way of life' (Jeffs 1988: 29). Since the 1960s however, because of various social changes and because of the nationalist and racist overtones in the ways 'the nation' had been presented to children, there has been a certain lack of frankness about the fact that at least some conception of 'the nation', some ability to apply the adjective 'national', is necessary to gain entry to most contemporary political and economic debates. Our discussion of theories of economic decline is but an illustration of this. Yet for a whole variety of reasons many educators in Britain have become extremely ambivalent about this concept and have tended to allow what are often their Right wing critics to articulate it as a cultural and sometimes political-racial unit.

Exactly what are the difficulties in attempting to introduce children to some conception of the national which would be useful for political and economic understanding? Again one is forced to use words like congruence and consistency to present the relationship between some contemporary educational and some political and economic discourse. On one side is a child-centred discourse which has its roots in both an anti-nationalism and anti-militarism of the founders of progressive education (viz. Selleck 1972) and the developmentalism of Piaget. On the other are a series of actual and theoretical developments which have cast doubt on the possibility of a national economy, or the state as a legitimate economic force.

Some research in the developmental tradition would certainly discourage teachers from believing that they could get very far with developing any sense of nation, society or community during the primary state of schooling. For example, Jahoda's original work with 6- to 11-year-olds (1963, 1964) could be taken as showing that young children had little conception of nation until 11 years of age, at least when asked some oddly fundamental questions as 'What is Britain?'

This is not the place to enter the complex debates about the methodological, epistemological and ontological presuppositions in Piagetian research. In the end all such development studies can show is, not that children *cannot* learn about these things, but that they do not, naturally, enter such conceptual worlds.

Many teachers have now become more aware of the problems of much Piagetian work in this field but there is another, related aspect of developing satisfactory initiatives in political-economic education. The dual emphasis on realism and experience can make it very difficult to explore with children the *inter-institutional* relations of an economic and political kind. Visits to *real* factories, depending on children's actual experience of shops and the local environment, or even giving them the experience of running their own mini-enterprise, may well produce pedagogic contexts which make it particularly hard to learn about the inter-institutional economic relationships within a given space or between different societies. This does not imply that children would have to be taught exclusively by a direct pedagogy when such issues were covered, but it is likely that inter-institutional relations could be better explored in 'unrealistic' settings. Such artifical contexts, simple models of contemporary communities, for example, complete with institutions of consumption and production, could be produced in such a way that there was a lower density of experiential reference. Here the 'realism effect' could depend more upon the children being involved in narratives or identifying with a position in the setting from which they could make calculations and play roles.

Another reason why it seems so difficult for teachers in state schools to deal with that group of political and economic concepts concerned with state and nation is that the previous conventions of representing 'the nation' to children now seem so contradicted by contemporary ideological, political and economic developments. Recent discussions about the nature of the national history curriculum have shown the depth and range of objections to any return to a representation of the past as the unfolding of a unified, national essence (Samuel 1989a). The publication of three volumes on the nature of British patriotism can only help to heighten our sensitivity to the cross pitfalls of naïveté which threaten any attempts to represent 'the nation' in schools (Samuel 1989b). The dangers are clear, but missing in most of this debate has been a consideration of how one could now represent national economic space, and how one could legitimately present notions, however simple, of the national and international economy. The matter is of some significance not least because a nationalist and over-inflated view of Britain may well have made its own contribution to post-war decline, causing over-expenditure on the military (Chalmers 1985) and pretensions about the value of sterling (Hall 1987).

In the past representations of the internal national economy have been confused with the attempted construction of cultural Englishness. Where reference was made to national economic space, it was shown to children as an interlocking system in which different regions or towns made their distinctive contributions to national wealth (Ahier 1988: 127–32). Children could learn that there were, within a coherent national economy, different places providing different, tangible goods – steel in Sheffield, engines in Coventry, and so on. Viewed externally the image of the economy in school texts has been in terms of what it exports and imports. When the history of the national economy has been outlined, there has been very little on structures or institutions. Oddly, the only genuine attempts to present children with the rudiments of a political–economic history were in the representations of the feudal village. Even books for very young children have included references to ownership, class, exchange, surplus and rent (Ahier 1988: 116). Capitalist agriculture, however, was usually described as the development of technologies only, and the growth of industry has excluded concern for banks, borrowing, saving, the formation of companies or trade unions.

Clearly all these representations are now inadequate. Not only was the image of Britain as the workshop of the world finally laid to rest in 1983 when the United Kingdom became a net importer of manufactured goods, but the last 15 years of de-industrialization, however explained, have had such differential effects on the regions and cities of Britain that links between localities and specific product have been, for the most part, destroyed. Old notions of the nation exporting those categories of goods which were in surplus, and importing those which were needed, are also outdated because the openness of the economy and the domin-ance of the multinational companies has developed two-way in similar products. However, the ultimate question is whether the difficulty in representing the national economy to future citizens stems from the fact that such a concept is now completely redundant.

Arguments to show the demise of national economies come from both the political Right and Left, partly as reactions to the declared failure of the Keynesian policies of the post-war period. To some on the Right, notions of a national economy conjure up thoughts of closed, state-dominated systems, thought to be crumbling all over the world in the face of economic liberalism and the urge of all people to be 'free'. Redwood's Popular Capitalism, for example (Redwood 1988), traces the spread of privatization, the growth of stock markets, and other signs of the flowering of enterprise as a global phenomenon, undermining previous notions of states as economic units. Those of another political persuasion refer to the evolution of a world system and argue that global capitalism is so pervasive and now so organized that what happens in any given state is determined by the world system (Wallerstein 1974) . . .

REFERENCES

Ahier, J. (1983) 'History and sociology of educational policy', in Ahier, J. and Flude, M. (eds) *Contemporary Education Policy*, Beckenham: Croom Helm.

Ahier, J. (1988) *Industry, Children and the Nation*, Lewes: Falmer Press.

Anderson, P. (1964) 'Origins of the present crisis', *New Left Review*, 23.

Anderson, P. (1968) 'Components of the national culture', *New Left Review*, 50.

Beck, J. (1983) 'Accountability, industry and education', in Ahier, J. and Flude, M. (eds) *Contemporary Education Policy*, Beckenham: Croom Helm.

Chalmers, M. (1985) *Paying for Defence: Military Spending and British Decline*, London: Pluto Press.

Fletcher, C. and Kipling, R. (1911) *A School History of England*, Oxford: Oxford University Press.

Frith, G. (1985) '"The time of your life": the meaning of the school story', in Steedman, C., Urwin, C. and Walkerdine, V. (eds) *Language, Gender and Childhood*, London: Routledge and Kegan Paul.

Hall, J. (1987) 'The State', in Causer, G. (ed.) *Inside British Society*, Brighton: Wheatsheaf Books.

Ingham, G. (1984) *Capitalism Divided? The City and Industry in British Social Development*, Basingstoke: Macmillan.

Jahoda, G. (1963) 'The development of children's ideas about country and nationality', *British Journal of Educational Psychology*, 33, 47–60, 143–53.

Jahoda, G. (1964) 'Children's concepts of nationality: a critical study of Piaget's stages', *Child Development*, 35.

Jamieson, I. (1985) *Industry in Education*, Harlow: Longman.

Jeffs, T. (1988) 'Preparing young people for participatory democracy', in Carrington, B. and Troyna, B. (eds) *Children and Controversial Issues*, Lewes: Falmer Press.

Marsland, D. (1988) *Seeds of Bankruptcy*, London: The Claridge Press.

Mathieson, M. and Bernbaum, G. (1988) 'The British disease: a British tradition?', *British Journal of Educational Studies*, xxv, 2.

Midwinter, E. (1971) 'Curriculum and the E.P.A. community school', in Hooper, R. (ed.) *Curriculum, Context, Design and Development*, Edinburgh: Oliver and Boyd.

Redwood, J. (1988) *Popular Capitalism*, London: Routledge.

Rose, J. (1984) *The Case of Peter Pan*, London: Macmillan.

Samuel, R. (1989a) 'New histories for old', in *History, The Nation and the Schools-Working Papers*, Ruskin College.

Samuel, R. (1989b) *Patriotism*, 3 vols., London: Routledge.

Selleck, R. (1972) *English Primary Education and the Progressives, 1914–1939*, London: Routledge and Kegan Paul.

Smith, D. (1986) *Industry Education in the Primary School*, School Curriculum Industry Project.

Smith, D. (1988) *Industry in the Primary School Curriculum*, Lewes: Falmer Press.

Stanworth, P. and Giddens, A. (1974) *Elites and Power in British Society*, Cambridge: Cambridge University Press.

Thompson, E. (1965) 'The peculiarities of the English', in Miliband, R. and Saville, J. (eds) *The Socialist Register*.

Thompson, F. (1984) 'English landed society in the nineteenth century', in Thane, P., Crossick, G. and Floud, R. (eds) *The Power of the Past*, Cambridge: Cambridge University Press.

Walkerdine, V. (1984) 'Developmental psychology and the child-centred pedagogy; the insertion of Piaget into early education', in Henriques, J., Holloway, W., Urwin, C., Venn, C. and Walkerdine, V., *Changing the Subject*, London: Methuen.

Wallerstein, I. (1974) *The Modern World System*, 2 vols., New York: Academic Press.

Wiener, M. (1981) *English Culture and the Decline of the Industrial Spirit, 1850–1980*, Cambridge: Cambridge University Press.

Part IV

Institutions and policies

Chapter 14

The changing role of the state in education provision

C. Chitty

Having been the last major country in Europe to create a national education system, England seems to take remarkably little pride in the schooling arrangements which cater for the vast majority of the nation's children. The media have long rejoiced in stories, many of them exaggerated or false, which betoken a crisis in our state schools (Chitty 1989), and the private sector is given every encouragement to prosper. Politicians of both major parties have found it politically useful to complain of insufficiently high standards in state schools; and few twentieth-century government ministers have educated their own children in the state sector. This paper examines the reasons for what appears to be a recurring aversion among policy makers in this country to the whole idea of the state having a pivotal role in education provision. While the situation is certainly not irredeemable, the events of recent years seem, if anything, to have intensified the pressure towards privatization and the gradual erosion of traditional state structures.

ENGLAND'S BACKWARDNESS: THE EVIDENCE AND POSSIBLE EXPLANATIONS

This country's overtly negative official attitude towards the achievements of the state education system, which has its origins in the *laissez-faire* individualism of the Victorian period, contrasts strongly with the enthusiasm of policy makers in the early modern period for making education a direct concern of the state. And it is worth stressing the interventionist role of the state in the sixteenth century before moving on to consider the reasons for the triumph of so-called voluntaryism in the nineteenth.

As Joan Simon has argued in *Education and Society in Tudor England*, published in 1966, it was at the Reformation that state intervention in English education really began. By the 1530s, education had long ceased to be the prerogative of the church; but it was during the period when Thomas Cromwell was all-powerful as Henry VIII's principal secretary

(1534–40) that educational reforms were promoted in the interests of the state. Cromwell's young protégés, who now found themselves in control of a developing machinery of state, were set the task of formulating concrete policies for enhancing the state's role and consolidating secular forms of government (Simon 1966). Such was their success that by the close of Henry's reign, in Joan Simon's words, 'there had been a wholesale transference of rights over schools to the Crown, bringing to a climax a long process of lay encroachment on ecclesiastical powers over education (*op. cit.*: 196). At the same time, no concerted programme for refounding schools was put into operation by the time of Henry's death; and it was in the short reign of his successor Edward VI (1547–53) that steps were taken towards establishing a new school system to meet the needs of a Protestant nation. So it can be argued that the Reformation brought about profound changes in outlook and administration, and not only in the church, which, in turn, required parallel changes in schooling and teaching. Reformation legislation – following on a long and gradual undermining of ecclesiastical jurisdiction – had effectively cleared the ground for the reorganizing of schools and colleges into a more co-ordinated system of education.

By the end of the seventeenth century, however, there were few remaining signs of this positive state interest in education, and we enter that period of a marked divergence between English educational development and that on the Continent. There was a brief interlude of educational expansion after the execution of Charles I in 1649; but the reforms of the revolutionary period were too closely associated with puritan and republican ideas to survive. Initiatives in educational reform passed to the dissenting academies which henceforth represented the most dynamic area of educational development.

Andy Green has argued that what most distinguishes English educational history in the 200-year period from 1660 to 1870 is 'the almost total absence of those state initiatives which were so significant in continental development' (Green 1990: 241). In Prussia, for example, Frederick II's compulsory attendance laws in 1763 marked the first important move in the direction of national education; and a national public system comprising elementary and secondary schools was essentially in place by the end of the 1830s. During Altenstein's period as Minister of Education (1817–38), elementary education was extended and regulated, developing a high degree of mechanical efficiency under centralized control (Samuel and Thomas 1949: 36).

In France, the central administrative apparatus for education was created by Napoleon with the laws founding the *Université* (the Napoleonic term for the whole system of schools and higher institutions) in 1806 and 1808. The Napoleonic *lycée* was created as early as 1802 giving the state a strategic control over secondary education; and it is possible to talk in terms of a full judicial and administrative framework for national education by the time of the Second Empire, which began life in 1852 (Moody 1978: 43). It is worth noting at this point that respect for the Revolutionary and Napoleonic concept of education as a public function of the state is still a significant factor in French educational thought. This sense of pride in former achievements comes through in the following extract from the Introduction to a bill of 1957 designed to reform the organization of schools:

> It was the Revolution which proclaimed officially, for the first time in France, 'the right to education as an essential right of all individuals' and the Nation's 'duty to instruct all its citizens'. These principles were totally new in the school situation of that period.
>
> (Quoted in Fraser 1963: 5)

In England, on the other hand, it was only in 1870 that the Forster Education Act – responding to the needs of a radically changing society – laid the first foundations of a *national* system of education. Yet even this important piece of legislation – designed to *fill the gaps* in existing provision – did not introduce compulsory education, just as it did not make education free. It was not until 1880 that compulsory attendance was finally introduced throughout the country, and not until 1891 that an act was passed to make most elementary education free (Simon 1965).

The reasons for England's backwardness in creating a national education system are both complex and hotly contested. Much controversy surrounds the claim made by some Marxist historians that nineteenth-century England failed to become a truly *bourgeois* state, and therefore lacked the incentive to develop a state system of education to meet *bourgeois* needs. This failure is itself often blamed on the unique quality of the seventeenth-century English Revolution.

Marx himself argued that the essential difference between the English Revolution and the French Revolution of 1789 was the existence in England (but not in France) of a 'permanent alliance between the middle class and the largest section of the great landowners' – an alliance which could be associated with sheep farming and which dated from the sixteenth century. According to Marx, early capitalism in England was strongest in the countryside where, particularly in the south and east, a large section of the gentry and yeomanry took part in production for the market. By 1640, the social forces let loose by or accompanying the rise of capitalism, especially in agriculture, could no longer be contained within the old political framework, except by the use of repressive policies which Charles I's Government simply did not have the means to enforce. The twin outcomes of the English Revolution were the establishment of conditions far more favourable to the development of capitalism than those which existed *before* 1640 and a reunion of the bourgeoisie with all sections of the nobility against religious, political and social radicalism (Marx 1971a: 92; Marx 1961: 717–44).

Marx's thesis has been elaborated on in a famous passage by the seventeenth-century historian Christopher Hill:

> In France economic and political divisions roughly corresponded with social: the unprivileged Third Estate opposed aristocracy and monarchy; the aristocracy took no part in trade and industry. But in England wool, cloth and agricultural production for the market split the ruling class itself: many gentlemen and even peers engaged in economic activities which would have been impossible for a French noble . . . The division in England is not Third Estate *versus* gentry and peerage, but country *versus* court. Court and government offered economic privilege to some merchants (monopolists, customs farmers, ruling oligarchies in London and other towns); and perquisites to many members of the landed class. On the other hand, those gentlemen and merchants excluded from economic privilege – and they included some of the richest and most go-ahead members of these social groups as well as the middling men – thought that greater freedom of economic development would be of advantage to themselves and the country.
>
> (Hill 1961: 102)

And Hill is here drawing on one of the conclusions reached by the late R.H. Tawney in an article published in 1941:

> The landowner living on the profits and rents of commercial farming, and the merchant or banker who was also a landowner, represented, not two classes, but one. Patrician and *parvenu* both owed their ascent to causes of the same order. Judged by the source of their incomes, both were equally *bourgeois*.

There are a number of interpretations of the class relations which secured the breakdown of the old order; but there seems to be wide acceptance that the true heirs of the seventeenth-century revolution in England were not the bourgeoisie as such, but the landed, albeit *capitalist*, gentry class who, it can be argued, retained their hegemony throughout the eighteenth and nineteenth centuries. The debate then centres on the precise *nature* of that hegemony. If it was primarily the political and cultural ascendancy of an essentially *landed* class, it would go some way towards accounting for the apparent dominance of aristocratic amateur values and the curious absence of that 'credentialist' or 'meritocratic' ethos which was such a marked influence on continental education. It was, after all, Martin Wiener's thesis in his influential book *English Culture and the Decline of the Industrial Spirit, 1850–1980*, published in 1981, that Britain's economic weakness was due to an anti-industrial culture with its roots in nineteenth-century aristocratic rule. If, on the other hand, as Marx argued, aristocratic hegemony was simply a mask disguising true bourgeois power – if, in fact, the landed aristocracy ruled as *delegates* of the bourgeois interest – it is not clear why there was not a greater attempt to create a truly *national* apparatus for middle-class education. Furthermore, while the aristocratic oligarchy in England was possibly unique in its absorption of upwardly mobile bourgeois families, such absorption was, by definition, available for only a minority; and, as Eric Hobsbawm has pointed out, there existed after 1830 large groups of men who recognized themselves as 'middle class', and yet did surprisingly little to win a system of 'middle-class' schools (Hobsbawm 1968: 65).

Andy Green has argued that other, and more convincing, explanations for England's 'backwardness' would have to include the deep infusion of liberal individualism in both the landed and middle classes. What separated Britain from the major continental states was not therefore the predominance of landed culture, but the power of the individualist creed, which meant that all sections of the ruling class shared a marked hostility to the state and were deeply suspicious of the idea of state control of education (*op.cit.* 237).

It was only in the second half of the nineteenth century – and particularly after 1870 – that a split developed in the Liberal Party concerning the role of the state in the amelioration of social problems and the creation of the good society. Traditional liberal theory had been based on a belief in freedom and diversity – and in the supreme virtue of limited government. Only gradually did liberal thought adapt to the rapid social changes of the nineteenth century, with the mood of *laissez-faire* giving way to the idea that the greatest freedom for every individual was possible *only* within the framework of the collective state.

At the same time, it is also true, as Eric Hobsbawm has argued, that England's early industrial development meant that there was never an equivalent in this country of that concerted drive towards development through the state that existed elsewhere in Europe. England did not need to use education in the pursuit of national economic development – because that development had taken place anyway *without the assistance of an educated population* (Hobsbawm 1968: 43–5).

Martin Wiener's thesis highlighting the English contempt for entrepreneurial values certainly goes some way towards accounting for the conservative, traditionalist ethos of the English public school which, as is well known, exerted such a powerful influence on all forms of secondary schooling in the Victorian era. The view persisted that the middle classes were well served by an education that paid little attention to the scientific and the technical. Yet the Wiener analysis needs to be considered alongside what we know of the nineteenth-century concern for the minimum of social regulation. Fearful of state control of education, the middle classes were quite prepared to educate their children in schools which reflected the culture of the rural upper class and, even after the principle of state intervention was conceded in 1870, did nothing to create a system of schools to cater for their needs.

THE GROWTH OF A NATIONAL SYSTEM: DIFFERENT INTERPRETATIONS

Forster's Education Act, which instituted, for the first time, state-*provided* and state-*maintained* elementary schools, gave responsibility for 'filling up the gaps' in school provision to around 2,500 newly created School Boards. These *ad hoc* bodies, directly elected and independent of existing forms of local government, were given considerable optional powers in the area of attendance; but a policy of 'permissive compulsion' was soon seen to have damaging limitations. In 1880 school attendance throughout the country was made compulsory at least until the age of 10, to be raised to 11 in 1893 and (except for children employed in agriculture) to 12 in 1899. In 1891, most parents were given the right of free elementary schooling for their children.

School Boards varied in size from that of London, which had some 55 members and soon controlled nearly 400 schools, to rural boards with only one school under their control. Between 1870 and 1900, the larger urban boards were particularly active and, as Richard Aldrich has written, played a major role in 'redefining elementary education in terms of universal schooling' (1982: 79). By the end of 1871, 117 School Boards had instituted by-laws requiring some degree of compulsory attendance. By 1900, nearly half the children who attended public elementary schools were in board schools; in large urban areas the proportion was often much higher.

The vast scope and achievements of the London School Board made it a national institution. It erected buildings which set standards for others to emulate; it established a system of school attendance officers, known somewhat euphemistically as 'visitors', who soon provided a wealth of detailed and reliable information about the lives of the urban poor; and it appointed its own medical officer to report on air space and the ventilation of classrooms and to examine children with special needs. Its debates and discussions were reported in *The Times*, which had declared at the inception of the Board in November 1870: 'No equally powerful body will exist in England outside Parliament, if power be measured by influence for good or evil over masses of human beings' (quoted in Armytage 1964). Between 1871 and 1903, the number of pupils in board schools in London rose from 1,117 to 549,677, while those in voluntary schools dropped from 221,401 to 213,297 (Rubinstein 1977).

In the large towns, the School Boards were often lively, progressive bodies with intelligent and committed members who regarded their service on the Boards as important social work. The schools they administered were regarded by many as a civilizing influence in the areas they served. Writing, for example, about the situation in South London, an HMI observed in 1882: 'Every new Board school erected in the midst of the crowded and joyless streets of Walworth or Peckham is eagerly welcomed by the parents, and becomes a new centre of civilization and intelligence' (quoted in Rubinstein 1977: 237).

Yet although the embryonic state education system (and it was only a tentative beginning) may have been a source of pride for many contemporary observers, the reforms introduced by Forster and the developments that then ensued have long been regarded by politicians and historians on the Far Right as an unnecessary and costly diversion from the true path that education should have followed in the second half of the nineteenth century: leaving it as a matter of purely private concern. According to Keith Joseph, for example, who was Margaret Thatcher's Secretary of State for Education from 1981 to 1986, the legislators made a big mistake in 1870; and the fundamental problem with the education system they inaugurated lies in the very fact that it is a *state* system:

> We have a bloody state system I wish we hadn't got. I wish we'd taken a different route in 1870. We got the ruddy state involved. I don't want it. I don't think we know how to do it. I certainly don't think Secretaries of State know anything about it. But we're landed with it. If we could move back to 1870, I would take a different route. We've got compulsory education, which is a responsibility of hideous importance, and we tyrannize children to do that which they don't want, and we don't produce results.
>
> (Quoted in Ball 1990: 62)

And Professor E.G. West has argued, in a book first published by the Institute of Economic Affairs in 1965, that, since Forster himself believed in 'selectivity' rather than 'universality' in the provision of social services, developments since 1870 actually represent a *betrayal* of the modest principles underpinning the 1870 Education Act (West 1965).

If the New Right rejects the whole argument that schooling should be provided by the state, another school of thought (with adherents within the Conservative Party) argues that even when a rudimentary system of state education was created after 1870, with some important refinements in 1902, the inertia associated with a *laissez-faire* philosophy was not entirely defeated and, consequently, insufficient was done to prepare youngsters to meet the requirements of a modern industrial civilization. This was the view put forward by Lord Annan, former Provost of University College, London in a BBC Radio Four 'Analysis' programme broadcast in March 1991:

Well, you see, in the nineteenth century and the twentieth century, right up to the 1944 Butler Act and even beyond that we have been *laissez-faire* in our attitude to education. In France, in Germany, the state ran education, the schoolmasters were civil servants; the dons, the professors in Prussia were civil servants; and, of course, we sneered at that because ... we prided ourselves on having a *laissez-faire* attitude to education. There was no Minister of Education: he was called the President of the Board of Education. Education was decentralized ... the universities were entirely independent: do what they wish – 'that's the only way we can get the freedom of mind to new ideas coming forward' – and so on and so forth. And it is that dogmatic attitude towards the fear of state education which is responsible for our current miseries

And Lord Annan's views were supported in the 'Analysis' programme by Correlli Barnett, Fellow of Churchill College, Cambridge, who went further by linking our nonchalant and *laissez-faire* approach to education with our complacency about our early industrial pre-eminence and our consequent failure to develop a national system of education and training along continental lines:

By the 1840s and 1850s, we had convinced ourselves that our enormous success in the first industrial revolution and our absolute supremacy at that time, say around 1850, was due to our particular native genius, the practical man who designed his own piece of equipment, and so on. When, in fact, it was a series of lucky historical accidents which had benefited us. And ... other countries, when they started to industrialize, did it far more as a conscious national operation, and they looked at us as a model, and they came and inspected us closely and they copied what they thought was good, but they also noted what they thought was not so good and you have for example in Europe, and especially Germany, the deliberate attempts to link a first-rate education and training system, first-rate scientific research establishments, to the development of great industries. And what, therefore, the Germans did in the 1840s and 1850s in education and training and scientific research paid off from the 1880s onwards in the conquest of new markets and things like chemicals and electricals, and we've never ever recovered our early lead.

If schooling for the next generation *had* a practical purpose after 1870, it was probably to train a privileged group of young men for service in the Empire – the one activity where state enterprise was practised between 1870 and 1939. It could, of course, be argued that Imperial Culture *was* Industrial Culture of a kind; or it could all be seen as a grand distraction from much-needed investment at home. What does at least seem clear is that it has become fashionable in some circles to hold the 'anti-industrial spirit' of the school system responsible for Britain's relative economic decline in the twentieth century.

THE OLD RIGHT AND THE NEW RIGHT, 1944–88

For at least 30 years after the end of the Second World War, both major parties in this country shared a basic commitment to the underlying principles of the Welfare State: a set of tacit assumptions that former cabinet minister Tony Benn has described as 'the welfare capitalist consensus' (Benn 1987). This involved a three-fold commitment to full employment, to the Welfare State itself, and to the coexistence of large public and private sectors in the economy. The Conservative and Labour parties often differed fiercely about specific details of policy; on a deeper level, their conceptions of political authority and social justice differed even more. They differed, however, within a structure of generally accepted values and assumptions. Above all, they believed in the concept of public provision.

As far as education was concerned, the dominating influence was the 1944 Education Act, which set up what is often referred to as a 'national system, locally administered'. What this amounted to was a tripartite 'partnership' between central government, local government and the individual schools and colleges. According to Vernon Bogdanor, the 'efficient secret' of the system was that no *one* individual participant should be able to enjoy a monopoly of power in the decision-making process:

> Power over the distribution of resources, over the organization and over the content of education was to be diffused amongst the different elements and no one of them was to be given a controlling voice . . . Such a structure . . . offered clear and obvious advantages, not only for the administrator concerned with the efficient working of the system, but also for the liberal, anxious to avoid the concentration of power, and the pluralist, insistent that different interests should be properly represented. For parallel to the formal relationships between central and local government, embodied in statute and convention, there grew up a network of professional communities whose role it was to soften the political antagonisms which might otherwise render the system unworkable . . . The diffused structure of decision-making led, it could be argued, to better decisions, because it ensured a wide basis of agreement before changes were made.
>
> (Bogdanor 1979)

The general emphasis of the post-war period was on expansion, and in education this meant a remarkable increase in the number of schools and teachers and of students in higher education. There was a relative absence of damaging political conflict in the 1950s and early 1960s which was itself greatly helped not only by the general climate of expansion, but also by the availability of sufficient resources to ensure the successful implementation of expansionist policies. Although the Conservative Governments of the 1950s were generally hostile to local experiments in comprehensive reorganization, there is much truth in the oft-repeated claim that from 1954, when Sir David Eccles was appointed Minister of Education, until the 1964 general election, when the Conservatives were defeated, government education policy was essentially non-partisan, and even, when Sir Edward Boyle was Minister of Education (1962–64), almost bi-partisan.

The post-war settlement is not, of course, without its critics on both the Right and the Left. Correlli Barnett, for example, has argued in *The Audit of War*, published in 1986, that post-war Britain made the big mistake of earmarking resources it did not possess for the creation of a 'New Jerusalem':

> Romantic idealists . . . right in the middle of the War . . . were, in fact, drawing up these blueprints for a 'New Jerusalem', in which you were going to have a beautiful society, in which all the ills of Victorian industrialism were going to be swept away, and so on and so on. You were going to have a free Health Service, Beveridge, and all that. But if you actually put all that alongside the fact that we were busted by the War, that we were absolutely bankrupt, you have this terrible gulf between these very expensive dreams and the fact that we had absolutely no resources.
>
> (Barnett 1986)

Tony Benn, on the other hand, has argued on a number of occasions that the post-war consensus was never based on a clear vision of a just society and actually served to conceal the factors at work in industry and the economy which were steadily undermining the state's ability to 'manage' capitalism:

> British capitalism, denied its traditional imperial markets, and reluctant to invest in the necessary re-equipment, began to fall behind in the race of markets, and became victim of a series of balance-of-payments crises, which were dealt with, by parties of both colour, by means of 'stop and go', a form of macro-economic masochism that undermined both business confidence and the power of labour.
>
> (Benn 1987: 303)

The economic base on which the 'welfare consensus' depended finally collapsed in the mid-1970s; but there were already signs in the late 1960s that the uneasy cross-party alliance on a number of welfare issues was beginning to fall apart, leaving little trace of that bi-partisan approach which had once facilitated the implementation of the comprehensive reform. This was due, in large measure, to increasing evidence of the exposed nature of Edward Boyle's position on the 'liberal' wing of the Conservative Party – a position which eventually became untenable, as large groups of right-wing back-benchers and constituency activists mobilized against the beleaguered Shadow Education Minister (Knight 1990). It was now widely held within the party that the Conservative Government had been defeated in 1964 not simply because of internal dissensions, nor because the public had become bored with it (though there was seen to be truth in both assertions), but because it had adopted economic and social policies which were a diluted version of its opponents' ideas. Nowhere did this appear to be more true than in the area of education policy – and Boyle was seen to be the chief culprit. At any rate, he was a convenient scapegoat. Matters came to a head at the 1968 Conservative Party Conference where Boyle was challenged to acknowledge that the party was hopelessly divided on such issues as secondary education, the grammar schools and reorganization, and where he made a passionate plea for moderation and consensus:

> I will join with you willingly and wholeheartedly in the fight against Socialist dogmatism wherever it rears its head. But do not ask me to oppose it with an equal and opposite Conservative dogmatism, because in education, it is dogmatism itself which is wrong.
>
> (Quoted in Corbett 1969)

The plea was unsuccessful, and the official motion on education was defeated.

By 1969, when Boyle relinquished the post of Shadow Education Minister, it was obvious that his largely non-partisan or even bi-partisan approach had lost the support of grass-roots activists in the party – and that it was simply no longer possible to paper over the cracks. Writing in *New Society* in May 1969, Anne Corbett argued that:

> However you express it – left versus right, consensus versus backlash, collectivists versus radicals, or just the informed versus the ignorant – the Tory Party in parliament and in the country is divided on education.

But at that time, according to Anne Corbett, the views of Boyle's many critics did not add up to 'a coherent rival philosophy'. Above all, there was a very real split on the Right of the party between the 'preservationists' who simply wanted to defend the old grammar schools, and the so-called 'voucher men' who wanted to experiment with new and untried ways of organizing education. The central issue concerned the role of the state in providing schools and allocating pupils to them on an equitable basis.

It was the 'preservationists' who dominated right-wing thinking until at least the mid-1970s. The first three Black Papers published in 1969 and 1970 were a vehicle for those Conservatives who wanted to put back the clock: to the days of formal teaching in the primary schools, of high academic standards associated with a traditional grammar-school education, and of well-motivated, hard-working and essentially conservative university students (Cox and Dyson 1969a,b, 1970). It was only in the last two Black Papers published in 1975 and 1977 that support was given to the introduction of educational vouchers and to the idea of much greater scope for parental choice of schools (Cox and Boyson 1975, 1977). By the mid-1970s, the politics of *reaction* had been replaced by the politics of *reconstruction*. The Old Right had given way to the New.

FREE MARKETEERS *VERSUS* CONSERVATIVE MODERNIZERS

The apparent triumph of New Right policies in the 1980s can be seen as one (albeit powerful) expression of a growing disillusionment with the major tenets of the post-war social democratic project. Foremost among the causes of the new mood of scepticism and anxiety was the economic down-turn of the early 1970s. The collapse of fixed exchange rates in 1971–72, followed by the quadrupling of the oil price in 1973, resulted in a generalized world recession and thereby undermined the policy regimes that had developed in the period of prosperity. In this country, as elsewhere, the 'crisis' produced a realignment of forces, both on the Left and on the Right. While Socialists in the Labour Party made little headway with the leadership which stuck to the tacit 'revisionism' of the 1950s and 1960s, their opponents on the Right found it comparatively easy to get their ideas debated in the higher echelons of the Conservative Party. Once Edward Heath had been removed as leader of the party in February 1975, a number of right-wing think-tanks set about the task of devising schemes for dismantling the party's commitment to the welfare capitalist consensus, and putting in its place an agenda recreating, at least in part, the classical market liberalism of the nineteenth century.

Yet it would be wrong to exaggerate the coherent nature of New Right philosophy or the extent to which the former Prime Minister and her allies succeeded in the 1980s in articulating a clear vision of the future. Thatcherism, and its revised version for the 1990s, can be seen as an uneasy attempt to link the principles of a free-market economy with an atavistic emphasis on the family, traditional moral values and the strong state. It involves rolling back the frontiers of the state in some areas, while pursuing policies of repression and coercion in others.

There is a marked hostility to all institutions which mediate between the individual and the state, so that the state emerges as the only collectivity in a society of individuals.

As far as education is concerned, the 1988 Act can be seen as an attempt to undermine and eventually *destroy* the power and influence of the local education authorities. Writing in *The Independent* on election day (11 June) 1987, education correspondent Peter Wilby forecast that: 'the return of a Conservative government today will mean the break-up of the state education system that has existed since 1944'. And the Right has certainly made no secret of its contempt for locally controlled education systems. The speech that former Education Secretary Kenneth Baker made to the 1986 Conservative Party Conference received sustained and rapturous applause at the point where he announced that the new City Technology Colleges would be completely independent of local education authority control. In an interview with *The Independent* in September 1987, Mrs Thatcher looked forward to a situation where 'most schools' would have chosen to opt out of local authority control and become, in her words, 'independent state schools'. And the right-wing Hillgate Group has argued that *all* schools should be owned by individual trusts, with their survival dependent on their ability to satisfy their customers (Hillgate Group 1986).

While the major provisions of the 1988 Act will clearly be instrumental in moving us towards a fully market-orientated system of public sector education, the National Curriculum – or rather its precise form in the legislation – can be seen as the brainchild of the 'neo-conservative' element within the New Right. This group of academics and intellectuals expounds a philosophy that is culturally supremacist and anti-egalitarian. The Neo-Conservatives see it as their main task to rescue 'British Culture' from its recent diminution by 'alien cultures'. The adoption of equal opportunities policies, the promotion of multi-culturalism and anti-racism, and the attempts to make schooling more relevant to the lives of working-class pupils are all seen as undermining the traditional values and hierarchical structures that have long been the dominant features of the English education system. The Neo-Conservatives of the Hillgate Group can make common cause with the Neo-Liberals in wanting to see the end of local autonomy; but their main complaint against the LEAs is that they have used their power 'to corrupt the minds and souls of the young' (Hillgate Group 1986: 18).

It is, however, too simplistic to see the debate within the Conservative Party as one between the Neo-Conservative and the Neo-Liberal elements of the New Right, an essential point of disagreement as far as education is concerned being the desirability or otherwise of a state-imposed national curriculum. As Ken Jones has pointed out, Conservatism in education is really 'three-headed', rather than 'double-faced' (1989). A group of Conservative Modernizers, led by David (now Lord) Young, and not really belonging to the New Right as such, became particularly influential during Keith Joseph's period at the DES – a factor which helps to account for Joseph's curious failure to implement the sort of privatizing measures favoured by his former allies in the right-wing think-tanks. The main aim of these 'modernizing' Conservatives was to see the school curriculum – and particularly the secondary curriculum – restructured in order to prepare pupils for work in an enterprise economy. Their main achievement in the field of curriculum initiatives was probably the introduction of the Technical and Vocational Education Initative (TVEI) in the Autumn of 1983. Unlike the Cultural Right – and particularly the Neo-Conservatives of the Hillgate Group – the 'modernizing' tendency has no time for the grammar-school tradition and, as we have seen, considers it to be largely responsible for Britain's long industrial decline. The modernizers find little to attract them in the Government's new National Curriculum, which is seen as offering pupils an education which is both book-bound and supremely irrelevant. The contradictions within the thinking of the Right are neatly illustrated by the fact that Keith Joseph – who was earlier quoted as wanting to see *no* state involvement in education – spent his time at the DES advocating that the state use its power and influence to make the curriculum more vocational, at least for the average and below-average pupils, and demanding that his civil servants read the works of Correlli Barnett and Martin Wiener (Annan 1990: 457).

CONCLUSION

It is hard to see how, irrespective of the political complexion of the government in power in the remaining years of the twentieth century, the educational developments of the last hundred or so years can be totally reversed. . . . The Right clearly hopes that, left to its own devices, the market can be relied on to create that stratification of schooling experience, both reflecting and reinforcing existing divisions in society, which is the 'real' agenda of both the Neo-Conservatives and the Neo-Liberals. Yet the project is fraught with difficulties. A Conservative government might one day feel strong enough to introduce a national system of education vouchers, but it would be more difficult to move to a situation where *all* schools, both primary and secondary, were owned and financed by individual trusts. At any rate, the choice before us in the 1990s is still the one outlined by Raymond Williams in *The Long Revolution* in 1961:

It is a question of whether we can grasp the real nature of our society, or whether we persist in social and educational patterns based on a limited ruling class, a middle professional class, a large operative class, cemented by forces that cannot be challenged and will not be changed. The privileges and barriers, of an inherited kind, will in any case go down. It is only a question of whether we replace them by the free play of the market, or by a public education designed to express and create the values of an educated democracy and a common culture (p. 176).

REFERENCES

Aldrich, R. (1982) *An Introduction to the History of Education*, London: Hodder & Stoughton.

Annan, N. (1990) *Our Age: the Generation That Made Post-War Britain*, London: Fontana.

Armytage, W.H.G. (1964) *Four Hundred Years of English Education*, Cambridge: Cambridge University Press.

Ball, S.J. (1990) *Politics and Policy Making in Education: Explorations in Policy Sociology*, London: Routledge.

Barnett, C. (1986) *The Audit of War: The Illusion and Reality of Britain as a Great Nation*, London: Macmillan.

Benn, T. (1987) British politics 1945–1987: a perspective, in P. Hennessy and A. Seldon (eds) *Ruling Performance: British Governments from Attlee to Thatcher*, Oxford: Basil Blackwell.

Bogdanor, V. (1979) Power and participation, *Oxford Review of Education* 5(2).

Chitty, C. (1989) *Towards a New Education System: the Victory of the New Right*, Lewes: Falmer Press.

Corbett, A. (1969) The Tory educators, *New Society*, 22 May.

Cox, C.B. and Boyson, R. (eds) (1975) *Black Paper 1975: The Fight for Education*, London: Dent.

Cox, C.B. and Boyson, R. (eds) (1977) *Black Paper 1977*, London: Maurice Temple Smith.

Cox, C.B. and Dyson, A.E. (eds) (1969a) *Fight for Education: A Black Paper*, London: Critical Quarterly Society.

Cox, C.B. and Dyson, A.E. (eds) (1969b) *Black Paper 2: The Crisis in Education*, London: Critical Quarterly Society.

Cox, C.B. and Dyson, A.E. (eds) (1970) *Black Paper 3: Goodbye Mr Short*, London: Critical Quarterly Society.

Fraser, W.R. (1963) *Education and Society in Modern France*, London: Routledge.

Green, A. (1990) *Education and State Formation: the Rise of Education Systems in England, France and the USA*, London: Macmillan.

Hill, C. (1961) *The Century of Revolution 1603–1714*, Edinburgh: Nelson.

Hillgate Group (1986) *Whose Schools? A Radical Manifesto*, London.

Hobsbawm E.J. (1968) *Industry and Empire: An Economic History of Britain Since 1750*, London: Weidenfeld & Nicolson.

Jones, K. (1989) *Right Turn: the Conservative Revolution in Education*, London: Hutchinson.

Knight, C. (1990) *The Making of Tory Education Policy in Post-War Britain, 1950–1986*, Lewes: Falmer Press.

Marx, K. (1961) *Capital*, Vol 1. *Moscow*: Foreign Languages Publishing House.

Marx, K. (1971a). A Review of Guizot's Book: Why has the English Revolution been Successful?, in K. Marx and F. Engels, *Articles on Britain*, Moscow: Progress Publishers.

Marx, K. (1971b) The British Constitution, in K. Marx and F. Engels, *Articles on Britain*, Moscow: Progress Publishers.

Moody, J. (1978) *French Education Since Napoleon*, New York: Syracuse University Press.

Rubinstein, D. (1977) Socialization and the London School Board 1870–1904: aims, methods and public opinion, in P. McCann (ed.), *Popular Education and Socialization in the Nineteenth Century*, London: Methuen.

Samuel, R. and Thomas, R. (1949) *Education and Society in Modern Germany*, London: Routledge.

Simon, B. (1965) *Education and the Labour Movement: 1870–1920*, London: Lawrence & Wishart.

Simon, J. (1966) *Education and Society in Tudor England*, Cambridge: Cambridge University Press.

Tawney, R.H. (1941) The rise of the gentry, *Economic History Review* 11(1).

West, E.G. (1965) *Education and the State: A Study in Political Economy*, London: Institute of Economic Affairs.

Wiener, M. (1981) *English Culture and the Decline of the Industrial Spirit, 1850 to 1980*, Cambridge: Cambridge University Press.

Williams, R. (1961) *The Long Revolution*, Harmondsworth: Penguin.

Chapter 15

New magistracies and commissariats

R. Morris

ORIGIN OF 'THE NEW MAGISTRACIES'

In 1981, I proposed, and nine years later elaborated, the concept of the 'new magistracies' in education (Morris 1981, 1990). I was referring originally to the school admissions appeals committees established under the Education Act 1980. I said of them:

> The panels of [elected] members and persons 'who have experience in education, are acquainted with the educational conditions in the area . . . or are parents of . . . pupils' will be a whole new magistracy.

The term was meant both in a classical Roman sense and as in the functions of the Justices of the Peace in county areas until the late nineteenth century. The term connoted not only adjudicatory but also administrative functions, and I applied it more generally in 1990 to locally established statutory bodies formed from the LEA but taking to themselves some of the authority's decision-making, or discretion:

- the revivified governing bodies of schools;
- bodies set up under arrangements approved by the Secretary of State to deal with complaints about curricular matters under s. 23 of the Education Reform Act;
- appeals committees for school admissions, exclusions and (at that time) special educational needs;
- and the standing advisory councils for religious education (SACREs), mandatory since the 1988 Act.

I identified as main characteristics of the new magistracies: their relative smallness (in comparison with education committees or major sub-committees); their being mostly appointed rather than elected; their dependence on the LEA for servicing; their operating where the LEA had overall or concurrent responsibilities; inclusion of an outside element in their membership (which is essentially lay); their exercise of powers by delegation or prescription; and their being a buffer or filter between

LEA and the Secretary of State. In that analysis, I concentrated on bodies within the education service narrowly defined, but I would since have added the training and enterprise councils, which, though not specified in legislation, have been created within the very broad powers which the Secretary of State for Employment enjoys under the Employment and Training Act 1973.

The new magistracies have been active, though some have been busier than others. Governing bodies have taken on much more than purely financial responsibilities under local management of schools. Though not generally at the forefront of LEAs' activities, SACREs have been getting on with their jobs, and have duly been reported on annually by the National Curriculum Council. The Bishop of Guildford (Chairman of the Church of England Board of Education) has expressed concern that '[a]s the LEA reduces its staff, and education committees disappear', the SACRE will suffer from lack of servicing and funding (Adie 1993). The local appeals committee will from 1994 be replaced, but only in cases involving special needs, by a branch of the Special Educational Needs Tribunal. The Government has, however, responded to representations by the Commissioner for Local Administration, the local authority associations and others that appeals committees of aided, special agreement and grant-maintained schools be brought under the supervision of the CLA (s. 269 of the new Act). The National Consumer Council has reported that the curricular complaints machinery is under-used because its existence is insufficiently known (Harris 1992).

In 1991 and 1992 Professors Jones and Stewart picked up the phrase 'new magistracies' (with attribution) and ran with it. They played it in the wider contexts of central and local government and the tendency of Ministers to prefer appointed bodies to local councils as executors of social and economic action. It is noteworthy that the newspapers have been giving some prominence to John Stewart's comments (1992) on the wide constitutional implications of the growth of the new magistracies.

THE NEW COMMISSARIATS

But I believe that, at least as far as education is concerned, an additional tier has to be described – that of the new commissariats – and distinguished from the magistracies. The new category includes the two funding authorities for schools, the FE Funding Councils (one for England, with regional advisory committees and their offices, and one FEFC for Wales), and the education associations, whom the Secretary of State may appoint, in the words of the new Act (s. 222(2)), 'to secure, so far as it is practicable to do so, the elimination of any deficiencies in the conduct of a school' found to be failing.

Characteristics of the commissariats are that: they are paid offices (it was tempting otherwise to label the education associations as stipendiary magistracies); the Secretary of State appoints the commissaries; funding comes from the national exchequer; and the commissariats have their own offices and staffs.

The commissariats exercise powers in place of the LEA, though there is some concurrence. For example, the Funding Agency for Schools (FAS) and the Schools Funding Council for Wales (SFCW) will be involved in a spectrum of responsibility alongside the LEA before the start of stage 3, the point at which by order of the Secretary of State, the *duty* to secure the provision of sufficient school places in the LEA's area passes from the LEA to the FAS and thereafter the LEA has only some defined *powers* to act. The FEFC and LEA are linked, by the FHE Act 1992, in a *chiasmus* of powers and duties; the one has the duty where the other has a power to secure FE provision, and vice versa. Both FAS and FEFC are given statutory functions for their areas, a phrase which the 1944 Act applied to the operations of the LEA, but, in the case of either quango, the 'area' is the whole of England (and the bailiwick of FEFCW and SFCW is all Wales). Both sorts of quangos astonishingly have responsibilities for individuals, the FEFC for students with special needs, and the FAS for children whose placement at a school has to be the subject of a direction.

I have chosen 'commissariat' as a label since its connotations are Continental and sufficiently various. 'Commissions' would mislead, since it is a term of art in UK systems, including the area of central government control over the functions of local authorities in default. 'Commissars' would have been unnecessarily pejorative.

It would probably be correct to place the School Curriculum and Assessment Authority (SCAA) in the 'new commissariat' category, even though its antecedents go back to the Secondary Schools Examination Council, the Curriculum Study Group and the Schools Council. The character of the most recent forebears, the tightening statutory remit, and the close attention apparently paid by ministers in selecting members – and the facility to correspond directly with schools over executive functions and policy matters – surely imply a commissary role.

The Lord Chancellor is to appoint to the SEN Tribunal those of its members who are required to be legally qualified, and the Secretary of State will appoint lay panellists. The procedural detail will be set out in regulations. As a more dignified body than the LEA appeals committee sitting on an SEN case, the Tribunal ranks as a new commissariat.

Most, but not all, of the new commissariats are quangos. They have to take instruction as deemed necessary by the Secretary of State. For example, the FEFC and the FEFCW, and the HE Funding Councils for England and for Wales may have imposed upon them by sections 7 and 68 respectively of the FHE Act 1992 grant conditions which in turn will place conditions on the funding allocated by the councils to institutions. The FAS and SFCW may be directed by the Secretary of State to cease funding a particular school. Under the Education Act 1993, the SCAA will have to comply with any directions made by the Secretary of State.

A parallel requirement is placed upon Her Majesty's Chief Inspectors in England and in Wales by sections 2(6) and 6(6) respectively of the Education (Schools) Act 1992 to 'have regard to such aspects of government policy as the Secretary of State may direct'. I am inclined to categorise OFSTED, the Office for Standards in Education, as a new commissariat, but the judgement may have to be revised in the light of how OFSTED works in practice. Though HMI has been around since 1839, OFSTED is a new commissariat principally because of the function to administer the new system of contracted-for inspections and because of the statutory removal of the LEA's right, under the 1944 Act, to carry out inspections of its own schools at large (s. 15 and sched. 5 of the Schools Act).

The first holder of the post of HMCI for England was quick to claim greater independence for his service than HMI under the old auspices (Sutherland 1993). In a letter to *The Independent*, Professor Sutherland was responding to two articles in that usually well-informed newspaper asserting that HMI had been abolished. The mistake has been repeated – even in the specialist *Times Educational Supplement* (Flesher 1993). It is, though, understandable. Responsibility for quality assurance in HE and FE has passed to the funding councils, and some of the old mystique of HMI has gone with the explicit duties set out in the Schools Act. The administrative responsibilities of OFSTED, however, are much greater than those of HMI hitherto: it has to make and maintain the register of those inspectors who are thereby qualified to lead inspectoral teams ('reggies'); it has to provide or commission training for all team members, including the lay inspectors; it lets the contracts for the periodic full inspections and superintends the processes and outcomes of inspection.

NEW MAGISTRACIES AND NEW COMMISSARIATS IN EDUCATION

Below is a tabulation of the new magistracies and commissariats.

New magistracies

School governing bodies.
Admissions and exclusions appeals committees.
SACREs.
Bodies to deal with curricular complaints.

New commissariats

The HE Funding Councils.
The FE Funding Councils.
The funding authorities for grant-maintained schools (the FAS in England will have been fully operational from 1 April 1994; the SFCW will be brought into being as and when needed).
The SEN Tribunal.
Education associations.
The SCAA.
OFSTED.

Other bodies

College governing bodies

Since 1989 HE, and since 1993 FE, colleges have enjoyed a greater measure of autonomy, with corporate status under the funding councils. Their detachment from LEA administration and their location in national funding arrangements qualify them as commissariats, though the Secretary of State's interest in gubernatorial appointments lapses after inauguration. I am inclined to regard grant-maintained school governing bodies as magistracies, because of their essentially local role.

Training and enterprise councils

TECs resemble new magistracies in their local nature, and the fact that the Secretary of State for Employment was involved in setting them up. It can be argued that the TEC carries out functions which could, and should, be those of the local authority exercising its economic-development and education powers; but the spirit of the times is such that ministers have preferred the *ad hoc* grouping of local employers' representatives. Such a body, with a role which also lies within the capacity of the local authority, looks like a new magistracy. TECs' functions, though, in administering national training schemes and disbursing departmental cash, and their having offices of their own, imply commissarial status. Mr Patten, Secretary of State for Education, has certainly seen them as alternatives to *national* administration, and he disregards the possible local government claim to a stake in the enterprise:

> The world of training has . . . been made more receptive to the needs and wishes of the individual. Employer-led . . . TECs are giving local people, not Whitehall civil servants, the chance to determine the

nature of training provision. And training credits are literally putting power into the pockets of the consumer.

(Patten 1993)

'*Reggies*' *as janissaries*

At the risk of being accused of fancifulness, I propose a third category: the janissaries. The Turkish origin of that word approximates to 'new militia', which seems apposite for the registered inspectors and their teams.

DEMOTION OF THE LEA

This paper has outlined the development of new or revitalised bodies in the public education service and the transfer of powers from LEAs to them. The following summarises the losses from local government – the debit side, as it were, of the account.

Losses from local government 1987–93, with particular reference to education

- Much financial discretion
- Schoolteachers' pay and other conditions of employment: national negotiations and collective agreements
- (LEA-sector) higher education, that is the polytechnics and other large colleges of HE
- Grant-maintained schools, as opting-out proceeds
- The unfettered power for the LEA to set schools' expenditure, and largely to control staffing establishments
- The power to regulate admissions numbers across schools in whole areas
- The right to inspect the LEA's schools at large
- Mainstream further education
- (Ultimately, as a result of the 1993 Act) The planning function for schools throughout the LEA's area
- Control of funds for teachers' in-service training
- The school curriculum, insofar as an LEA may have exercised much leadership or control in recent years
- The capacity to innovate

The list represents a massive territorial loss, which was belatedly signalled by government amendments to the recent Education Bill. The legislative contortions which accompanied the process of amendment ('Clause Zero') were because the House of Lords refused to accept changes which would have denied the universities the institutional safeguards for academic freedom won after hard debate on the Education Reform Bill and already tested once in the courts. In that process, however, the measure of institutional freedom gained by FE colleges in the FHE Act 1992 has been put in doubt.

Sections 1 and 2 of the Education Act 1993 have, from 1 October 1993, replaced s. 1(1) of the 1944 Act, which read (in its most recent reformulation):

> It shall be the duty of the Secretary of State for Education to promote the education of the people of England and Wales [though, under Transfer Orders, responsibility for schooling and FE in Wales is largely a matter for the Secretary of State for Wales] and the progressive development of institutions devoted to that purpose. and to secure the effective execution by local authorities, under his control and direction, of the national policy for providing a varied and comprehensive educational service in every area.

In the new Act. s. 1 re-enacts the promotional duty, but s. 2 uses more leaden language and omits specific reference to LEAs:

> 1   The Secretary of State shall exercise his powers in respect of those bodies in receipt of public funds which:
>
>   (a) carry responsibility for securing that the required provision for primary, secondary or further education is made in schools, or institutions within the further education sector, in or in any area of England and Wales, or
>   (b) conduct schools or institutions within the further education sector in England and Wales,
>
> for the purpose of promoting primary, secondary and further education in England and Wales.

I do not regret having described this language as 'banker's banausic'. Subsection (2) is unexceptionable, though of a declaratory rather than prescriptive nature:

> 2   He shall, in the case of his powers to regulate the provision made in schools and institutions within the further education sector in England and Wales, exercise his powers with a view, among other things, to improving standards, encouraging diversity and increasing opportunities for choice.

A non-statutory signal of the significant constitutional changes has been given in ministerial statements. At Lords Second Reading of the Education Reform Bill, Baroness Hooper, then a Parliamentary Under-Secretary of State at DES, had denied that the proposals in the legislation would undermine LEAs; rather, they would be given 'a new strategic role' in their localities (19 April 1988, col. 1467). That role has been a short one. At Report Stage in the Lords in the summer of 1993, a defeat the government temporarily suffered was over amendments moved by Lord Judd (Labour) and Baroness Williams (Liberal Democrat), effectively restoring to LEAs within the framework of the Bill a strategic-planning function despite the numbers of grant-maintained schools and activities of the FAS in their areas. The amendments were negated in the Commons, and the Minister of State (Baroness Blatch) then explained the reason to the Lords:

> Those amendments . . . gave a continuing strategic role to the [LEA]. That role was inconsistent with the new regime embodied in the Bill as a whole and inconsistent in particular with the autonomy of schools, especially those which have opted to leave their LEAs. . . .
>
> (26 July 1993, col. 963)

It may be thought remarkable that the removal of a substantial power from a tier of the constitution, albeit within a particular service, should have been achieved by government relatively easily.

REFERENCES

Adie, Rt Rev. M. (1993) 'Value Inadequate', *Education*, 29 Jan., p. 71.

Flesher, T.J. (1993) 'HMI's demise exaggerated', *Times Educational Supplement*, 3 Sept.

Harris, N. (1992) *Complaints About Schooling*, National Consumer Council, pp. 119–24.

Jones, G. and Stewart, J. (1991) 'Government is being weakened by being split into small units', *Local Government Chronicle*, 8 March, p. 15.

Jones, G. and Stewart, J. (1992) 'Selected not Elected', *Local Government Chronicle*, 13 Nov., p. 15.

Morris, R. (1981) 'Education', *Local Government Studies Annual Review 81*, 7(2): 93.

Morris R. (1990) 'Power: Local Gains and Losses', Ch. 8 of R. Morris (ed.) *Central and Local Control of Education After the Education Reform Act 1988*, Longman.

Patten, Rt Hon. J. (1993) *The Home Front in a New Century*, Conservative Political Centre, p. 13.

Stewart, J. (1992) *Accountability to the Public*, European Policy Forum, p. 7.

Sutherland, S. (1993) 'School Inspectors Alive and Well', *The Independent*, 31 Dec.

Chapter 16

The policy process and the processes of policy

R. Bowe and S.J. Ball, with A. Gold

INTRODUCTION

In the field of educational policy studies the 'placing' of schools, teachers and students in the policy process, has been largely achieved by theoretical fiat. On the one hand there has been extensive work on the generation of policy. This has remained, for the most part, within the province of macro-based theoretical analyses of policy documents and the activities and organization of groups of policy-makers. Concern here has been with the representation or exclusion of interests in the political process and the struggles of activists, pressure groups and social classes within that arena (Kogan 1975; Ball 1990). In these conceptualizations schools remain either marginal to the policy process or they are 'represented' via the teaching unions. The voices of the heads, senior managers, classroom teachers or the students remain, for the most part, strangely silent. On the other hand, there has been a growing body of literature investigating the 'implementation' of policy. This has often taken the form of detailed analyses (micro-based ethnographies for example) of how the 'intentions' behind policy texts become embedded in schooling or, more frequently, of how aspects of the schooling situation 'reflect' wider developments in the political and economic arena. There has also been a somewhat smaller body of literature that has celebrated the potential power of teachers and/or students to subvert the heavy hands of the economy or the State. Here the silent voices are heard, but they speak either as theoretically overdetermined mouthpieces of a world beyond their control or as potentially free and autonomous resisters or subverters of the status quo.

This separation between investigations of the *generation* and the *implementation* of policy, has tended to reinforce the 'managerial perspective' on the policy process, in the sense that the two are seen as distinctive and separate 'moments'; generation followed by implementation (Alford and Friedland 1988). This distortion produces accounts of the policy process as linear in form; whether top-down, bottom-up or allowing for a 'relative autonomy' of the bottom from the top. Thus, state control theories (Dale 1989) portray policy generation as remote and detached from implementation. Policy then 'gets done' to people by a chain of implementors whose roles are clearly defined by legislation. In policy studies generally this sort of 'linear' conception of policy has been further encouraged, post-1979, by what has been increasingly referred to as the Thatcher 'style' of government and its avowed intention to break down the corporatism of the 'social democratic' consensus (CCCS 1981). The lack of wide consultation prior to legislation on the trade unions, the health service and in education was seen as evidence of a new, non-corporatist style in action. Thus, for example, Lawton has talked of the pulling apart of the old 'partnership' between the DES (Department of Education and Science), the LEAs (local education authorities) and the teachers and its substitution by a fragmented policy process in which the new policy makers appear remote from the educational scene; a scene which, nonetheless, the policy makers are trying to control more tightly (Lawton 1984). Thus, he considers the politicos (ministers, political advisers, etc.), the bureaucrats (DES officials) and the professionals, HMI (Her Majesty's Inspectorate) to have become increasingly 'disconnected' from the policy receivers (LEAs, schools and teachers) (Lawton 1984). If we take this 'tightening grip' (Lawton 1984) thesis further then the shift appears to have been taking place for some time. The growth of centrally administered policies, TVEI (the Technical and Vocational Education Initiative) run by the MSC (Manpower Services Commission, later to become the Training Agency), ESGs (Educational Support Grants) run by the DES, both on a 'bid and deliver' basis, would be examples of the State's growing control of education. The culmination being the Educational Reform Act 1988 with its centrally 'determined' policy prescription that gives the DES and the Secretary of State extensive new powers to direct the work of LEAs and schools. In this analysis the changing language of the policy process would be illustrative of deeper structural changes in the relationship of the State to educational institutions. Thus from the TVEI and ESGs, which introduced the 'delivery' of educational change, external 'monitoring', 'management' and 'evaluation' (Dale *et al.* 1990), we go through to NCC (National Curriculum Council) documents which pick up that language and also talk about the 'implementation by headteachers . . . of the National Curriculum', 'absorption by individual teachers of the National Curriculum', 'delivery of his or her (student's) entitlement' etc., etc. (see, for example, *National Curriculum: From Policy to Practice*, DES 1989).

There seems little doubt that there has been a State control element in the Government's approach to policy construction and a strong desire to exclude practitioners (or their 'representatives', the trade unions) (see

Ball 1990). Furthermore, we would accept that in the legislation the Government's promotion of parents and the market over the claims of the 'educational lobby', and its language of 'implementation' are all attempts to continue to exclude certain voices from the policy process. Nonetheless we want to suggest that it would be politically naive and analytically suspect to begin from the assumption that it has been possible to make that exclusion total; either in terms of policy generation or in terms of implementation. The example of TVEI is itself particularly telling in this respect.

POLICY ANALYSIS AND THE STATE-CONTROL MODEL

As a policy externally imposed upon schools TVEI was initially seen as a classic example of a 'top-down' model of curriculum reform; however, the actual experiences of researchers and teachers told a somewhat different tale. TVEI reached the statute books as an initiative of Margaret Thatcher, Lord Young and Sir Keith Joseph. It was well financed and required schools and LEAs to submit projects for scrutiny prior to finance being made available. Yet many have pointed out that the MSC's need to secure the co-operation of the 'educational lobby' actually produced curriculum development in schools that was far closer to the educationalist (mostly school-based) than the occupationalist (mostly MSC-based) model of the curriculum (Dale *et al.* 1990). The point is that the transformations that may come about as legislative texts are recontextualized may, in some cases, be dramatic. McCulloch (1986) argues, for example, that the utilitarian rhetoric and objectives that accompanied the launching of the initiative have been *subverted* via their incorporation into mainstream education. Although TVEI was successfully established in the context of Thatcherite politics at the national level, at the local level it gave way to a revival of more liberal notions of educational practice (Gleeson 1989: 88–9). Saunders (1985), referring to TVEI, has suggested three broad categories to indicate how schools generally responded to this externally initiated change:

1 Adaptive extension: A strong interpretation of TVEI – it has been used to change the whole curriculum.
2 Accommodation: TVEI adapted to fit the general shape of the existing curriculum structure.
3 Containment: TVEI absorbed by the existing school pattern.

While there are many problems with a static and uniform categorization of this kind (schools may shift position over time and different departments may respond differently and financial and staffing constraints may inhibit response) it nonetheless serves to underline the ways in which detailed curricular planning and implementation may be driven by different interpretations of change. In reading the literature on TVEI one is struck by the extent to which an externally 'imposed' policy was appropriated by the teaching profession for very different purposes to those intended by the policy. The implication is that the 'capacity' of the State to reach into the schools has to be judged via the use practitioners make of policy initiatives and, consequently, the extent of State control resulting from the 1988 Act actually remains an empirical question. Indeed we would go further and agree with West's observation about *Learning to Labour* (Willis 1977) and extend it to the sociology of education more generally:

> There is a relative lack of serious examination of institutional or organization mediations between capital and the classrooms experienced by the lads. Although other CCCS work does begin to address such issues of educational policy, professional alliances, etc., we still have little idea of how such national policy issues and processes connect to schools and classrooms, and how the latter connect to such groups as the lads.
>
> (West 1983)

Thus, despite the very real sense in which teachers have been excluded from the 'production' of the Reform Act 1988, we still want to argue that a State control model distorts the policy process. Indeed it seems to us that the image implicit in the conception of distinct and disconnected sets of policy-makers and policy implementors actually serves the powerful ideological purpose of reinforcing a linear conception of policy in which theory and practice are separate and the former is privileged. The language of 'implementation' strongly implies that there is, within policy, an unequivocal governmental position that will filter down through the quasi-state bodies (presently the NCC and the subject working parties) and into the schools. (The LEAs are placed in a marginal position, but are essentially seen to be supporting schools in their endeavours.) It is clearly in the Government's interest to promote such a view. Consequently, this top-down, linear model is hardly the best starting point for research into the practical effects of the ERA. *Who* becomes involved in the policy process and *how* they become involved is a product of a combination of administratively based procedures, historical precedence and political manoeuvring, implicating the State, the State bureaucracy and continual political struggles over access to the policy process; it is not *simply* a matter of implementors following a fixed policy text and 'putting the Act into practice'. One key task for policy analysis is to grasp the significance of the policy as a text, or series of texts, for the different contexts in which they are used.

POLICY RESEARCH AND THE ANALYSIS OF POLICY TEXTS

The translation of educational policy into legislation produces a key text (the Act). This, in turn, becomes a 'working document' for politicians, teachers, the unions and the bodies charged with responsibility for 'implementing' the legislation. Although questions about the status and the nature of particular policy texts remain empirical ones, we have found the work of Roland Barthes a useful, conceptual starting point here. He has argued that:

> literature may be divided into that which gives the reader a role, a function, a contribution to make, and that which renders the reader idle or redundant, 'left with no more than the poor freedom to accept or reject the text' and which thereby reduces him to that apt but impotent symbol of the bourgeois world, an inert consumer to the author's role as producer.
>
> (Hawkes 1977: 113)

This latter sort of text he refers to as 'readerly', and the signifier/signified relationship is clear and inescapable; there is the minimum of opportunity for creative interpretation by the reader. An initial reading of National Curriculum texts, for example, and their technical language of levels, attainment targets, standardized attainment testing and programmes of study, might suggest just such a readerliness. However, the NCC has also published secondary texts, the Non-Statutory Guidelines, which suggest the National Curriculum texts are to be interpreted more like Barthes' alternative 'writerly' texts, which self-consciously invite the reader to 'join-in', to co-operate and co-author. In the language of TVEI, to feel a sense of 'ownership'. But this free play is a matter of degree in the interpretation and reading of these texts rather than any kind of open freedom of action. Barthes has also argued that: 'writerly texts require us to look at the nature of language itself, not through it at a preordained "real world"' (Hawkes 1977: 118).

We have been acutely aware that the very invention of a new proposed 'reality' for schooling in terms of attainment targets, etc., draws attention to the language itself, and to its adequacy as a way of thinking about and organizing the way pupils learn. 'Making sense' of new texts leads people into a process of trying to 'translate' and make familiar the language and the attendant embedded logics. In this process they place what they know against the new. Readerly texts, however, presuppose and depend upon presumptions of innocence, upon the belief that the reader will have little to offer by way of an alternative. Teachers may feel battered and coerced, they may have been softened up for change, but they are also suspicious and cynical and professionally committed in ways that hardly form the basis for 'innocence'. Finally, Barthes suggests that the reading of writerly texts involves two kinds of 'pleasure', the straightforward pleasure of reading and the *jouissance*, the ecstasy or bliss which arise from the sense of breakdown or interruption. The latter coming from the critical and creative response to the text, the seeing through to something beyond. While this might produce for some a sense of discomfort and loss, it also opens up possibilities for 'gaps' and 'moments' of progressive and radical insertion, for example the breakdown of transmission teaching, subject boundaries and formal examining and their replacement with cross-curricular work, investigations and group and process-based assessments. What it is also vital to recognize then is that these readerly and writerly texts are the products of a policy process, a process that we have already indicated emerges from and continually interacts with a variety of interrelated contexts. Consequently texts have clear relationships with the particular contexts in which they are used. This applies as much to national debates as to exchanges in schools between teachers and the individual approaches developed by teachers to meet the requirements of the National Curriculum.

In looking at the 1988 Act a number of authors have already pointed out, it is not a text that is capable of only one interpretation and the various elements that make up the Act (the National Curriculum, LMS, Open Enrolment, Opting Out, etc.) empower different bodies, groups and individuals in different ways (Bash and Coulby 1989; Jones 1989; Whitty 1989), empowerment depending not only upon the 'tightness' or otherwise of the legislation but also upon the possibilities and the limits of particular contexts and settings. In effect the ERA is being constantly rewritten as different kinds of 'official' texts and utterances are produced by key actors or agencies of government – Programmes of Study, Attainment Targets, Subject Working Party Reports, NCC Reports, etc., etc. Thus a whole variety and criss-cross of meanings and interpretations are put into circulation. Clearly these textual meanings influence and constrain 'implementors' but their own concerns and contextual constraints generate other meanings and interpretations. Thus while textual analysis:

> Makes it possible to understand knowledge production as a chain or series of transformative activities which range from the social organization of text industries, to the activities of text producers, through the symbolic transformations of the text itself, and to the transformative interaction between text and reader, or school knowledge and student.
>
> (Wexler 1982: 286)

As Wexler goes on to point out, it is crucial that such analysis is critically informed by a political and social analysis that seeks to uncover some of the processes whereby such texts are generated. Texts, structures and agencies of control need to be attended to. The state control model actually tends to freeze policy texts and exclude the contextual slippages that occur throughout the policy cycle. Instead we would want to approach legislation as but one aspect of a *continual* process in which the loci of power are constantly shifting as the various resources implicit and explicit in texts are recontextualized and employed in the struggle to maintain or change views of schooling.

This leads us to approach policy as a discourse, constituted of possibilities and impossibilities, tied to knowledge on the one hand (the analysis of problems and identification of remedies and goals) and practice on the other (specification of methods for achieving goals and implementation). We see it as a set of claims about how the world should and might be, a matter of the 'authoritative allocation of values'. Policies are thus the operational statements of values, statements of 'prescriptive intent' (Kogan 1975: 55). They are also, as we conceive it, essentially contested in and between the arenas of formation and 'implementation'. While the construction of the policy text may well involve different parties and processes to the 'implementing' process, the opportunity for re-forming and re-interpreting the text means policy formation does not end with the legislative 'moment'; 'for any text a plurality of readers must necessarily produce a plurality of readings' (Codd 1988: 239).

In our ethnographically-based study of policy our concern has been to explore policy-making, in terms of the processes of value dispute and material influence which underlie and invest the formation of policy discourses, as well as to portray and analyse the processes of active interpretation and meaning-making which relate policy texts to practice. In part this involves the identification of resistance, accommodation, subterfuge and conformity within and between arenas of practice and the plotting of clashes and mismatches between contending discourses at work in these arenas, e.g. professionalism vs. conformity, autonomy vs. constraint, specification vs. latitude, the managerial vs. the educational. Furthermore it is important to acknowledge that policy intentions may contain ambiguities, contradictions and omissions that provide particular opportunities for parties to the 'implementation' process, what we might term 'space' for manoeuvre (Wallace 1988). We want, briefly, to illustrate this approach by looking at the National Curriculum.

THE NATIONAL CURRICULUM AS TEXT AND THE POLITICAL CONTEXT

In a very real sense generation and implementation are continuous features of the policy process, with generation of policy . . . still taking place after the legislation has been effected; both within the central State and within the LEAs and the schools. What is more, these different contexts of policy recreation are connected directly by their varying capacities to affect the work of each other. In our research on the ERA we have been constantly aware of the extent to which people in schools and LEAs discuss the alternative 'readings' of the broader political picture and the pronouncements of politicians, the policy 'implementing' bodies such as the NCC and SEAC (Secondary Examinations and Assessment Council) and the officials of the DES. These discussions provided varying interpretations of what 'they' (the legislators and the 'implementing bodies') wanted and varying views of what possibilities or limits these might create for the LEAs or the schools.

> Well when the first document came out, about '87, the red book I think, people immediately saw that as a very much back-to-basics, back to single subject definitions, especially percentages of each one. But now that the programmes of study are beginning to evolve, or at least the attainment targets and so on have shown they're not, and attainment targets emphasize cross-curricular links, people are moving now away from this subject definition again, towards the concept of cross-co-operation, and cross-curricular links and in fact I'm quite hopeful that the National Curriculum will be a stimulus for curriculum development, not a hindrance for it.
>
> (Deputy Head, Flightpath, 6 March 1990)

Thus the National Curriculum text enters into, as a new element, the *bricolage* of teaching, the cobbling together of bits and pieces into a 'pedagogic discourse' (Bernstein 1986). As a text it is decontextualized from its original location and then recontextualized into a new assemblage. The pedagogic discourse so constructed consists of 'the rules regulating the production, distribution, reproduction, inter-relation and change of what counts as legitimate pedagogic texts' (Atkinson 1985: 171). In the generation and 'implementation' of policy the nature of policy contexts (classrooms, departments, schools, LEAs, NCC, SEAC, DES, 'think tanks', working parties, etc., etc.) and the relations between them become crucial to our understanding of how texts operate; although we must also remain aware of the ways in which texts change contexts and the relations between contexts. As Shilling points out, education policy is a dialectical process; 'policy outcomes are reliant upon the cooperation of the state, and an array of non-state organizations and individuals' (Shilling 1988: 11), and importantly, in the case of TVEI, he argues that the outcomes: 'are constrained not only by the potential power schools are able to exercise as "front-line" organizations (Shilling 1986), but by fiscal and other institutional constraints . . .' (Shilling 1988: 11).

Texts carry with them both possibilities and constraints, contradictions and spaces. The reality of policy in practice depends upon the compromises and accommodations to these in particular settings. Thus our conception of policy has to be set against the idea that policy is something that is simply done to people; although we accept that particular policy texts will differ in their degree of explicit recognition of the active (rather than passive) relationship between intended, actual and policy-in-use. One example is to be found in the recent statements, related to the National Curriculum, that are giving particular emphasis to the active participation of teachers. In various quarters teachers are being encouraged to 'make the National Curriculum their own'. There is an interesting and difficult double paradox in this in terms of education policy and politics. On the one hand the ERA and the NC are the outcome of a now typical process of macho, Thatcherite policy-making which rides roughshod over the interests and sensibilities of the teachers. In addition, years of strident critique from Government has sapped public confidence in, and the morale of, teachers. On the other hand, the implementation of the NC relies heavily upon the goodwill, commitment and energy of teachers. They must make it work. Since the Act came on to the statute books a number of senior Tory politicians have been engaged in a propaganda exercise to 'talk-up' teachers and praise their efforts and talents. Kenneth Baker, then Secretary of State for Education, in the 1989 inaugural IBM Education Lecture at the Royal Society, asserted: 'I doubt that any country starts with a better or more effective teacher force than we have in Britain. Our teachers stand comparison anywhere in professionalism, dedication and imagination.' He then went on to say: 'The achievement in schools in the last three years in bringing in the new GCSE examination to a successful introduction is witness to that. The professional work now going on in schools all over the country to prepare the way for introducing the national curriculum inspires confidence that that too will be a job well done' (*TES* 1989). And the then Prime Minister herself, in a widely reported interview with the *Sunday Telegraph* on 15 April 1990, stated:

> Going on to the other things in the curriculum, when we first started on this, I do not think I ever thought they would do the syllabus in such detail as they are doing now. Because I believe there are thousands of teachers who are teaching extremely well. And I always felt that when we had done the core curriculum, the core syllabus, there must always be scope for each teacher to use her own methods, her own experience, the things which she has learned and he or she really knows how to teach.

A report of this was headlined in the following Friday's *Times Educational Supplement*, 'Mrs. Thatcher signals "U-turn" on curriculum'. In the article the reporters suggested the Prime Minister was concerned about the National Curriculum becoming too prescriptive. What was remarkable was her frequently repeated reference to the teaching force,

> So I did not really feel that the core curriculum or any subject should take up all the time devoted to that subject, because otherwise you are going to lose the enthusiasm and the devotion and all of the extras that a really good teacher can give out of her own experience.
>
> (*TES* 1990)

The point is of course, as Shilling notes, that the State must rely upon teachers to 'deliver' the curriculum. Consequently, to sustain a singular, National Curriculum requires either teacher acceptance and understanding, 'lock, stock and barrel', or a system for effectively policing teachers. A question of either 'winning the hearts and minds' of the workers at the chalkface – 'The commitment of individual teachers will be crucial in making it happen' (DES 1989, Secn. 9.14) – or creating the means whereby the State has the capacity to control and discipline the workforce specifically and directly. While there are clearly many elements of the latter embedded in the ERA, with 'implementation' at the forefront of governmental concern, it is now strategically necessary, or perhaps inevitable, that proactive readings of the NC text be encouraged (what might be described as developing a degree of tolerance without fostering a sense of latitude). Thus, Duncan Graham, Chairman of the NCC until the summer of 1991, has said that, 'getting the National Curriculum off the ground will involve the talents of universities, colleges, LEAs and schools', and added; referring to the NCC itself, 'we have a highly professional Council which covers the main interests in the education service, with two exceptions all educationalists, people with practical hard-line experience of education, and it's turning out to have a gratifying mind of its own' (Talk at King's College, 18 January 1989).

However, the dilemma, tolerance without latitude, which the NCC as an organization represents and embodies, is never far from the surface. In the same talk Duncan Graham spoke of teachers as 'far more worried about their own position than the children passing through'. Teachers cannot be but must be trusted. This dilemma is increasingly evident in the official and semi-official texts which 'speak' the National Curriculum to schools. The recontextualization of policy in this case takes place in two stages, from Government, to agencies of sub-government (HMI, NCC, in-service and initial teacher education) and thence to the arenas of practice. The openness/closeness of text and the reactivity/proactivity of readings is a problem in both transitions. Thus the politics surrounding the work of the Subject Working Groups and the contradictory pressures on the NCC, alongside the emergent compromises in the ERA (Ball 1990; Whitty 1989) mean the work of the DES and the NCC has two very different audiences. On one side there are the hawkish factions in the Conservative Party, on the other side are the teachers and the educational establishment. The first group must remain convinced that the National Curriculum will discipline teachers, raise standards and not pander to 'entrenched orthodoxies' (CPS 1988: 6). The second must be reassured that the National Curriculum will not become a vehicle for the 'loony Right' and will achieve a level of educational respectability. There have already been difficulties on both sides particularly in relation to the constitution and work of the NC Subject Working Parties. The Right have been disappointed with the work of the Science, Mathematics and English Groups (and the Kingman Report 1988) and the permanent members of the educational establishment are severely disgruntled with the reports of the English, Geography and History Working Parties. As regards the former, the Centre for Policy Studies have offered their own alternative *Correct Core* and comment:

> The CPS Core Curriculum sets out curricula for English, Maths and Science. In order to ensure that pupils leave school literate, numerate and with a modicum of scientific knowledge, it should not extend beyond these three core subjects, nor attempt more than set minimum standards in basic knowledge and technique.
>
> It is regrettable that these aims appear recently to have been abandoned by those in charge of producing and implementing education policy. As the following pages show, the official committees, the DES and Her Majesty's Inspectorate no longer adhere to the belief that teachers should teach and pupils should learn a simple body of knowledge and a simple set of techniques.
>
> (CPS 1988: 59)

This perhaps serves to underline our view that policy, as knowledge and practices, as a discourse, is contested. It also points up the significance of influence in and control over critical sites of text production and recontextualization in the policy process. In this case the Subject Working Parties themselves and the NCC are prime examples of such crucial sites. To an extent the New Right have found themselves excluded until recently and thus limited in the effect they might have upon the production of 'official discourse' in these arenas. (They are, however, influential elsewhere in the whole policy process in education and they have gained some representation in SEAC, most recently with the replacement of the SEAC chair, Philip Halsey, by former No. 10 Policy Unit Head, Brian (Lord) Griffiths and also on the NCC, following the resignation of Duncan Graham, with the appointment of David Pascall, member of Margaret Thatcher's policy unit in the mid-1980s.) Consequently, even with a highly detailed piece of legislation on the statute books, educational policy *is still being generated and implemented both within and around the educational system* in ways that have intended and unintended

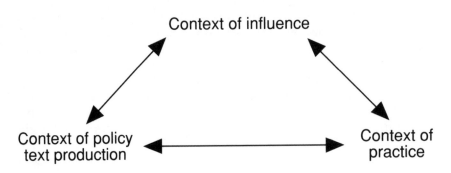

Figure 16.1 Contexts of policy-making

consequences for both education and its surrounding social milieu. As a result the ERA and its attendant texts are in one respect an expression of sets of political 'intentions' and a political resource for continuing national debates, and in another a micro-political resource for teachers, LEAs and parents to interpret, re-interpret and apply to their particular social contexts.

CHARACTERIZING THE POLICY PROCESS

We want to end this chapter by indicating how we might move away *analytically* from a State control model, while still recognizing that the State, LEAs and schools are differentially empowered, over time, within the policy process. By introducing the notion of a continuous policy cycle we have tried to draw attention towards the work of policy recontextualization that goes on in the schools. However, researching the school setting actually requires us to consider not only the National Curriculum but also how the various elements that make up the ERA, LMS, Open Enrolment, opting out, etc., empower different bodies, groups and individuals in different ways. An heuristic representation of the policy process is represented in Figure 16.1. (This is the development of an earlier formulation in which, reading from the top and anti-clockwise, the contexts were labelled intended, actual and policy-in-use. We have broken away from this formulation because the language introduced a rigidity we did not want to imply, e.g. there are many competing intentions that struggle for influence, not only one 'intention' and 'actual' seemed to us to signal a frozen text, quite the opposite to how we wanted to characterize this aspect of the policy process.)

We envisage three primary policy contexts, each context consisting of a number of arenas of action, some public, some private (see Figure 16.1). The first context, the *context of influence*, is where public policy is normally initiated. It is here that policy discourses are constructed. It is here that interested parties struggle to influence the definition and social purposes of education, what it means to be educated. The private arenas of influence are based upon social networks in and around the political parties, in and around Government and in and around the legislative process. Here key policy concepts are established (e.g. market forces, National Curriculum, opting out, budgetary devolution), they acquire currency and credence and provide a discourse and lexicon for policy initiation. This kind of discourse forming is sometimes given support, sometimes challenged by wider claims to influence in the public arenas of action, particularly in and through the mass media. In addition there are a set of more formal public arenas: committees, national bodies, representative groups which can be sites for the articulation of influence. Clearly in trying to understand the education policy-making of the last three Conservative Governments it is important to be aware of the considerable 'capture' of influence by the New Right think tanks that operate in and around the Conservative Party (see Ball 1990; Knight 1991). But it is also vital to appreciate the ebb and flow in the fortunes of and the changes in personnel of the DES, and to recognize the increasing 'ministerialization' of policy initiation (see Ball 1990). As we noted earlier, this contrasts starkly with the virtual exclusion of union and local authority representatives from arenas of influence and the much diminished and discredited contribution from the educational establishment.

This context of influence has a symbiotic but none the less uneasy relation to the second context, the *context of policy text production*. Because while influence is often related to the articulation of narrow interests and dogmatic ideologies, policy texts are normally articulated in the language of general public good. Their appeal is based upon claims to popular (and populist) commonsense and political reason. Policy texts therefore *represent* policy. These representations can take various forms: most obviously 'official' legal texts and policy documents; also formally and informally produced commentaries which offer to 'make sense of' the 'official' texts, again the media is important here; also the speeches by and public performances of relevant politicians and officials; and 'official' videos are another recently popular medium of representation. Many of those towards whom policy is aimed rely on these secondhand accounts as their main source of information and understanding of policy as intended. But two key points have to be made about these ensembles of texts which represent policy. First, the ensembles and the individual texts are not necessarily internally coherent or clear. The expression of policy is fraught with the possibility of misunderstanding, texts are generalized, written in relation to idealizations of the 'real world', and can never be exhaustive, they cannot cover all eventualities. The texts can often be contradictory (compare National Curriculum statutory guidance with NCC produced Non-Statutory Guidance), they use key terms differently, and they are reactive as well as expository (that is to say, the representation of policy changes in the light of events and circumstances and feedback from arenas of practice). Policy is not done and finished at the legislative moment, it evolves in and through the texts that represent it, texts have to be read in relation to the time and the particular site of their production. They also have to be read with and against one another – intertextuality is important. Second, the texts themselves are the outcome of struggle and compromise. The control of the representation of policy is problematic. Control over the timing of the publication of texts is important. A potent and immediate example of struggle in arenas of text production is that which goes on (as noted already) in relation to National Curriculum working party reports (Ball 1990). The interchange of documents between the NCC, SEAC and the DES is also a case in point. Groups of actors working within different sites of text production are in competition for control of the representation of policy. Most of these struggles go on behind closed doors but occasional glimpses of the dynamics of conflict are possible. What is at stake are attempts to control the meaning of policy through its representation.

Policies then are textual interventions but they also carry with them material constraints and possibilities. The responses to these texts have 'real' consequences. These consequences are experienced within the third main context, the *context of practice*, the arena of practice to which policy refers, to which it is addressed. The key point is that policy is not simply received and implemented within this arena rather it is subject to interpretation and then 'recreated'. . . .

Practitioners do not confront policy texts as naive readers, they come with histories, with experience, with values and purposes of their own, they have vested interests in the meaning of policy. Policies will be interpreted differently as the histories, experiences, values, purposes and interests which make up any arena differ. The simple point is that policy writers cannot control the meanings of their texts. Parts of texts will be rejected, selected out, ignored, deliberately misunderstood, responses may be frivolous, etc. Furthermore, yet again, interpretation is a matter of struggle. Different interpretations will be in contest, as they relate to different interests (Ball 1987), one or other interpretation will predominate, although deviant or minority readings may be important. Rizvi and Kemmis (1987: 29) underline this point:

> Because the participants in the contests which shape the evolution of a program start from different positions of relative power, the program, as it emerges, is disorted by the exercise of power, and freezes certain dominant ways of thinking into its structure.

But we must not see power in relation to policy as a fixed dimension. In patterns of contestation claims to power will always be tested in process, power is an outcome. Rizvi and Kemmis (1987: 28) also make the important point that contestation is not a problem as such, it should not be seen as untoward or extraordinary:

> Processes of contestation should not be thought to be unusual, and certainly not reprehensible. In fact contestation is a perfectly usual means through which ideas are developed and tested. In social life in general, different ideas, practices and forms of organization all have their advocates, and the evolution of social forms takes place through a struggle between supporters of different positions.

In all this authoritative interpretations may be at a premium. For many practitioners their response to texts will be constructed on the basis of 'interpretations of interpretations' (Rizvi and Kemmis 1987: 14). In a similar way the evaluation of policy in practice or of practitioner responses will be the outcome of contested interpretations. Evaluation is a way of making sense of practice for particular purposes. The definition of those purposes and the control or the machinery of evaluation are what is important. Thus it seems far more appropriate to talk of policies as having 'effects' rather than 'outcomes'. The policy process is one of complexity, it is one of policy-making and remaking. It is often difficult, if not impossible to control or predict the effects of policy, or indeed to be clear about what those effects are, what they mean, when they happen. Clearly, however, interpretations are not infinite, clearly also, as noted already, different material consequences derive from different interpretations in action. Practitioners will be influenced by the discursive context within which policies emerge. Some will have an eye to personal or localized advantage, material or otherwise, which may stem from particular readings of policy texts. But to reiterate, the meanings of texts are rarely unequivocal. Novel or creative readings can sometimes bring their own rewards. New possibilities can arise when 'national' policies intersect with local initiatives. Equally . . . different aspects of the same policy ensemble may contradict to the extent that certain well established readings of texts may have very different consequences and implications for practice.

REFERENCES

Alford, R. and Friedland, R. (1988) *Powers of Theory: Capitalism, the State, and Democracy*, Cambridge: Cambridge University Press.

Atkinson, P. (1985) *Language, Structure and Reproduction*, London: Methuen.

Ball, S.J. (1987) *The Micro-politics of the School*, London: Methuen.

Ball, S.J. (1990) *Politics and Policy-making in Education: Explorations in Policy Sociology*, London: Routledge.

Bash, L. and Coulby, D. (1989) *The Education Reform Act: Competition and Control*, London: Cassell.

Bernstein, B. (1986) 'On pedagogic discourse' in J.G. Richardson (ed.) *Handbook of Theory and Research for the Sociology of Education*, New York: Greenwood.

CCCS (Centre for Contemporary Cultural Studies) (1981) *Unpopular Education*, London: Hutchison.

Codd, J. (1988) 'The construction and deconstruction of educational policy documents', *Journal of Education Policy*, 3 (5): 235–48.

CPS (Centre for Policy Studies) (1988) *The Correct Core*, London: Centre for Policy Studies.

Dale, R. (1989) *The State and Education Policy*, Milton Keynes: Open University Press.

Dale, R., Bowe, R., Harris, D., Loveys, M., Moore, R., Shilling, C., Sykes, P., Trevitt, J. and Vasecchi, V. (1990) *The TVEI Story: Policy, Practice and the Preparation of the Workforce*, Milton Keynes: Open University Press.

DES (1989) *National Curriculum: From Policy to Practice* (Sections 4.3. and 9), London: HMSO.

Gleeson, D. (1989) *The Paradox of Training: Making Progress out of Crisis*, Milton Keynes: Open University Press.

Hawkes, T. (1977) *Structuralism and Semiotics*, London: Methuen.

Jones, K. (1989) *Right Turn*, London: Radius.

Kingman Report (1988) *Report of the Committee of Inquiry into the Teaching of English Language*, London: HMSO.

Knight, C. (1991) *The Making of Tory Education Policy in Post-War Britain, 1950–1986*, London: Falmer Press.

Kogan, M. (1975) *Educational Policy-Making*, London: Allen & Unwin.

Lawton, D. (1984) *The Tightening Grip: Growth of Central Control of the School Curriculum*, Bedford Way Papers 21, London: Heinemann Educational.

McCulloch, G. (1986) 'Policy, politics and education: the Technical and Vocational Education Initiative', *Journal of Education Policy*, 1 (1): 35–52.

Rizvi, F. and Kemmis, S. (1987) *Dilemmas of Reform*, Geelong: Deaking Institute for Studies in Education.

Saunders, M. (1985) *Emerging Issues for TVEI Implementation*, 2nd edn, Lancaster: University of Lancaster.

Shilling, C. (1986) 'Implementing the contract – the Technical and Educational Vocational Initiative', *British Journal of Sociology of Education*, 7 (4): 397–414.

Shilling, C. (1988) 'Thatcherism and education: the dialectics of political control'. Paper given to the International Sociology of Education Conference, Westhill College, Birmingham.

TES (1989) 'Another crusade that must be won', *Times Educational Supplement*, 26 May.

TES (1990) 'Mrs Thatcher signals U turn on curriculum' and 'What the Prime Minister said', *Times Educational Supplement*, 20 April.

Wallace, M. (1988) 'Innovation for all: management development in small primary schools', *Education Management and Administration*, 16 (1): 15–24.

West, G. (1983) 'Phenomenon and form in interactionist and neo-Marxist qualitative educational research', in S. Walker and L. Barton (eds) *Gender, Clan and Education*, Lewes: Falmer Press.

Wexler, P. (1982) 'Structure, text and subject: a critical sociology of school knowledge', in M. Apple (ed.) *Cultural and Economic Reproduction in Education*, London: Routledge & Kegan Paul.

Whitty, G. (1989) 'The New Right and the National Curriculum: state control or market forces', *Journal of Education Policy*, 4 (4): 329–42.

Willis, P.E. (1977) *Learning to Labour*, Farnborough: Saxon House.

Chapter 17

Market discipline versus comprehensive education

A case study of a London comprehensive school struggling to survive in the education market place

S. Gewirtz

The Education Reform Act (ERA) 1988 established in England and Wales a new structure of school provision with the mechanisms of open enrolment, *per capita* funding and site-based management combining to create a quasi market. Schools (as producers) are now supposed to compete for the custom of children and their parents (as consumers) and the funding of schools is heavily dependent on their success in attracting 'customers'. In addition, the national curriculum, testing and the publication of league tables of raw exam results represent key political controls on the market. This political-market-oriented restructuring of the education system has implications for the values and cultures which operate within schools and it is with those implications that this chapter is concerned. I want to consider the case of one school in particular, Northwark Park, an undersubscribed London comprehensive school whose staff and governors find themselves having to confront the issue of institutional survival in the market context. I will discuss the value conflicts in which they are becoming enmeshed and consider the implications of market-induced cultural shifts for patterns of social inequality. Before doing so I want to briefly raise some concerns about the way in which policy implementation has been conceptualised in some recent research and writing on the ERA.

RECENT ANALYSES OF THE IMPACT OF ERA – THE 'CELEBRATION OF INDETERMINACY'

The conceptualisation of implementation which I am concerned about – what might be called the 'celebration of indeterminacy' – places a great deal of emphasis on complexity, '*ad hoc*ery', messiness and unpredictability; it is an analytical trend which appears to be informed by particular variants of postmodern theory. This kind of conceptualisation is adopted by Richard Bowe and Stephen Ball (1992) in their book, *Reforming Education and Changing Schools* (see also Ball and Bowe 1992) – a case-study of the early impact on secondary schools of the national curriculum and local management of schools: 'The policy process', they suggest, 'is one of complexity, it is one of policy-making and remaking. It is often difficult, if not impossible to control or predict the effects of policy, or to be clear about what those effects are, what they mean when they happen' (Bowe and Ball with Gold 1992: 23). This perspective seems to have been quite influential on other analyses of recent education policy developments. Halpin and Fitz, for instance, explicitly endorse it (1990: 172) as do Raab (1992) and Penney and Evans (1992). The 'celebration of indeterminacy', it would seem, is becoming an orthodoxy in current analyses of the implementation of ERA.

I don't disagree that the process of policy implementation is messy, complex, *ad hoc* and results in unintended and unforeseen outcomes. This is because those who frame policies cannot control precisely how they are interpreted and put into practice on the ground. However I want to argue that it is possible to overstate the messiness, complexity and '*ad hoc*ery' associated with policy implementation. This kind of conceptualisation obscures patterns of domination and oppression which are being exacerbated by recent policy developments.

The conceptualisation of implementation employed by Bowe and Ball draws on the work of discourse theory. Discourse theory 'interprets discourse as a site and object of struggle where different groups strive for hegemony and the production of meaning and ideology' (Best and Kellner 1991). The following extracts from Bowe and Ball with Gold (1992) illustrate their approach:

> We would want to approach legislation as but one aspect of a continual process in which the loci of power are constantly shifting as the various resources implicit and explicit in texts are recontextualised and employed in the struggle to maintain or change views of schooling.
>
> This leads us to approach policy as a discourse, constituted of possibilities and impossibilities. . . . While the construction of the policy text may well involve different parties and processes to the 'implementing' process, the opportunity for re-forming and re-interpreting the text means policy formation does not end with the legislative 'moment'; 'for any text, a plurality of readers must necessarily produce a plurality of readings'.
>
> (Codd 1988: 239)

> [P]olicy is not simply received and implemented within [the context of practice] rather it is subject to interpretation and then 'recreated' . . . . Practitioners do not confront policy texts as naive readers, they come with histories, with experience, with values and purposes of their own, they have vested interests in the meaning of policy. Policies will be interpreted differently as the histories, experiences, values, purposes and interests which make up any arena differ. The

simple point is that policy writers cannot control the meanings of their texts. Parts of texts will be rejected, selected out, ignored, deliberately misunderstood, responses may be frivolous etc. . . . we must not see power in relation to policy as a fixed dimension. In patterns of contestation claims to power will always be tested in the process, power is an outcome.

(Wallace 1990: 22)

It is our contention that it is in the micro-political processes of the schools that we begin to see not only the limitations and possibilities State policy places upon schools but, equally, the limits and possibilities practitioners place upon the capacity of the State to reach into the daily lives of schools.

(*ibid.*: 85)

I do not disagree with any of these statements. What I am concerned about is the degree of emphasis. So much emphasis is placed on the interpretability of texts, the unpredictability of policy outcomes, the complexity of the policy process, the ability of individuals working in schools to respond creatively to the ERA, that broad patterns of oppression and domination created by the Act are obscured. Bowe and Ball appear to be tacitly adopting a Foucaultian conception of power:

Power's condition of possibility . . . must not be sought in the primary existence of a central point, in a unique source of sovereignty from which secondary and descendent forms would emanate; it is the moving substrate of force relations which, by virtue of their inequality, constantly engender states of power, but the latter are always local and unstable. The omnipresence of power: not because it has the privilege of consolidating everything under its invincible unity, but because it is produced from one moment to the next, at every point, or rather in every relation from one point to another. Power is everywhere; not because it embraces everything, but because it comes from everywhere.

(Foucault 1990: 93)

[A]s soon as there is a power relation, there is a possibility of resistance. We can never be ensnared by power: we can always modify its grip in determinate conditions and according to precise strategy

(Foucault 1988: 123)

And they are open to the same criticisms that have been made about Foucault's work:

Foucault rarely analyzes the important role of macro-powers such as the state or capital. While in *Madness and Civilisation* and *Discipline and*

Punish he occasionally points to the determining power of capitalism, and in *The History of Sexuality* he sees the state as an important component of 'biopower', macrological forces are seriously under-theorized in his work. In Foucault's defence, it could be argued that his intention is to offer novel perspectives on power as a diffuse, disciplinary force, but his microperspectives nevertheless need to be more adequately conjoined with macroperspectives that are necessary to illuminate a wide range of contemporary issues and problems such as state power (as manifested in oppressive laws or increasingly powerful surveillance technologies) and the persistence of class domination and the hegemony of capital.

As Poulantzas (1978) observes, Foucault seriously understates the continued importance of violence and overt repression. For Poulantzas, by contrast, '*State-monopolized physical violence permanently underlies the techniques of power and mechanisms of consent: it is inscribed in the web of disciplinary and ideological devices; and even when not directly exercized, it shapes the materiality of the social body upon which domination is brought to bear*' (1978: 81). Poulantzas does not deny the validity of Foucault's perspective of disciplinary power, he only insists that it wrongly abstracts from state power and repression which, for Poulantzas, are the conditions of possibility of disciplinary society.

(Best and Kellner 1991: 71–2)

My point is that Bowe, Ball and Gold emphasise 'the limits and possibilities practitioners place upon the capacity of the State to reach into the daily lives of schools' at the expense of exposing the way in which State policy in the form of ERA and the market it has created imposes a highly constraining disciplinary framework on schools and local school systems. The material consequences of that disciplinary framework are the exacerbation of inequalities of provision along class lines.

The 'celebration of indeterminacy' approach to research is not only diversionary. It also carries with it the potential to function in a legitimatory way. The ERA is justified by its proponents partly on the grounds that it is more democratic, that it is effecting a decentralisation of power: headteachers and governors are being empowered, according to government rhetoric, at the expense of local authorities many of which have for too long, so the argument goes, abused their power; and parents are being empowered in relation to schools and local authorities. I am concerned that research which overemphasises the diffusion of power inadvertently reinforces and supports New Right versions of the market.

In this chapter I want to put the emphasis back where I feel it should belong on the disciplinary workings and effects of the *state*-constructed market and on the implications of those effects for patterns of social inequality.

MARKET DISCIPLINE VERSUS COMPREHENSIVE EDUCATION

By using a case-study approach I want to illustrate how the market functions as a system of rewards and punishments, a disciplinary framework, fostering particular cultural forms and socio-psychological dispositions and marginalising others (see Figure 17.1)

Within a market culture it is acceptable for there to be winners and losers, access to resources which is differentiated but unrelated to need, hierarchy, exclusivity, selectivity, and for producers to utilise whatever tactics they can get away with to increase their market share and to maximise profits. In short, there is pressure on individuals (both producers and consumers) to be motivated first and foremost by self-interest. The social psychology of the market discourages the universalism and collectivism that in theory underpinned comprehensivism, whereby the educational needs of all children in an area, regardless of class, 'race', gender or ability, would be met by the local neighbourhood school. And the principles of comprehensivism may be further seen to be undermined by the controls which the government have placed on the market. The national curriculum, testing at four key stages and the publication of those test results in the form of league tables represent potentially powerful mechanisms for influencing the way schools function in the market place. If schools are rewarded for having good test results, there is an incentive, for instance, for schools to select their students (where they are able) on the basis of ability. Funding shortages provide an additional incentive to select: 'less able' children and children for whom English is a second language, for instance, are more expensive to educate than 'more able' children who are proficient in English. Funding constraints also threaten other aspects of comprehensivism because adequate mixed ability teaching and the integration of children with special needs are expensive ways of organising learning.

The extent to which individual schools are able to resist the culture of the market depends largely on their market position. A heavily oversubscribed school is least likely to face a situation in which it needs to change what it is already doing in order to attract pupils. Where schools are unsuccessful in market terms (i.e. they are undersubscribed) the potential for resistance is lowest and market-induced ethical dilemmas are therefore most pronounced. This is the case with Northwark Park.

Comprehensive Values → **Market Values**

Comprehensive Values	Market Values
Led by agenda of social and educational concerns	Led by agenda of image/ budgetary concerns
Oriented to serving community needs	Oriented to attracting 'motivated' parents/ 'able' children
Emphasis on student need	Emphasis on student performance
Resource emphasis on 'less able'/ SEN	Resource emphasis on 'more able'
Mixed ability	Setting
Integrationist	Exclusivist
Caring ethos	Academic ethos
Emphasis on good relationships as basis of school discipline	Emphasis on extrinisic indicators of discipline, e.g. uniform
Cooperation amongst schools	Competition between schools

Figure 17.1 Values Drift

Northwark Park

Northwark Park is undersubscribed and under pressure. An ex-Inner London Education Authority (ILEA) school, it is located on the eastern edge of Northwark where it abuts the neighbouring authority, Streetley. It takes about one-third of its children from primary schools in that authority. The school's intake is predominantly working class although there is a small core of white middle-class children, described to us by staff in the school as having liberal/left-wing parents who choose the school because it is local, comprehensive and non-uniform: '. . . and a lot of them have been involved in Labour Party politics, educational and housing issues, that kind of thing and basically believe very much [in] a local authority' (Headteacher).

Approximately 45 per cent of the children are white, 45 per cent are Afro–Carribean and the other 10 per cent is made up of other ethnic minorities including children with a South Asian background and African, Chinese and East European students. The school's poor market position could well have something to do with its short and rocky history. It was opened in 1986 as an amalgamation of two schools, one of which itself was the product of an earlier amalgamation. In 1991 the school was one of four in the authority threatened with closure. Although it won its campaign to stay open, the uncertainty surrounding its possible closure was harmful in terms of recruitment. Northwark Park also suffers from a reputation of being 'tough' because, as the headteacher put it: 'each time it got going as a mixed school, they amalgamated it with a boys school. Therefore it has fought actually the image of a boys school for quite some time.' And its location near to Broughton tube station and Broughton High Street and adjacent to a pub with a history of drug activity are other factors beyond the control of the school which are seen to be affecting its reputation.

However, the impression one gets from spending time in the school is actually very different from its rough, tough, macho reputation. The school building is small and carpeted and the atmosphere is calm, quiet and relaxed. The following comment by the NAS/UWT representative is typical of how the school was described by its teachers and confirms what we ourselves have observed: 'the school has always been a very friendly school. It's not the sort of school that you feel much physical intimidation . . . students are very friendly, staff are very friendly.'

Northwark Park has a stable and experienced staff but, therefore, also an expensive staff leading to speculation amongst some members of staff that senior management might, in the context of formula funding, be forced to make redundancies. . . .

An expensive staff means less money for other (non-human) resources, like books: 'We barely have enough really to replace damaged books these days' (Maths Teacher). Undersubscription of course compounds the funding shortages. Whilst money is in short supply in the school, the needs of many of the children are great. Like many city schools, Northwark Park has a high turnover of children: '. . . we had a lot of first generation immigrants coming into the area, so we tend to take those obviously, because we're a school that's got vacancies, so they tend to get pushed here, and then you get a lot of families who will settle for a year or so and then move out, so we lose a lot of children' (Head of Year Seven). The intake of the school is skewed towards 'lower ability' children (in 1992 Northwark Park had the second lowest intake of band one children in the LEA and the highest proportion of band three children); and the school-based education welfare officer has contact with a high proportion of the children in the school. She has just over a hundred open cases in a school with less than 700 on roll, not counting those children she works with on a casual basis, and estimates that 'a sixth probably of the school . . . sometime or another is referred'. She attributes this high proportion to the reputation the school has as a caring school and the selective nature of another local school:

> It's known as a small caring school and a school that's known as caring, I think gets a high proportion of children with problems and because Hutton which is our nearest secondary school in Northwark, has always had a much higher profile so they have always been in the position where they can pick and choose a lot more.

The education welfare service within the authority as a whole is under review which is likely to mean cuts and, since amalgamation in 1986, the special needs department at Northwark Park has also been progressively reduced in size:

> As our staffing has shrunk and shrunk . . . from about five full timers down to two full timers, it's basically down to the basics of English and Maths, and some Science if we can, not all classes get it. . . . We're an easier area to cut obviously than others because we're not an area of the curriculum, as such.

> (Head of Special Needs)

An additional effect of cuts over the last few years has been an increase in class sizes in certain subjects and the use of teachers to teach subjects they are not trained to teach in:

> . . . now in this school it is not recognised that practical subjects require smaller classes. . . . We've got people who usually teach art and come in here to do odd periods which is very – well they've got no commitment to the department, they show no interest in the department, so basically it drags the department down.

> (Technology Teacher)

Thus the combination of a high level of need amongst the children, pre-ERA cuts in special needs provision and particular curriculum areas, undersubscription, *per capita* funding and a parsimonious local authority mean that the school's resources are extremely stretched. Northwark Park is a school fighting for its survival. If it ignores the market it dies. Given its undersubscription and its overall funding position the school has little option but to take competition for students very seriously. 'The system is now changing, which means we . . . cannot stay as we were. We will have to perform in some way in order to survive' (Teacher Governor).

However, the need to change in response to new conditions throws up ethical dilemmas. The school's staff and governors have traditionally been ardently committed to comprehensive education but, as noted above, the new market structure of educational provision is not conducive to the retention of a comprehensive culture. There is, therefore, a significant mismatch between the established culture of the school and the culture of the market, and the sharpness of this dichotomy produces dilemmas in the school's response. . . .

Northwark Park is committed to the integration of children with special needs, and, as we have already seen, it has a reputation for being a caring school. The staff have been particularly concerned to promote equal opportunities for girls: some all-boys groups were introduced 'so that girls' experience of the classroom would not be that they were swamped' (Headteacher) and times are set aside when only girls can use the library. Another crucial element which characterised Northwark Park as a comprehensive school was its policy on mixed ability teaching, whereby all lessons in all subjects and years were taught in mixed-ability classes. The other elements which are part of the culture of Northwark Park include: a commitment to cooperation with other local schools; a relaxed and friendly atmosphere in the school; good relationships between students and staff; and no uniform.

Clearly I would be presenting too romantic a view if I were to portray Northwark Park pre-ERA as a model comprehensive school. Whilst the staff express a commitment to comprehensive values, it would be naive not to question the relationship between rhetoric and practice, and the school is not without its internal critics. There is a general concern expressed by a number of members of staff, including the new Headteacher, Barbara Swallow, that the school has traditionally failed to challenge children academically:

> I think in the past there were schools [and she is clearly implying that Northwark Park was one of these] weren't there, that saw its image as a caring school and there was always a kind of sub text to that, which meant a not very high achieving school.
>
> (Headteacher)

> ... we do get on reasonably well with the students ... but a lot of
> Northwark Park is that we don't challenge, as a staff we don't
> challenge, and I think that's been one of our failings in the past ...
>
> (Head of Year Seven)

The Chair of Governors in particular is concerned about what he
believes to be low expectations of working-class and especially black
boys in the school:

> ... there are issues like the performance of black boys in an area
> where there isn't work for black youths where, counter to the sort of
> as it were gender direction, it's the boys who very much get the worst
> out of the school, and out of the job market. ...
>
> [The Head's] view is that the staff have almost sort of a corporate
> profile about what they think they're about, which needs to be
> budged. Firstly, they think they're there to help the underprivileged
> working-class kids, and to that extent they resent the high-flying kids
> from middle-class homes who come and seem to do well in the school
> ... and I think she thinks that their attitude to both is wrong, that
> they need a far more systematic and less condescending approach to
> the bulk of the kids who come to the school ...
>
> (Chair of Governors)

Similar doubts about opportunities for black children to perform well in
the school were voiced by one of the parent governors. There is also a
concern that the school alienates black and Asian parents who are
reluctant to become involved in the school:

> we haven't got very many black staff here so at a parents' evening, if
> a black parent does come to a parents' evening, they'll only see a
> couple of Asian, two Asian teachers and one black teacher, out of the
> whole of ... forty-nine staff. So the school is very white, the senior
> management is totally white, it's nearly all male.
>
> (Teacher Governor)

Like many comprehensive schools, then, there would seem to be at
Northwark Park a gap between comprehensive values and comprehensive practice within the school. But the gap is acknowledged, particularly
by certain governors including the Chair and apparently by the Head
too, and one of the questions I want to address here is the conflict
between the desire to narrow this gap and the need to survive in the
local education market place.

The staff are *reluctantly implicated* in the market. They don't like it, but
they are part of it and most recognise the need to respond to it.

I don't think you can have a premise that you have winners and losers in education. I don't think society can afford to run on those sort of principles . . . and I think this sort of, this market place business is potentially very dangerous. I mean we have to respond to it, that's the problem, that's why we're sort of running round in circles at the moment, because we can't just take the moral high ground and say, we will have nothing to do with that, we have to be part and parcel of it.

(Deputy Head)

I don't believe in parental choice at all, I think really parents should send their children to the local school. I don't believe in private education either. But it's there and it's staying so we have to make the best.

(Head of Sixth Form)

But how do they deal with this *reluctant implication*, how do they 'make the best' of it? Ideally they want to hang on to their principles, to the comprehensive ethos, whilst becoming more successful in the market place – it's a fragile balance and there are varying degrees of sacrifice which the staff and governors are prepared to make. It is possible to visualise a *value spectrum* along which individuals drift. On one end of the spectrum are those who are reluctant to change, resistant to abandoning any of their principles. The governing body of the school has on it a majority of left-wing members strongly opposed to any value drift. The Chair of Governors, Dan Kennedy, for instance, has been active in socialist education politics for many years. An ex-ILEA sub-committee chair, he is also a governor of a secondary school in Streetley, a past vice-chair of governors at Streetley College and Secretary of the Streetley Socialist Education Association. As we have already seen, he is particularly concerned about what he believes to be low expectations of black and working-class children by teachers at Northwark Park. The governors are seen as constituting the school's ethical conscience:

I think the governors, our governors, are quite political and are by and large. They are former ILEA governors, so they are, I mean they are political, they are left-wing, by and large, and I don't think for one moment they approve of the sort of market place philosophy in education, and I think it just is taking them some time and will take them some time, to come to terms with what it implies.

(Deputy Head)

The Head believes that some governors will just give up, rather than compromise their values. 'I think there are some who will probably just stop being governors, because they hate the situation so much.' But the abdication of 'comprehensive governors' may only speed up and exacerbate the insidious disciplinary and value effects of the market.

Some of the staff share the governors' opposition to abandoning the key elements of the school's comprehensive culture. . . .

The Headteacher (who operates at the point of interface between the old and the new values) has drifted further along the value spectrum, arguing that the community school is incompatible with a competitive structure of provision:

> I think that it's the kind of school, with the kind of staff and governors, who would like to see, the governors would certainly like to see a community school, and I think it's taking a lot of people, quite a long time, to think themselves into . . . the different situation, that the '90s are not like the '70s . . . and the community school is not going to happen with LMS and with GMS schools and we have to take on the competition, whether we like it or not.

However, she still wants to hang on to aspects of comprehensivism but without the community part. The elements she wants to adhere to are a broad curriculum, a comprehensive intake, and equal opportunities policies for gender and 'race'. John Fox, the Deputy cited earlier, would seem to be located even further along the value spectrum towards a more ready acceptance of participation in the market place. He appeared to be toying with the idea of a shift towards a more grammar school-type ethos to enable the school to sell itself better. He described – admiringly it would appear – changes which have occurred in the nearby opted out girls school, Martineau:

> I'm not saying it's lost its comprehensive ideals, but Kath Davies, who is the head there, in my view has set herself up as near as damn it to a traditional girls' grammar school. . . . I mean it's obviously attracted a lot of people. You know, you can imagine trying to put that across here and I think you might run into difficulties.

The market then sets comprehensive school values against institutional survival and thus against jobs and livelihoods: the market, as a disciplinary framework, is fostering the social psychology of self-interest which is in direct conflict with the collectivist, universalistic psychology conducive to a comprehensive system of provision. In the rest of the chapter I want to look at specific key examples of conflicts which have arisen in the school out of the clash between comprehensive and market values, between the culture of collectivism and the social psychology of self-interest.

Expanding the intake

All of the conflicts I want to look at stem from the pressure on Northwark Park to expand its intake. The new local structure of provision has involved schools opting out, early signs of informal selection and fears that Northwark Park will become a sink school:

> I fear that what will happen is that Hutton, which is a mixed school, and that Martineau, which is a girls school, will grow and grow and grow in strength . . . and what will happen is then we will go back to being a secondary modern school.
>
> (Head of Year Seven)

There seems to be a general recognition that the school must attract a more diverse clientele. But there seem to be different conceptions of what particular sections of the community the school should be targeting. The Head commented in one interview that, 'I'm not saying we're looking for middle-class parents . . . but we're looking for motivated parents'. Yet elsewhere in the interview her concern does seem to be for the school to appeal to middle-class parents. The head talked about the possibility of beginning to attract South Asian children: 'I think that we have not tried very hard to get into the Asian community. It's an area we ought to do some more work on.' John Fox, the Deputy Head, expresses a desire to attract the newly affluent working-class or lower middle-class parents:

> we always have had, and still do have, a nucleus of what I suppose you would call sort of very middle-class, very sort of politically aware parents, who consciously send their kids here because they like certain aspects of the school, but what we miss out on is other sort of, a lot of that sort of middle band of people who have, you know, real sort of aspirations for themselves and for their children as well. I don't know what you'd call them . . . like electricians and plumbers and people like that who are enjoying a certain sort of affluence, you know. They tend to avoid us and I'm not sure why that is.
>
> . . .

Cutting across these varied (but not necessarily incompatible) visions of who the school should be targeting are conflicting rationales for the expansion. It is at this juncture that comprehensive values begin to vie with market-induced values. . . . The attempt to attract more 'motivated' parents is defended by other members of staff as being essential if the school is to remain comprehensive. A comprehensive school, it is argued, is dependent on there being a 'balanced' or comprehensive intake:

> If you can attract a good range of intake, if you're full, and without, still within the comprehensive ideal, have a range of ability, rather than being weighted at the bottom, then I suppose by and large all the students benefit from that sort of balance.
>
> (Deputy Head)

I think what people here would say is that every school should take its share of problem families, problem children, children with special educational needs, we don't not want those children at all, but a school which is full of children like that, very easily becomes a sink school, because nobody puts the resources in that you need to deal – that's why secondary modern schools didn't work.

(Headteacher)

Yet there is a fine line between wanting to expand one's intake in order for it to remain comprehensive, and wanting to expand it in order for it to become selective. Dan Kennedy (Chair of Governors) suggests that Martineau, the nearby grant-maintained school, has already crossed that line: 'I think you'll find that you get so much double talk about what people think they're doing or what they say they're doing . . . I mean the opting out schools say they're opting out in order to preserve comprehensive education.' What Kennedy is hinting at here is that some schools, whilst claiming they want to remain comprehensive and whilst keeping an ability spread, are in fact selecting on the basis of motivation. They are, in other words, adopting the kinds of informal admissions policies used by some of the voluntary-aided ILEA schools and more recently and formally by City Technology Colleges. . . . In some of the comments made by staff at Northwark Park, it is already possible to detect an ambiguity on the question of selection. Alongside arguments about a balanced intake being necessary if the school is going to continue to function as a comprehensive are arguments which hint at a desire to be selective or to somehow gain in status within the local economy of schooling: 'Ideally every school wants to be oversubscribed, so it does have some control over who comes in . . . to be in a position to say, no' (Acting Deputy Head).

Reviewing mixed ability

Last year the school conducted a review of its mixed-ability policy. Prior to the review, all classes were mixed ability in all subjects and all years. The review may be understood as a response to the combination of a range of disciplinary mechanisms: the publication of raw results in the form of league tables, the structure of the national testing at key stages three and four, the effects of under-resourcing on class sizes and special needs provision, the policy of Northwark's inspectorate and the introduction of teacher appraisal. . . .

The result of the review was a decision that individual departments would decide on whether or not to introduce setting. So far only science has decided to do so, but it is felt that modern languages and perhaps maths and humanities will follow. Whilst the introduction of setting in some subjects, might have the offshoot, as the Headteacher put it, of attracting parents and might also serve to raise the academic performance of *some* children, there is clearly a downside with respect to the achievement of 'less able' children and children with special needs: 'you then get the development of the label of failure and the D-Stream culture. The movement that is there in the mixed-ability class is lost' (Head of Special Needs).

It is most unlikely that the introduction of differential testing at key stages three and four and setting will solve the problem of low teacher expectations of working-class and particularly black children and restricted opportunities for them. In fact it is likely to do the opposite – to aggravate the problem (see Tomlinson 1987; DES 1981; Ball 1981; Lacey 1970; Barker–Lunn 1969; and Hargreaves 1967). As Tomlinson (1987: 106) has pointed out:

> Although ability is supposedly the major criterion for placement in subject and examination levels, ability is an ambiguous concept and school conceptions of ability can be affected by perceptions that pupils are members of particular social or ethnic groups and by the behaviour of individual pupils. Factors related to class, gender, ethnicity, and behaviour *can* be shown to affect the placement of pupils at option time, even those of similar ability.

Tomlinson (1987: 106) has also drawn attention to the disadvantages associated with placement in lower level examination classes 'as employment possibilities dwindle and higher level credentials are required for further and higher education and training and in new types of manual work'.

The integration of children with special needs

Like many state schools since Warnock, Northwark Park has progressively moved away from the remedial approach to special needs provision, where children with special needs were mainly withdrawn from mainstream classes and taught a virtually separate curriculum, towards a more integrated approach with an emphasis on in-class support. But there are signs, which I have already alluded to, that the trend towards integration may be receding because of market forces and the associated shift of resources away from children with special needs.

I have already pointed to the introduction of setting in some subjects which constitutes an obvious barrier to integration. I have also referred to the contraction of the special needs department resulting in a reduced capacity for in-class support for children with special needs. In addition to these developments, the 'reorganisation' of special needs provision in the local authority as a whole, whilst presented by the authority as a policy designed to enhance integration, has in practice meant that off-site support has now been reduced also. This has given rise to fears that: '. . . there probably won't even be enough to cover the statutory work that we do. . . . No doubt there will be children next year who have got statements who won't have the support they are legally entitled to' (Head of Special Needs).

But it is not just a shortage of resources and a local authority apparently more concerned about challenging the able than stretching the 'less able' which puts pressure on the ability of the school to provide for special needs adequately. There are other disciplinary mechanisms at work here which function to stunt the development of integrative policies. The desire that the school should be attractive to 'motivated' parents with 'able' children combines with inadequate resourcing to function as a disincentive for good special needs provision and the integration of children with special needs. The Deputy Head commented:

> it's a fairly contentious thing to say but I think special educational needs could suffer. I think people will be less tolerant, because that sort of provision is expensive, so it's eating up your money and your time, and if you're being asked to produce a good set of examination results, then you want as much of your resourcing as possible to be directed at that.
>
> . . .

So in the area of special needs, educational considerations are beginning to be accommodated to commercial ones.

Once again, then, funding shortages, local authority policy towards provision for the 'less able', *per capita* funding, national testing, the publication of league tables of raw scores and the subsequent concern to attract more 'able' children into the school combine to form a disciplinary framework which works against the culture of comprehensivism, and in this particular instance integration.

The question of exclusions

Governors and staff at Northwark Park have observed an increase in the rate of permanent exclusions from other local schools. . . .

National and local statistics would appear to support these impressions, with permanent exclusions rising and a disproportionate number of black boys being excluded. Whilst local oversubscribed schools are able to exclude, Northwark Park is, as we have already seen, under pressure to accept the excluded:

> Our school is attracting a very large number of usually expelled, displaced fifteen year olds, who've missed the option level, so they're

coming into our school. Our exam results as a result will be quite seriously affected by the number who've joined us after the beginning of the tenth year and therefore are almost bound to have a restricted exam potential. . . .

(Chair of Governors)

There are divergent views within school about the educational merits and demerits of permanent exclusion. The EWO is opposed to exclusion on the grounds that it does not benefit the excluded child because the source of the problem which led to exclusion in the first place is not confronted: '. . . if a child is not attending because they don't have you know meaningful relationships with children in the school, or they don't know the staff very well . . . moving them to another school is not going to solve that'.

There are a group of teachers within the school, however, who would like the school's exclusion policy to be tightened up. At an in-service training day in which the school development plan was discussed some members of staff were critical of senior management for not taking up effectively complaints about a core of disruptive students who were seen to be absorbing a disproportionate amount of teacher time and consequently damaging the learning of other children. At the feedback session on the day there was a heated discussion between the Head and a number of teachers about this group of students which focused on the issue of exclusions:

One teacher pointed out that these children were disrupting other students on a regular basis and another commented that the number of GCSE grade As in one particular class was lowered because of the presence of a disruptive pupil in that class. The Head reported that she had presented to the governors the exclusion figures since January and that they thought they were high. A teacher responded: 'They don't have to deal with them. Let them come into the classes and deal with it.'

(Observation notes)

There is clearly a resource dimension to the arguments of these teachers. If class sizes were smaller and there was less pressure on teacher and senior management time and resources more generally, then other strategies might be more easily found to deal with this group of children. But on the whole, as far as the teaching staff are concerned, the debate is essentially about the *educational* advantages or disadvantages of exclusion.

At management level, however, it would seem that on the issue of exclusion, as in other areas, educational questions are being increasingly subordinated to commercial, market-oriented ones. The debate within management about whether or not to exclude is centred on the question of whether it is a good or bad marketing strategy and about the financial implications of excluding. Oversubscribed schools can easily replace their excluded students with students on their waiting lists. But if Northwark Park excludes, they are unlikely to get a replacement and will simply lose the money attached to the excluded pupil: 'I mean each child now is worth money and you've got to be pretty desperate to actually suggest a parent changes school for a child' (Head of Year Seven).

Belonging to a local system

It is argued at Northwark Park that an essential part of being a comprehensive school is belonging to a local system of comprehensive schools. The local system in Northwark is dissolving. The break up of ILEA was perhaps the first nail in the coffin but the reforms of the ERA are accelerating the dissolution. Many Northwark teachers are trying to resist the fragmentation that the market fosters. The Head of Sixth Form at Northwark Park is part of a group of Northwark Heads of Sixth Form trying to maintain links:

> ... I don't like being in a situation where we're competing for students. Luckily my colleagues in sixth forms in other schools, locally, we've more or less agreed that we won't poach from each others' schools so that if a fifth year student from another school applies to the sixth form here, I would get back to his or her school, and tell them that is the case. As I say, we've got a general agreement, there is a small group of us, little group but there's one school in particular in the LEA that seems to take anybody, and has always been the first one to try and poach. That's their policy. It's a bigger school and some people think the best school, but that's been going on for some while.
>
> (Head of Sixth Form)

But however much individual teachers would like to continue cooperating with other schools, the odds are increasingly against it happening because the new deregulated structure of school provision is not conducive to cooperation. This is ... because it encourages competition which is already leading to the souring of relations between some schools. ...

Also once schools opt out (three have already done so in Northwark and three others are in the process of doing so) professional contact between teachers in different sectors becomes difficult to maintain: 'We have official meetings at the Teachers' Centre about four or five times a year and then unofficial contacts. ... But the group is narrowing because of the opting out' (Head of Sixth Form). ...

And of course the fragmentation of the local system of schooling has very obvious effects on the pupils, as is apparent in the following example given by the Head of Sixth Form:

I don't agree with formula funding. I think it's not the way to fund education for a start. It's made very, it's a very stark choice. You, know, one student is worth so many pounds, there's a very strong pressure therefore, to accept students who would be better advised to go elsewhere. And sometimes we have truthfully, we have had one or two in the sixth form who perhaps should not have been in the sixth form, but they were here because they wanted to be and it was very useful to have them to boost the numbers, and boost our income. . . .

The opt-out option

The opting-out debate at Northwark Park is complicated. Ethical dilemmas are closely bound up with tactical considerations. When the school was threatened with closure, the staff and governors voted to call a parental ballot on going grant-maintained as a way of saving the school, but the threat was removed, the school canvassed for a no vote, and the parents voted no. The issue didn't go away however. Opting out is potentially a means of holding on to some of the school's existing values in the face of the LEA's hostility to comprehensivism. It also might increase the chances of a balanced intake, both because it might make the school more popular with middle-class parents and because it would mean they wouldn't have to accept children excluded from the other grant-maintained schools. On the other hand, going grant-maintained means contributing to the break up of the LEA system. In addition, there is the practical matter of which course of action brings with it more money, since the LEA are offering financial bribes to its remaining schools if they stay in.

The opting-out issue brings into sharp relief the opposition between comprehensive principles and the psychology of self-interest which the new market structure creates. Some teachers were not prepared to concede to market forces, to drift further along the value spectrum, by supporting the opt-out move, even in the extreme case of the school's survival depending on such a concession. The NUT Rep. was amongst the minority who voted against going for a parental ballot when the school was being threatened with closure. He did not want to be part of a school whose only commitment was to survival:

I was opposing it because of the way it undermines national agreements on working conditions and everything else, and because I believe that schools should be part of an education system and once you're opted out, you're not part of anything, your only real commitment is to self-preservation, keeping your institution going. You know, schools should be planned, they should be part of the wider community. . . .

The NAS/UWT Rep. adopted a similar position. . . .

While the threat of closure by the LEA has been removed, some of the arguments for going grant-maintained still remain. There is the recurring worry that the school will otherwise become a 'sink' school open to all the children excluded from other local schools and once again institutional survival takes precedence over the needs of children, in this instance excluded ones:

> . . . we've got four other schools in Northwark that have gone grant-maintained, and that puts peculiar pressure on to the school. And there are other implications for the school as well, such as . . . I mean this is a very simplistic one, but a very true one, if a child is expelled from a grant-maintained school, the authority cannot direct another grant-maintained school to pick them up. If we, as we think may happen, in two years are one of the only state schools left in Northwark, we will be directed to pick up all those children. Now we could easily become a sink school. . . .
>
> (Teacher Governor)

If the school opted out, it would have additional funds but would have to compete directly with its larger, better perceived opted-out neigh-bours. Opting out would mean abandoning the comprehensive ILEA history of the school entirely. Survival within the Northwark LEA system and the offer of capital funds involves acceptance of specialisation and selection. The management of the school believe that there is room for manoeuvre within the LEA scheme. But here comprehensivism is under threat from a different set of pressures. At present compromise seems the only alternative to decline and perhaps eventual closure. Heads they win, tails you lose.

CONCLUSION

The case of Northwark Park illustrates how the market rewards shrewd-ness rather than principles and encourages commercial rather than educational decision-making. This is evidenced, in particular, by the staff's comments on exclusions, integration and sixth-form provision. This reflects a fundamental value shift in the UK education system: concern for social justice is being replaced by concern for institutional survival, collectivism with individualism, cooperation with suspicion, and need with expediency.

Whilst certain interests and needs are privileged in the education market place, others are marginalised via the systematic restructuring of school provision. The market introduced by the ERA is not a neutral mechanism of resource allocation, nor is it apolitical: it is a form of 'ordered competition' (Hayek 1980) with *particular* social and economic goals embedded in it. We have seen that the market introduced by ERA functions as a disciplinary mechanism via the provision of incentives and disincentives. Open enrolment and *per capita* funding, poor resourcing, the testing of children at four key stages and the publication of league tables of those results are crucial components of that mechanism. Research on parental choice indicates that exam results are only one of several criteria seen by parents as being important in helping them decide on a secondary school for their children (Stillman and Maychell 1986; Coldron and Boulton 1991; Hunter 1991; West and Varlaam 1991; Ball *et al.* 1993). Yet the publication of league tables of results and the publicity surrounding their publication mean that *schools* are paying *particular* attention to test results. Low levels of funding mean that schools are pressured into maximising their results in the cheapest ways possible. Admitting only those students who are likely to perform well in tests and excluding those who are likely to perform badly are the most cost-effective means for (oversubscribed) schools to boost their positions in the league tables; and setting is a cheaper way of organising learning than mixed-ability grouping. Another element of the disciplinary mechanism, which is further encouraging the more widespread adoption of setting practices, is the introduction of differential testing at key stages three and four. Teacher appraisal is an additional component. Still in its infant stages, we have yet to see precisely what effects it will have, but, as Dan Kennedy, Northwark Park's Chair of Governors put it, the incentive will be for teachers to concentrate on 'the areas that they're going to be marked in and if it means that they haven't got the time to look at other areas, then they'll abandon that'.

If the education market is leading to more selection than it is also likely to lead to greater segregation *between* schools along social class lines. This is because, where oversubscribed schools are allowed to select pupils, modes of selection tend to favour children from middle-class backgrounds. And a drift away from mixed-ability teaching is likely to result in greater social class and 'racial' segregation *within* schools through setting (Tomlinson 1987; DES 1981; Ball 1981; Lacey 1970; Barker-Lunn 1969; and Hargreaves 1967). Middle-class children may benefit from such a reorganisation, given the more generous resourcing of oversubscribed schools (where such children are likely to be concentrated) and given 'the contextual effect of school mean [socio-economic status] on individual attainment' (Echols *et al* 1990). Working-class and ethnic minority children, who are more likely to be represented amongst those designated 'less able', are likely to be congregated in the most poorly resourced schools and in the lowest sets. The restructuring of educational provision along market lines, therefore, has significant implications for social justice and educational opportunity.

Northwark Park is a 'critical case' which illustrates how difficult it is for schools to resist the discipline imposed by the market. It is a school whose staff and governors are ideologically committed to the principle of comprehensive education. Thus, if there were any potential for strategies to be developed which would enable schools to retain immunity from market pressures, than one would expect Northwark Park to have developed and utilised them. But, as we have seen, in order to survive in the market place, the school management and staff are having to consider cultivating a more middle-class intake and abandoning some of the key components of comprehensivism – namely mixed-ability teaching, a commitment to the integration of children with special educational needs and being non-selective.

So, to return to the concern I began with – about accounts which appear to celebrate indeterminacy – it is vital to note that whilst the ERA may be a text open to different and creative interpretations, particular interpretations carry with them material rewards whilst others incur punishment. The ultimate sanction for teachers in schools which do not conform to market demands is unemployment and all of the attendant hardships of unemployment. The fact that he or she may have responded 'creatively' to texts emanating from the central state will be of little comfort to the teacher who is made unemployed as a result. Whilst unemployment is not a form of physical violence it is nevertheless a form of violence, and a weapon which can be utilised by the state to ensure conformity. Like physical violence, it:

> permanently underlies the techniques of power and mechanisms of consent: it is inscribed in the web of disciplinary and ideological devices; and even when not directly exercized, it shapes the materiality of the social body upon which domination is brought to bear.
>
> (Poulantzas 1978: 81)

It is of course possible, in critiquing the 'celebration of indeterminacy', to go too far the other way, to portray the state as all-powerful and to suggest that state-policy can never be successfully contested. We must not fall into this trap either, but nor should we underestimate the enormity of the task of contestation.

REFERENCES

Ball, S.J. (1981) *Beachside Comprehensive: a Case Study of Secondary Schooling*, Cambridge: Cambridge University Press.

Ball, S.J. and Bowe, R. (1992) 'Subject departments and the "implementation" of

National Curriculum policy: an overview of the issues' *Journal of Curriculum Studies* 24(2): 97–115.

Ball, S.J., Bowe, R. and Gewirtz, S. (1995) 'Circuits of Schooling: A sociological exploration of parental choice of school in social class contexts', *Sociological Review* 43 (1).

Barker-Lunn, J. (1969) *Streaming in the Primary School*, Slough: NFER.

Best, S. and Kellner, D. (1991) *Postmodern Theory: Critical Interrogations*, Basingstoke: Macmillan.

Bowe, R. and Ball, S. with Gold (1992) *Reforming Education and Changing Schools: Case Studies in Policy Sociology*, London: Routledge.

Codd, J. (1988) 'The construction and deconstruction of educational policy documents', *Journal of Education Policy* 3(5): 235–8.

Coldron, J. and Boulton, P. (1991) '"Happiness" as a criterion of parents' choice of school', *Journal of Education Policy* 6(2): 169–78.

Department of Education and Science (1981) *West Indian Children in Our Schools*, London: HMSO.

Echols, F., McPherson, A. and Williams, J.D. (1990) 'Parental choice in Scotland', *Journal of Education Policy* 5(3): 207–22.

Foucault, M. (1988) in Kritzman, L.D. (ed.) *Michel Foucault: Politics, Philosophy and Culture*, New York: Semiotext(e).

Foucault, M. (1990) *The History of Sexuality: Volume 1: An Introduction*, Harmondsworth: Penguin.

Halpin, D. and Fitz, J. (1990) 'Researching grant-maintained schools', *Journal of Education Policy* 5(2): 167–80.

Hayek, K. (1980) *Individualism and Economic Order*, University of Chicago Press.

Hargreaves, D. (1967) *Social Relations in a Secondary School*, London: Routledge & Kegan Paul.

Hunter, J. (1991) 'Which school? A study of parents' choice of secondary school', *Educational Research* 33(1): 31–41.

Lacey, C. (1970) *Hightown Grammar*, Manchester University Press.

McPherson, A.F. and Williams, J.D. (1987) 'Equalisation and improvement: some effects of comprehensive reorganisation in Scotland', *Sociology* 21(4): 509–39.

Penney, D. and Evans, J. (1992) 'From "Policy" to "Practice": the development and implementation of the National Curriculum for physical education'. Presented at CEDAR International Conference, University of Warwick, 10–12 April.

Petch, A. (1986) 'Parents' reasons for choosing schools', in Stillman, A. (ed.) *The Balancing Act of 1980: Parents, Politics and Education*, Slough: NFER.

Poulantzas, N. (1978) *State, Power, Socialism*, London: New Left Books.

Raab, C. (1992) 'Where are we now: some reflections on the sociology of education policy'. Paper presented at ESRC-funded seminar on Methodological and Ethical Issues Associated with Research into the 1988 Education Reform Act, University of Warwick, 29 April.

Stillman, A. and Maychell, K. (1986) *Choosing Schools: Parents, LEAs and the 1980 Education Act*, Windsor: NFER-Nelson.

Tomlinson, S. (1987) 'Curriculum option choices in multi-ethnic schools', in Troyna, B. *Racial Inequality in Education*, London: Tavistock Publications.

Wallace, M. (1990) *Coping with Multiple Innovations in Schools*, School of Education, University of Bristol.

West, A. and Varlaam, A. (1991) 'Choosing a secondary school: parents of junior school children', *Educational Research* 33(1): 22–30.

Chapter 18

Equal opportunities

The curriculum and the subject

L. Jones and R. Moore

INTRODUCTION

A major feature of the reforms which have taken place in educational
policy over the 1980s is the changing attitude to 'equality of opportunities'. The achievement of 'equality' is no longer the guiding principle
behind educational reform. Indeed, its pursuit has been identified by the
'New Right' as a major cause of an alleged lowering of academic and
social standards. It has been associated with progressive permissiveness,
and the erosion of traditional authority and respectful attitudes and
values. More specifically, within the public and political debates of the
period, equal opportunity (EO) policies in the 'race' and gender areas
became a prime target for attack from elements of the media.

The educational reforms of the 1980s included both a major ideological
shift in the approach to and understanding of 'equality' in education and
an assault upon policies and curriculum developments which aimed at
promoting equal opportunities. We want to argue that, in addition,
there is an increasing awareness of problems internal to the position
which has underpinned EO policies over the past decade.[1]

Rather than simply defend these earlier positions, we believe that the
most productive response to the current climate of hostility to equal
opportunities is to critically engage with these internal problems and
seek to extend our understanding of how the educational process may be
involved in producing socially differentiated outcomes.

EQUAL OPPORTUNITIES AND THE EDUCATIONAL
PROCESS

Equal opportunities strategies have typically taken the curriculum as
their major focus and have attributed discriminatory effects (mainly
against female and black pupils) to its content and to the manner of its
transmission in the classroom. On this basis, debates have revolved
around issues such as what should be 'in' National Curriculum history

and whether or not an 'anglocentric' bias would be detrimental to ethnic minority pupils or whether the 'masculinised' character of school science is the major cause of the 'underachievement' by girls.

It should be noted, however, that both the supporters and the opponents of EO policies share in common an assumption concerning their potential efficacy. 'New Right' critics dislike progressive measures such as multicultural and anti-sexist education precisely because of the effects they attribute to them. Their disagreement is ideological. They reject the aims of EO policies and the (for them) undesirable consequences of their implementation (e.g. Hiskett 1988).

In this respect both camps can be seen as differing fundamentally from a third position which questions these assumptions about effects. There are two distinct approaches here. The first is associated with 'school effectiveness' research[2] which identifies aspects of school organisation rather than curriculum or teaching style, as the major factor creating differences in educational outcomes; and the second is based upon a critical analysis of the assumptions of EO approches in relation to how the curriculum as a central dimension of the teaching–learning process might be involved in generating educational inequality.[3] It is in terms of this latter perspective that we are writing here.

The concern with EO has been associated with efforts to identify the causes of inequality (in relation to class, gender and 'race') and to suggest remedies. The familiar types of policies from LEAs and schools in the late 1970s and 1980s are based on these understandings of the causes of the social differentiation of educational attainment. Hence, the structure of educational differences is associated with theories concerning the manner in which the educational process generates distinctive forms of social differentiation. In these terms EO policies and the associated 'good practices' are seen as solutions to the problems created for girls or black pupils by unreconstructed curricula and teaching methods.

Policies and paradigms

Although assumptions about the effects of the educational process can be seen as underpinning EO policies and approaches, we would suggest that the major debates in the area over the past decade have tended to neglect this central issue in favour of a concern with the wider social origins of discriminatory practices. The debates around multicultural *v.* anti-racist education or liberal *v.* radical feminist positions, for instance, have taken as their major point of difference the manner in which racism or sexism is built into the social system and, consequently, the form and degree of social or educational change necessary to make any 'real' difference. The basic character of these distinctions is encapsulated in the 'race' area, in that between concerns with 'life-styles' (multiculturalism) or 'life-chances' (anti-racism) (Troyna 1989: 155), and in gender in the uses of the concept of 'patriarchy' as an explanatory principle.

Without in any way intending to dismiss the importance of these concerns in principle, we feel that there has been a tendency to deduce the effective features of classroom processes from broader depictions of social order. This has resulted in a counter-productive simplification of the relationships and processes involved. Wolpe, for example, in a criticism of the way in which 'patriarchy' has been used in this fashion, says that,

> The starting point for radical analysis is the notion of patriarchy. The contruction of reality is premissed on this basis. In accordance with patriarchal relations all boys are seen to be privileged in schools, as contrasted with all girls. Boys, it is argued, are accorded a higher status by virtue of their being male. This dominance permeates all relations in the school and is particularly manifest in the classroom.
>
> The result of this emphasis is a plethora of data . . . which is said to express patriarchal power. . . . For example . . . teachers' behaviour is said to have the effect of lowering girls' self-esteem thereby affecting their performance in school.
>
> (Wolpe 1988: 143)

In a similar fashion, Carrington and Short (1989) have suggested that the much used formula, 'racism = power + prejudice',

> . . . rests upon a number of untenable assumptions: power in British society is in the hands of white people; as a consequence of colonialism (which has left an indelible mark on their consciousness) only white people can be racist; and all white people (including antiracists and others who do not consciously hold racist attitudes) cannot escape the influence of racism because institutional practices and procedures are loaded in their favour.
>
> (pp. 16–17)

Associated with this type of account is the 'negative self-image' or 'low self-esteem' explanation of supposed black 'underachievement', which is similar to that alluded to by Wolpe, above, in relation to girls.

In addition to these problems of generalisation and simplification, the various approaches which these debates have generated in the 'race' and gender areas have tended, despite their differences, to rely upon a particular (usually implicit) model of how the educational process creates differential patterns of attainment through the effects of sexist and racist curricula and teaching upon pupil 'self-image'. We will argue that EO policy and practice has been powerfully influenced by a largely unexamined educational paradigm which links attainment and the teaching–learning process to a particular theory of identity formation.

The notion of 'stereotyping' is central to the model of the teaching–learning process which tends to underpin curriculum developments in the EO area. Although the term is widely distributed in EO educational literature, it is rare to find any sustained, critical discussion of what it means in terms of the characteristics of the processes it implies or the model of the pupil it assumes. This lack of discussion may well be indicative of the manner in which the model and its cluster of concepts ('stereotype', 'internalisation', 'negative self-image', 'low self-esteem', 'teacher expectations', 'self-fulfilling prophecy', 'underachievement') have become part of the taken-for-granted assumptions of educationalists and teachers as to how the educational process 'works' in this respect.

We would also suggest that it is the model most frequently transmitted to students in teacher-training institutions and most likely to be spontaneously invoked by teachers in order to explain social differentiation along 'race' and gender lines.

POSITIVE IMAGES

Much of what has come to count as 'good practice' in the EO area makes sense in terms of the assumptions of the 'negative self-image' account of educational differentiation and the apparent 'underachievement' of girls and black pupils. Perhaps the most typical expression of this approach in practice is the anti-sexist or anti-racist 'checklist'. The strategy of which it is a part seeks to identify negative stereotypes in teaching materials or teachers' behaviour and replace them with alternatives which will promote 'positive images' of the groups in question. It assumes a linkage between 'image' and 'self-image' facilitated by the manner in which the teaching-learning process functions simultaneously as a process of identity formation. . . .

In their critical review of the history of the approach Reeves and Chevannes (1988) describe how American educationalists in the 1960s and 1970s attempted to 'explain the poor educational performance of blacks in terms of damage caused to the "black identity" by the widespread racism in white society and institutions such as the school' (p. 190). Drawing upon work in psychology and on symbolic interactionist ideas of sociology, this 'identity theory' attributed a 'negative self-image' to black people as a result of their internalisation of white racist ideology and imagery.

In another recent critical review of the 'negative self-image' model of the black pupil, Coultas (1989) has argued that 'the conclusions of the original research on the self-esteem of black pupils were false because they were based on patronising and racist assumptions' (p. 292). This research failed to acknowledge the extent to which black people can draw upon their own cultural resources to counter the effects of white racism and construct identities and enjoy self-esteem independently of its influence.

However, this should not be taken as simply implying that black people have their own alternative stock of 'positive images'. Self-esteem is not a simple attribute which individuals have more or less of any more than 'selves' are simple, unitary entities experienced in a static form, regardless of context or circumstances. As we shall argue later, criticisms such as that of Coultas' are pointing towards a quite different understanding of the learning process in the classroom and of identity and 'the self'.

Essentially, what this approach does, in both the 'race' and gender areas, is to conflate an explanation of differential patterns of educational attainment with a theory of identity formation. It does it in such a way that girls and blacks are presented as simply the passive victims of patriarchy or racism (Wolpe 1988: 138), their self-images and attainments reflecting the consciousness, behaviour and interests of men or whites. The educational process and the curriculum (both formal and hidden) in particular, is taken as the vehicle of influences shaping pupil identities and, so, their patterns of attainment.

Rather than the issues which have traditionally preoccupied advocates of multicultural and anti-racist education, or liberal and radical feminists, the key concern, we suggest, should be the theory of the subject and the reception of educational knowledge implicit in such accounts of the pupil and the teaching–learning process.

THE MODEL AND ITS LIMITATIONS

We are arguing that EO policies and curriculum developments in the recent past have typically been underpinned by a theory of social differentiation in education. This theory associates the acquisition of school knowledge with identity formation on the basis of the internalisation of stereotypically 'appropriate' raced and gendered 'images' principally transmitted through the curriculum and reinforced by 'teacher expectations' and the influences of various 'significant others' in the family, peer group and media.

This paradigm can be seen as constructed from a dated body of psychological and sociological theory and research strongly influenced by symbolic interactionist models of socialisation.[4] We will now look at the assumptions of this paradigm in more detail by considering the following extract from Davina Cooper's (1989) critical account of events surrounding Haringey Council's positive images of homosexuality policy.

This is a particularly interesting illustration of EO policy in that it brings together a number of associated issues. Within the context of the public and political debates of the eighties it can be seen as extremely radical at the level of the issue (gay rights). From the Authority's point of view the policy was logically consistent with their broader EO strategy and was understood in terms of a broad social mandate to provide equal opportunities in education. However, it also generated a media orchestrated 'moral panic' typical of the politicisation of educational issues by the 'New Right' at the time.

Our principal interest, here, is in the manner in which this example illustrates the assumed linkage between learning and identity formation. Cooper provides the following account of the rationale for the approach as put forward in the policy statement *Mirrors Round the Walls – Respecting Diversity* (Haringey Educational Service 1988). Although the document is exceptional in referring to gay issues, it is in other respects representative of policy statements in the equal opportunities area generally in terms of its principles, rhetoric and underlying explanatory model.

> 'Positive images' is not a term specific to lesbians and gay men. Rather it refers to the need for role models for all sections of the community who internalise societal prejudice and derogatory stereotypes about themselves. Underlying this perceived educational need are principles of meritocracy and the self-fulfilling prophecy: that if adults and society in general project a negative image of certain young people, they will not succeed to the full extent of their capabilities. This has been shown why Black, working class students and young women often underachieve in non-traditional areas of study.   (p. 48)

The reference to 'principles of meritocracy and the self-fulfilling prophecy' combines the dual concern of educators with a social mandate for equality of opportunities and a particular understanding of the teaching–learning process.

The following points can be drawn from this:

1 we see the familiar terminology of 'stereotypes', 'role models', 'internalisation', 'the self-fulfilling prophecy', 'low expectations';
2 these terms are associated with a causal/explanatory theory of underachievement by black, working-class and female students.

Beyond the section we have quoted:

3 There is a distinction between the particular needs of the 'victims' of stereotyping, and those of all pupils and society in general. This is similar to distinctions made in the multicultural area between the particular needs of ethnic minority pupils and the general aims for all pupils (Halstead 1988).
4 There is the implicit assumption that (a) society should be diversified,

and (b) that respect for and encouragement of diversity is a good thing. Both these claims are contested by cultural conservatives.

In these respects, the document is typical of EO policy statements.

Our basic criticisms of the model outlined can be summarised as follows. Essentially, the causal/explanatory process assumed is:

Stereotype → Internalisation → Self-image → Attainment

The implicit assumptions of the model are:

1 the simple, 'given' nature of the message incorporated in the stereotype, either as an 'image' encountered directly in a text or in the behaviour of a prejudiced individual;
2 its unmediated reception and acceptance by the pupil;
3 its automatic subjective effect upon the pupil in terms of identity formation (the translation of 'image' into 'self-image') and the unitary, essentialist nature of the self that this implies.[5]

The model effectively decontextualises these processes by ignoring the complex interactive setting of the classroom, the collective strategies that pupils adopt there and the wider cultural resources upon which they draw.[6]

The associated socialisation model tends to assume that social categories and their meanings are unitary, consensual, fixed, stable and enduring (Billig et al. 1988; Potter and Wetherell 1987). The idea that girls, for instance, avoid school science because it is perceived as 'unfeminine' presupposes a given definition of 'femininity' (and of 'science') in terms of which this behaviour is intelligible. On the assumption that girls simply internalise this particular model of femininity and that their identities (self-images) are constructed accordingly, the stereotype in itself provides the rationality principle for their behaviour and an 'explanation' of gender differences in this area of the curriculum.

In terms of pupil/teacher relationships there is an assumption that prejudiced teachers consistently act towards certain pupils in a 'biased' fashion which is not only perceptible as such to those pupils, but also affects them in such a way that they uncritically incorporate this view within their own 'self-image' and under-achieve as a result.

The 'good practice' implied by this model entails substituting alternative 'positive' images for the negative ones embodied in the stereotypes assumed to be routinely encountered in the home, the media, and in unreconstructed school texts and practices. In that it aims to make up for the deficiencies of the child's experience and to act positively upon the 'self-image' of the black or female pupil the educational model is essentially compensatory and 'therapeutic' (Stone 1981; Sarup 1986) and can lead to the systematic underestimation of pupils' academic aspirations and potential. We would agree with John Ahier's (1991) view that,

> What is mistaken in this whole enterprise is the belief that you can track down some socially damaging cultural element, be it racism or ruralism, by the content analysis of educational or other texts, and then put it right by re-writing the books, reversing the values and including the excluded. (p. 129)

The essence of the 'mistake' to which Ahier refers is the view that images have a fixed form in relation to the object which they represent and that, on this basis, they are automatically 'absorbed' into pupil consciousness, determining their view of their own self and of others. The checklist device associated with 'positive image' approaches presumes precisely that images can be identified in this unproblematical, stereo-typical form, their effects taken for granted and negative influences neutralised by the substitution of positive alternatives.

IMPLICATIONS

We have been arguing that EO policies and practices have tended to be based on an understanding of educational inequality which relates social differentiation in education to identity formation structured by the teaching–learning process. As a result of the manner in which this model relies upon the notion of 'stereotypes' and their internalisation, the curriculum has tended to be singled out for special attention as the repository of positive or negative 'images'.

The focus tends to be upon these 'images' in themselves rather than on what pupils 'do' with them or how their meanings might be deconstructed and reconstructed within the teaching process. Meaning has tended to be taken for granted, as simply 'given' in either a negative or positive form rather than seen as provisional and renegotiable in terms of a multiplicity of interpretive possibilities. On this basis, the central issue is seen as having to do with substituting one repertoire of images for another rather than with a critical exploration of the complexities of discourse and of meaning construction.

Although its theoretical origins are rarely made explicit, it is clear from its terminology that the standard EO paradigm is based on a set of ideas derived from, by now, dated psychological and sociological work (Reeves and Chevannes 1988; Wineburg 1991), largely in the symbolic interactionist tradition. These ideas concerning 'teacher expectations', 'labelling', 'self-fulfilling prophecies', etc. [classically associated with Rosenthal and Jacobson's *Pygmalion in the Classroom* (1968)] have retained their hold despite considerable and long-standing reservations by sociologists and social psychologists (Furlong 1985; Wood 1988).

In both disciplines, theories of the subject, identity formation and representation have undergone considerable development (Potter and Wetherell 1987; Giddens 1991). The major problem with the standard EO paradigm is its reliance upon essentialist models of 'image', 'identity' and 'self' which simplify the very processes with which teachers could most productively engage in the classroom.

Rather than taking meanings for granted, social psychologists and sociologists are increasingly drawing upon the insights of discourse theory and semiotics in order to grasp the complexities of their construction (Potter and Wetherell 1987). As far as the classroom is concerned, this involves a focus upon the ways in which, within the learning process, pupils actively construct meaning rather than passively receive (more or less successfully) a pre-given curriculum (Pollard 1990).

On the basis of their work with the Cultural Studies Project in schools in Southwark, Haddock and Cohen (1991) argue that,

> There is a need to move away from over-simple, prescriptive notions of positive versus negative images and accept that to attempt to replace one by the other is to fail to acknowledge the multiplicity of selves that children – and adults – deploy as they negotiate different aspects of their lives in various settings. To impose an over-restrictive view of what is a 'positive image' on the complexity of their experience can both alienate and confuse children. They may not recognise their lived experience within it. To accept that a plurality of aspirations is possible is to recognise that there may be conflicts between them and this enables children to explore the complexity of their experience in a way that reflects their day to day lives with their inevitable contradictions.
>
> (pp. 3–4)

The concern is to move from an approach which treats curriculum content as the major issue on the assumption that its meanings and effects can be automatically deduced from an evaluation of its positive or negative status, to one which attempts to engage with its logic in use in everyday life and the classroom. From this point of view, it is pedagogy and the development of teaching method (Troyna 1989) that is the key concern. However, for this to be successful it is necessary, we would argue, that developments be based on deeper theoretical understandings of the self, identity formation, meaning and the learning process.

NOTES

1 To a considerable extent, these problems reflect the undermining of key substantive assumptions. More sophisticated, statistical analyses, for instance, have made it impossible to sustain the view that black pupils simply 'under-

achieve' (Kysel 1988) and ethnographic studies question how far they have 'negative self-images' and 'low self-esteem' (Coultas 1989). The compulsory aspect of the National Curriculum will modify the differential pattern of attainment between girls and boys, but the central issue in the gender area is to do with how schooling might inculcate traditional constructions of gender.

2 Particularly relevant to the concerns of this paper is Smith and Tomlinson (1989).

3 Both in terms of its theoretical contribution and through its school-based research and teaching resources, Phil Cohen's 'Cultural Studies Project' (based at the London University Institute of Education) exemplifies this approach (Cohen 1988, 1991; Haddock and Cohen 1991). See, also Ahier (1988, 1991) and Carrington and Short (1989).

4 The origins and history of this approach are well reviewed in Reeves and Chevannes (1988), Coultas (1989) and Wineburg (1991) (see also Stone 1981).

5 A major reference for the critical development of the theory of the subject is Henriques et al. (1984). See also, Billig et al. (1988), Ahier (1988) and Cohen (1991).

6 On the construction of meaning in the classroom and pupil strategies, see, for instance, Woods (1990).

REFERENCES

Ahier, J. (1988) *Industry, Children and the Nation*, Lewes: Falmer Press.

Ahier, J. (1991) 'Explaining economic decline and teaching children about industry: some unintended continuities', in R. Moore and J. Ozga (eds) *Curriculum Policy*, Oxford: Pergamon.

Billig, M., Condor, S., Edwards, D., Gane, M., Middleton, D. and Radley, A. (1988) *Ideological Dilemmas*, London: Sage.

Carrington, B. and Short, G. (1989) *Racism and the Primary School*, Windsor: NFER-Nelson.

Cohen, P. (1988) 'The perversions of inheritance', in P. Cohen and H. Bains (eds) *Multi-racist Britain*, Basingstoke: Macmillan.

Cohen, P. (1991) *Monstrous Images, Perverse Reasons*, London: ULIE.

Coultas, V. (1989) 'Black girls and self-esteem', *Gender and Education* 1(3): 283–94.

Cooper, D. (1989) 'Positive images in Haringey: a struggle for identity', in C. Jones and P. Mahony (eds) *Learning Our Lines*, London: The Woman's Press Ltd.

Furlong, V.J. (1985) *The Deviant Pupil*, Milton Keynes: Open University Press.

Giddens, A. (1991) *Modernity and Self-identity*, Cambridge: Polity Press.

Haddock, L. and Cohen, P. (1991) *Anansi Meets Spiderwoman and Other Stories*, London: ULIE.

Halstead, M. (1988) *Education, Justice and Cultural Diversity*, Lewes: Falmer Press.

Haringey Education Service (1988) *Mirrors Round the Walls – Respecting Diversity*, Haringey, Curriculum Working Party on Lesbian and Gay Issues in Education

Henriques, J., Holloway, W., Urwin, C., Venn, C. and Walkerdine, V. (1984) *Changing the Subject*, London: Methuen.

Hiskett, M. (1988) 'Should sons and daughters be brought up differently? Radical feminism in schools', in D. Anderson (ed.) *Full Circle*, London, Social Affairs Unit.

Kysel, F. (1988) 'Ethnic background and examination results', *Educational Research* 30(2): 83–9.

Pollard, A. (1990) 'Towards a sociology of learning in primary schools', *British Journal of Sociology of Education* 11(3): 241–56.

Potter, J. and Wetherell, M. (1987) *Discourse and Social Psychology*, London: Sage.

Reeves, F. and Chevannes, M. (1988) 'The ideological construction of black underachievement', in M. Woodhead and A. McGrath (eds) *Family, School and Society*, London: Hodder & Stoughton.

Rosenthal, R. and Jacobson, L. (1968) *Pygmalion in the Classroom*, New York: Holt, Rinehart & Winston.

Sarup, M. (1986) *The Politics of Multiracial Education*, London: Routledge & Kegan Paul.

Smith, D. and Tomlinson, S. (1989) *The School Effect*, London: Policy Studies Institute.

Stone, M. (1981) *The Education of the Black Child in Britain*, Glasgow: Fontana.

Troyna, B. (1989) 'Beyond multiculturalism: towards the enactment of antiracist education in policy, provision and pedagogy, in B. Moon, P. Murphy and J. Raynor (eds) *Policies for the Curriculum*, London: Hodder & Stoughton.

Wineburg, S. (1991) 'The self-fulfillment of the self-fulfilling prophecy', in D. Anderson and B. Biddle (eds) *Knowledge for Policy*, Lewes: Falmer Press.

Wolpe, A.-M. (1988) 'Experience' as analytical framework: does it account for girls' education?' in M. Cole (ed.) *Bowles and Gintis Revisited*, Lewes: Falmer Press.

Wood, D. (1988) *How Children Think and Learn*, Oxford: Basil Blackwell.

Woods, P. (ed.) (1990) *The Happiest Days? How Children Cope with School*, Lewes: Falmer Press.

Index